# The Red Seas

## VOL.1 - UNDER THE BANNER OF KING DEATH

THE RED SEA... ...D STEVE YEOWELL

# The Red Seas

## VOL. 1 - UNDER THE BANNER OF KING DEATH

**IAN EDGINTON**
Writer

**STEVE YEOWELL**
Artist

Creative Director and CEO: Jason Kingsley
Chief Technical Officer: Chris Kingsley
*2000 AD* Editor in Chief: Matt Smith
Graphic Design: Simon Parr & Luke Preece
Marketing and PR: Keith Richardson
Repro Assistant: Kathryn Symes

Graphic Novels Editor: Jonathan Oliver
Designer: Simon Parr
Original Commissioning Editor: Matt Smith

Published by Rebellion, The Studio, Brewer Street, Oxford OX1 1QN.
www.rebellion.co.uk

ISBN 13:978-1-905437-49-8
Printed in Malta by Gutenberg Press
Manufactured in the EU by LPPS Ltd., Wellingborough, NN8 3PJ, UK.
First printing: November 2007
10 9 8 7 6 5 4 3 2 1

A CIP catalogue record for this book is available from the British Library.

For information on other *2000 AD* graphic novels, or if you have any comments on this book, please email books@2000ADonline.com

To find out more about 2000 AD, visit www.2000ADonline.com

# INTRODUCTION

## "Fifteen Men on a Dead Man's Chest…" Or… How I discovered my inner pirate.

### By Ian Edginton

I'm a writer. It's official. My name's on the front of this book and everything. Actually, I'm fortunate enough to have my name on the front of several books but this is one of the few that I've written where I can trace a direct line back to the influences that started me writing in the first place.

It was 1979 and I was ill. I'd been in and out of school for months. The Head thought I was bunking off and decided to call my bluff by having me checked over by a doctor. Turned out I had glandular fever. Had it for a couple of months in fact. Oh, how we chuckled! I only had a very mild case but still had to take a further six months off, with blood tests every few weeks to see how I was doing. I got tired easily but that was all.

To pass the time, I read voraciously. Books and comics. Science fiction, fantasy and horror. I saw a lot of movies. I vividly remember going to afternoon matinees, eating sherbet lemons and Everton mints and sitting next to old ladies who smelt faintly of talc and digestive biscuits, Together we watched such classics as Richard (*Jaws*) Kiel as Golob in *The Humanoid* and the sultry Caroline Munro in *Starcrash*.

But I digress…

I also watched a phenomenal amount of television. Back then the BBC threw anything on in the afternoons to fill their scheduling, including old films. Lots and lots of old films. It's where I first became acquainted with *The Day the Earth Stood Still, Dr. Strangelove, King Kong,* and *Earth vs Flying Saucers.* I also relished non-sci-fi films like *Singing in the Rain, Pick-up on South Street* and *The Third Man.* Then one afternoon, I caught what I thought was a period drama that had me riveted.

It was Errol Flynn in *The Sea Hawk.*

I still get goose bumps when I hear the stirring opening bars of Erich Korngold's score for 'Strike for the Shores of Dover.'

Okay, I know it's not actually a pirate movie but it has all the credentials! I made certain to keep an eye on the listings for other pirate movies, not realising how thin on the ground they were. There was Flynn again as *Captain Blood.* Robert Newton as Blackbeard the Pirate. Yul Brynner as Jean Lafitte in *The Buccaneer* and the superb Burt Lancaster as the Crimson Pirate.

There's something about pirates that has a particular pull on the British psyche. I think it's because we're an island nation. Whenever we wanted to go somewhere, the sea was in the way and so we became adept in crossing it to steal other people's stuff. There's a roguery and romance to pirates that has little to do with history and everything with high adventure. The pirate is like the cowboy. Both only existed in a pure form for a narrow span of years, yet secured their place in our hearts and imaginations for decades to come.

Hence, fifteen years on I was in the Marvel offices in New York, pitching *Red Seas* for what would be the last series ever in Marvel's Epic line. I'd previously written a *Terminator* series for Dark Horse and this was my next big step up the ladder. UK artist Phil Winslade was assigned the art chores but another project he was involved with, *Goddess* by Garth Ennis over at DC, dragged on interminably. Instead of replacing the artist, Marvel shut Epic down early and I returned to the salt mines.

A decade or so later artist Steve Yeowell and I were chatting about working together when I mentioned *Red Seas.* The rest of the conversation went by in a blur as we threw ideas around ten to the dozen. I forwarded the outline to Matt Smith who approved it within twenty-four hours, the fastest turnaround I've ever had on a proposal!

The story seemed to strike a chord with 'two-thou' readers and I'm pleased to say we've never looked back. The world of *Red Seas* has broadened over the subsequent series, as I've worked in my love of the novels of Verne, Wells and Burroughs and the films of the genius that is Ray Harryhausen. However, at their heart they still remain ripping yarns! It's been a long voyage getting here but rest assured, we're not done yet.

Ian Edginton
October, 2007

# UNDER THE BANNER OF KING DEATH

Script: Ian Edginton
Art: Steve Yeowell
Letters: Annie Parkhouse

Originally published in *2000 AD* Progs 1313 - 1321

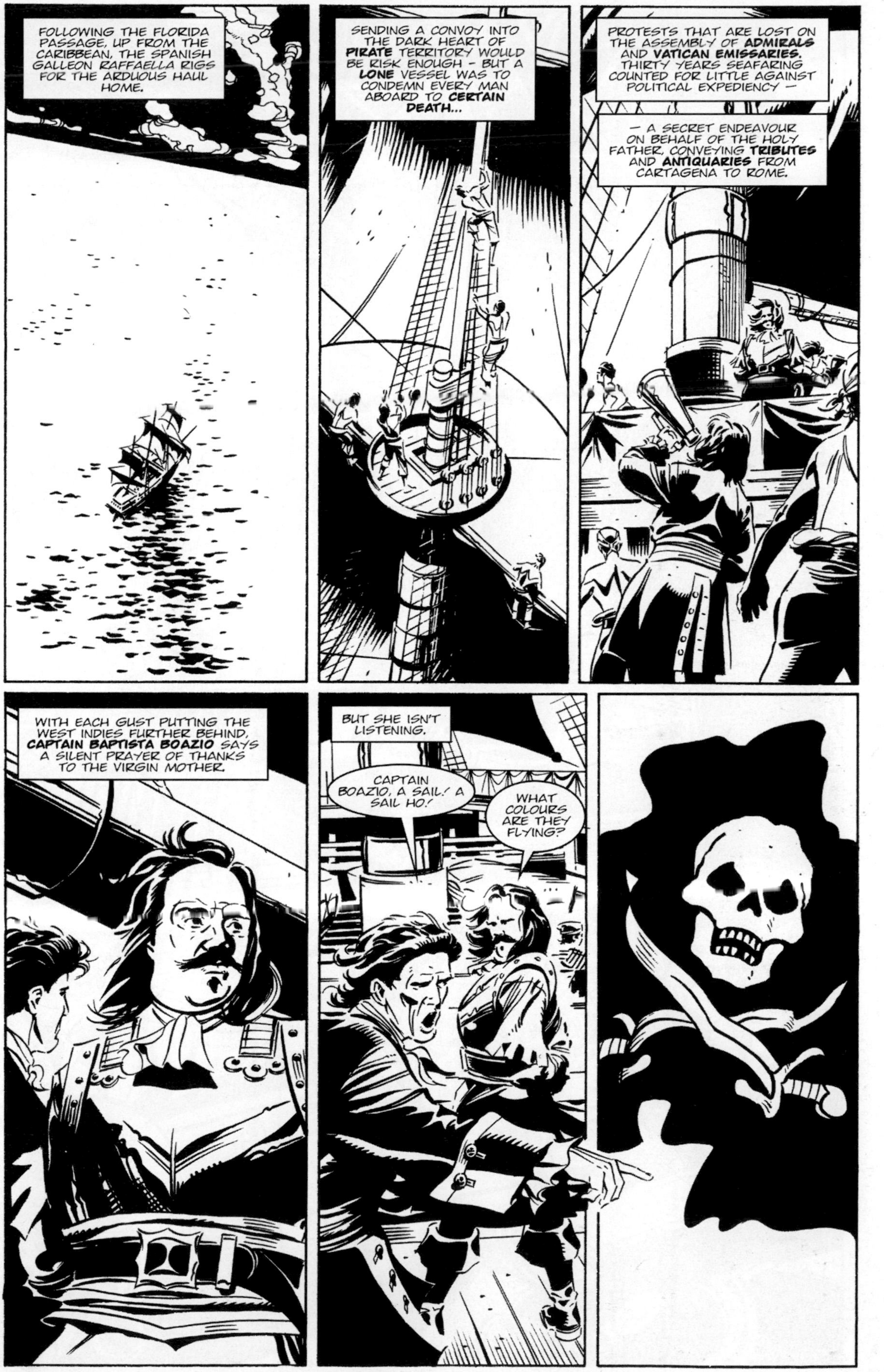
FOLLOWING THE FLORIDA PASSAGE, UP FROM THE CARIBBEAN, THE SPANISH GALLEON RAFFAELLA RIGS FOR THE ARDUOUS HAUL HOME.
SENDING A CONVOY INTO THE DARK HEART OF PIRATE TERRITORY WOULD BE RISK ENOUGH – BUT A LONE VESSEL WAS TO CONDEMN EVERY MAN ABOARD TO CERTAIN DEATH...
PROTESTS THAT ARE LOST ON THE ASSEMBLY OF ADMIRALS AND VATICAN EMISSARIES. THIRTY YEARS SEAFARING COUNTED FOR LITTLE AGAINST POLITICAL EXPEDIENCY –
– A SECRET ENDEAVOUR ON BEHALF OF THE HOLY FATHER, CONVEYING TRIBUTES AND ANTIQUARIES FROM CARTAGENA TO ROME.
WITH EACH GUST PUTTING THE WEST INDIES FURTHER BEHIND, CAPTAIN BAPTISTA BOAZIO SAYS A SILENT PRAYER OF THANKS TO THE VIRGIN MOTHER.
BUT SHE ISN'T LISTENING.
CAPTAIN BOAZIO, A SAIL! A SAIL HO!
WHAT COLOURS ARE THEY FLYING?

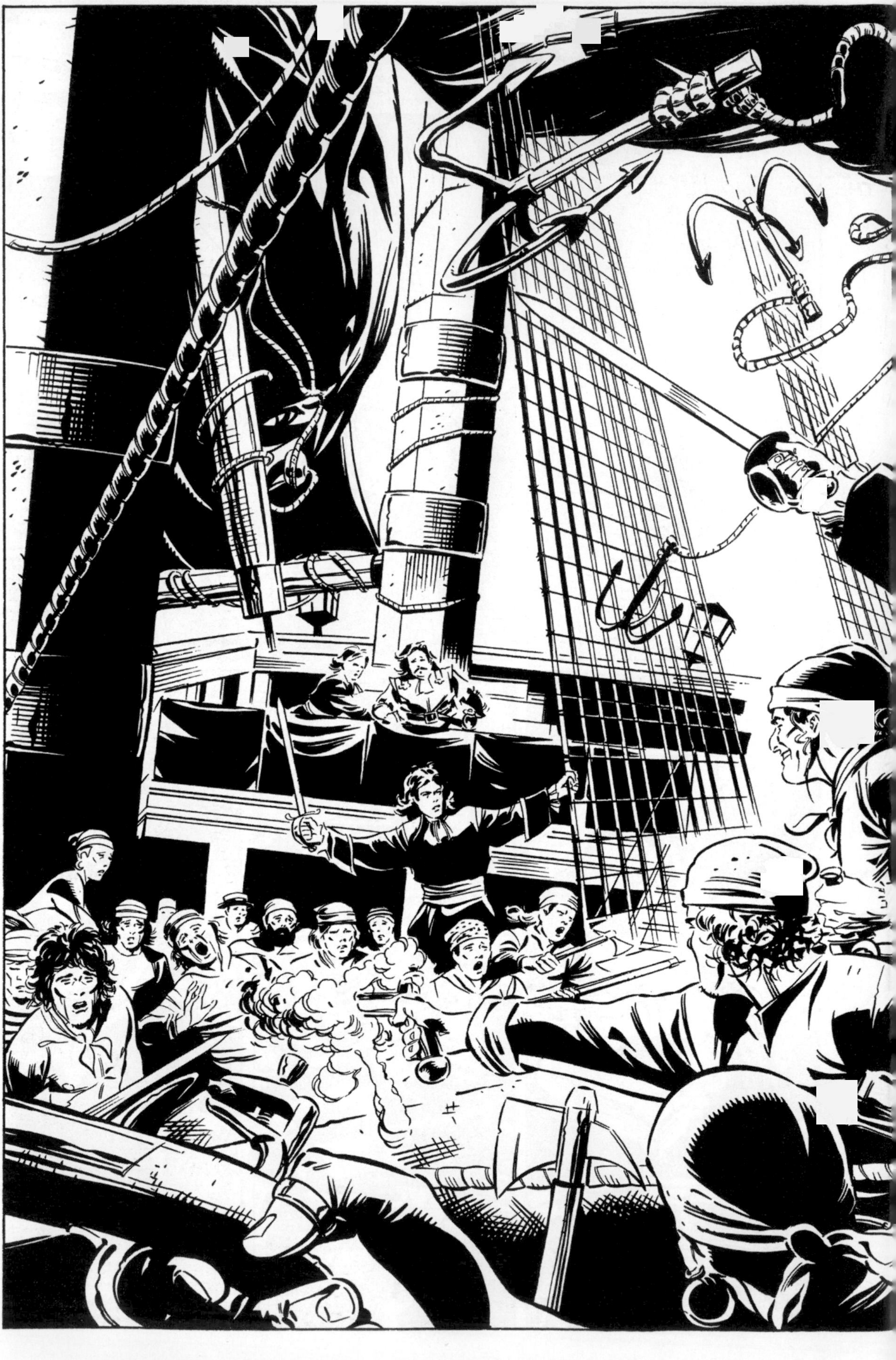

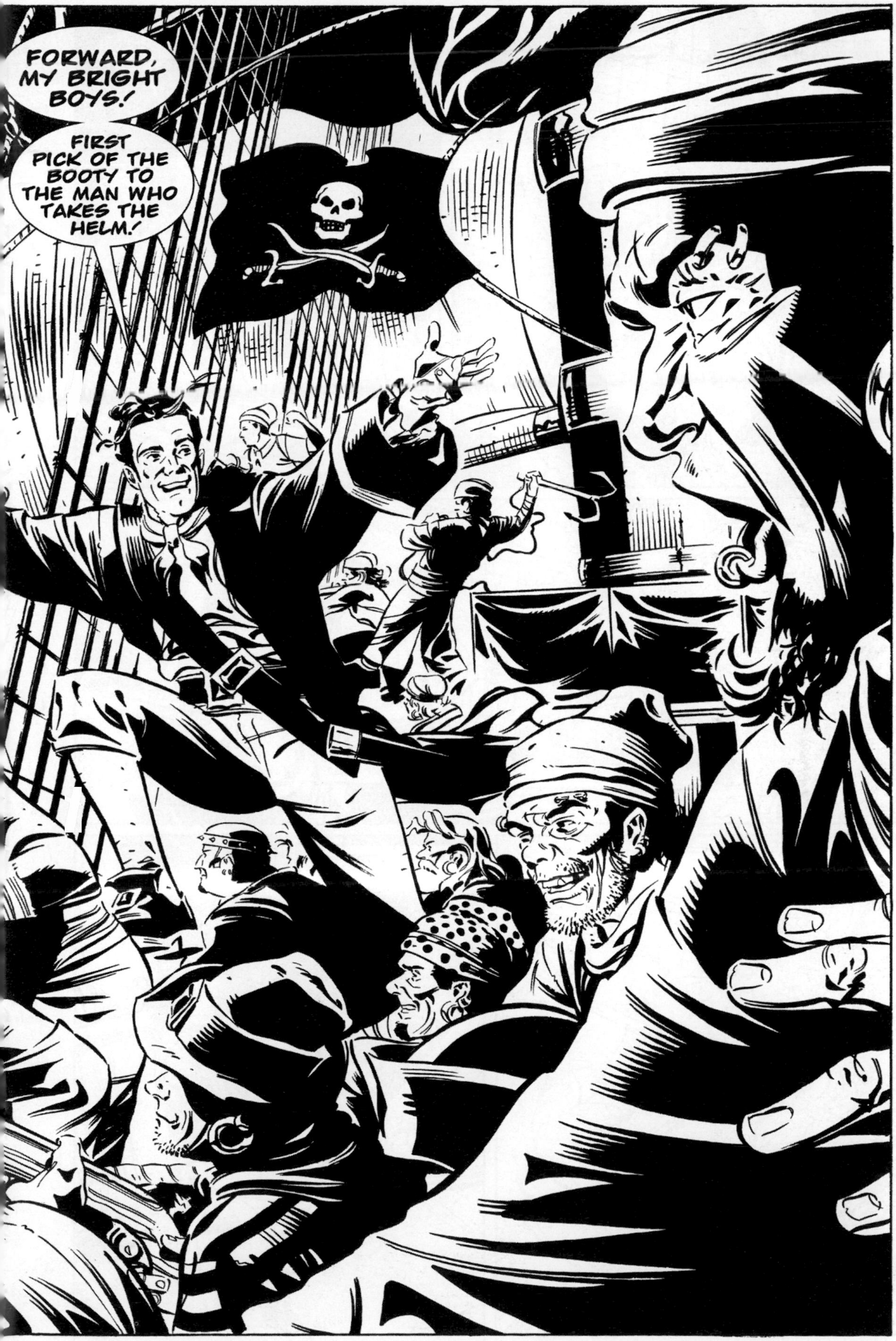
FORWARD, MY BRIGHT BOYS!
FIRST PICK OF THE BOOTY TO THE MAN WHO TAKES THE HELM!

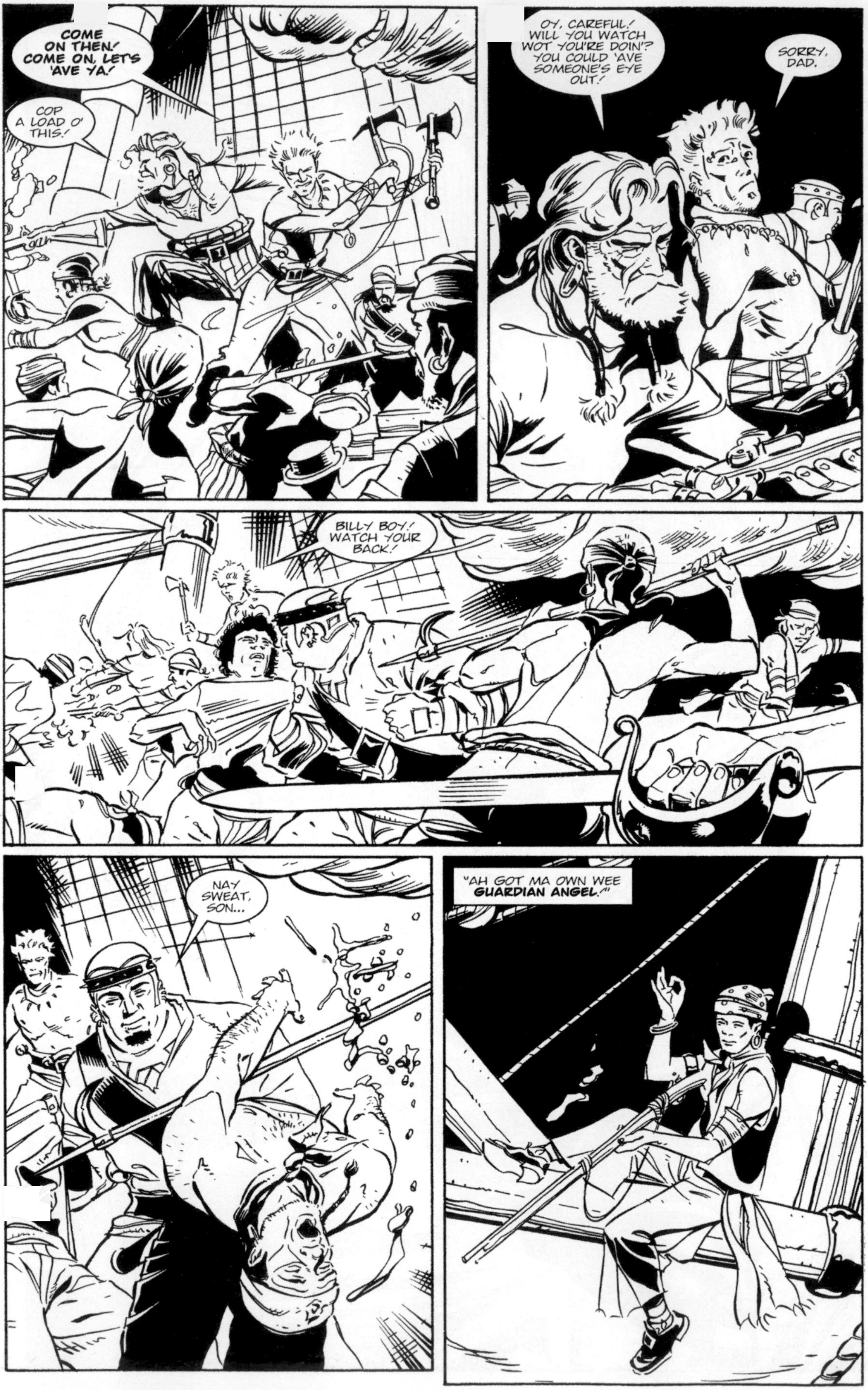
COME ON THEN! COME ON, LET'S 'AVE YA!
COP A LOAD O' THIS!
OY, CAREFUL! WILL YOU WATCH WOT YOU'RE DOIN'? YOU COULD 'AVE SOMEONE'S EYE OUT!
SORRY, DAD.
BILLY BOY! WATCH YOUR BACK!
NAY SWEAT, SON...
"AH GOT MA OWN WEE GUARDIAN ANGEL."

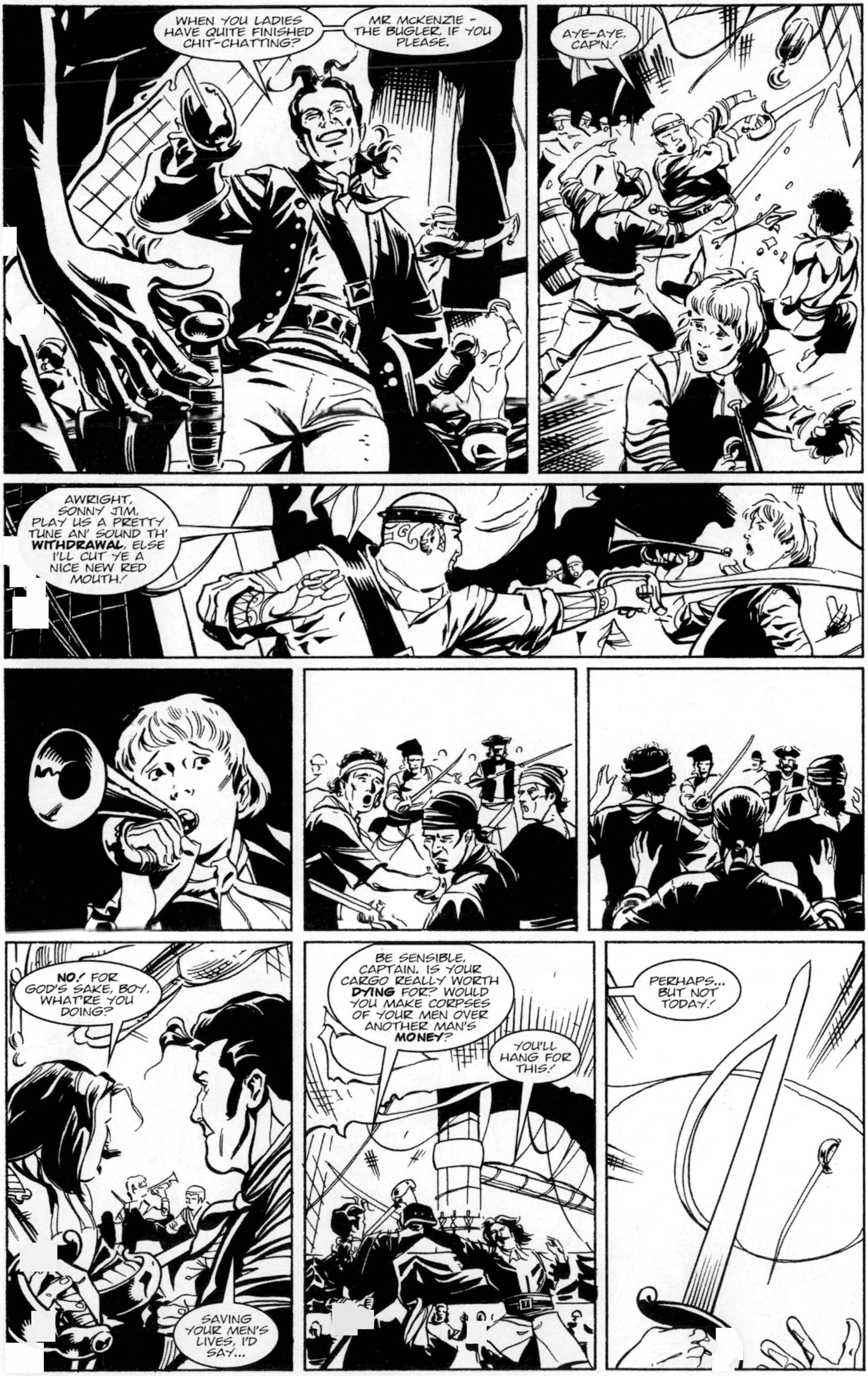
WHEN YOU LADIES HAVE QUITE FINISHED CHIT-CHATTING?
MR McKENZIE - THE BUGLER, IF YOU PLEASE.
AYE-AYE, CAP'N!
AWRIGHT, SONNY JIM, PLAY US A PRETTY TUNE AN' SOUND TH' **WITHDRAWAL**, ELSE I'LL CUT YE A NICE NEW RED MOUTH!
**NO!** FOR GOD'S SAKE, BOY, WHAT'RE YOU DOING?
SAVING YOUR MEN'S LIVES, I'D SAY...
BE SENSIBLE, CAPTAIN. IS YOUR CARGO REALLY WORTH **DYING** FOR? WOULD YOU MAKE CORPSES OF YOUR MEN OVER ANOTHER MAN'S **MONEY**?
YOU'LL HANG FOR THIS!
PERHAPS... BUT NOT TODAY!

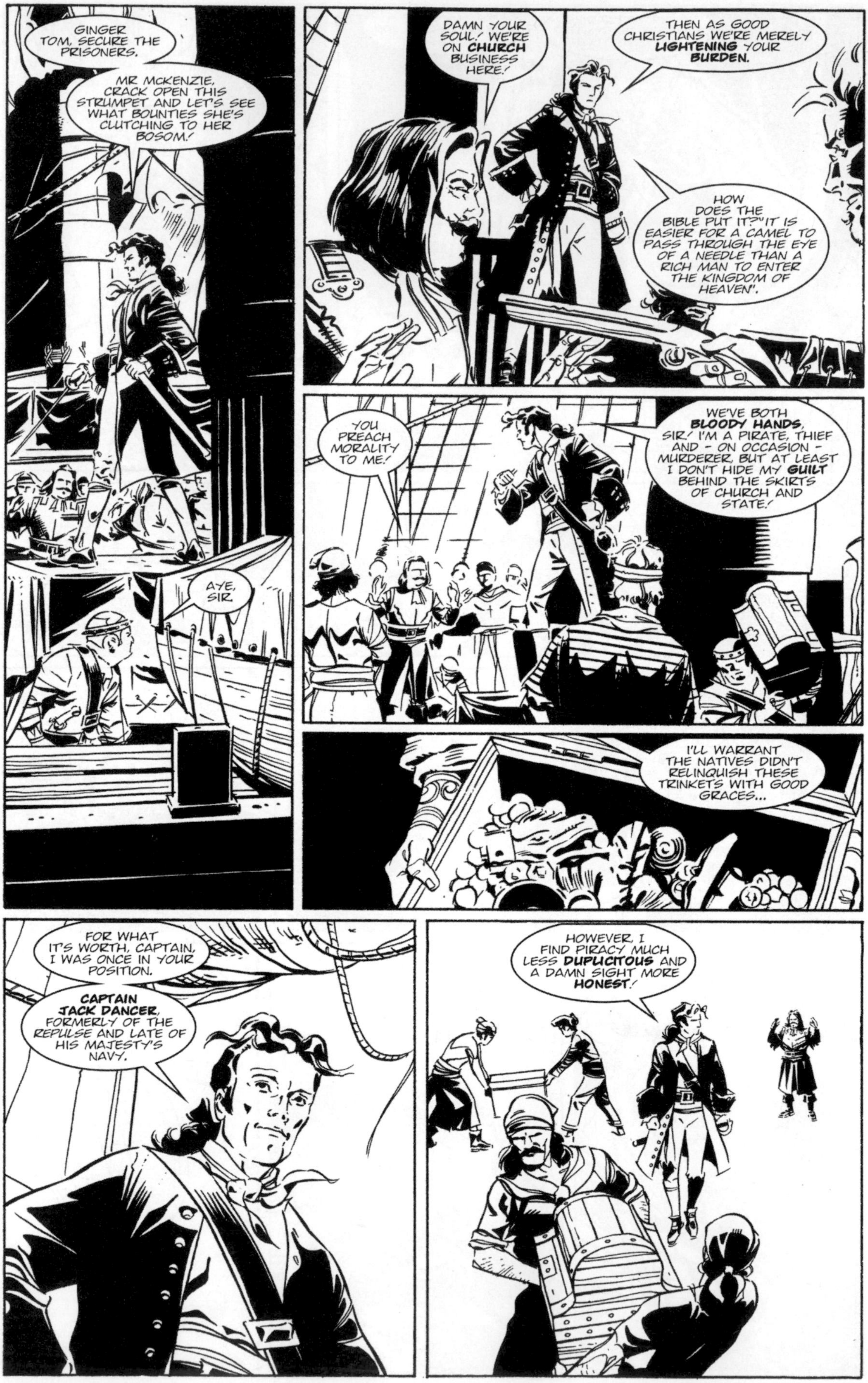
GINGER TOM, SECURE THE PRISONERS.
MR MCKENZIE, CRACK OPEN THIS STRUMPET AND LET'S SEE WHAT BOUNTIES SHE'S CLUTCHING TO HER BOSOM!
AYE, SIR.
DAMN YOUR SOUL! WE'RE ON **CHURCH** BUSINESS HERE!
THEN AS GOOD CHRISTIANS WE'RE MERELY **LIGHTENING** YOUR **BURDEN.**
HOW DOES THE BIBLE PUT IT? "IT IS EASIER FOR A CAMEL TO PASS THROUGH THE EYE OF A NEEDLE THAN A RICH MAN TO ENTER THE KINGDOM OF HEAVEN".
YOU PREACH MORALITY TO ME!
WE'VE BOTH **BLOODY HANDS**, SIR! I'M A PIRATE, THIEF AND - ON OCCASION - MURDERER, BUT AT LEAST I DON'T HIDE MY **GUILT** BEHIND THE SKIRTS OF CHURCH AND STATE!
I'LL WARRANT THE NATIVES DIDN'T RELINQUISH THESE TRINKETS WITH GOOD GRACES...
FOR WHAT IT'S WORTH, CAPTAIN, I WAS ONCE IN YOUR POSITION.
**CAPTAIN JACK DANCER**, FORMERLY OF THE REPULSE AND LATE OF HIS MAJESTY'S NAVY.
HOWEVER, I FIND PIRACY MUCH LESS **DUPLICITOUS** AND A DAMN SIGHT MORE **HONEST**!

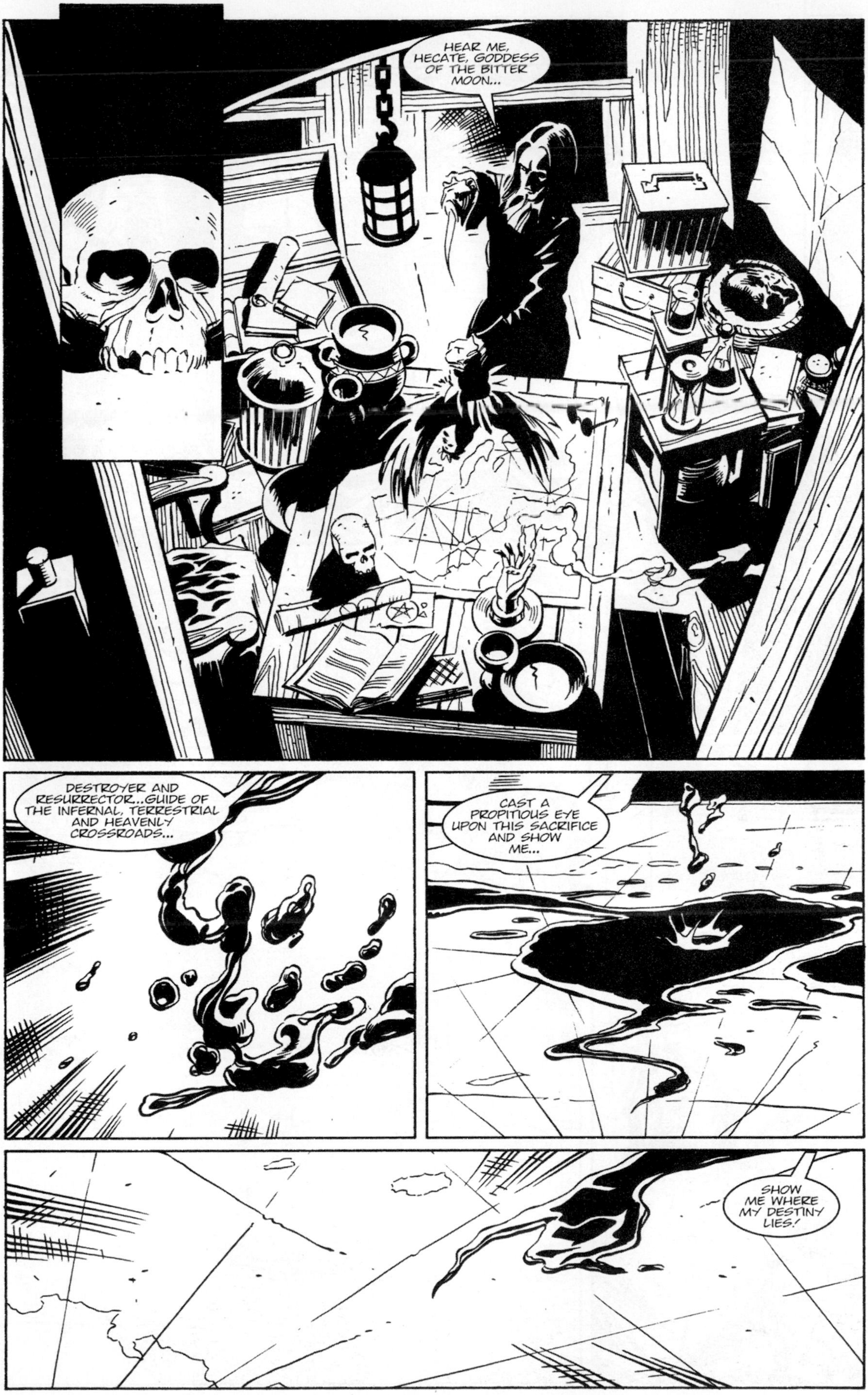
HEAR ME, HECATE, GODDESS OF THE BITTER MOON...
DESTROYER AND RESURRECTOR...GUIDE OF THE INFERNAL, TERRESTRIAL AND HEAVENLY CROSSROADS...
CAST A PROPITIOUS EYE UPON THIS SACRIFICE AND SHOW ME...
SHOW ME WHERE MY DESTINY LIES!

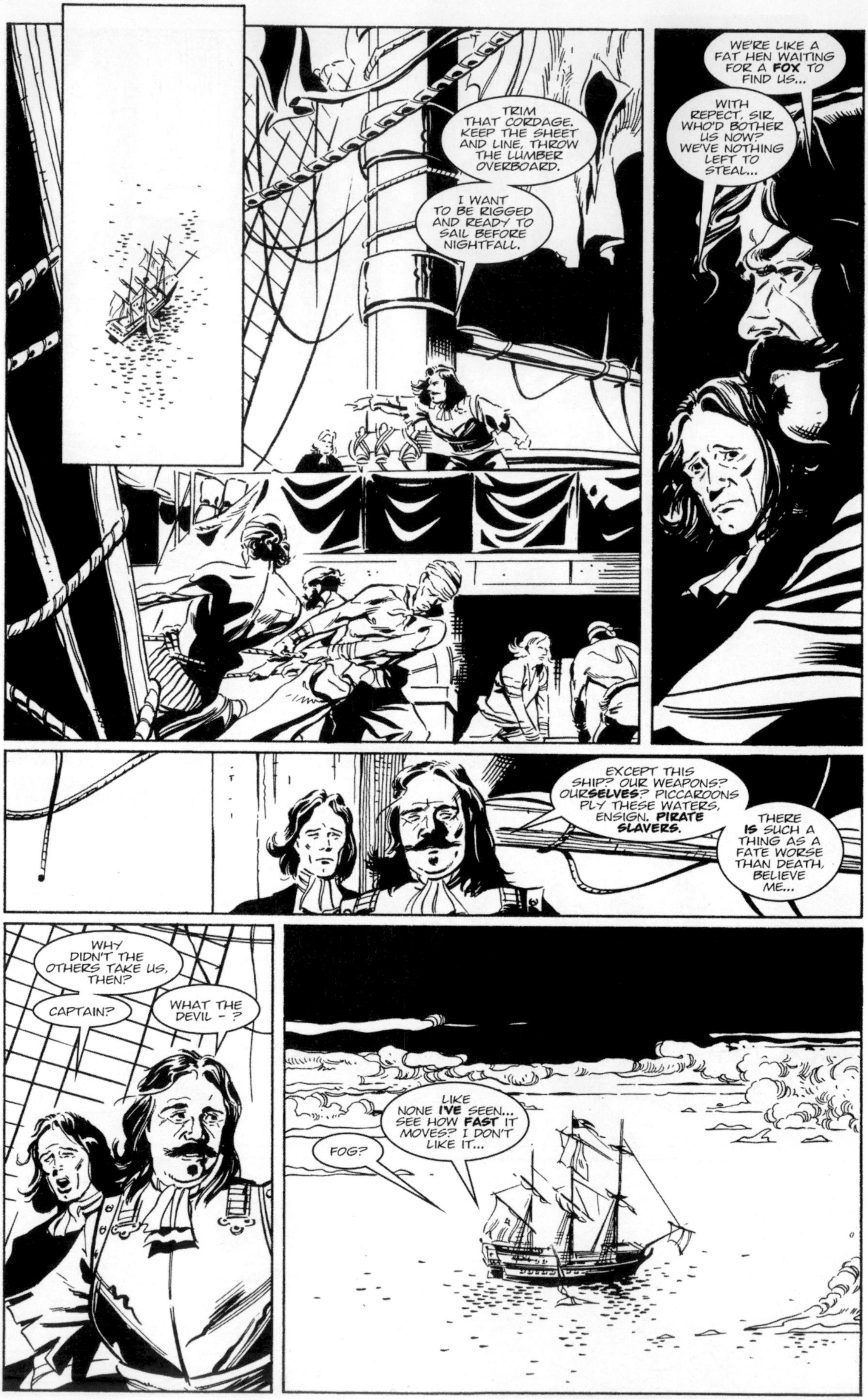
TRIM THAT CORDAGE. KEEP THE SHEET AND LINE, THROW THE LUMBER OVERBOARD.
I WANT TO BE RIGGED AND READY TO SAIL BEFORE NIGHTFALL.
WE'RE LIKE A FAT HEN WAITING FOR A FOX TO FIND US...
WITH REPECT, SIR, WHO'D BOTHER US NOW? WE'VE NOTHING LEFT TO STEAL...
EXCEPT THIS SHIP? OUR WEAPONS? OURSELVES? PICCAROONS PLY THESE WATERS, ENSIGN. PIRATE SLAVERS.
THERE IS SUCH A THING AS A FATE WORSE THAN DEATH, BELIEVE ME...
WHY DIDN'T THE OTHERS TAKE US, THEN?
CAPTAIN?
WHAT THE DEVIL - ?
FOG?
LIKE NONE I'VE SEEN... SEE HOW FAST IT MOVES? I DON'T LIKE IT...

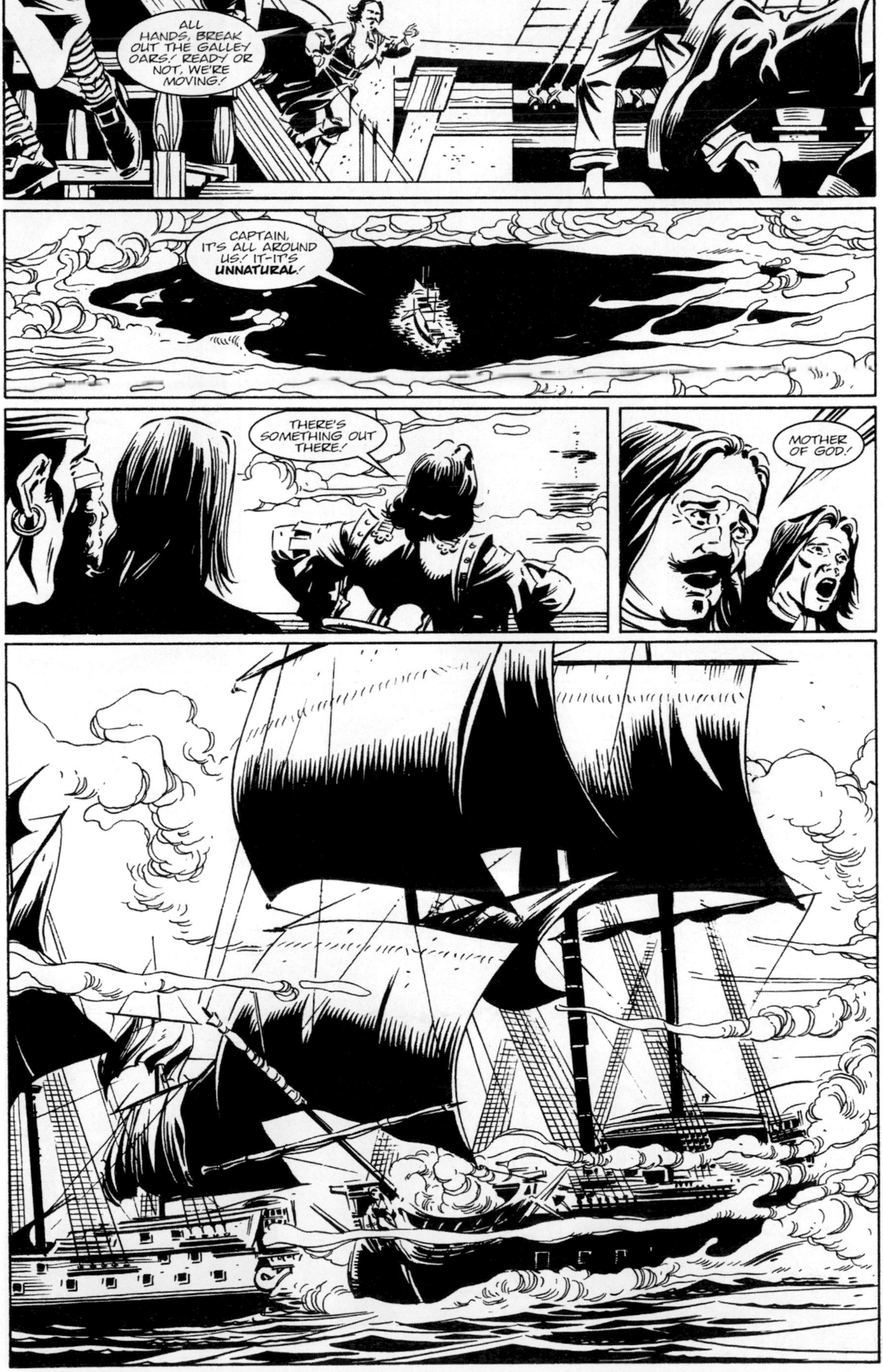
ALL HANDS, BREAK OUT THE GALLEY OARS! READY OR NOT, WE'RE MOVING!
CAPTAIN, IT'S ALL AROUND US! IT-IT'S **UNNATURAL**!
THERE'S SOMETHING OUT THERE!
MOTHER OF GOD!

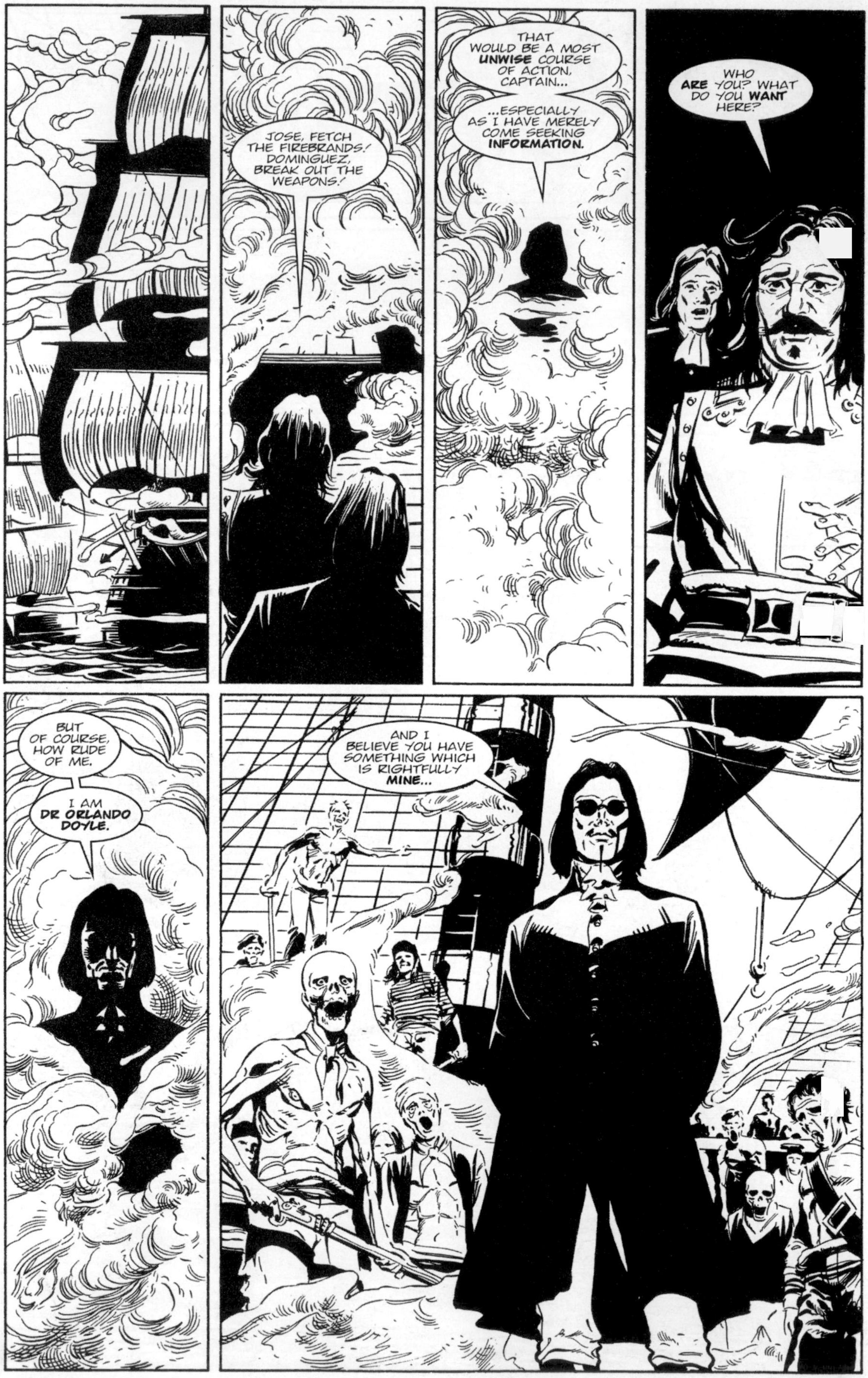
JOSE, FETCH THE FIREBRANDS! DOMINGUEZ, BREAK OUT THE WEAPONS!
THAT WOULD BE A MOST **UNWISE** COURSE OF ACTION, CAPTAIN...
...ESPECIALLY AS I HAVE MERELY COME SEEKING **INFORMATION**.
WHO **ARE** YOU? WHAT DO YOU **WANT** HERE?
BUT OF COURSE, HOW RUDE OF ME.
I AM **DR ORLANDO DOYLE**.
AND I BELIEVE YOU HAVE SOMETHING WHICH IS RIGHTFULLY **MINE**...

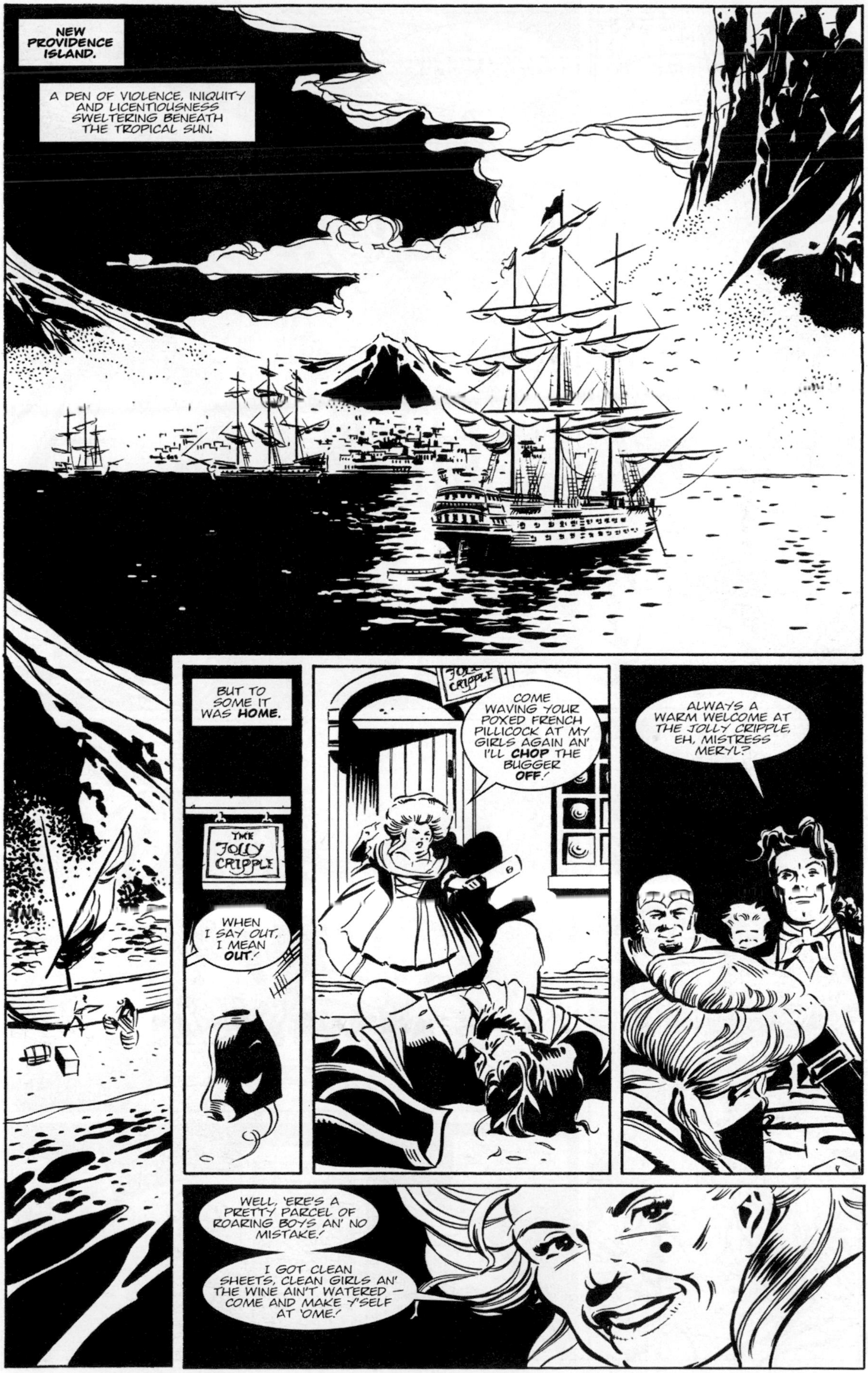
NEW PROVIDENCE ISLAND.
A DEN OF VIOLENCE, INIQUITY AND LICENTIOUSNESS SWELTERING BENEATH THE TROPICAL SUN.
BUT TO SOME IT WAS HOME.
THE JOLLY CRIPPLE
WHEN I SAY OUT, I MEAN OUT!
JOLLY CRIPPLE
COME WAVING YOUR POXED FRENCH PILLICOCK AT MY GIRLS AGAIN AN' I'LL CHOP THE BUGGER OFF!
ALWAYS A WARM WELCOME AT THE JOLLY CRIPPLE, EH, MISTRESS MERYL?
WELL, 'ERE'S A PRETTY PARCEL OF ROARING BOYS AN' NO MISTAKE!
I GOT CLEAN SHEETS, CLEAN GIRLS AN' THE WINE AIN'T WATERED — COME AND MAKE Y'SELF AT 'OME!

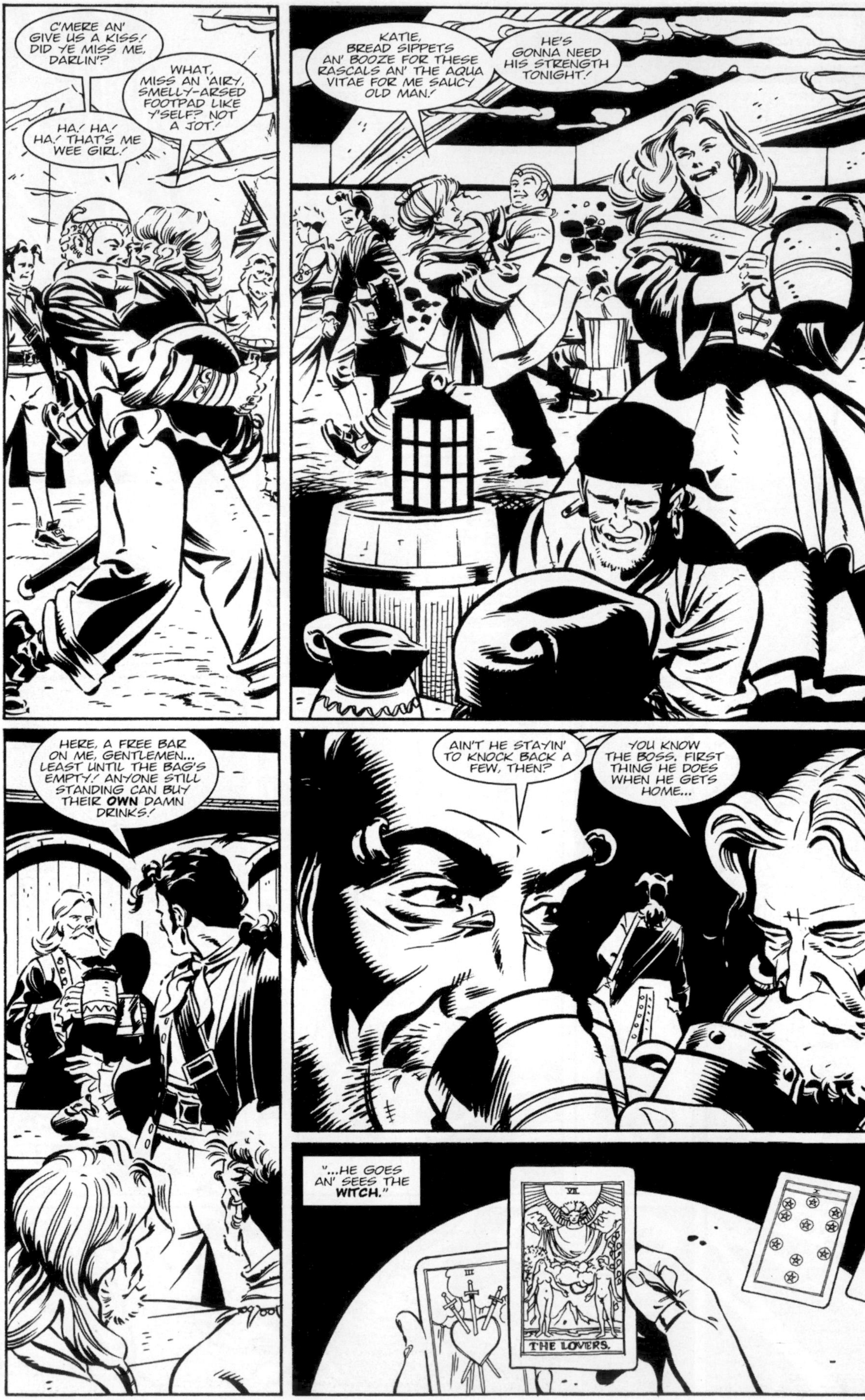
C'MERE AN' GIVE US A KISS! DID YE MISS ME, DARLIN'?
WHAT, MISS AN 'AIRY, SMELLY-ARSED FOOTPAD LIKE Y'SELF? NOT A JOT!
HA! HA! HA! THAT'S ME WEE GIRL!
KATIE, BREAD SIPPETS AN' BOOZE FOR THESE RASCALS AN' THE AQUA VITAE FOR ME SAUCY OLD MAN!
HE'S GONNA NEED HIS STRENGTH TONIGHT!
HERE, A FREE BAR ON ME, GENTLEMEN... LEAST UNTIL THE BAG'S EMPTY! ANYONE STILL STANDING CAN BUY THEIR **OWN** DAMN DRINKS!
AIN'T HE STAYIN' TO KNOCK BACK A FEW, THEN?
YOU KNOW THE BOSS. FIRST THING HE DOES WHEN HE GETS HOME...
"...HE GOES AN' SEES THE **WITCH**."
THE LOVERS.

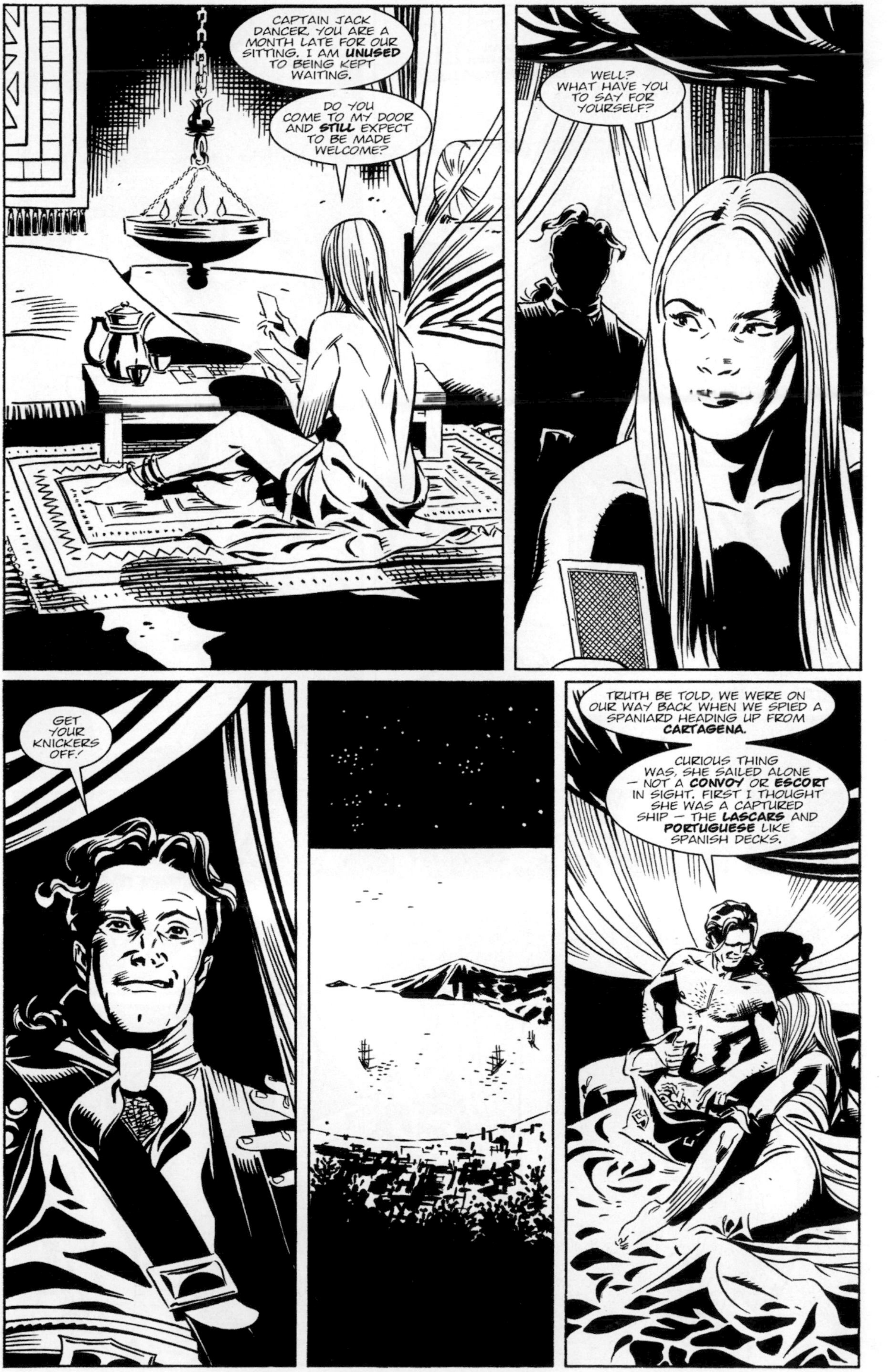
CAPTAIN JACK DANCER, YOU ARE A MONTH LATE FOR OUR SITTING. I AM **UNUSED** TO BEING KEPT WAITING.
DO YOU COME TO MY DOOR AND **STILL** EXPECT TO BE MADE WELCOME?
WELL? WHAT HAVE YOU TO SAY FOR YOURSELF?
GET YOUR KNICKERS OFF!
TRUTH BE TOLD, WE WERE ON OUR WAY BACK WHEN WE SPIED A SPANIARD HEADING UP FROM **CARTAGENA**.
CURIOUS THING WAS, SHE SAILED ALONE — NOT A **CONVOY** OR **ESCORT** IN SIGHT. FIRST I THOUGHT SHE WAS A CAPTURED SHIP — THE **LASCARS** AND **PORTUGUESE** LIKE SPANISH DECKS.

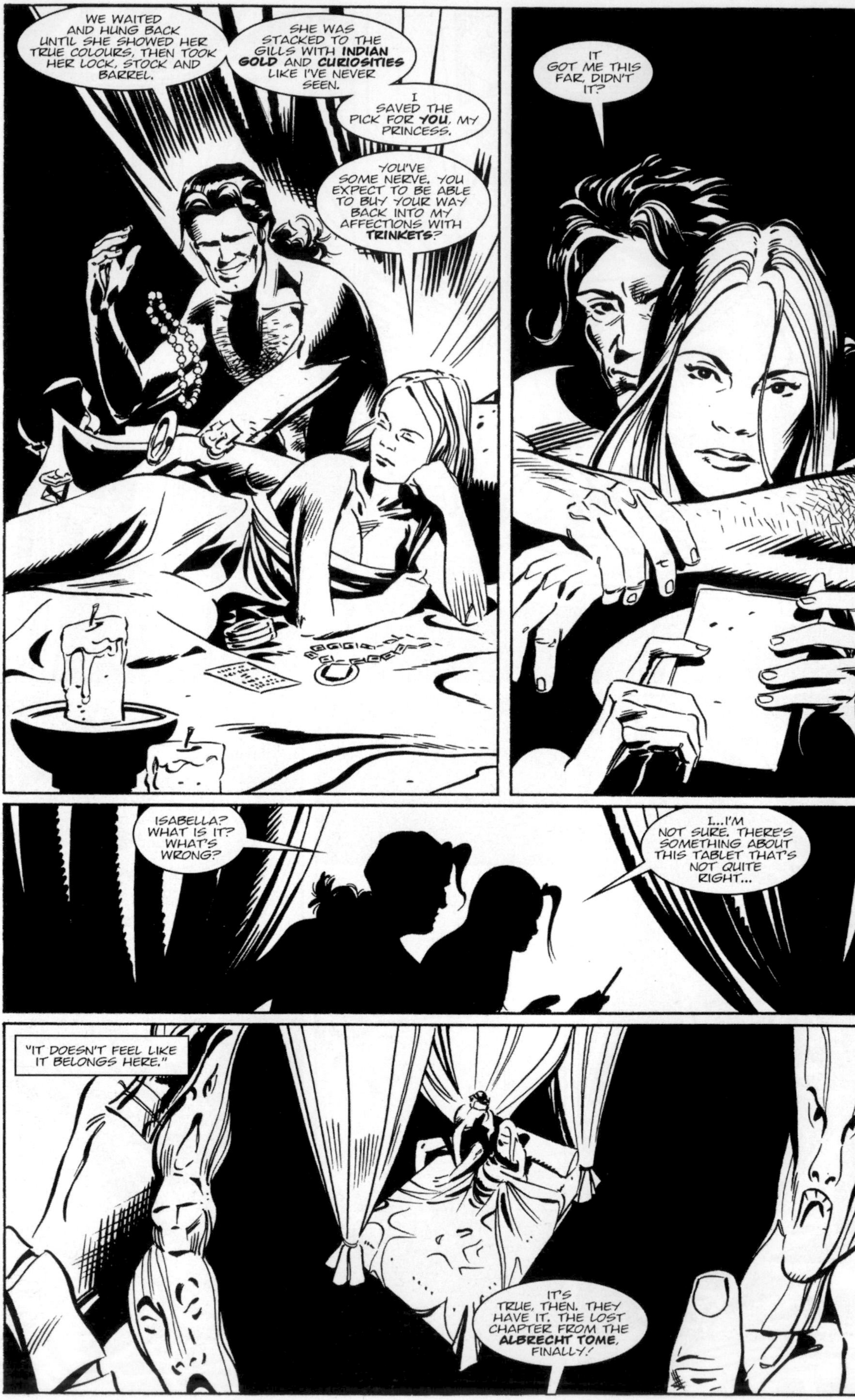
WE WAITED AND HUNG BACK UNTIL SHE SHOWED HER TRUE COLOURS, THEN TOOK HER LOCK, STOCK AND BARREL.
SHE WAS STACKED TO THE GILLS WITH INDIAN GOLD AND CURIOSITIES LIKE I'VE NEVER SEEN.
I SAVED THE PICK FOR YOU, MY PRINCESS.
YOU'VE SOME NERVE. YOU EXPECT TO BE ABLE TO BUY BACK YOUR WAY BACK INTO MY AFFECTIONS WITH TRINKETS?
IT GOT ME THIS FAR, DIDN'T IT?
ISABELLA? WHAT IS IT? WHAT'S WRONG?
I...I'M NOT SURE. THERE'S SOMETHING ABOUT THIS TABLET THAT'S NOT QUITE RIGHT...
"IT DOESN'T FEEL LIKE IT BELONGS HERE."
IT'S TRUE, THEN. THEY HAVE IT. THE LOST CHAPTER FROM THE ALBRECHT TOME, FINALLY!

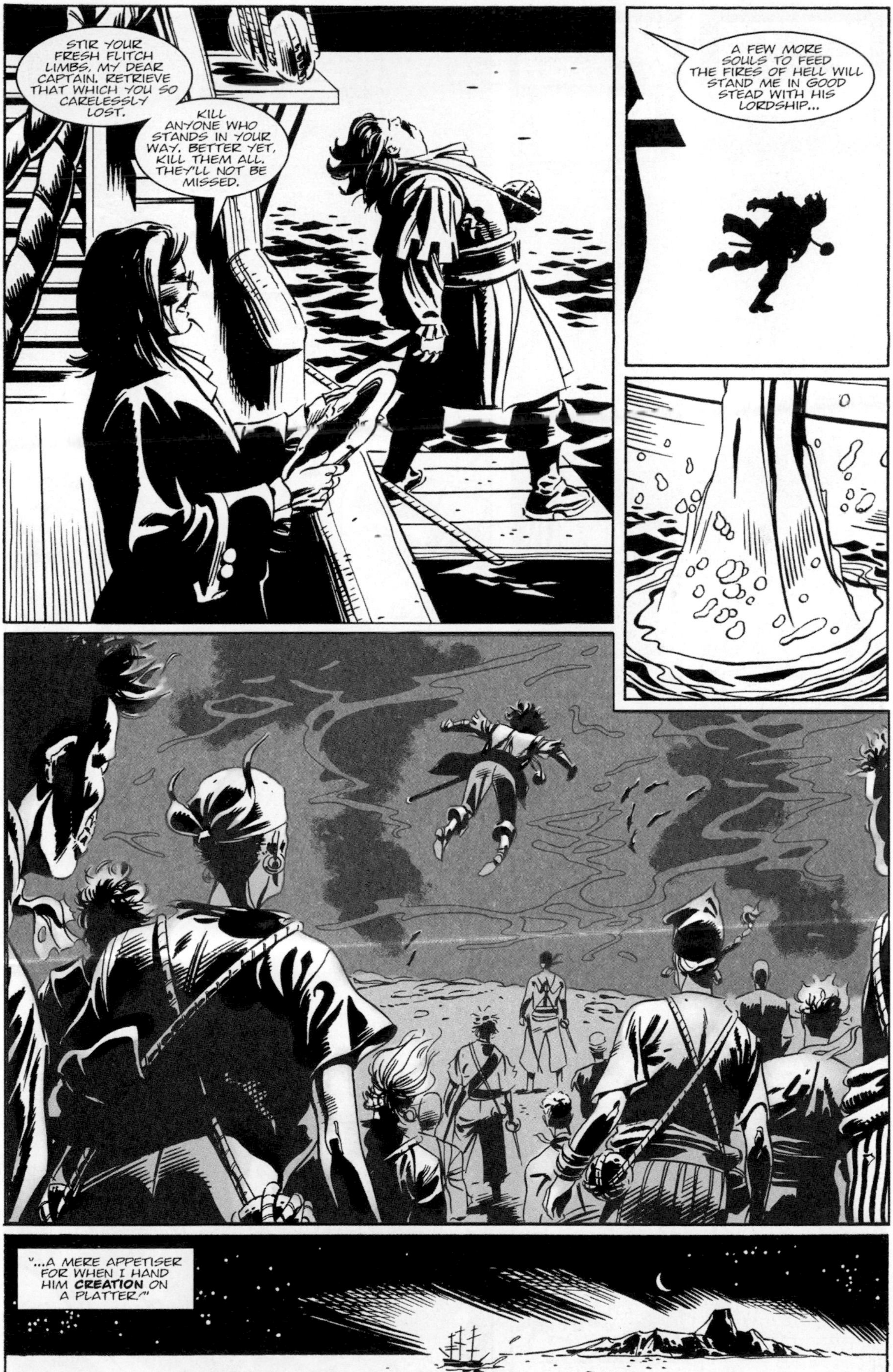
STIR YOUR FRESH FLITCH LIMBS, MY DEAR CAPTAIN. RETRIEVE THAT WHICH YOU SO CARELESSLY LOST.
KILL ANYONE WHO STANDS IN YOUR WAY. BETTER YET, KILL THEM ALL. THEY'LL NOT BE MISSED.
A FEW MORE SOULS TO FEED THE FIRES OF HELL WILL STAND ME IN GOOD STEAD WITH HIS LORDSHIP...
"...A MERE APPETISER FOR WHEN I HAND HIM CREATION ON A PLATTER."

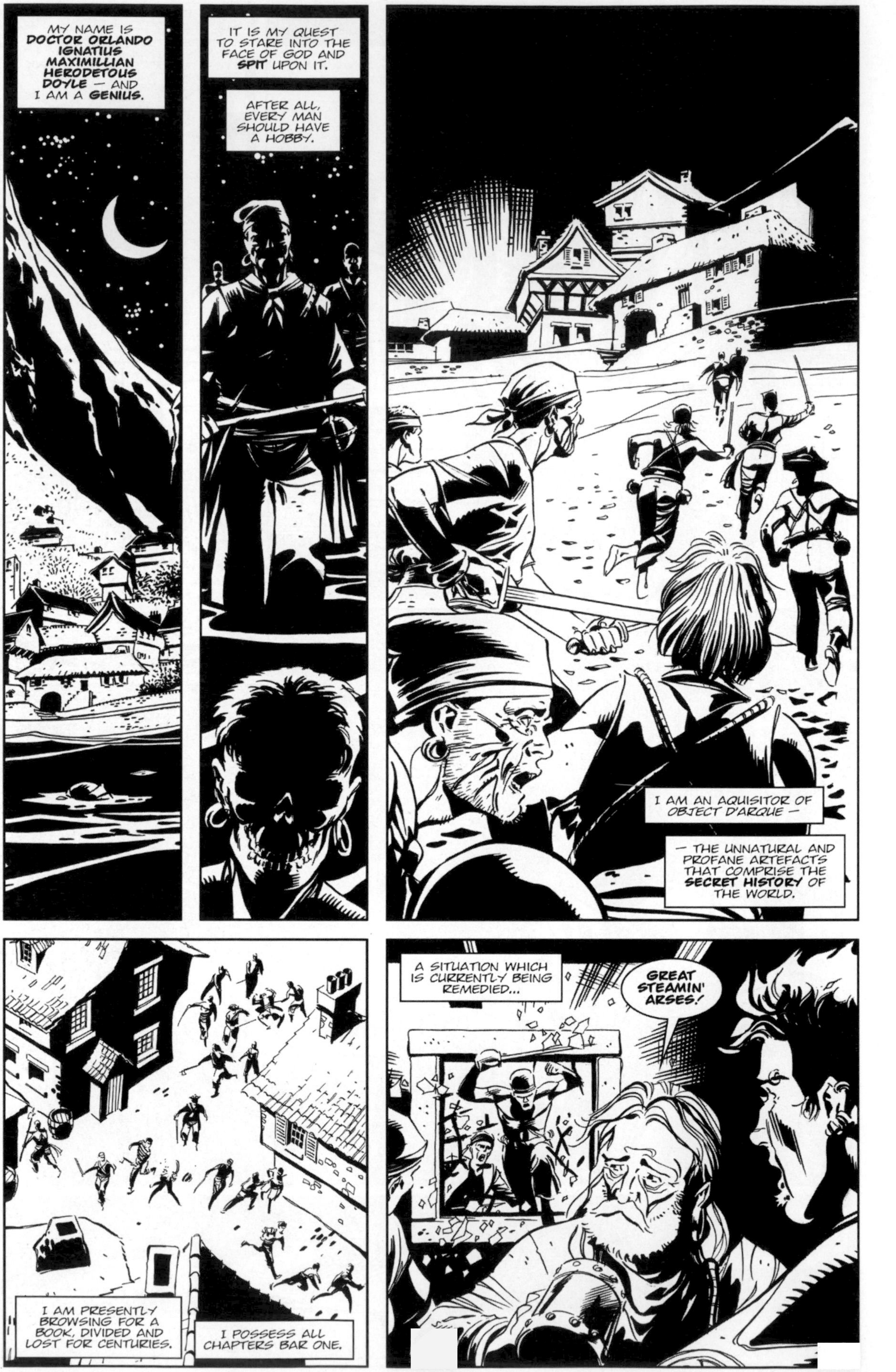
MY NAME IS DOCTOR ORLANDO IGNATIUS MAXIMILLIAN HERODETOUS DOYLE — AND I AM A GENIUS.
IT IS MY QUEST TO STARE INTO THE FACE OF GOD AND SPIT UPON IT.
AFTER ALL, EVERY MAN SHOULD HAVE A HOBBY.
I AM AN AQUISITOR OF OBJECT D'ARQUE —
— THE UNNATURAL AND PROFANE ARTEFACTS THAT COMPRISE THE SECRET HISTORY OF THE WORLD.
I AM PRESENTLY BROWSING FOR A BOOK, DIVIDED AND LOST FOR CENTURIES.
I POSSESS ALL CHAPTERS BAR ONE.
A SITUATION WHICH IS CURRENTLY BEING REMEDIED...
GREAT STEAMIN' ARSES!

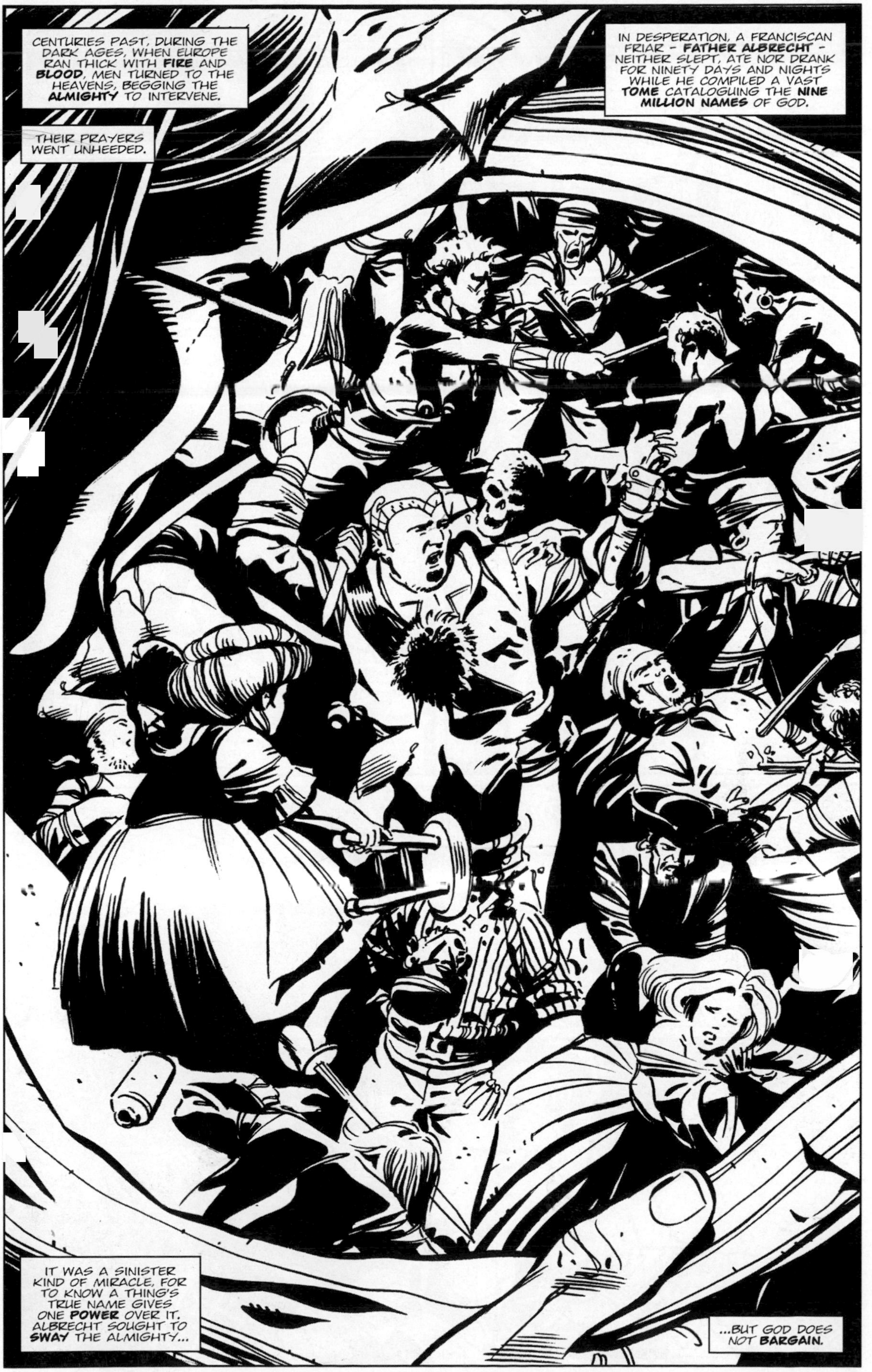
CENTURIES PAST, DURING THE DARK AGES, WHEN EUROPE RAN THICK WITH FIRE AND BLOOD, MEN TURNED TO THE HEAVENS, BEGGING THE ALMIGHTY TO INTERVENE.
THEIR PRAYERS WENT UNHEEDED.
IN DESPERATION, A FRANCISCAN FRIAR - FATHER ALBRECHT - NEITHER SLEPT, ATE NOR DRANK FOR NINETY DAYS AND NIGHTS WHILE HE COMPILED A VAST TOME CATALOGUING THE NINE MILLION NAMES OF GOD.
IT WAS A SINISTER KIND OF MIRACLE, FOR TO KNOW A THING'S TRUE NAME GIVES ONE POWER OVER IT. ALBRECHT SOUGHT TO SWAY THE ALMIGHTY...
...BUT GOD DOES NOT BARGAIN.

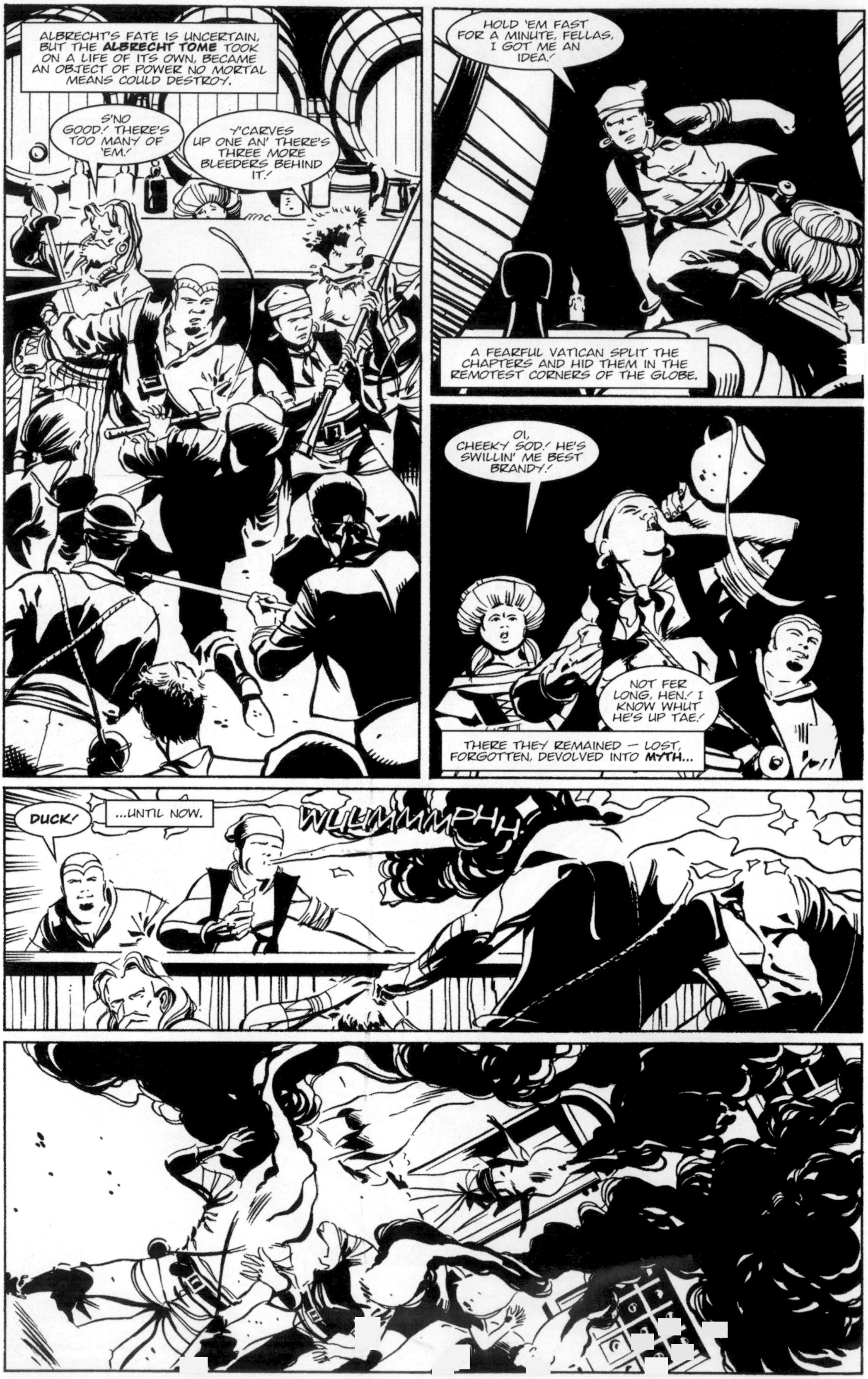
ALBRECHT'S FATE IS UNCERTAIN, BUT THE **ALBRECHT TOME** TOOK ON A LIFE OF ITS OWN, BECAME AN OBJECT OF POWER NO MORTAL MEANS COULD DESTROY.
S'NO GOOD! THERE'S TOO MANY OF 'EM!
Y'CARVES UP ONE AN' THERE'S THREE MORE BLEEDERS BEHIND IT!
HOLD 'EM FAST FOR A MINUTE, FELLAS, I GOT ME AN IDEA!
A FEARFUL VATICAN SPLIT THE CHAPTERS AND HID THEM IN THE REMOTEST CORNERS OF THE GLOBE.
OI, CHEEKY SOD! HE'S SWILLIN' ME BEST BRANDY!
NOT FER LONG, HEN! I KNOW WHUT HE'S UP TAE!
THERE THEY REMAINED — LOST, FORGOTTEN, DEVOLVED INTO **MYTH**...
DUCK!
...UNTIL NOW.
WUUMMMPHH

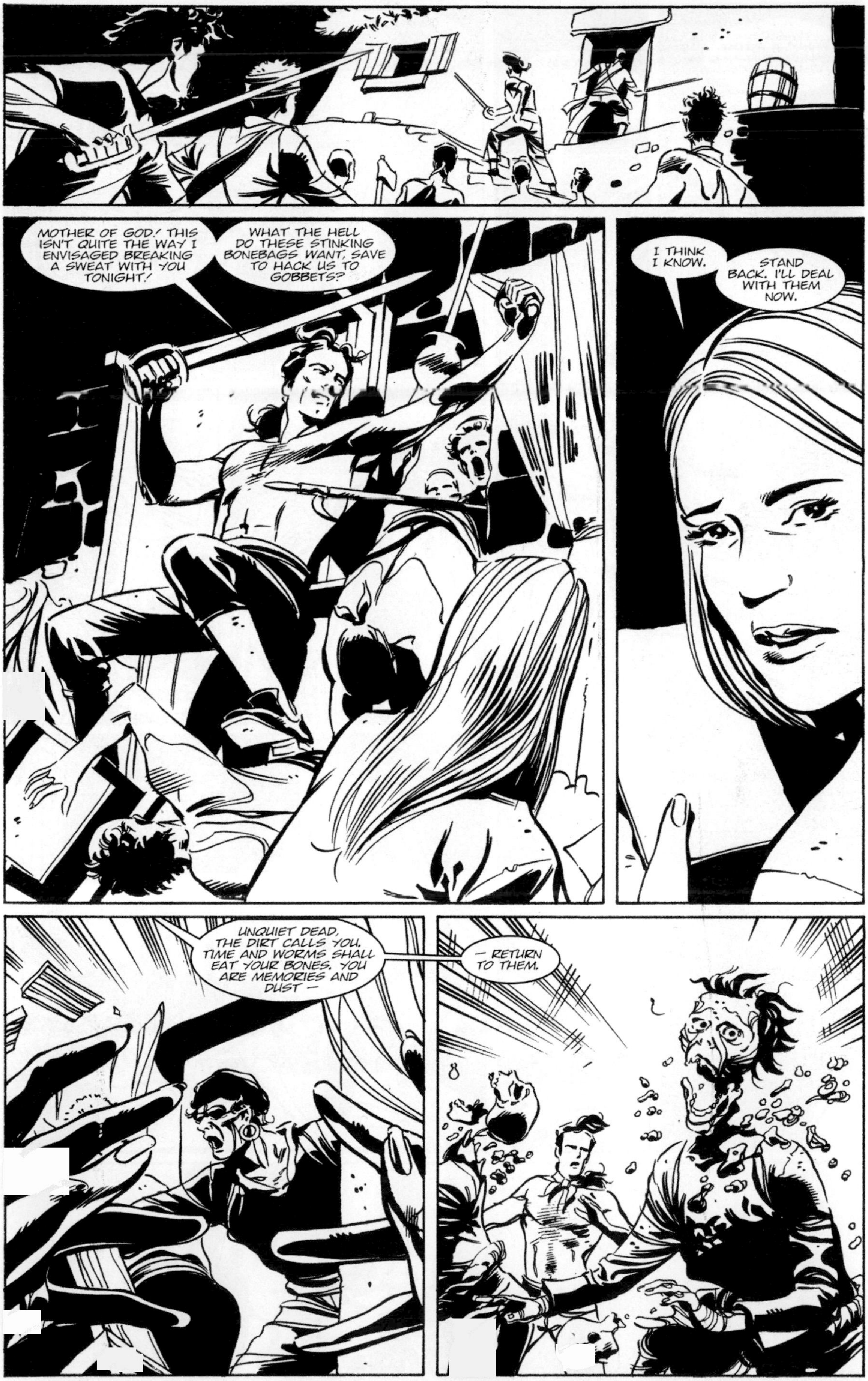
MOTHER OF GOD! THIS ISN'T QUITE THE WAY I ENVISAGED BREAKING A SWEAT WITH YOU TONIGHT!
WHAT THE HELL DO THESE STINKING BONEBAGS WANT, SAVE TO HACK US TO GOBBETS?
I THINK I KNOW.
STAND BACK. I'LL DEAL WITH THEM NOW.
UNQUIET DEAD, THE DIRT CALLS YOU. TIME AND WORMS SHALL EAT YOUR BONES. YOU ARE MEMORIES AND DUST —
— RETURN TO THEM.

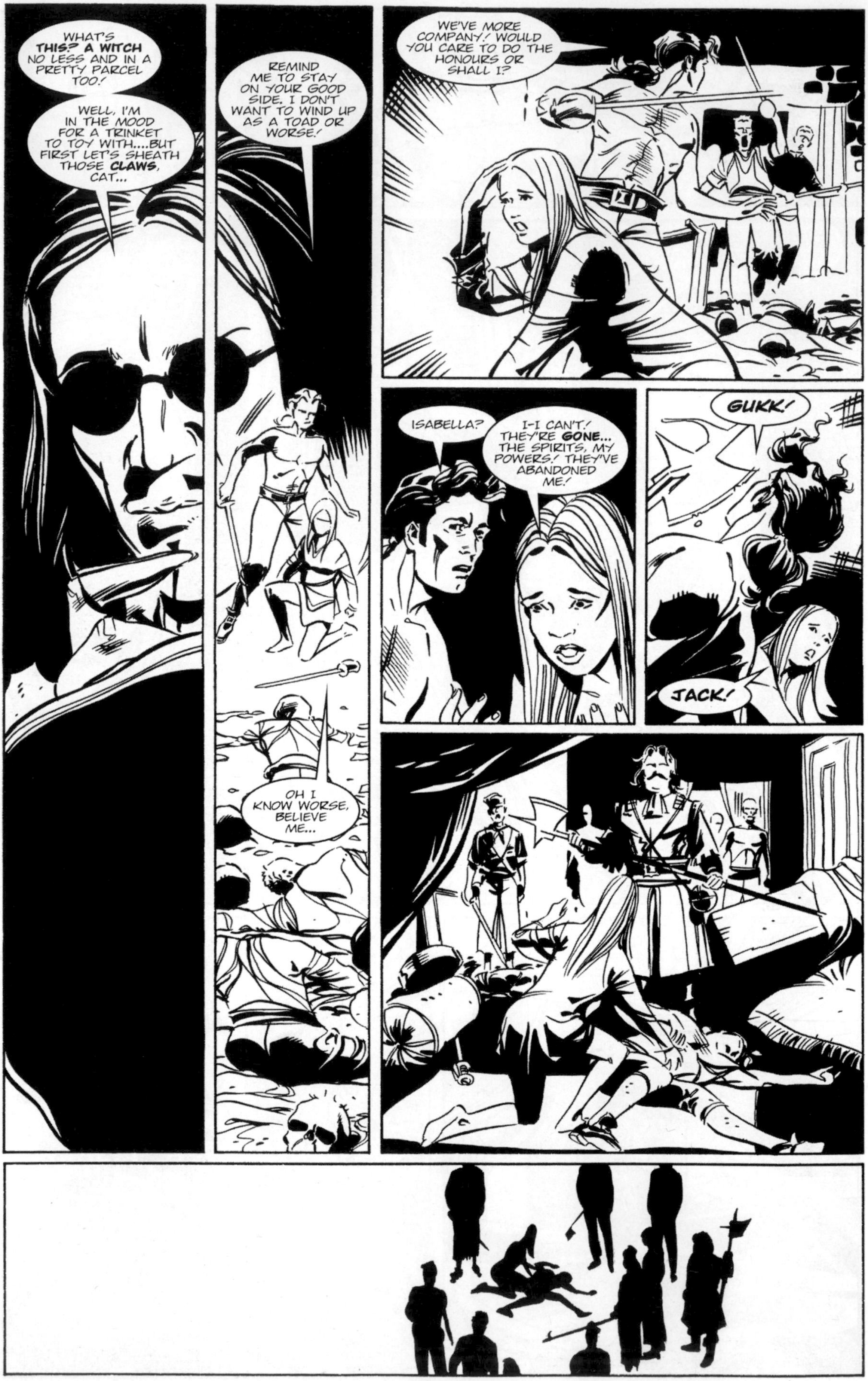
WHAT'S THIS? A WITCH NO LESS AND IN A PRETTY PARCEL TOO!
WELL, I'M IN THE MOOD FOR A TRINKET TO TOY WITH....BUT FIRST LET'S SHEATH THOSE CLAWS, CAT...
REMIND ME TO STAY ON YOUR GOOD SIDE. I DON'T WANT TO WIND UP AS A TOAD OR WORSE!
OH I KNOW WORSE, BELIEVE ME...
WE'VE MORE COMPANY! WOULD YOU CARE TO DO THE HONOURS OR SHALL I?
ISABELLA?
I-I CAN'T! THEY'RE GONE... THE SPIRITS, MY POWERS! THEY'VE ABANDONED ME!
GUKK!
JACK!

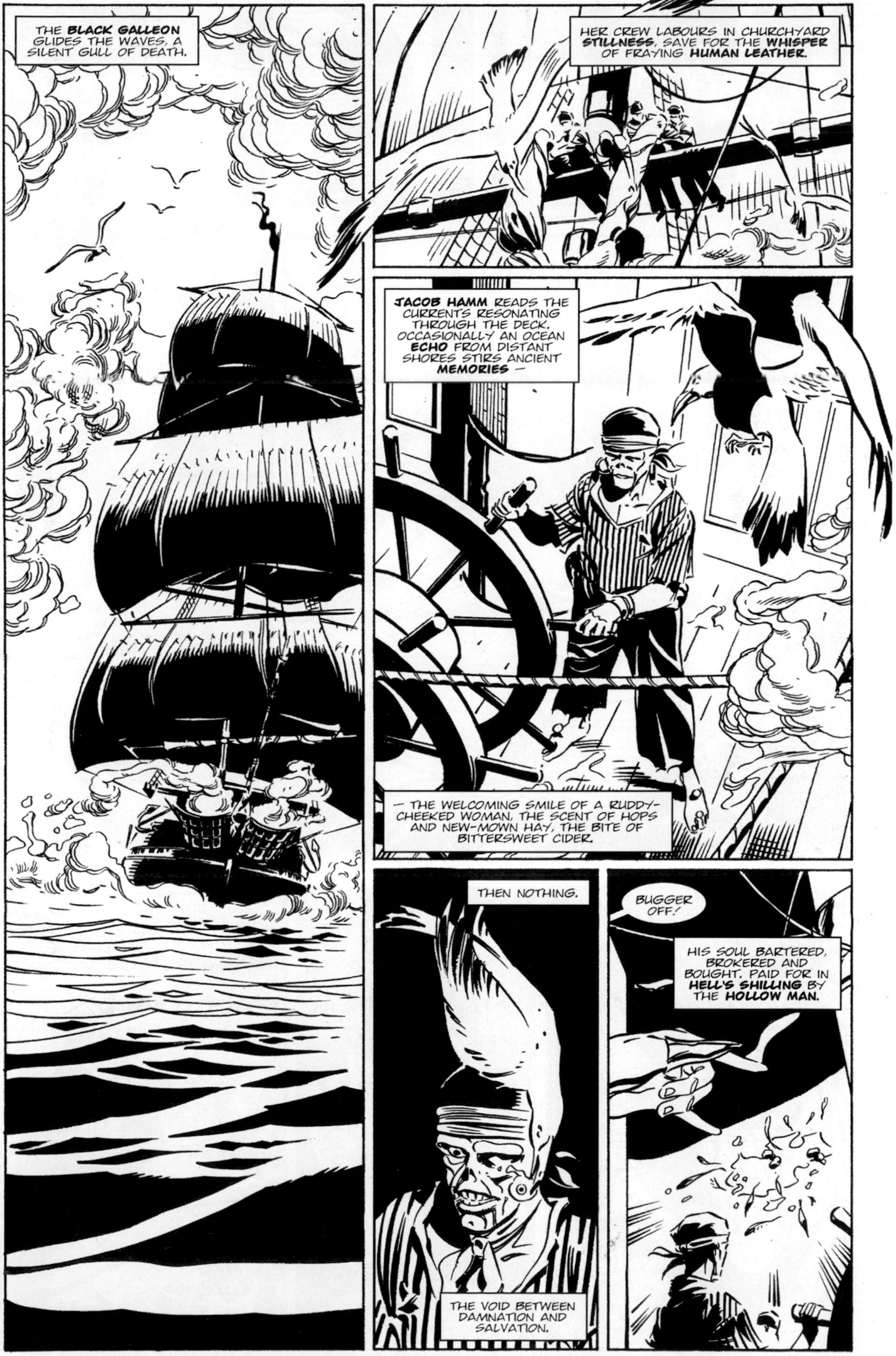
THE BLACK GALLEON GLIDES THE WAVES, A SILENT GULL OF DEATH.
HER CREW LABOURS IN CHURCHYARD STILLNESS, SAVE FOR THE WHISPER OF FRAYING HUMAN LEATHER.
JACOB HAMM READS THE CURRENTS RESONATING THROUGH THE DECK. OCCASIONALLY AN OCEAN ECHO FROM DISTANT SHORES STIRS ANCIENT MEMORIES –
– THE WELCOMING SMILE OF A RUDDY-CHEEKED WOMAN, THE SCENT OF HOPS AND NEW-MOWN HAY, THE BITE OF BITTERSWEET CIDER.
THEN NOTHING.
THE VOID BETWEEN DAMNATION AND SALVATION.
BUGGER OFF!
HIS SOUL BARTERED, BROKERED AND BOUGHT. PAID FOR IN HELL'S SHILLING BY THE HOLLOW MAN.

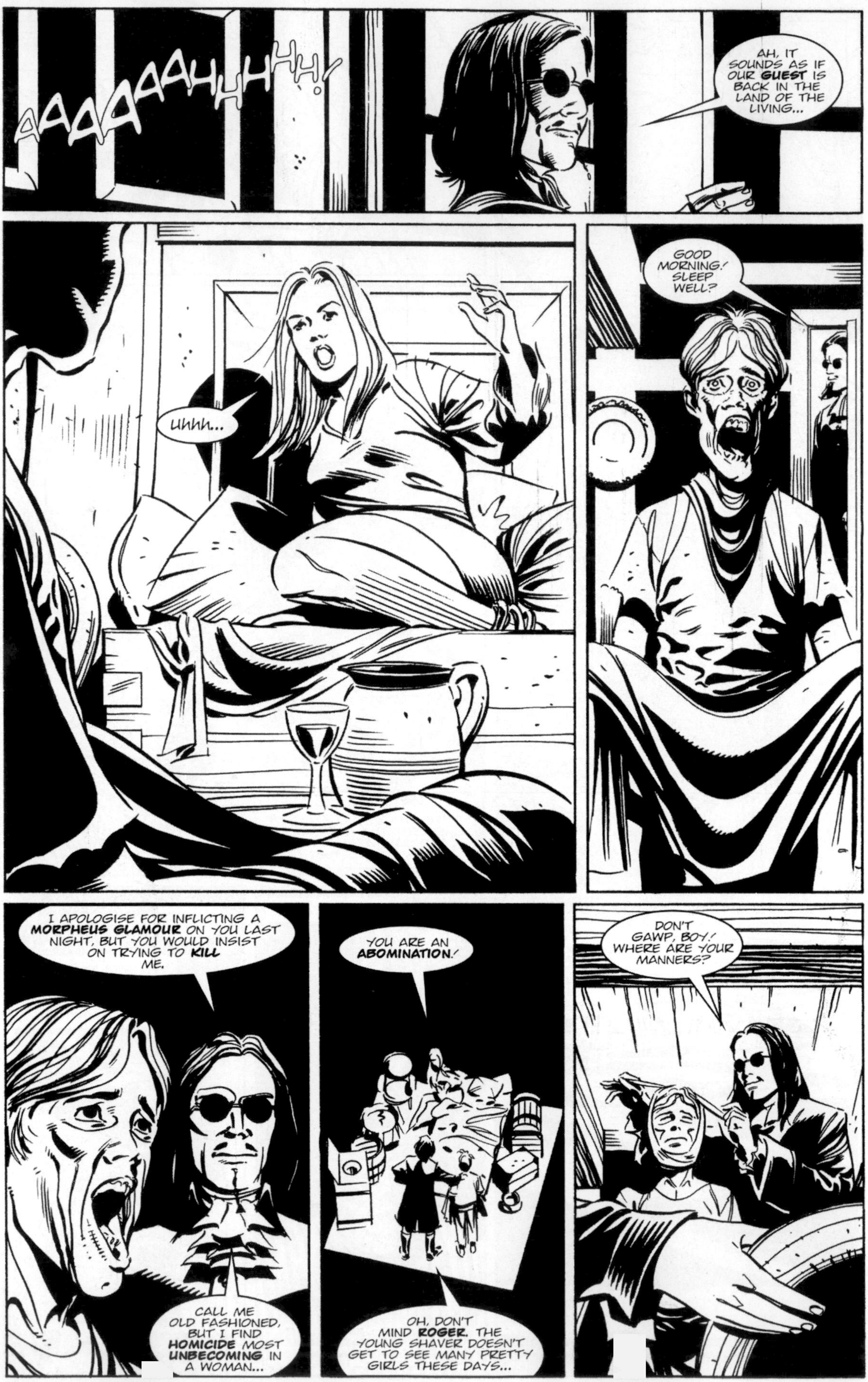
AAAAAAAHHHHHH!
AH, IT SOUNDS AS IF OUR GUEST IS BACK IN THE LAND OF THE LIVING...
UHHH...
GOOD MORNING! SLEEP WELL?
I APOLOGISE FOR INFLICTING A MORPHEUS GLAMOUR ON YOU LAST NIGHT, BUT YOU WOULD INSIST ON TRYING TO KILL ME.
CALL ME OLD FASHIONED, BUT I FIND HOMICIDE MOST UNBECOMING IN A WOMAN...
YOU ARE AN ABOMINATION!
OH, DON'T MIND ROGER. THE YOUNG SHAVER DOESN'T GET TO SEE MANY PRETTY GIRLS THESE DAYS...
DON'T GAWP, BOY! WHERE ARE YOUR MANNERS?

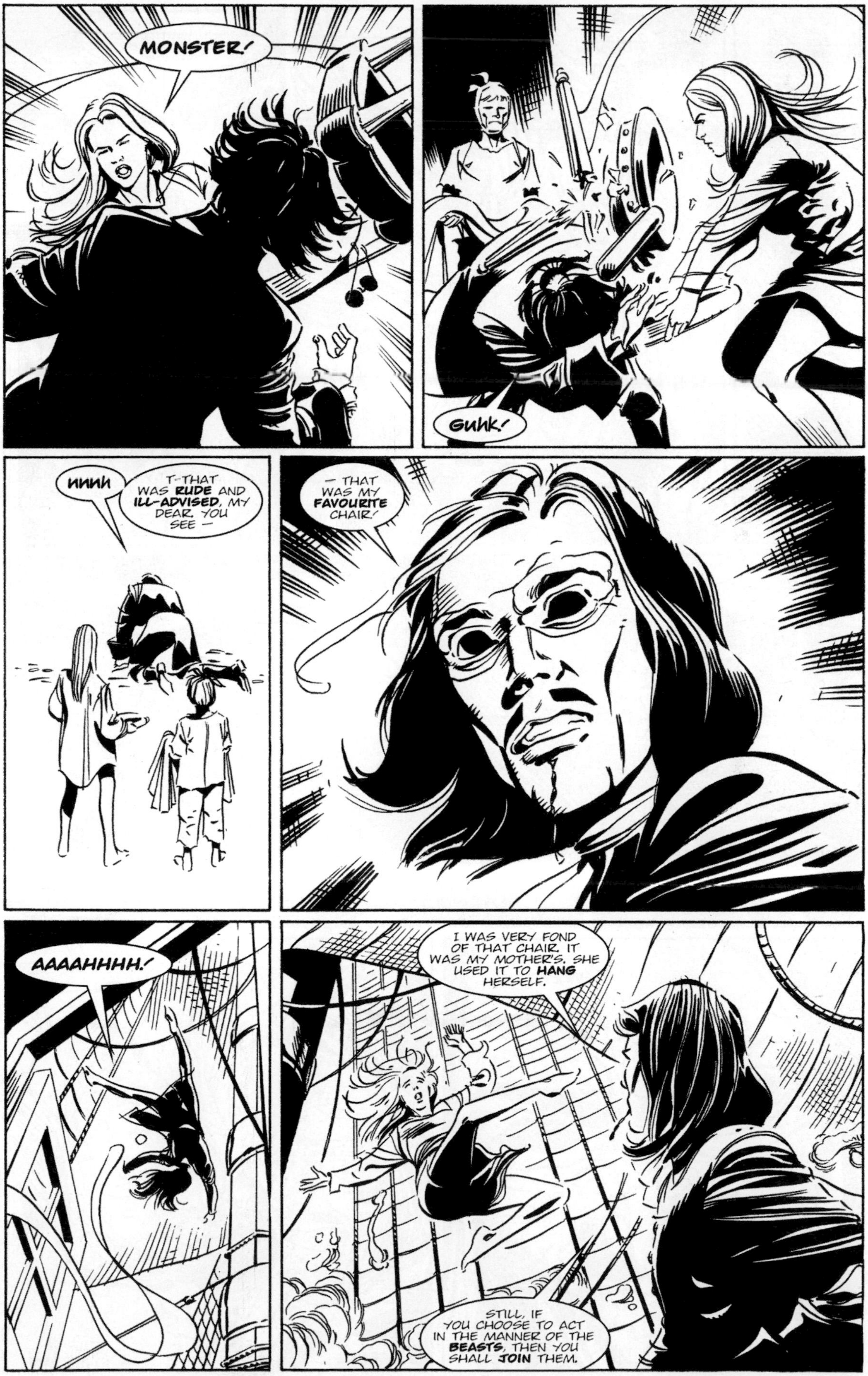
MONSTER!
GUHK!
UNNH
T-THAT WAS RUDE AND ILL-ADVISED, MY DEAR, YOU SEE —
— THAT WAS MY FAVOURITE CHAIR!
AAAAHHHH!
I WAS VERY FOND OF THAT CHAIR. IT WAS MY MOTHER'S. SHE USED IT TO HANG HERSELF.
STILL, IF YOU CHOOSE TO ACT IN THE MANNER OF THE BEASTS, THEN YOU SHALL JOIN THEM.

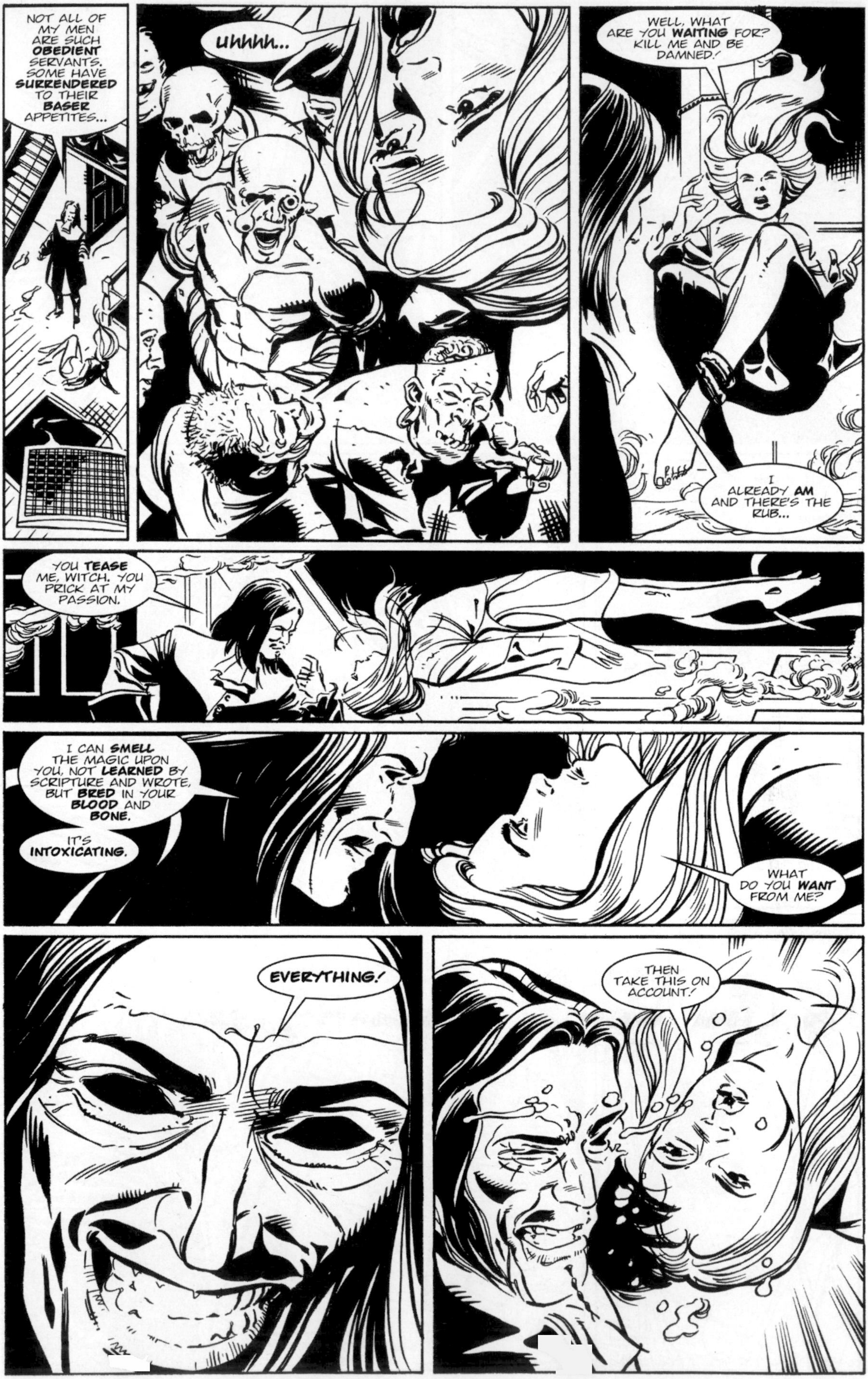
NOT ALL OF MY MEN ARE SUCH OBEDIENT SERVANTS. SOME HAVE SURRENDERED TO THEIR BASER APPETITES...
UHHHH...
WELL, WHAT ARE YOU WAITING FOR? KILL ME AND BE DAMNED!
I ALREADY AM AND THERE'S THE RUB...
YOU TEASE ME, WITCH. YOU PRICK AT MY PASSION.
I CAN SMELL THE MAGIC UPON YOU, NOT LEARNED BY SCRIPTURE AND WROTE, BUT BRED IN YOUR BLOOD AND BONE.
IT'S INTOXICATING.
WHAT DO YOU WANT FROM ME?
EVERYTHING!
THEN TAKE THIS ON ACCOUNT!

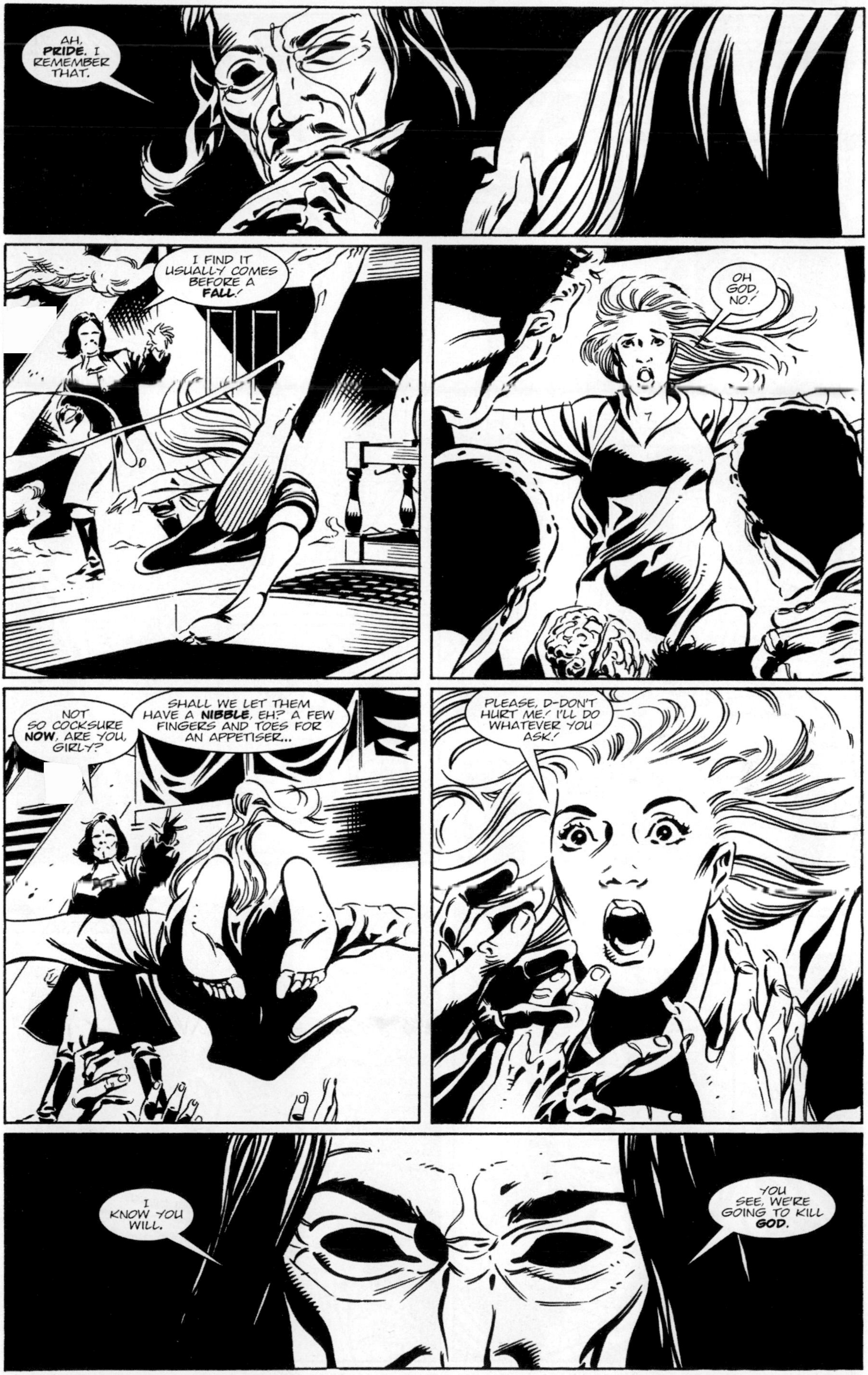
AH, PRIDE. I REMEMBER THAT.
I FIND IT USUALLY COMES BEFORE A FALL!
OH GOD, NO!
NOT SO COCKSURE NOW, ARE YOU, GIRLY?
SHALL WE LET THEM HAVE A NIBBLE, EH? A FEW FINGERS AND TOES FOR AN APPETISER...
PLEASE, D-DON'T HURT ME! I'LL DO WHATEVER YOU ASK!
I KNOW YOU WILL.
YOU SEE, WE'RE GOING TO KILL GOD.

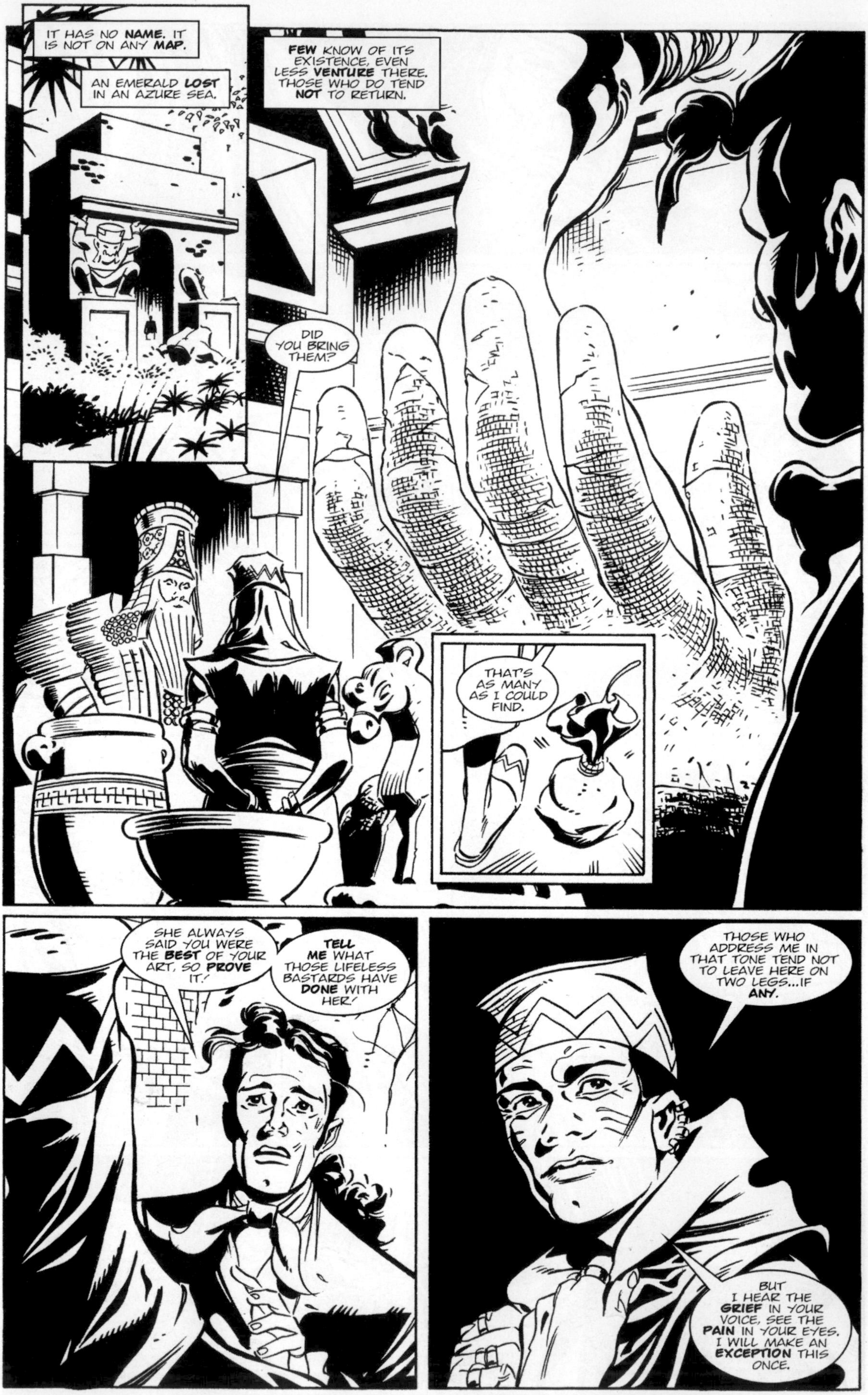
IT HAS NO NAME. IT IS NOT ON ANY MAP.
AN EMERALD LOST IN AN AZURE SEA.
FEW KNOW OF ITS EXISTENCE, EVEN LESS VENTURE THERE. THOSE WHO DO TEND NOT TO RETURN.
DID YOU BRING THEM?
THAT'S AS MANY AS I COULD FIND.
SHE ALWAYS SAID YOU WERE THE BEST OF YOUR ART, SO PROVE IT!
TELL ME WHAT THOSE LIFELESS BASTARDS HAVE DONE WITH HER!
THOSE WHO ADDRESS ME IN THAT TONE TEND NOT TO LEAVE HERE ON TWO LEGS...IF ANY.
BUT I HEAR THE GRIEF IN YOUR VOICE, SEE THE PAIN IN YOUR EYES. I WILL MAKE AN EXCEPTION THIS ONCE.

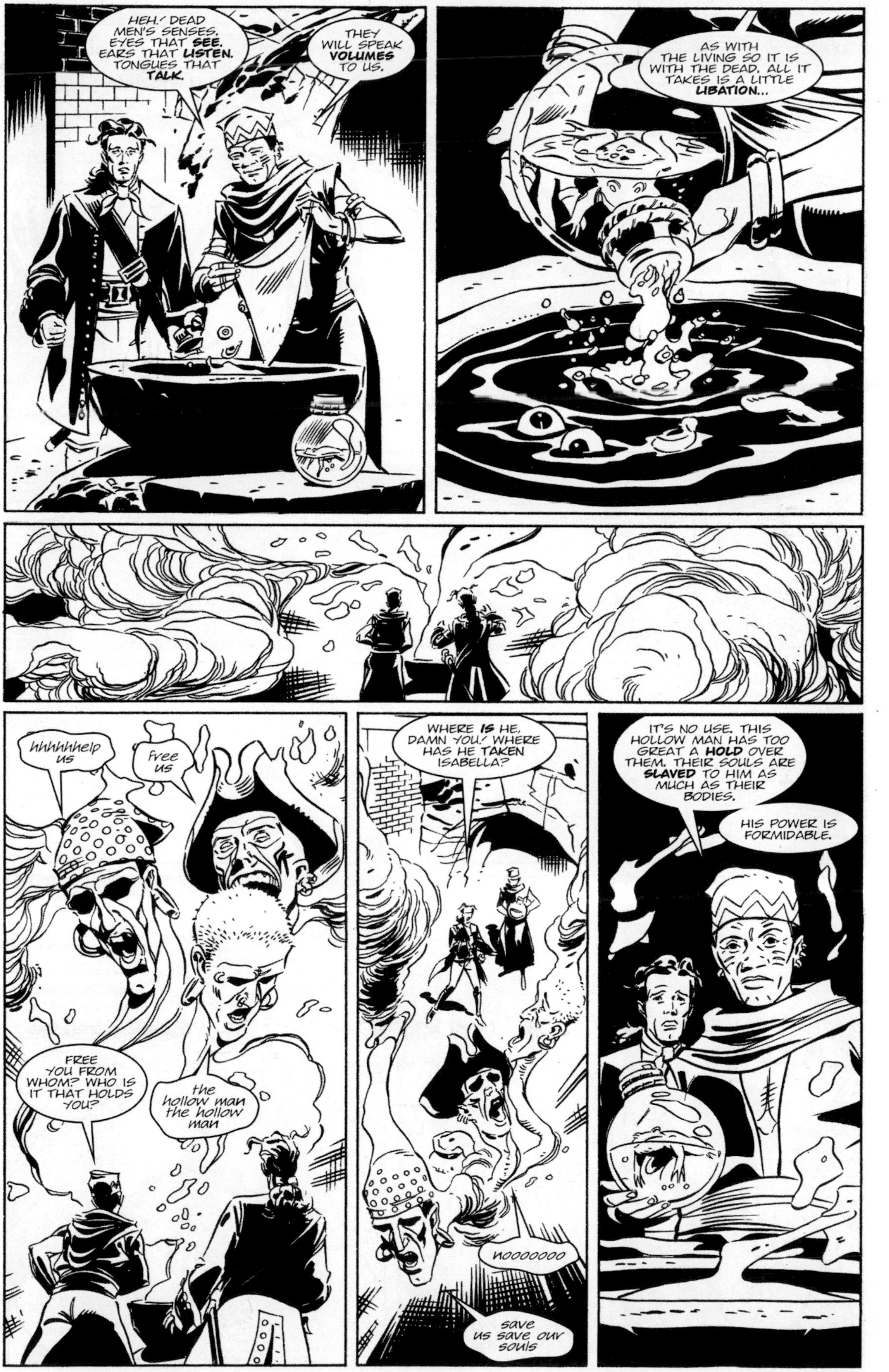
HEH! DEAD MEN'S SENSES. EYES THAT SEE. EARS THAT LISTEN. TONGUES THAT TALK.
THEY WILL SPEAK VOLUMES TO US.
AS WITH THE LIVING SO IT IS WITH THE DEAD. ALL IT TAKES IS A LITTLE LIBATION...
hhhhhhelp us
free us
FREE YOU FROM WHOM? WHO IS IT THAT HOLDS YOU?
the hollow man the hollow man
WHERE IS HE, DAMN YOU! WHERE HAS HE TAKEN ISABELLA?
nooooooo
save us save our souls
IT'S NO USE. THIS HOLLOW MAN HAS TOO GREAT A HOLD OVER THEM. THEIR SOULS ARE SLAVED TO HIM AS MUCH AS THEIR BODIES.
HIS POWER IS FORMIDABLE.

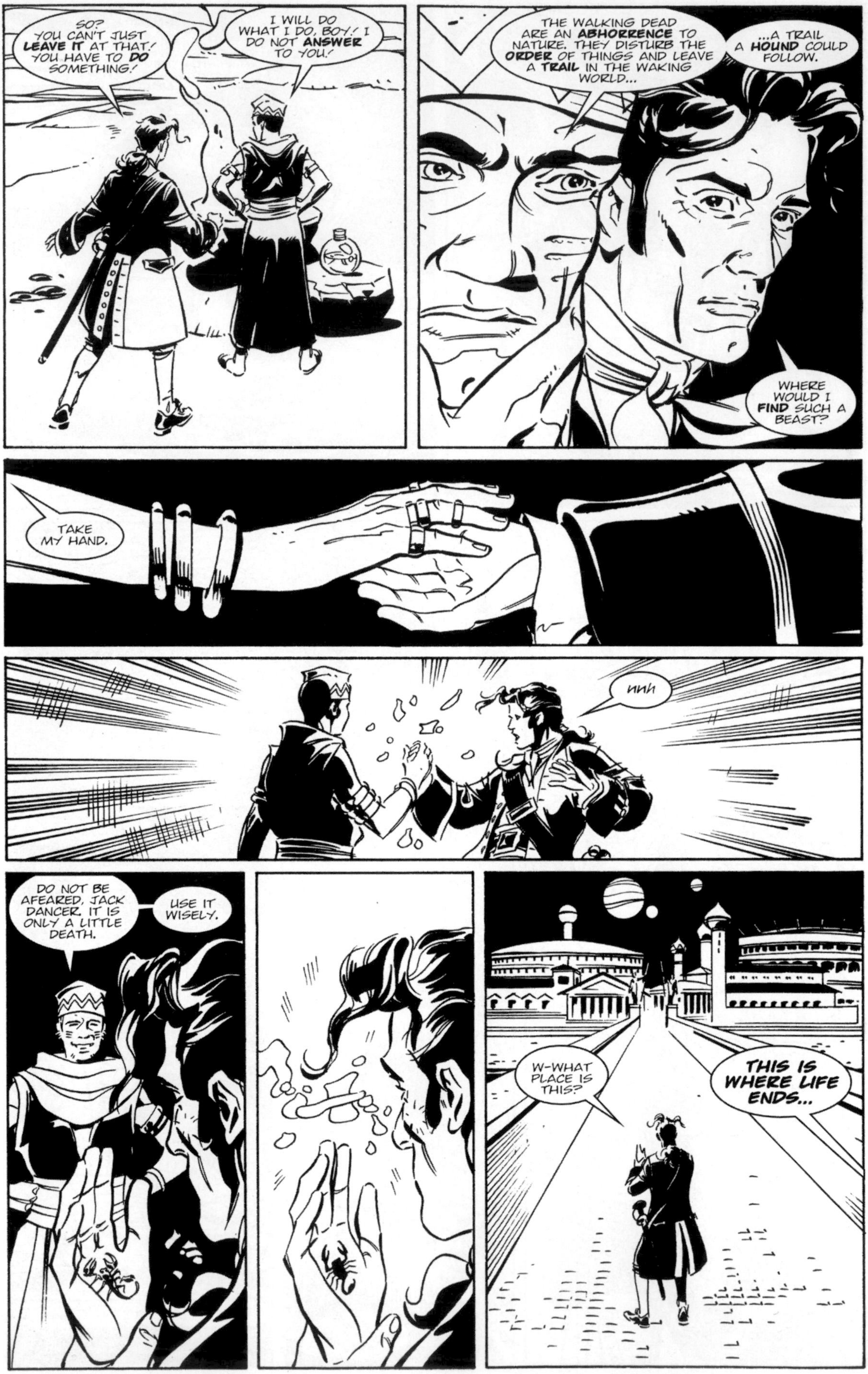
SO? YOU CAN'T JUST LEAVE IT AT THAT! YOU HAVE TO DO SOMETHING!
I WILL DO WHAT I DO, BOY! I DO NOT ANSWER TO YOU!
THE WALKING DEAD ARE AN ABHORRENCE TO NATURE. THEY DISTURB THE ORDER OF THINGS AND LEAVE A TRAIL IN THE WAKING WORLD...
...A TRAIL A HOUND COULD FOLLOW.
WHERE WOULD I FIND SUCH A BEAST?
TAKE MY HAND.
UNH
DO NOT BE AFEARED, JACK DANCER. IT IS ONLY A LITTLE DEATH.
USE IT WISELY.
W-WHAT PLACE IS THIS?
THIS IS WHERE LIFE ENDS...

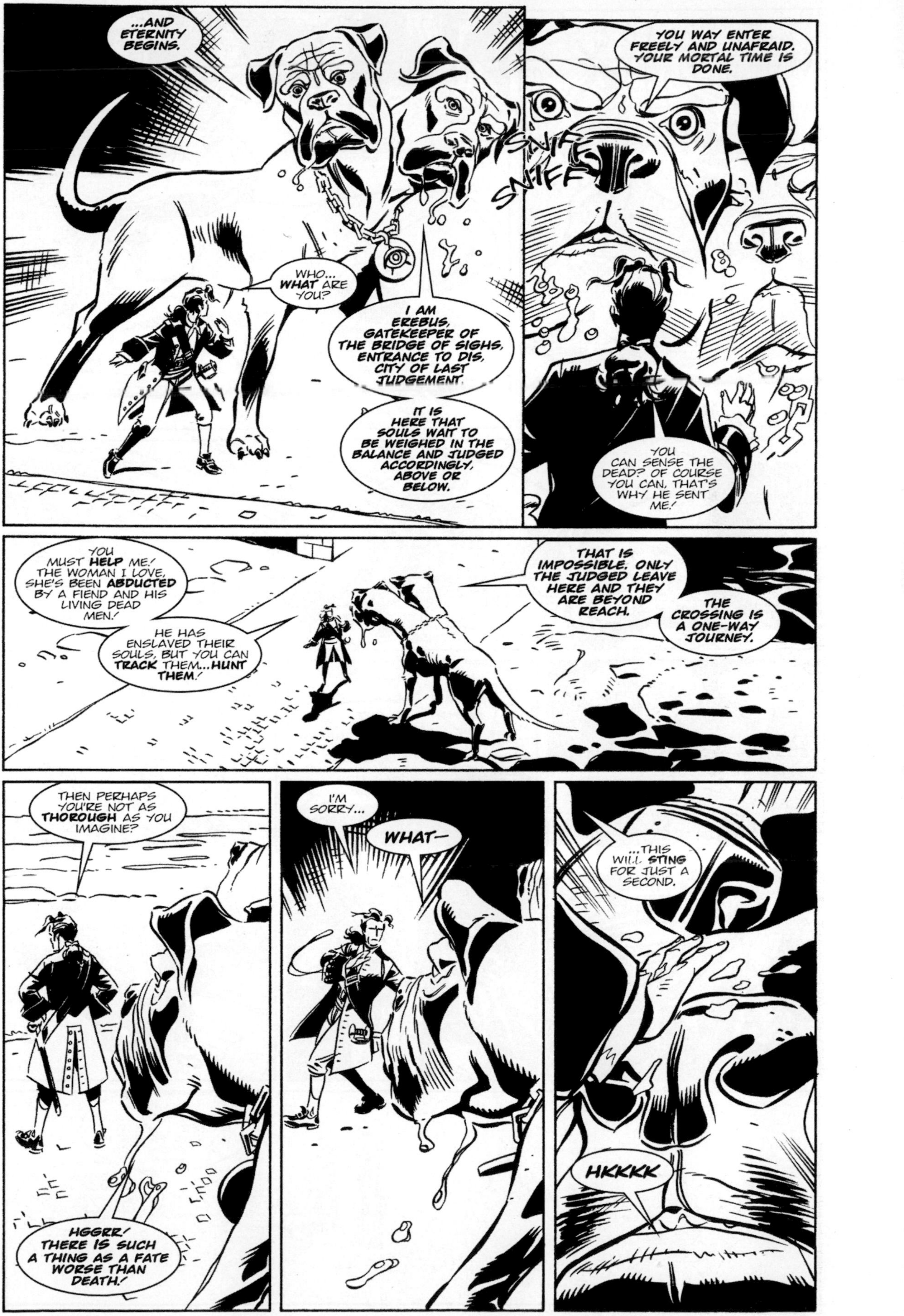
...AND ETERNITY BEGINS.
WHO... WHAT ARE YOU?
I AM EREBUS, GATEKEEPER OF THE BRIDGE OF SIGHS, ENTRANCE TO DIS, CITY OF LAST JUDGEMENT.
IT IS HERE THAT SOULS WAIT TO BE WEIGHED IN THE BALANCE AND JUDGED ACCORDINGLY, ABOVE OR BELOW.
YOU WAY ENTER FREELY AND UNAFRAID. YOUR MORTAL TIME IS DONE.
SNIFF SNIFF
YOU CAN SENSE THE DEAD? OF COURSE YOU CAN, THAT'S WHY HE SENT ME!
YOU MUST HELP ME! THE WOMAN I LOVE, SHE'S BEEN ABDUCTED BY A FIEND AND HIS LIVING DEAD MEN!
HE HAS ENSLAVED THEIR SOULS, BUT YOU CAN TRACK THEM...HUNT THEM!
THAT IS IMPOSSIBLE. ONLY THE JUDGED LEAVE HERE AND THEY ARE BEYOND REACH.
THE CROSSING IS A ONE-WAY JOURNEY.
THEN PERHAPS YOU'RE NOT AS THOROUGH AS YOU IMAGINE?
HGGRR! THERE IS SUCH A THING AS A FATE WORSE THAN DEATH!
I'M SORRY...
WHAT—
...THIS WILL STING FOR JUST A SECOND.
HKKKK

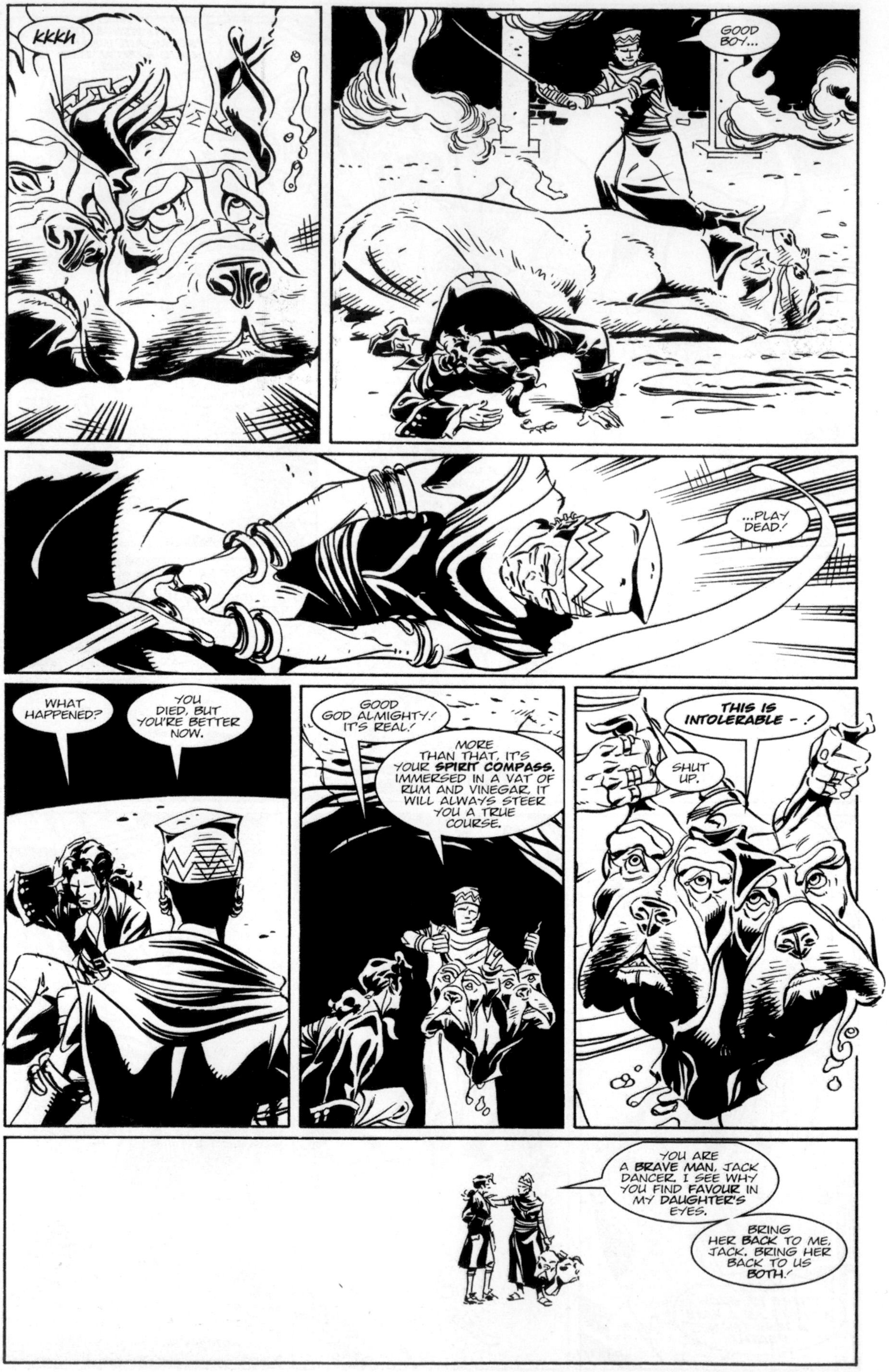
KKKH
GOOD BOY...
...PLAY DEAD!
WHAT HAPPENED?
YOU DIED, BUT YOU'RE BETTER NOW.
GOOD GOD ALMIGHTY! IT'S REAL!
MORE THAN THAT, IT'S YOUR SPIRIT COMPASS. IMMERSED IN A VAT OF RUM AND VINEGAR, IT WILL ALWAYS STEER YOU A TRUE COURSE.
THIS IS INTOLERABLE--!
SHUT UP.
YOU ARE A BRAVE MAN, JACK DANCER. I SEE WHY YOU FIND FAVOUR IN MY DAUGHTER'S EYES.
BRING HER BACK TO ME, JACK. BRING HER BACK TO US BOTH!

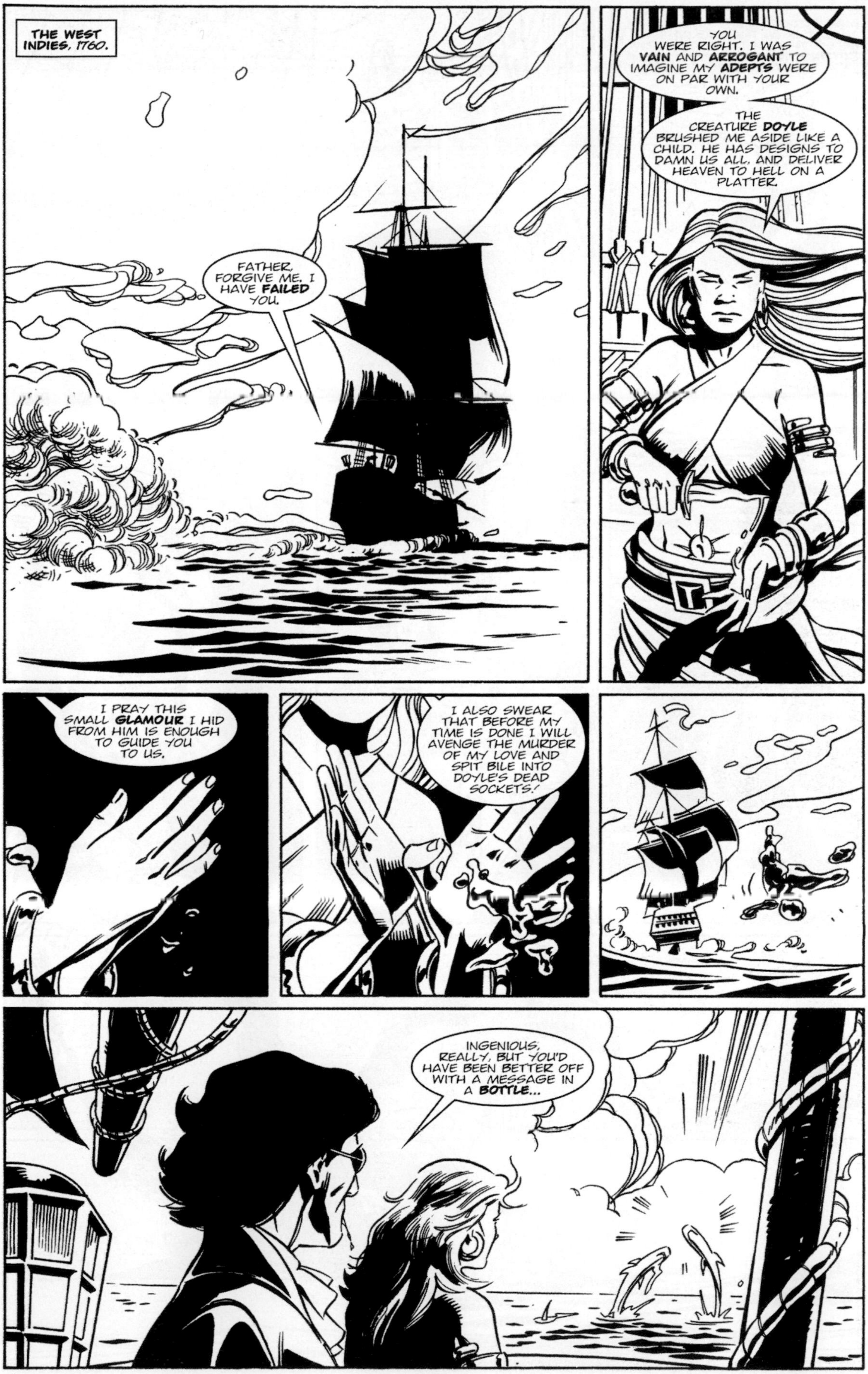
THE WEST INDIES, 1760.
FATHER, FORGIVE ME. I HAVE FAILED YOU.
YOU WERE RIGHT. I WAS VAIN AND ARROGANT TO IMAGINE MY ADEPTS WERE ON PAR WITH YOUR OWN.
THE CREATURE DOYLE BRUSHED ME ASIDE LIKE A CHILD. HE HAS DESIGNS TO DAMN US ALL, AND DELIVER HEAVEN TO HELL ON A PLATTER.
I PRAY THIS SMALL GLAMOUR I HID FROM HIM IS ENOUGH TO GUIDE YOU TO US.
I ALSO SWEAR THAT BEFORE MY TIME IS DONE I WILL AVENGE THE MURDER OF MY LOVE AND SPIT BILE INTO DOYLE'S DEAD SOCKETS!
INGENIOUS, REALLY, BUT YOU'D HAVE BEEN BETTER OFF WITH A MESSAGE IN A BOTTLE...

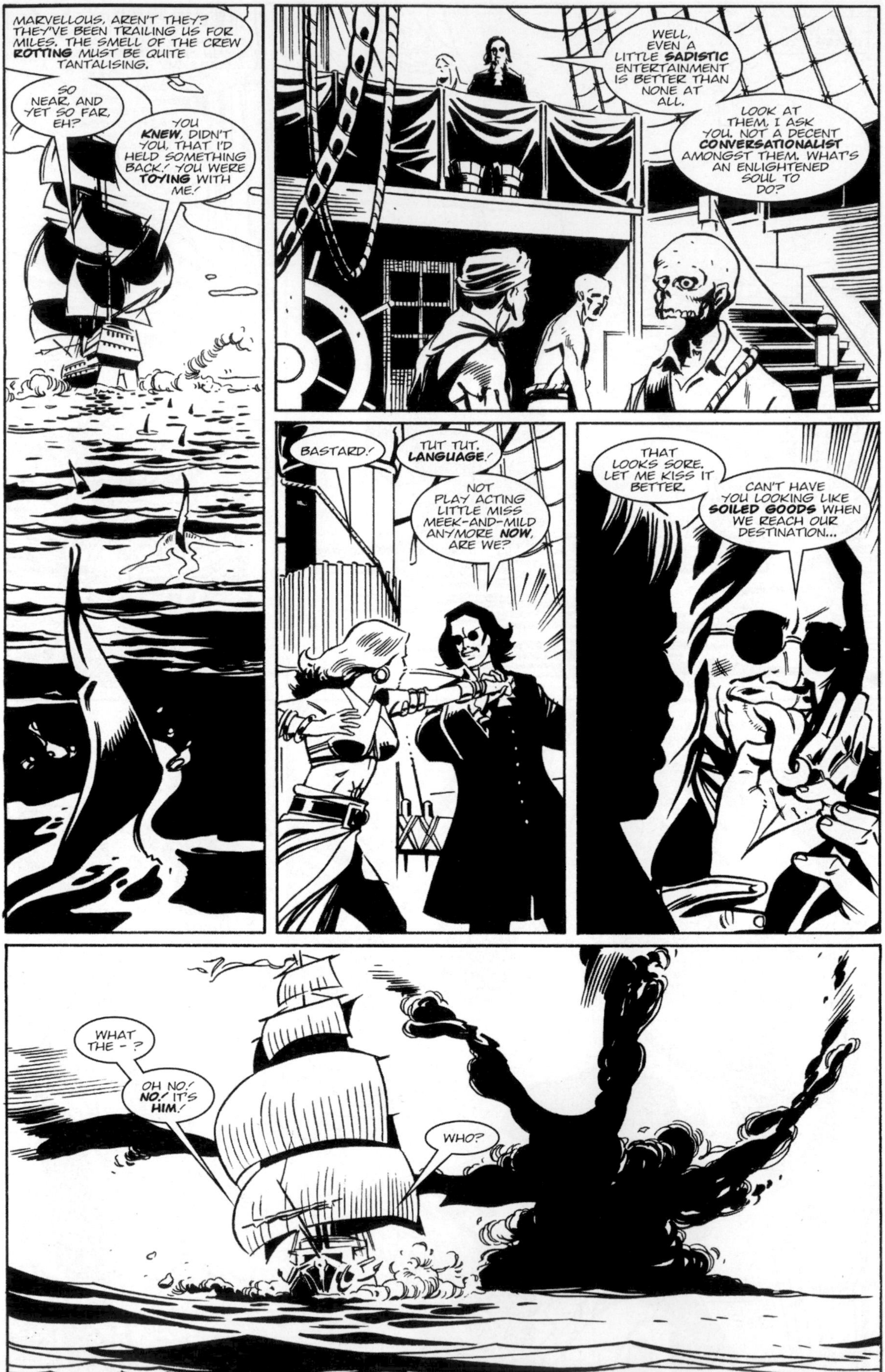
MARVELLOUS, AREN'T THEY? THEY'VE BEEN TRAILING US FOR MILES. THE SMELL OF THE CREW **ROTTING** MUST BE QUITE TANTALISING.
SO NEAR, AND YET SO FAR, EH?
YOU **KNEW**, DIDN'T YOU, THAT I'D HELD SOMETHING BACK! YOU WERE **TOYING** WITH ME!
WELL, EVEN A LITTLE **SADISTIC** ENTERTAINMENT IS BETTER THAN NONE AT ALL.
LOOK AT THEM, I ASK YOU. NOT A DECENT **CONVERSATIONALIST** AMONGST THEM. WHAT'S AN ENLIGHTENED SOUL TO DO?
BASTARD!
TUT TUT. **LANGUAGE**!
NOT PLAY ACTING LITTLE MISS MEEK-AND-MILD ANYMORE **NOW**, ARE WE?
THAT LOOKS SORE. LET ME KISS IT BETTER.
CAN'T HAVE YOU LOOKING LIKE **SOILED GOODS** WHEN WE REACH OUR DESTINATION...
WHAT THE - ?
OH NO! **NO!** IT'S **HIM**!
WHO?

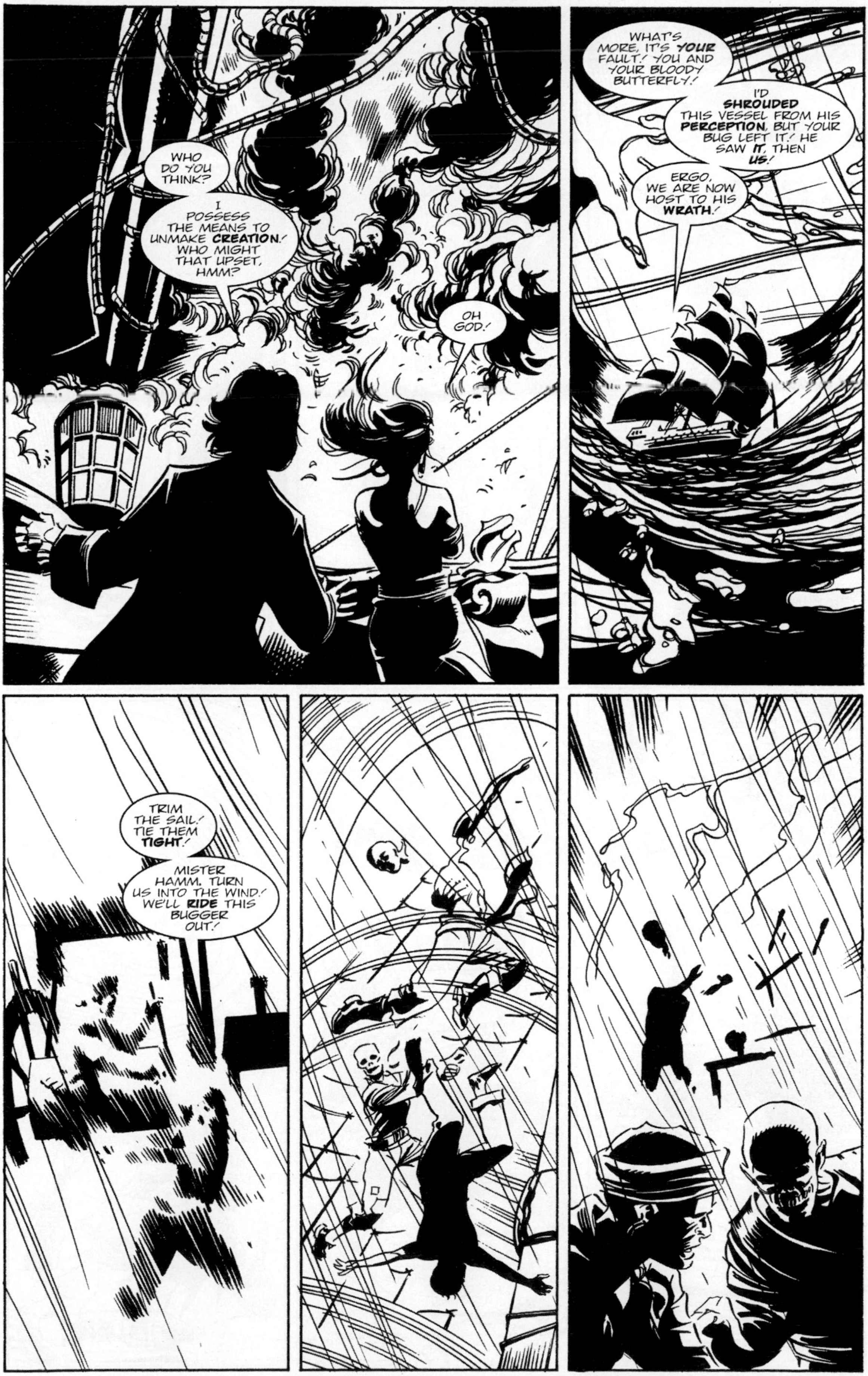
WHO DO YOU THINK?
I POSSESS THE MEANS TO UNMAKE CREATION! WHO MIGHT THAT UPSET, HMM?
OH GOD!
WHAT'S MORE, IT'S YOUR FAULT! YOU AND YOUR BLOODY BUTTERFLY!
I'D SHROUDED THIS VESSEL FROM HIS PERCEPTION, BUT YOUR BUG LEFT IT! HE SAW IT, THEN US!
ERGO, WE ARE NOW HOST TO HIS WRATH!
TRIM THE SAIL! TIE THEM TIGHT!
MISTER HAMM, TURN US INTO THE WIND! WE'LL RIDE THIS BUGGER OUT!

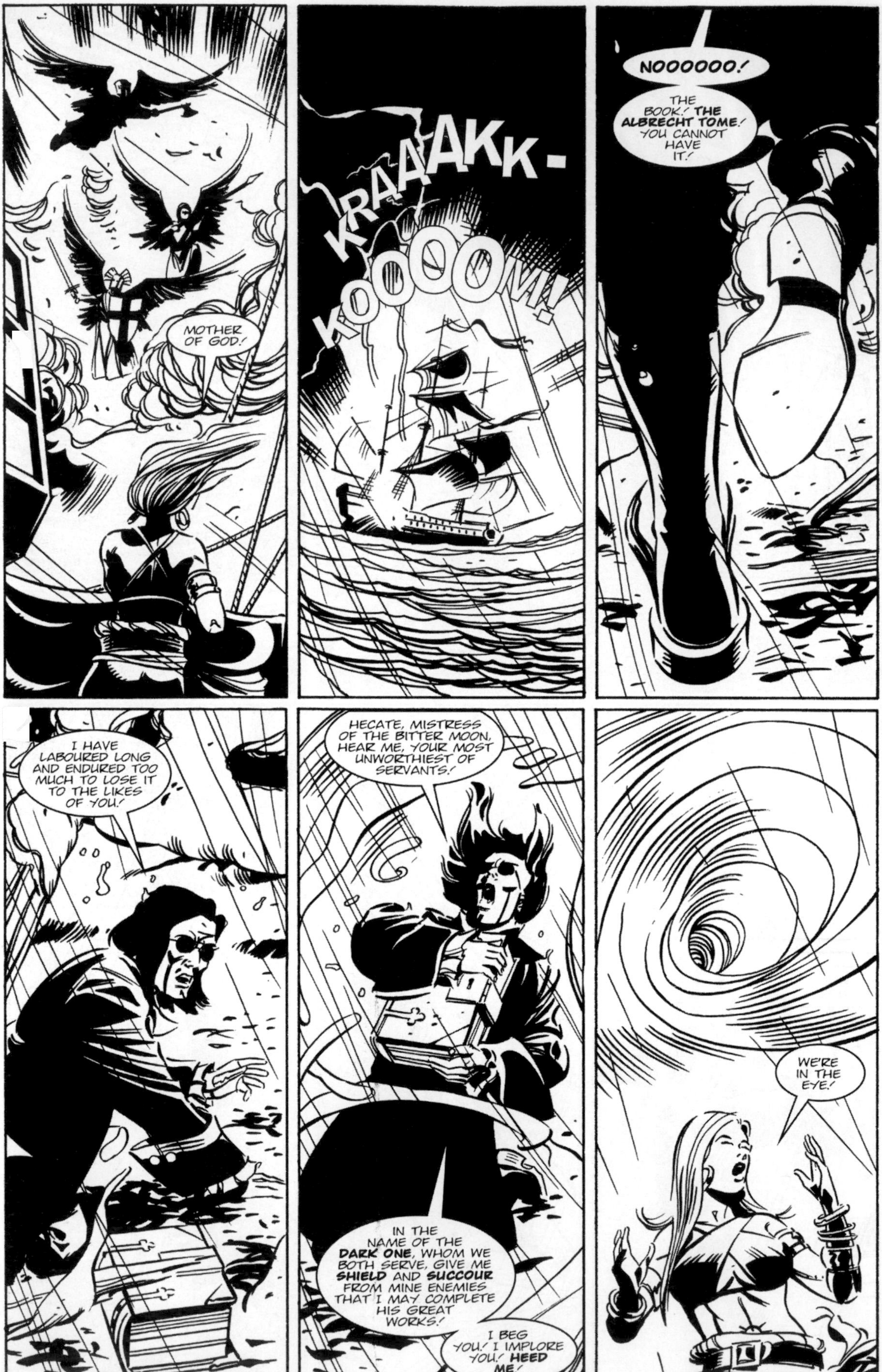

MOTHER OF GOD!
KRAAAKK-KOOOOOM!!
NOOOOOO!
THE BOOK! THE ALBRECHT TOME! YOU CANNOT HAVE IT!
I HAVE LABOURED LONG AND ENDURED TOO MUCH TO LOSE IT TO THE LIKES OF YOU!
HECATE, MISTRESS OF THE BITTER MOON, HEAR ME, YOUR MOST UNWORTHIEST OF SERVANTS!
IN THE NAME OF THE DARK ONE, WHOM WE BOTH SERVE, GIVE ME SHIELD AND SUCCOUR FROM MINE ENEMIES THAT I MAY COMPLETE HIS GREAT WORKS!
I BEG YOU! I IMPLORE YOU! HEED ME!
WE'RE IN THE EYE!

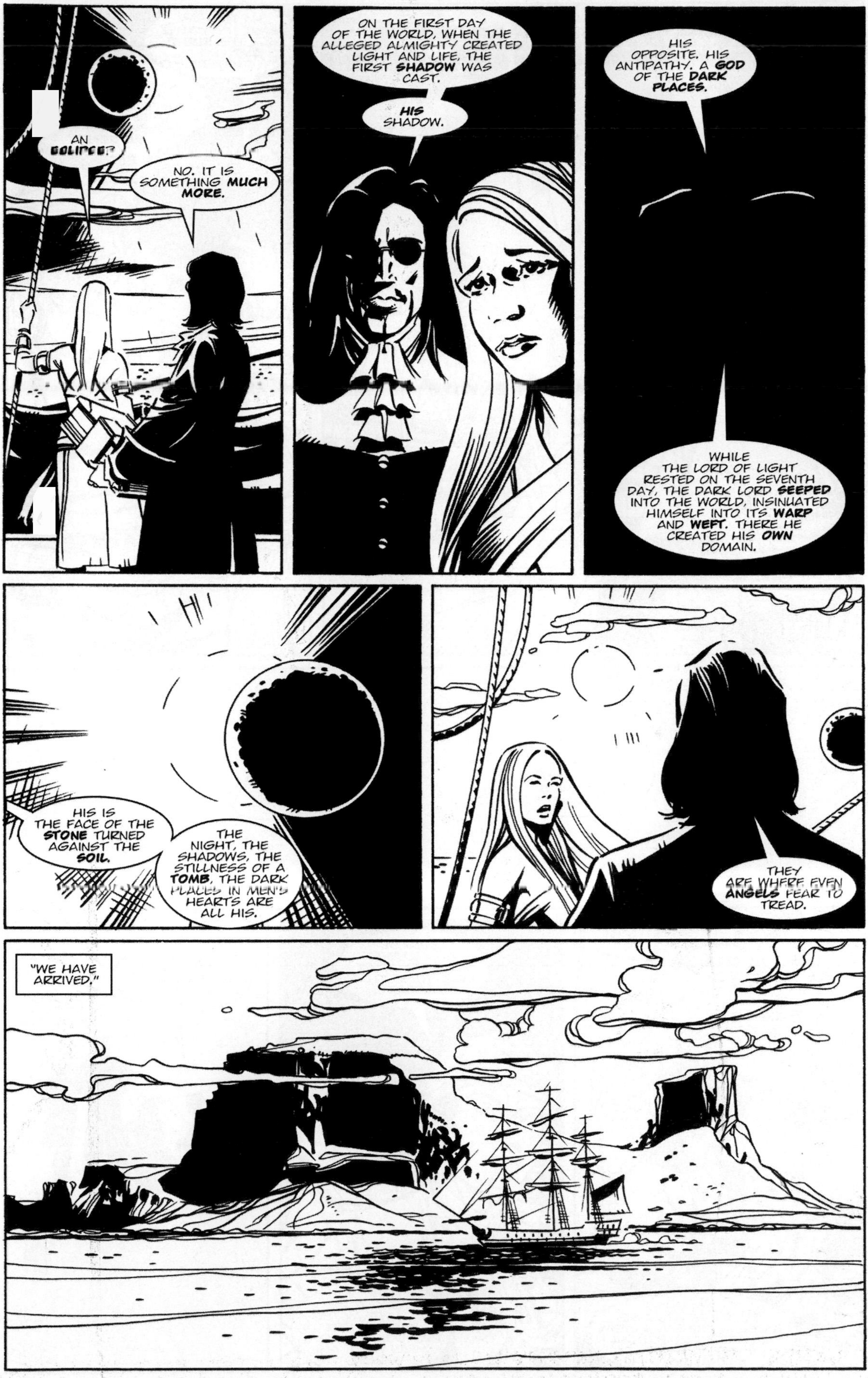
AN ECLIPSE?
NO. IT IS SOMETHING MUCH MORE.
ON THE FIRST DAY OF THE WORLD, WHEN THE ALLEGED ALMIGHTY CREATED LIGHT AND LIFE, THE FIRST SHADOW WAS CAST.
HIS SHADOW.
HIS OPPOSITE. HIS ANTIPATHY. A GOD OF THE DARK PLACES.
WHILE THE LORD OF LIGHT RESTED ON THE SEVENTH DAY, THE DARK LORD SEEPED INTO THE WORLD, INSINUATED HIMSELF INTO ITS WARP AND WEFT. THERE HE CREATED HIS OWN DOMAIN.
HIS IS THE FACE OF THE STONE TURNED AGAINST THE SOIL.
THE NIGHT, THE SHADOWS, THE STILLNESS OF A TOMB, THE DARK PLACES IN MEN'S HEARTS ARE ALL HIS.
THEY ARE WHERE EVEN ANGELS FEAR TO TREAD.
"WE HAVE ARRIVED."

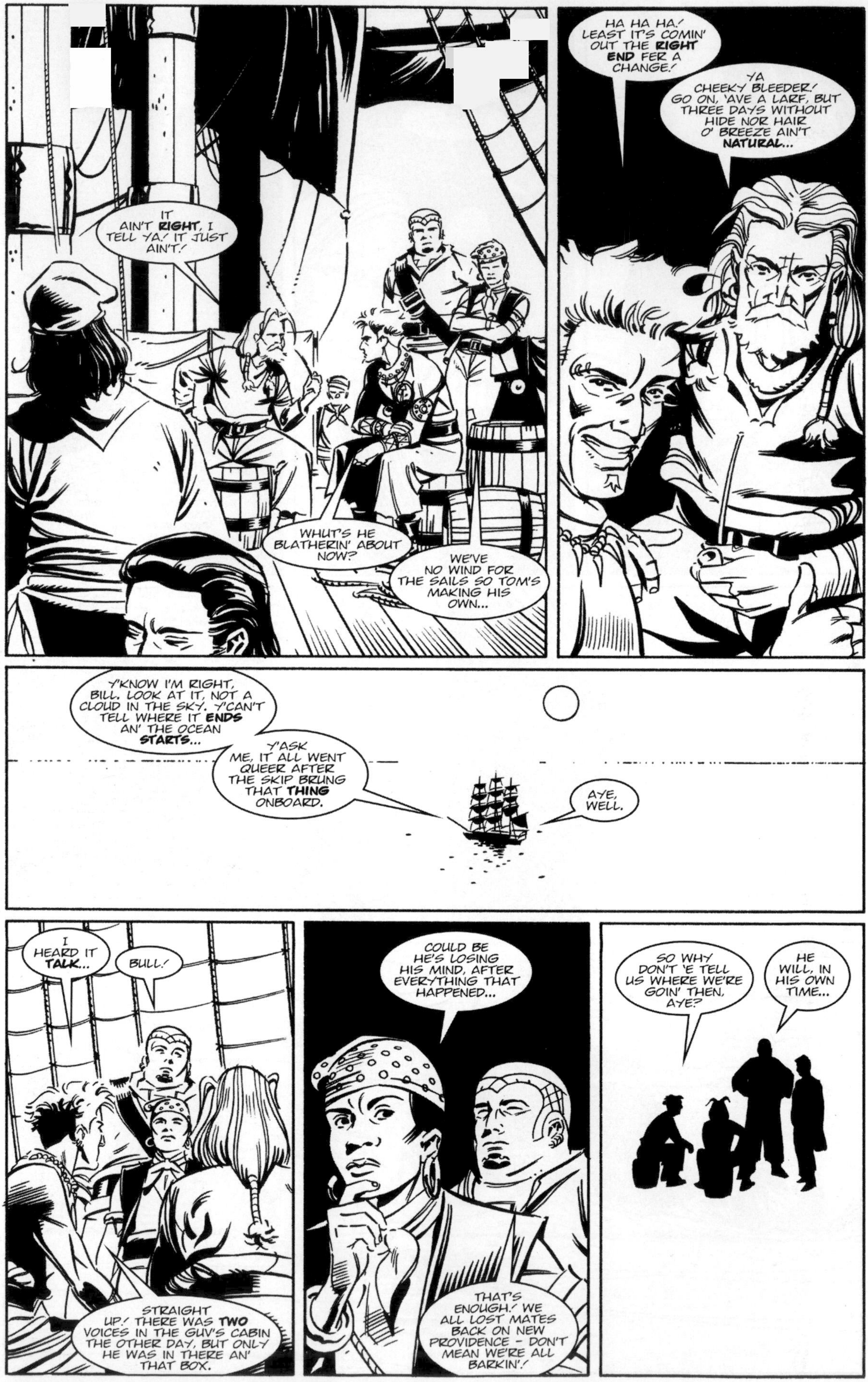

IT AIN'T RIGHT, I TELL YA! IT JUST AIN'T!
WHUT'S HE BLATHERIN' ABOUT NOW?
WE'VE NO WIND FOR THE SAILS SO TOM'S MAKING HIS OWN...
HA HA HA! LEAST IT'S COMIN' OUT THE RIGHT END FER A CHANGE!
YA CHEEKY BLEEDER! GO ON, 'AVE A LARF, BUT THREE DAYS WITHOUT HIDE NOR HAIR O' BREEZE AIN'T NATURAL...
Y'KNOW I'M RIGHT, BILL. LOOK AT IT, NOT A CLOUD IN THE SKY. Y'CAN'T TELL WHERE IT ENDS AN' THE OCEAN STARTS...
Y'ASK ME, IT ALL WENT QUEER AFTER THE SKIP BRUNG THAT THING ONBOARD.
AYE, WELL.
I HEARD IT TALK...
BULL!
STRAIGHT UP! THERE WAS TWO VOICES IN THE GUV'S CABIN THE OTHER DAY, BUT ONLY HE WAS IN THERE AN' THAT BOX.
COULD BE HE'S LOSING HIS MIND, AFTER EVERYTHING THAT HAPPENED...
THAT'S ENOUGH! WE ALL LOST MATES BACK ON NEW PROVIDENCE - DON'T MEAN WE'RE ALL BARKIN'!
SO WHY DON'T 'E TELL US WHERE WE'RE GOIN' THEN, AYE?
HE WILL, IN HIS OWN TIME...

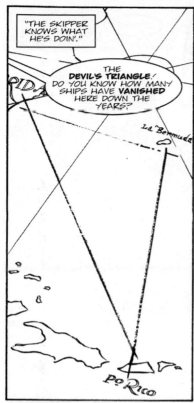

"THE SKIPPER KNOWS WHAT HE'S DOIN'."

THE DEVIL'S TRIANGLE! DO YOU KNOW HOW MANY SHIPS HAVE VANISHED HERE DOWN THE YEARS?

Id. Bermuda

P'o Rico

NO, I'M A DOG.

ARE YOU CERTAIN WE'LL FIND THE HOLLOW MAN HERE?

PUT IT THIS WAY, IF I HAD A TAIL, I'D WAG IT.

THAT WAS A HINT, BY THE WAY.

BUT WHY HERE?

BECAUSE THIS IS WHERE IT ALL BEGAN. THE ALMIGHTY MADE IT FIRST SO HE HAD SOMEWHERE TO STAND WHILE HE CRAFTED THE WORLD.

IT IS THE FIRST AND OLDEST PIECE OF CREATION. REALITY IS TIRED AND THIN HERE. THINGS CAN PASS BACK AND FORTH WITH EASE.

THINGS?

THERE ARE WORLDS OTHER THAN THIS ONE, JACK DANCER, AS WELL YOU KNOW...

A SAIL! SAIL HO!

WHERE?

OFF T'STARBOARD, CAPT'N. JUST APPEARED OUTTA NOWHERE.

THAT'S NO SAIL, IT'S —

OH MY GOD!

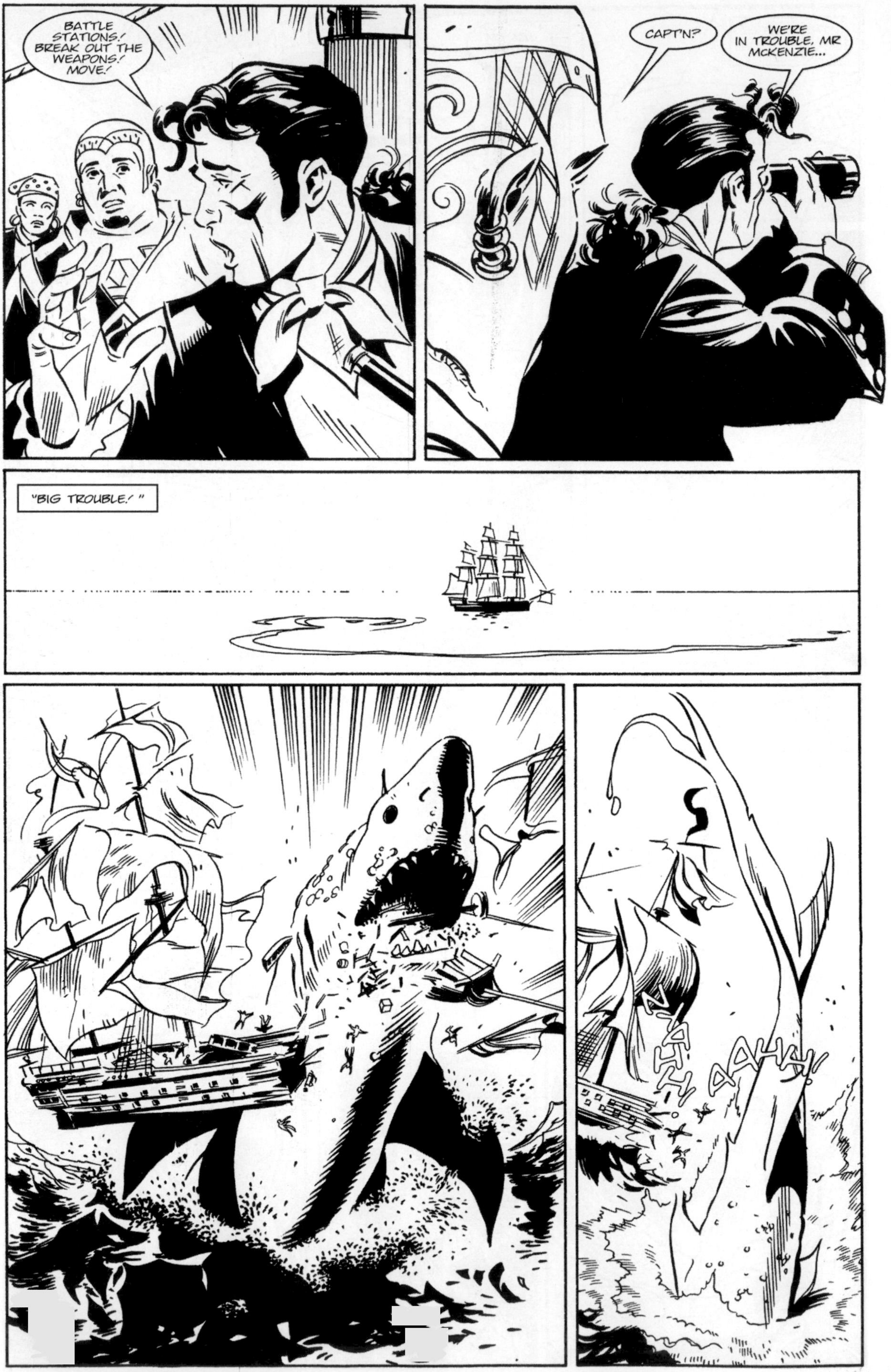
BATTLE STATIONS! BREAK OUT THE WEAPONS! MOVE!
CAPT'N?
WE'RE IN TROUBLE, MR McKENZIE...
"BIG TROUBLE!"
AAHH! AAHH!

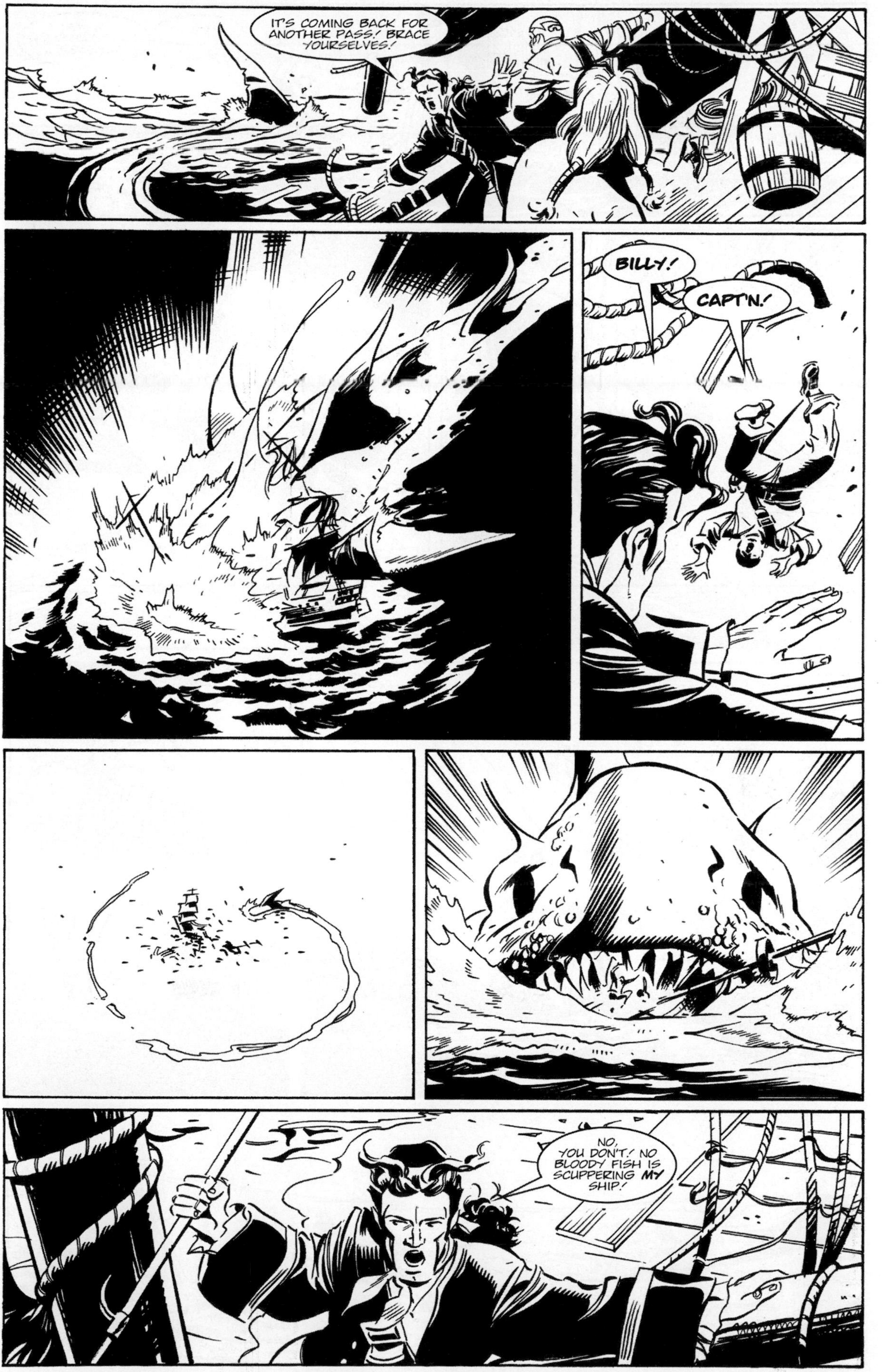
IT'S COMING BACK FOR ANOTHER PASS! BRACE YOURSELVES!
BILLY!
CAPT'N!
NO, YOU DON'T! NO BLOODY FISH IS SCUPPERING MY SHIP!

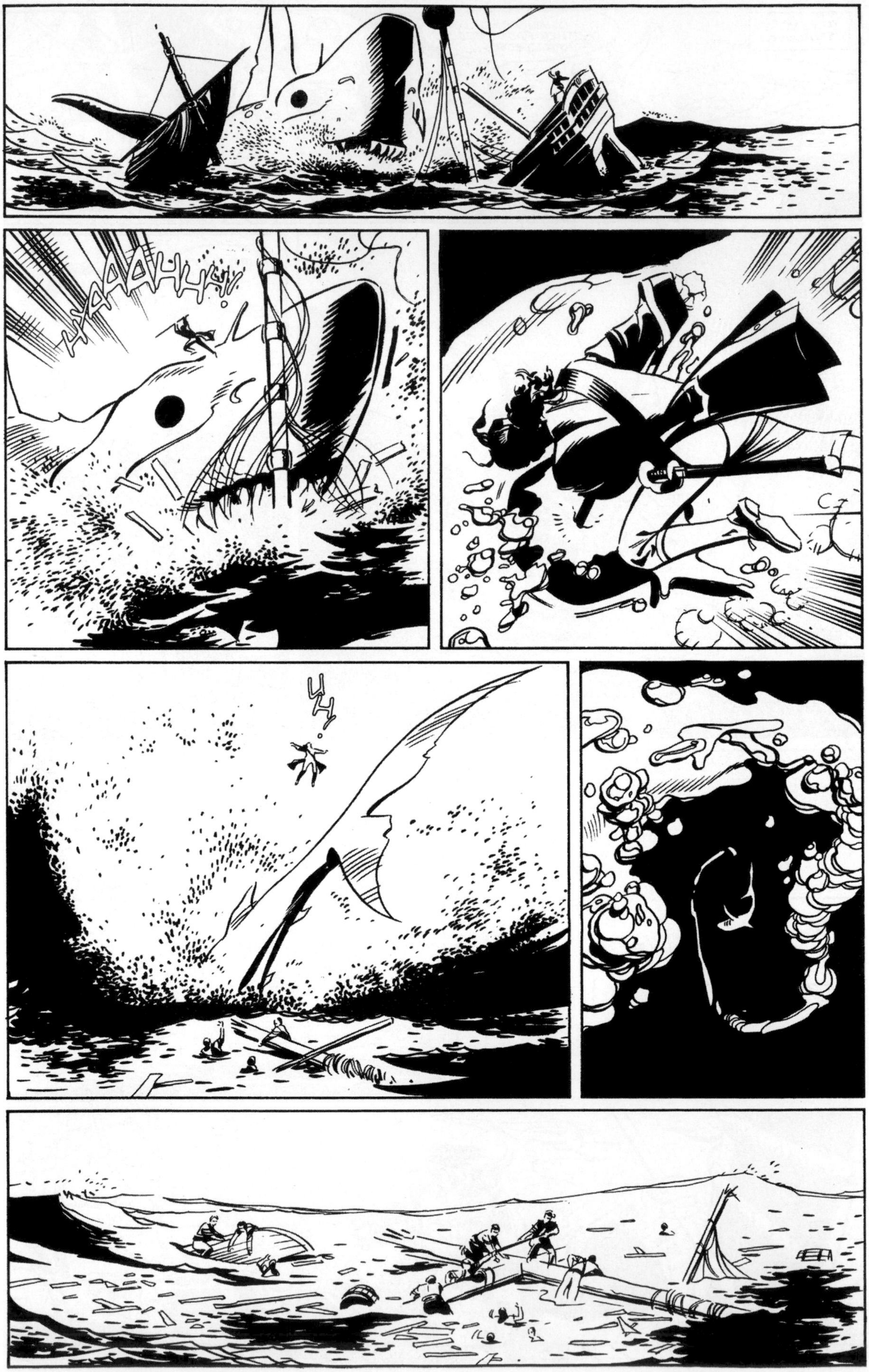
HYAAAHHH!!
UH!

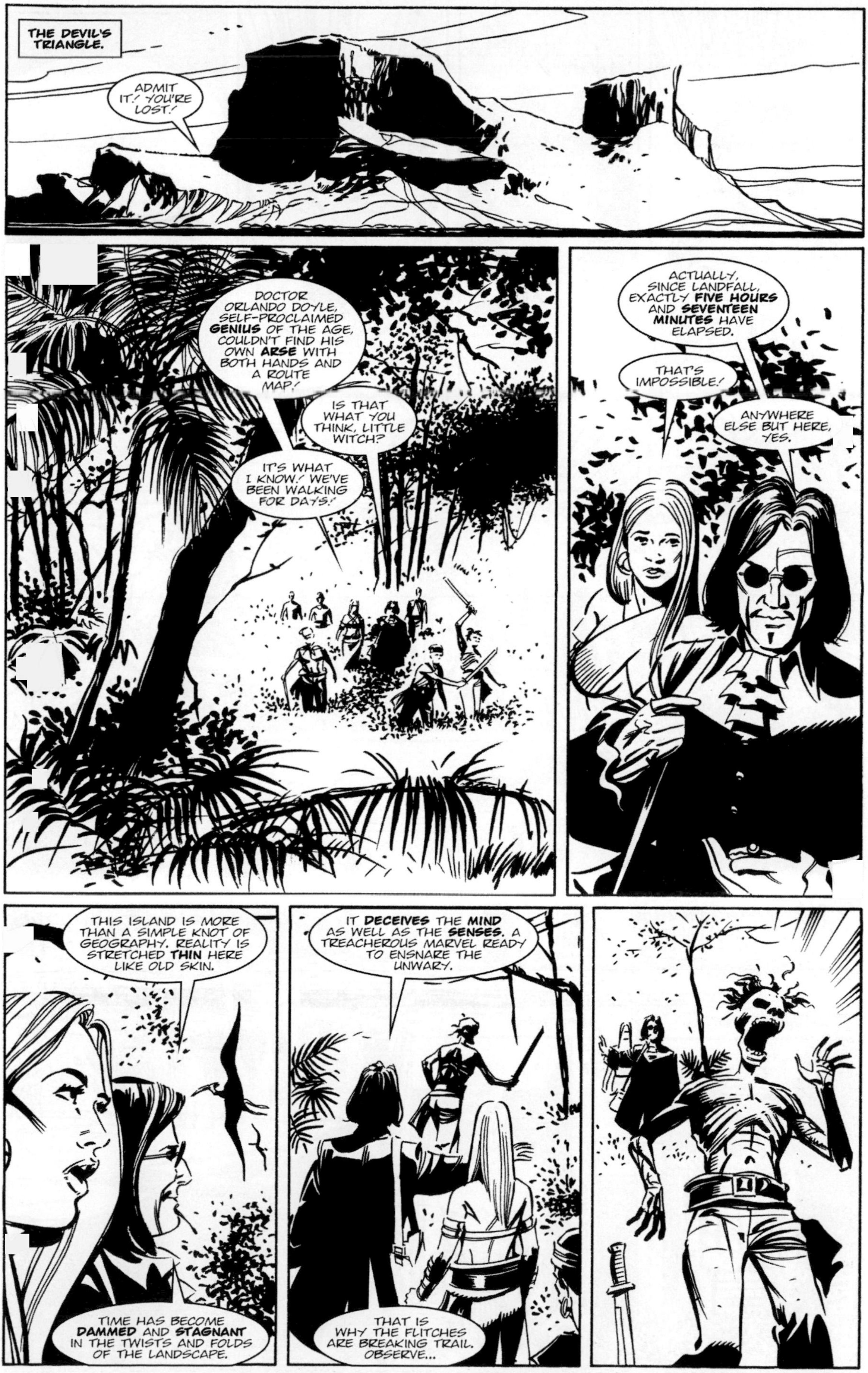
THE DEVIL'S TRIANGLE.
ADMIT IT! YOU'RE LOST!
DOCTOR ORLANDO DOYLE, SELF-PROCLAIMED GENIUS OF THE AGE, COULDN'T FIND HIS OWN ARSE WITH BOTH HANDS AND A ROUTE MAP!
IS THAT WHAT YOU THINK, LITTLE WITCH?
IT'S WHAT I KNOW! WE'VE BEEN WALKING FOR DAYS!
ACTUALLY, SINCE LANDFALL, EXACTLY FIVE HOURS AND SEVENTEEN MINUTES HAVE ELAPSED.
THAT'S IMPOSSIBLE!
ANYWHERE ELSE BUT HERE, YES.
THIS ISLAND IS MORE THAN A SIMPLE KNOT OF GEOGRAPHY. REALITY IS STRETCHED THIN HERE LIKE OLD SKIN.
TIME HAS BECOME DAMMED AND STAGNANT IN THE TWISTS AND FOLDS OF THE LANDSCAPE.
IT DECEIVES THE MIND AS WELL AS THE SENSES. A TREACHEROUS MARVEL READY TO ENSNARE THE UNWARY.
THAT IS WHY THE FLITCHES ARE BREAKING TRAIL. OBSERVE...

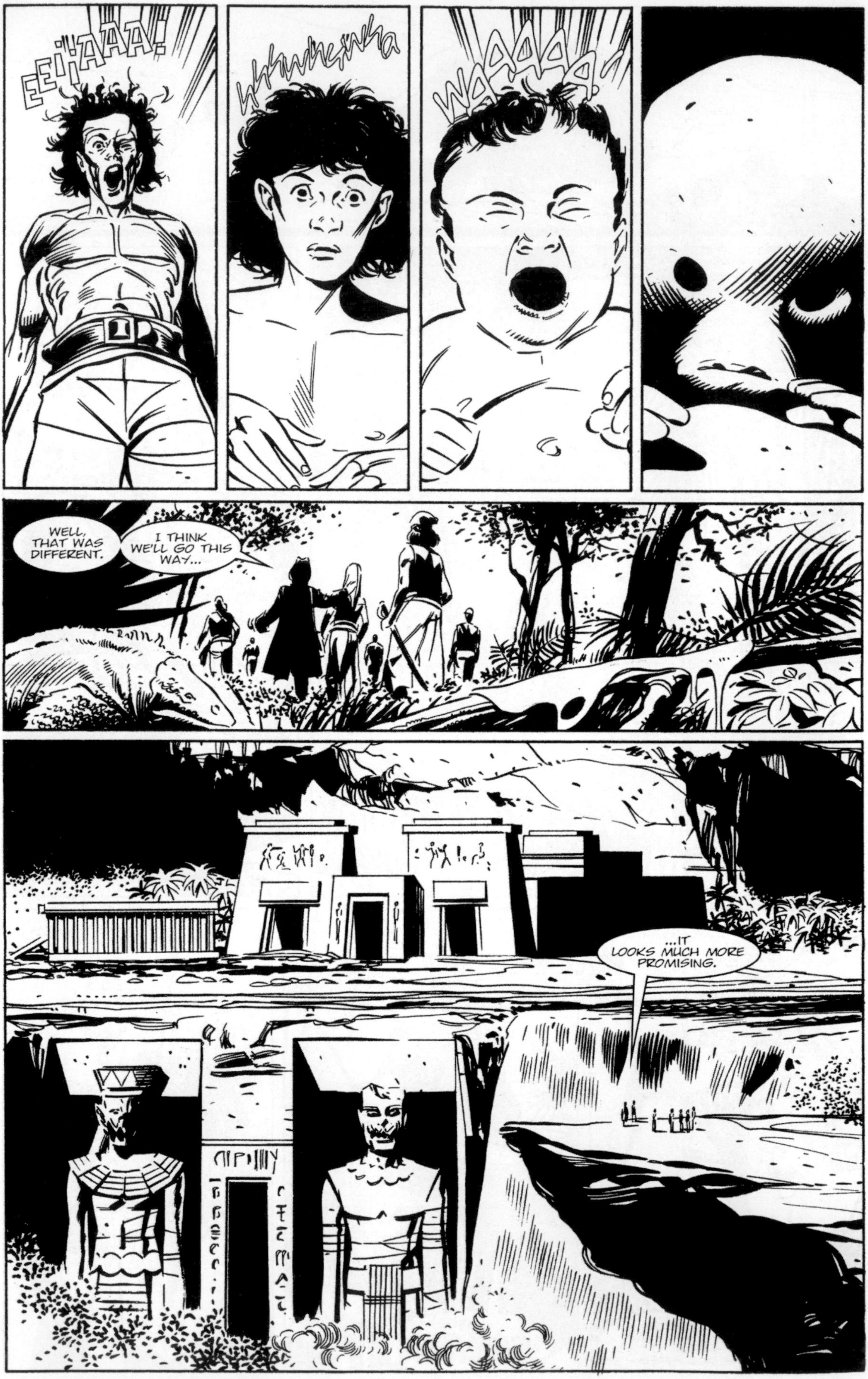
EEIIAAAA!
WAAAAA!
WELL, THAT WAS DIFFERENT.
I THINK WE'LL GO THIS WAY...
...IT LOOKS MUCH MORE PROMISING.

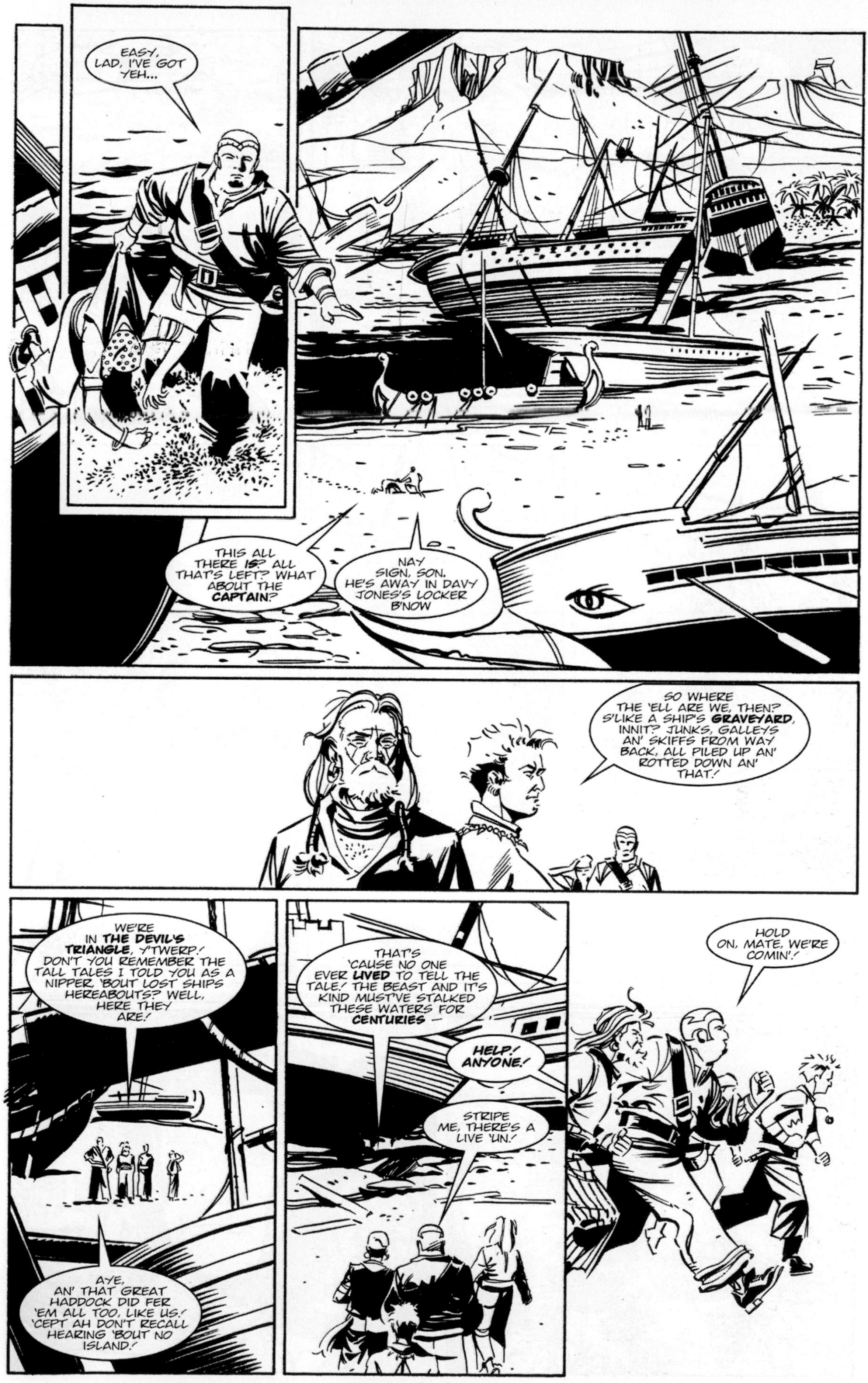
EASY, LAD, I'VE GOT YEH...
THIS ALL THERE IS? ALL THAT'S LEFT? WHAT ABOUT THE CAPTAIN?
NAY SIGN, SON. HE'S AWAY IN DAVY JONES'S LOCKER B'NOW
SO WHERE THE 'ELL ARE WE, THEN? S'LIKE A SHIP'S GRAVEYARD, INNIT? JUNKS, GALLEYS AN' SKIFFS FROM WAY BACK, ALL PILED UP AN' ROTTED DOWN AN' THAT!
WE'RE IN THE DEVIL'S TRIANGLE, Y'TWERP! DON'T YOU REMEMBER THE TALL TALES I TOLD YOU AS A NIPPER, 'BOUT LOST SHIPS HEREABOUTS? WELL, HERE THEY ARE!
AYE, AN' THAT GREAT HADDOCK DID FER 'EM ALL TOO, LIKE US! 'CEPT AH DON'T RECALL HEARING 'BOUT NO ISLAND!
THAT'S 'CAUSE NO ONE EVER LIVED TO TELL THE TALE! THE BEAST AND IT'S KIND MUST'VE STALKED THESE WATERS FOR CENTURIES –
HELP! ANYONE!
STRIPE ME, THERE'S A LIVE 'UN!
HOLD ON, MATE, WE'RE COMIN'!

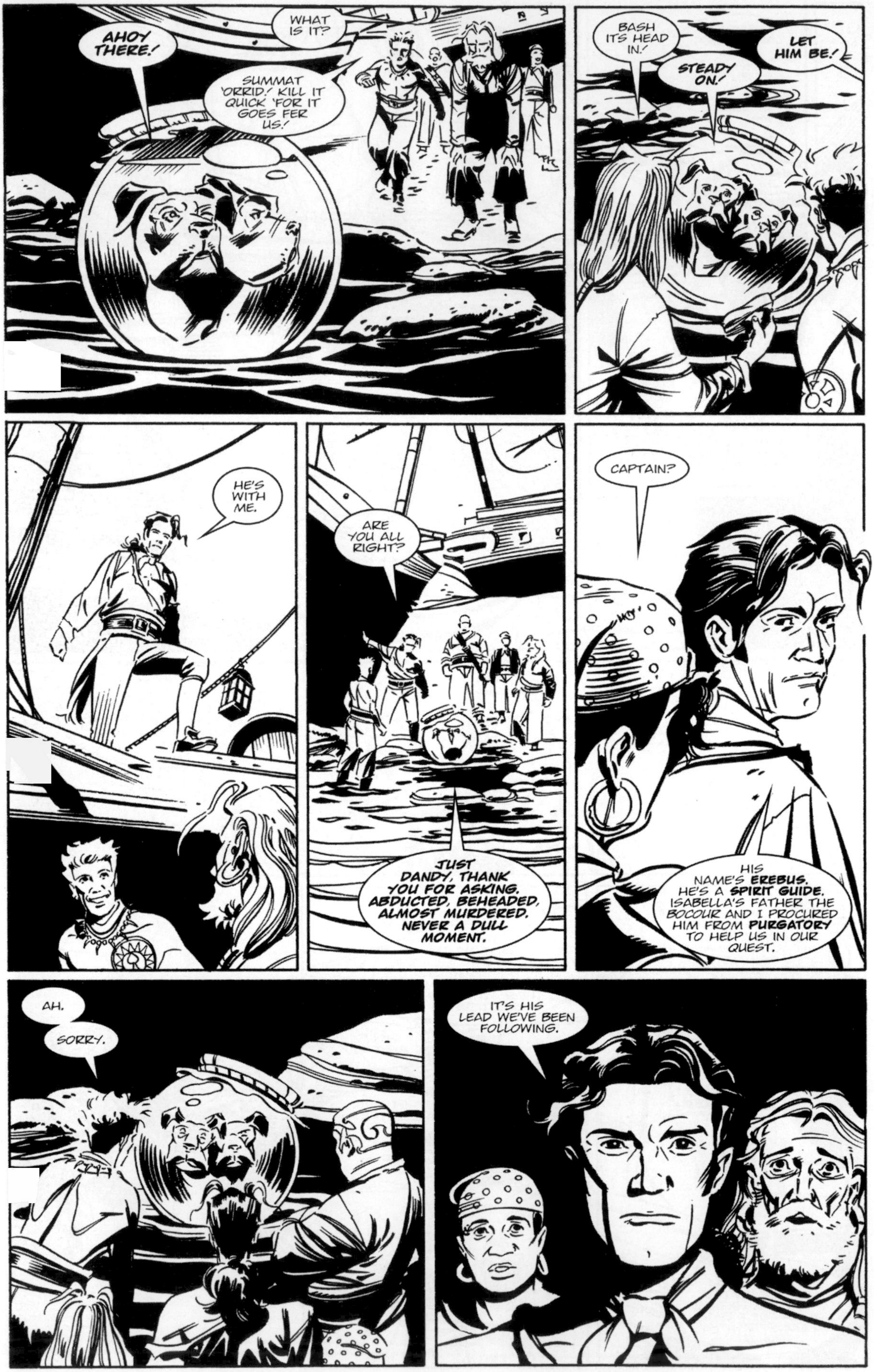

AHOY THERE!
WHAT IS IT?
SUMMAT 'ORRID! KILL IT QUICK 'FOR IT GOES FER US!
BASH ITS HEAD IN!
STEADY ON!
LET HIM BE!
HE'S WITH ME.
ARE YOU ALL RIGHT?
JUST DANDY, THANK YOU FOR ASKING. ABDUCTED, BEHEADED, ALMOST MURDERED. NEVER A DULL MOMENT.
CAPTAIN?
HIS NAME'S EREBUS. HE'S A SPIRIT GUIDE. ISABELLA'S FATHER THE BOCOUR AND I PROCURED HIM FROM PURGATORY TO HELP US IN OUR QUEST.
AH.
SORRY.
IT'S HIS LEAD WE'VE BEEN FOLLOWING.

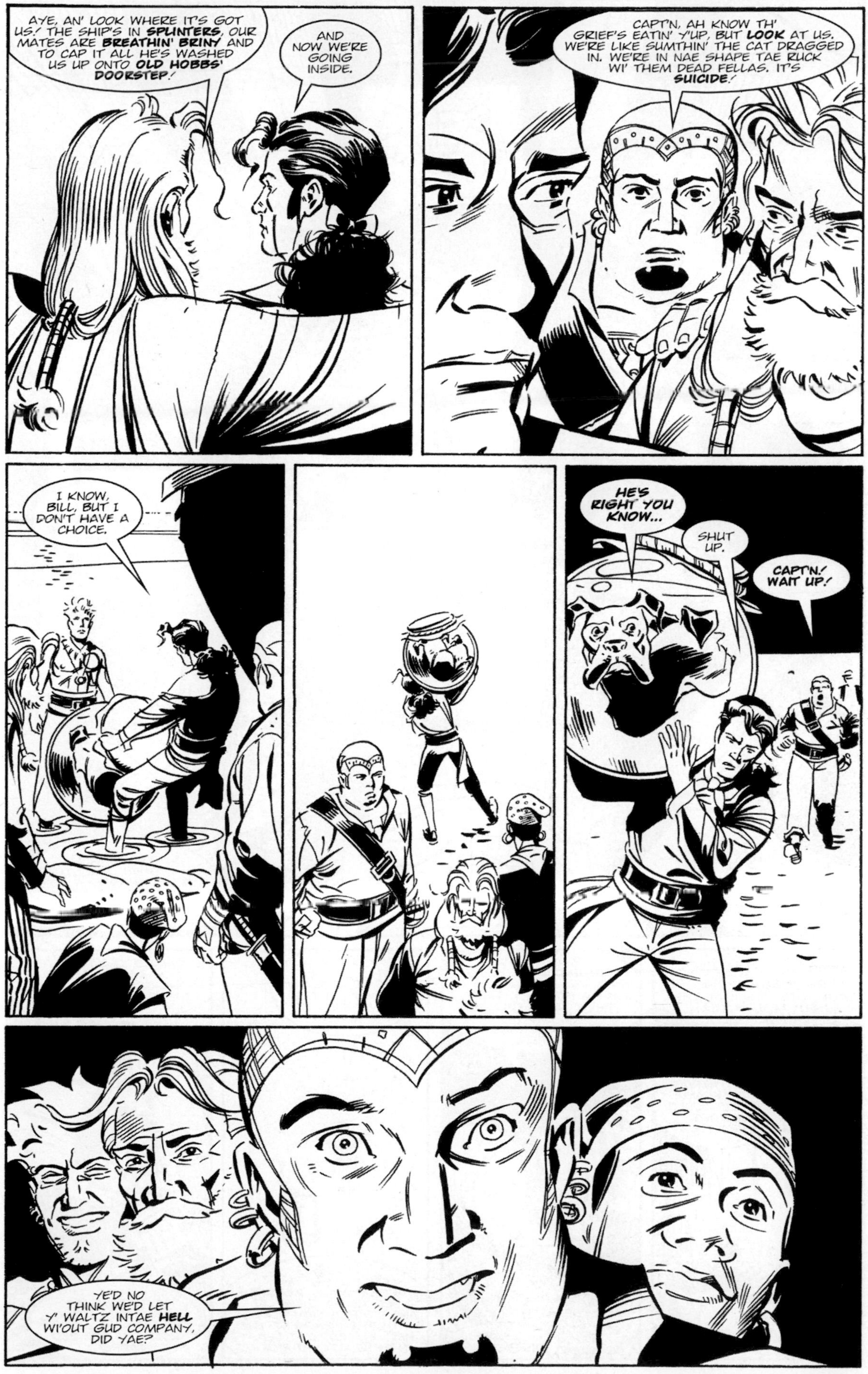

AYE, AN' LOOK WHERE IT'S GOT US! THE SHIP'S IN SPLINTERS, OUR MATES ARE BREATHIN' BRINY AND TO CAP IT ALL HE'S WASHED US UP ONTO OLD HOBBS' DOORSTEP!
AND NOW WE'RE GOING INSIDE.
CAPT'N, AH KNOW TH' GRIEF'S EATIN' Y'UP, BUT LOOK AT US. WE'RE LIKE SUMTHIN' THE CAT DRAGGED IN. WE'RE IN NAE SHAPE TAE RUCK WI' THEM DEAD FELLAS. IT'S SUICIDE!
I KNOW, BILL, BUT I DON'T HAVE A CHOICE.
HE'S RIGHT YOU KNOW...
SHUT UP.
CAPT'N! WAIT UP!
YE'D NO THINK WE'D LET Y' WALTZ INTAE HELL WI'OUT GUD COMPANY, DID YAE?

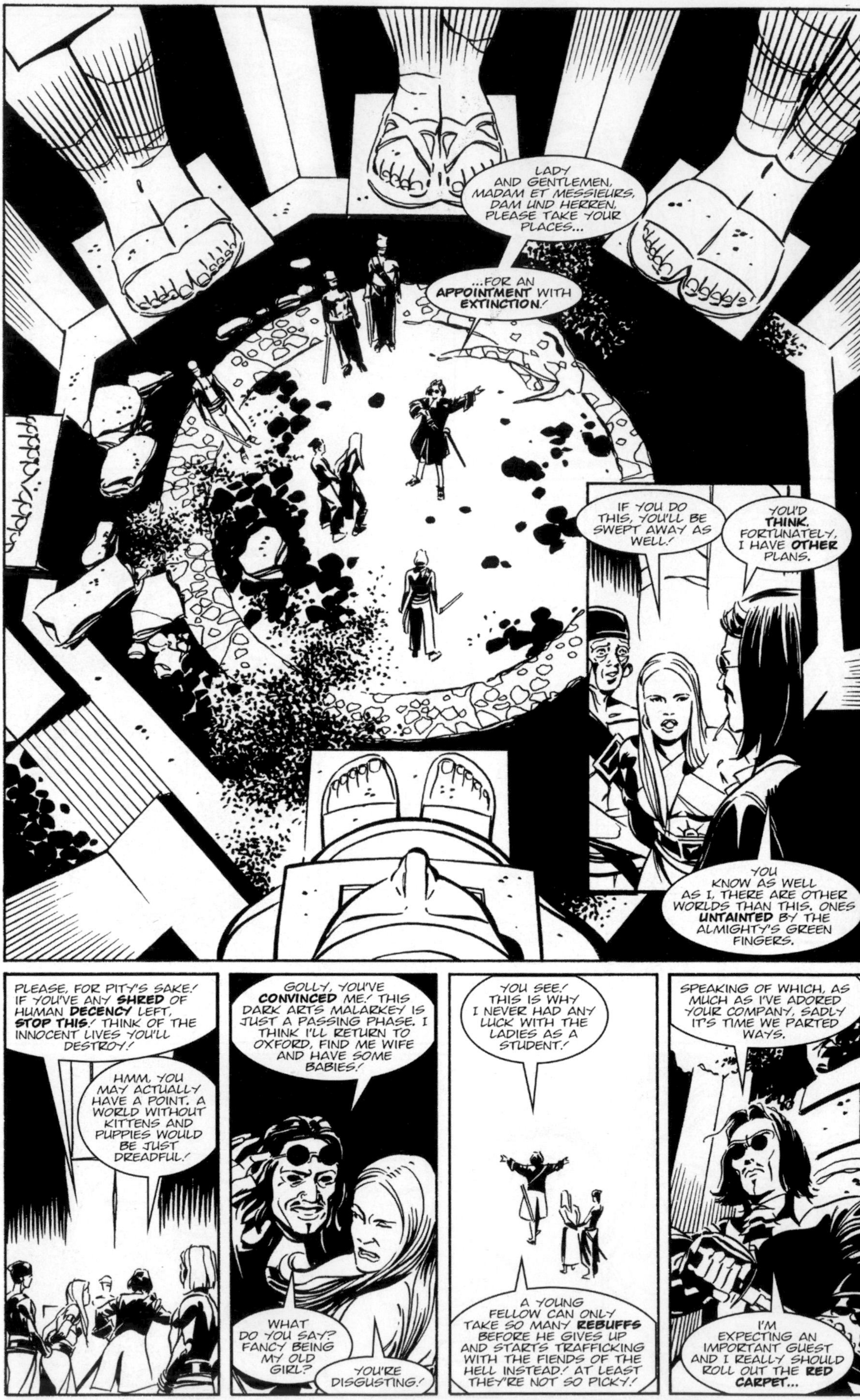
LADY AND GENTLEMEN, MADAM ET MESSIEURS, DAM UND HERREN, PLEASE TAKE YOUR PLACES...
...FOR AN **APPOINTMENT** WITH **EXTINCTION**!
IF YOU DO THIS, YOU'LL BE SWEPT AWAY AS WELL!
YOU'D **THINK**. FORTUNATELY, I HAVE **OTHER** PLANS.
YOU KNOW AS WELL AS I, THERE ARE OTHER WORLDS THAN THIS. ONES **UNTAINTED** BY THE ALMIGHTY'S GREEN FINGERS.
PLEASE, FOR PITY'S SAKE! IF YOU'VE ANY **SHRED** OF HUMAN **DECENCY** LEFT, **STOP THIS**! THINK OF THE INNOCENT LIVES YOU'LL DESTROY!
HMM, YOU MAY ACTUALLY HAVE A POINT. A WORLD WITHOUT KITTENS AND PUPPIES WOULD BE JUST DREADFUL!
GOLLY, YOU'VE **CONVINCED** ME! THIS DARK ARTS MALARKEY IS JUST A PASSING PHASE. I THINK I'LL RETURN TO OXFORD, FIND ME WIFE AND HAVE SOME BABIES!
WHAT DO YOU SAY? FANCY BEING MY OLD GIRL?
YOU'RE DISGUSTING!
YOU SEE! THIS IS WHY I NEVER HAD ANY LUCK WITH THE LADIES AS A STUDENT!
A YOUNG FELLOW CAN ONLY TAKE SO MANY **REBUFFS** BEFORE HE GIVES UP AND STARTS TRAFFICKING WITH THE FIENDS OF THE HELL INSTEAD! AT LEAST THEY'RE NOT SO PICKY!
SPEAKING OF WHICH, AS MUCH AS I'VE ADORED YOUR COMPANY, SADLY IT'S TIME WE PARTED WAYS.
I'M EXPECTING AN IMPORTANT GUEST AND I REALLY SHOULD ROLL OUT THE **RED CARPET**...

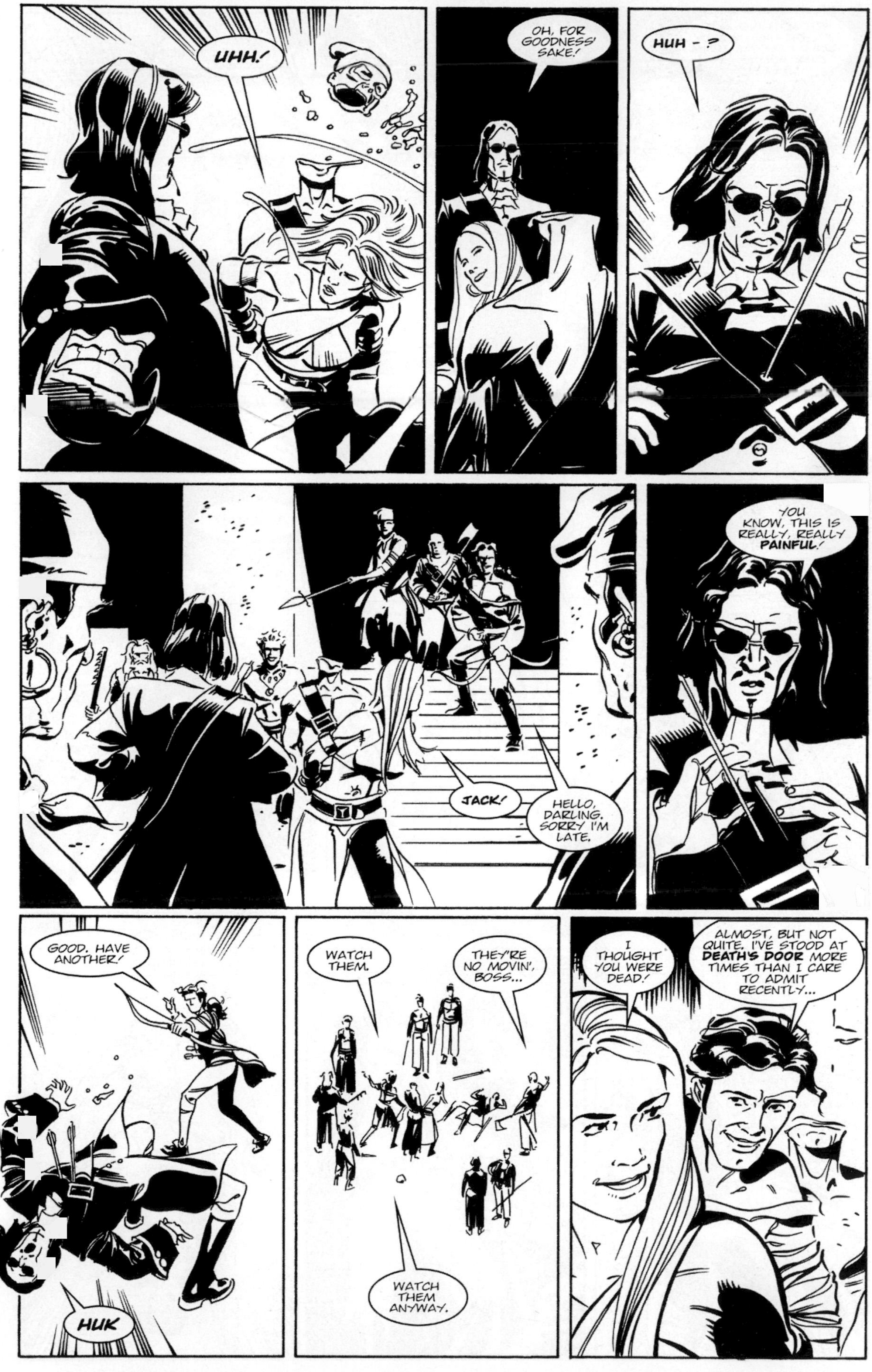
UHH!
OH, FOR GOODNESS' SAKE!
HUH - ?
JACK!
HELLO, DARLING. SORRY I'M LATE.
YOU KNOW, THIS IS REALLY, REALLY PAINFUL!
GOOD. HAVE ANOTHER!
HUK
WATCH THEM.
THEY'RE NO MOVIN', BOSS...
WATCH THEM ANYWAY.
I THOUGHT YOU WERE DEAD!
ALMOST, BUT NOT QUITE. I'VE STOOD AT DEATH'S DOOR MORE TIMES THAN I CARE TO ADMIT RECENTLY...

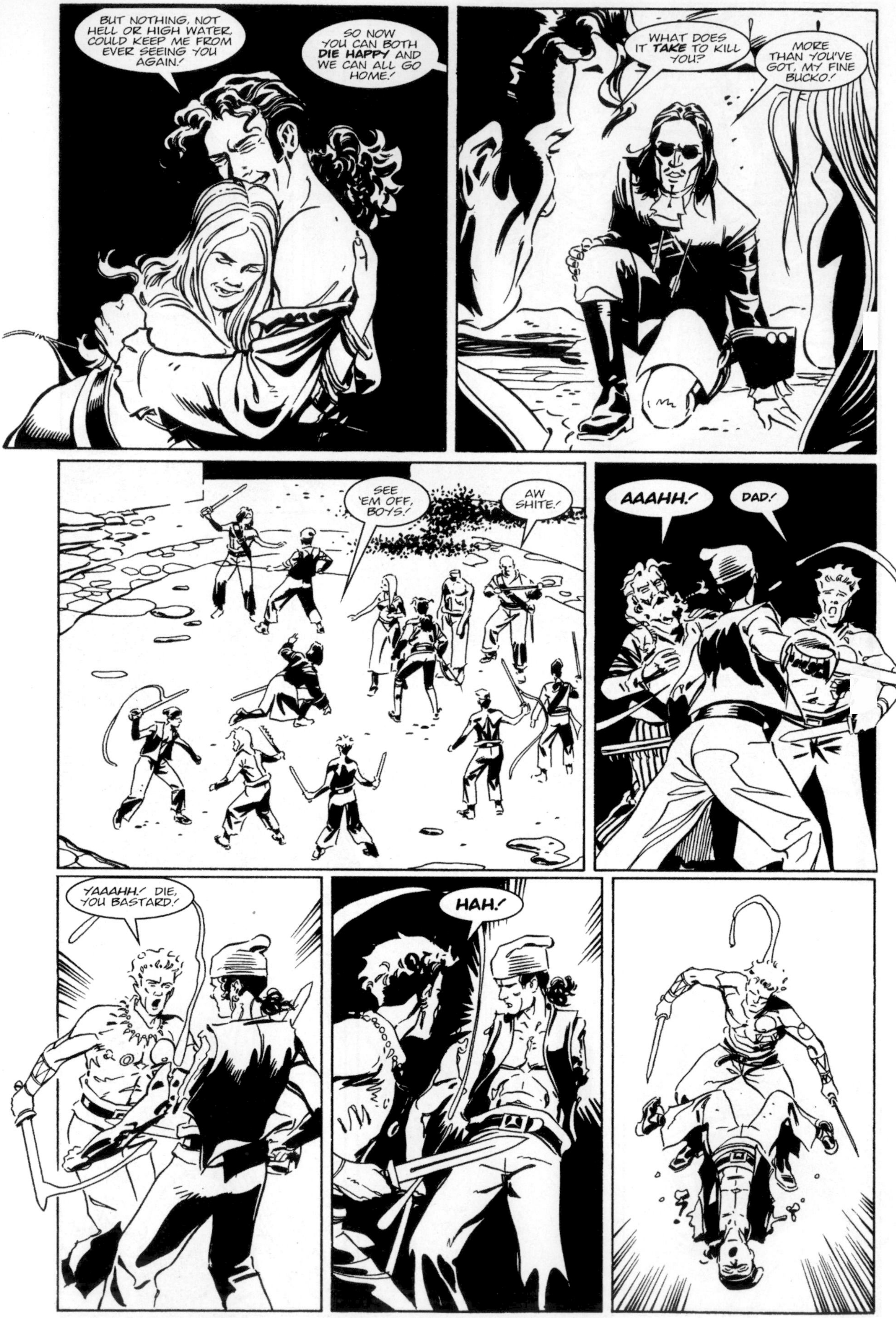
BUT NOTHING, NOT HELL OR HIGH WATER, COULD KEEP ME FROM EVER SEEING YOU AGAIN.!
SO NOW YOU CAN BOTH DIE HAPPY AND WE CAN ALL GO HOME.!
WHAT DOES IT TAKE TO KILL YOU?
MORE THAN YOU'VE GOT, MY FINE BUCKO.!
SEE 'EM OFF, BOYS.!
AW SHITE.!
AAAHH.!
DAD.!
YAAAHH.! DIE, YOU BASTARD.!
HAH.!

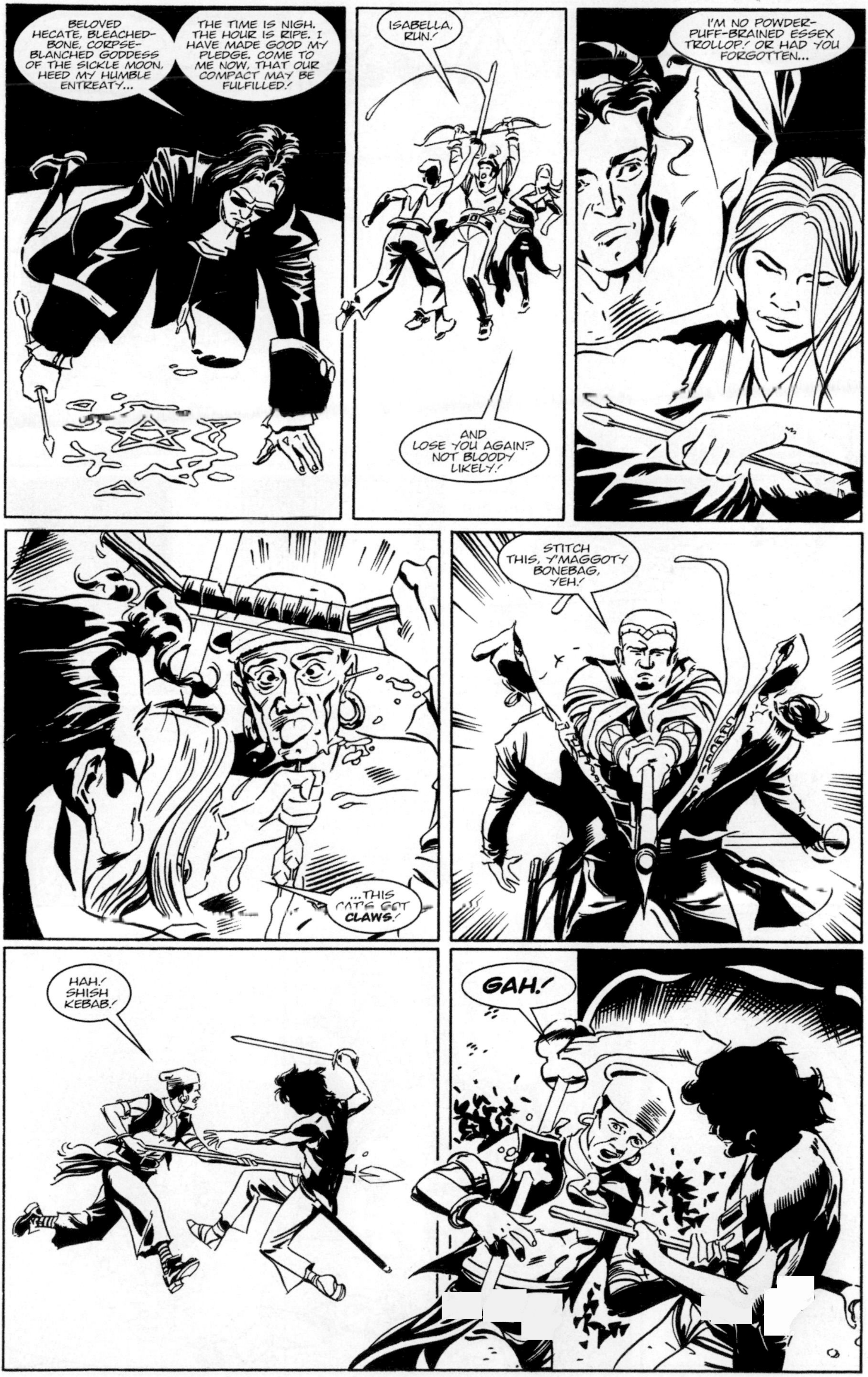

BELOVED HECATE, BLEACHED-BONE, CORPSE-BLANCHED GODDESS OF THE SICKLE MOON, HEED MY HUMBLE ENTREATY...
THE TIME IS NIGH. THE HOUR IS RIPE. I HAVE MADE GOOD MY PLEDGE. COME TO ME NOW, THAT OUR COMPACT MAY BE FULFILLED!
ISABELLA, RUN!
AND LOSE YOU AGAIN? NOT BLOODY LIKELY!
I'M NO POWDER-PUFF-BRAINED ESSEX TROLLOP! OR HAD YOU FORGOTTEN...
...THIS CAT'S GOT CLAWS!
STITCH THIS, Y'MAGGOTY BONEBAG, YEH!
HAH! SHISH KEBAB!
GAH!

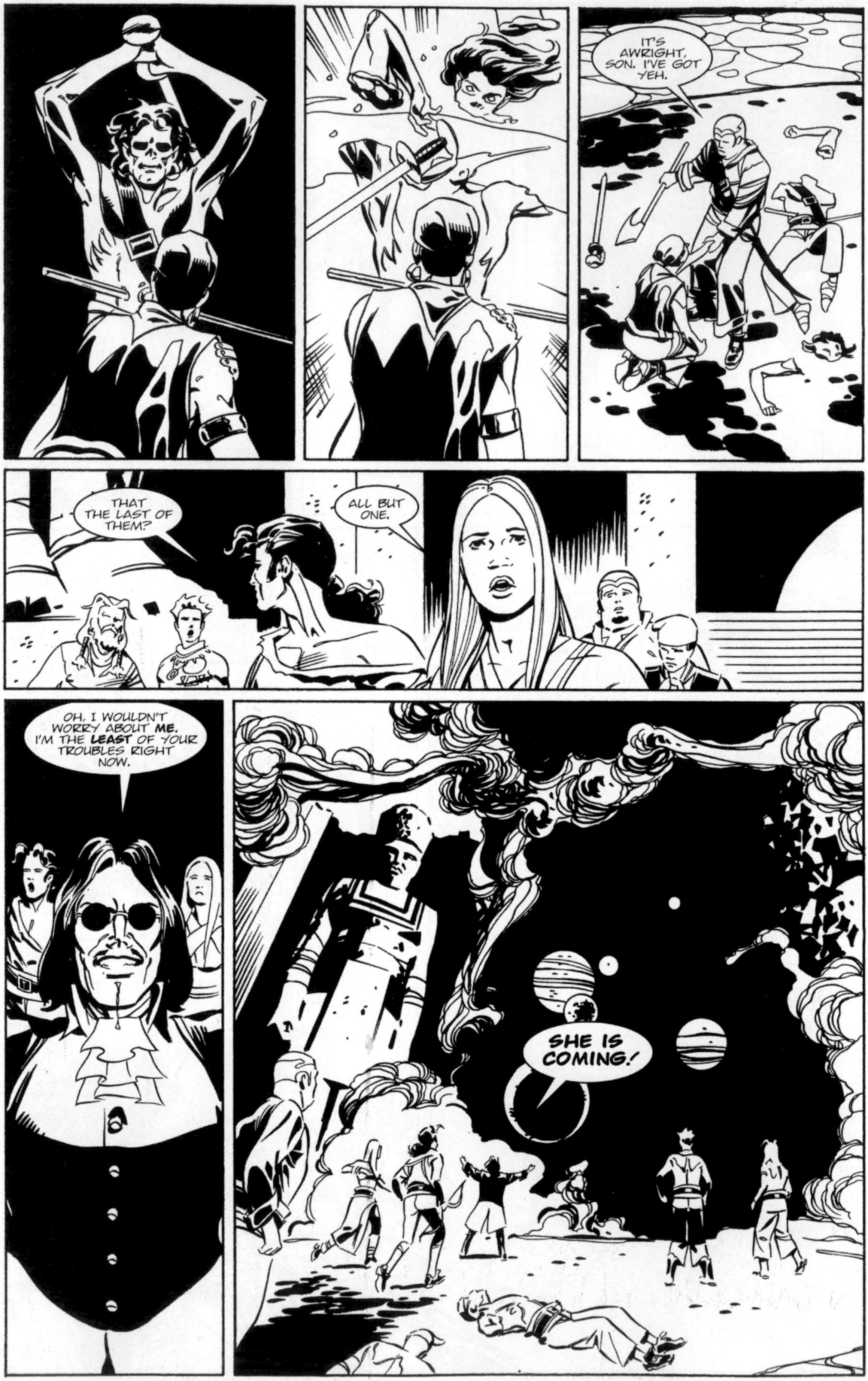
IT'S AWRIGHT, SON. I'VE GOT YEH.
THAT THE LAST OF THEM?
ALL BUT ONE.
OH, I WOULDN'T WORRY ABOUT **ME**. I'M THE **LEAST** OF YOUR TROUBLES RIGHT NOW.
SHE IS COMING!

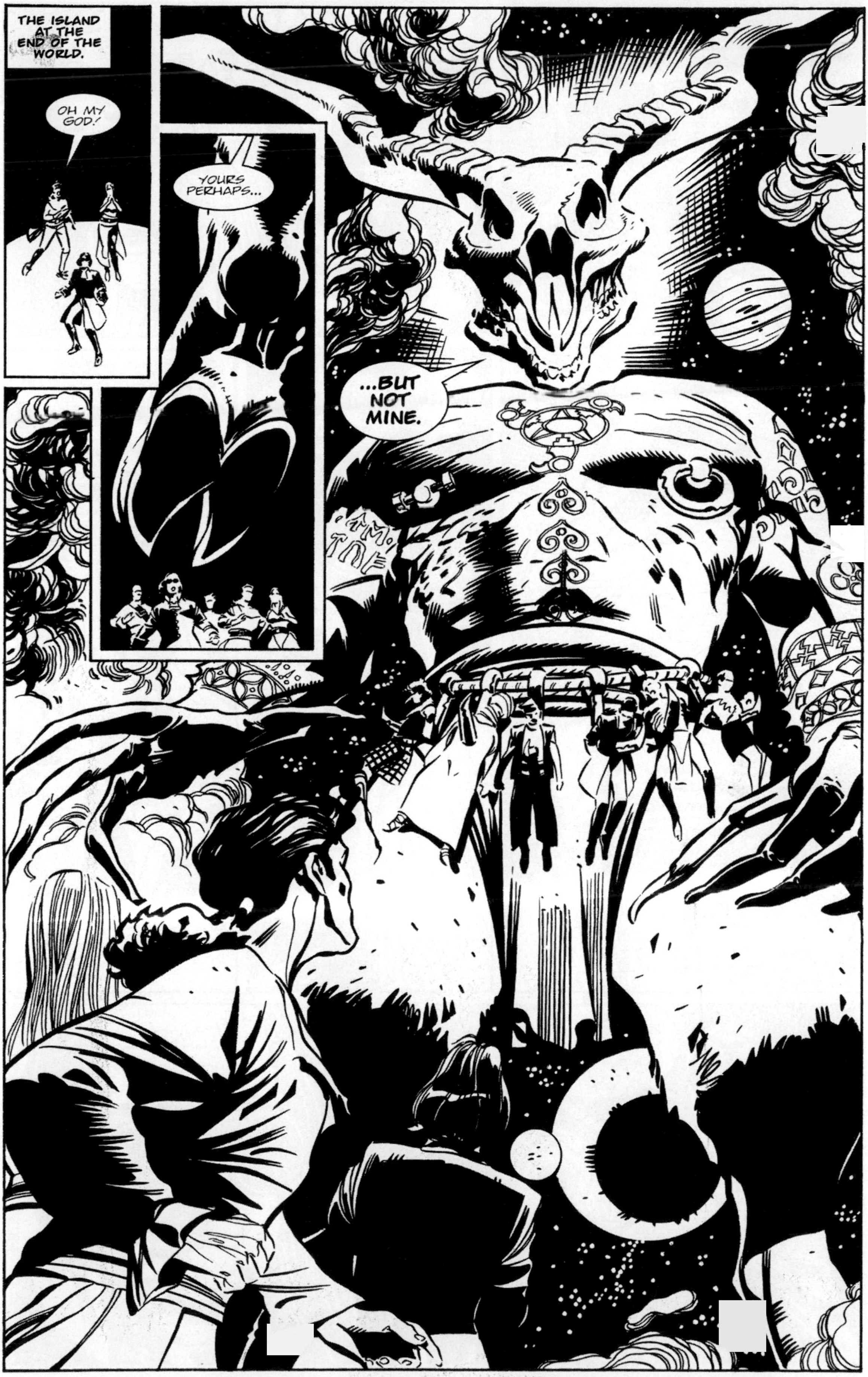
THE ISLAND AT THE END OF THE WORLD.
OH MY GOD!
YOURS PERHAPS...
...BUT NOT MINE.

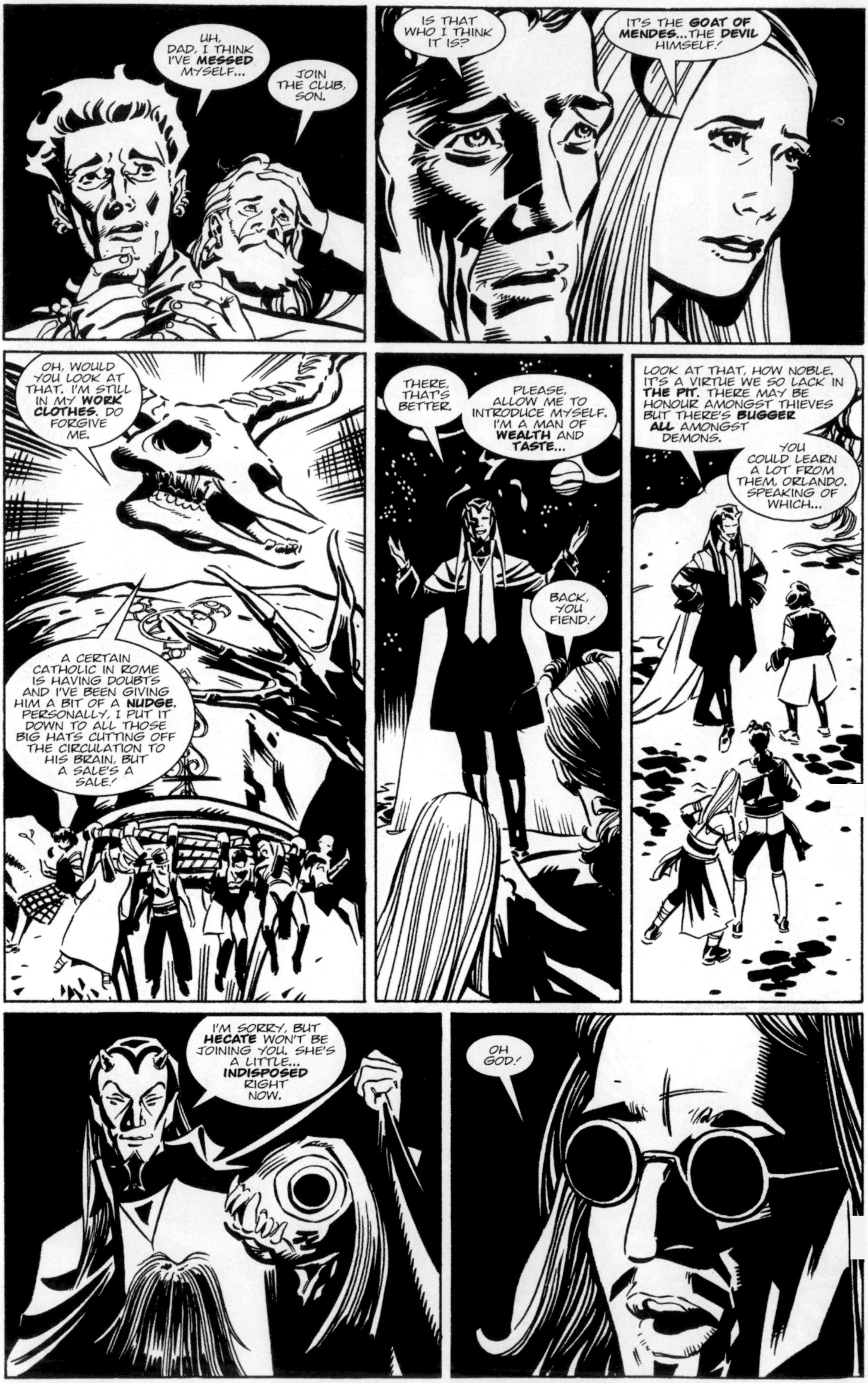

UH, DAD, I THINK I'VE **MESSED** MYSELF...
JOIN THE CLUB, SON.
IS THAT WHO I THINK IT IS?
IT'S THE **GOAT OF MENDES**...THE **DEVIL** HIMSELF!
OH, WOULD YOU LOOK AT THAT. I'M STILL IN MY **WORK CLOTHES**. DO FORGIVE ME.
A CERTAIN CATHOLIC IN ROME IS HAVING DOUBTS AND I'VE BEEN GIVING HIM A BIT OF A **NUDGE**. PERSONALLY, I PUT IT DOWN TO ALL THOSE BIG HATS CUTTING OFF THE CIRCULATION TO HIS BRAIN, BUT A SALE'S A SALE!
THERE, THAT'S BETTER.
PLEASE, ALLOW ME TO INTRODUCE MYSELF. I'M A MAN OF **WEALTH** AND **TASTE**...
BACK, YOU FIEND!
LOOK AT THAT, HOW NOBLE. IT'S A VIRTUE WE SO LACK IN **THE PIT**. THERE MAY BE HONOUR AMONGST THIEVES BUT THERE'S **BUGGER ALL** AMONGST DEMONS.
YOU COULD LEARN A LOT FROM THEM, ORLANDO. SPEAKING OF WHICH...
I'M SORRY, BUT **HECATE** WON'T BE JOINING YOU. SHE'S A LITTLE... **INDISPOSED** RIGHT NOW.
OH GOD!

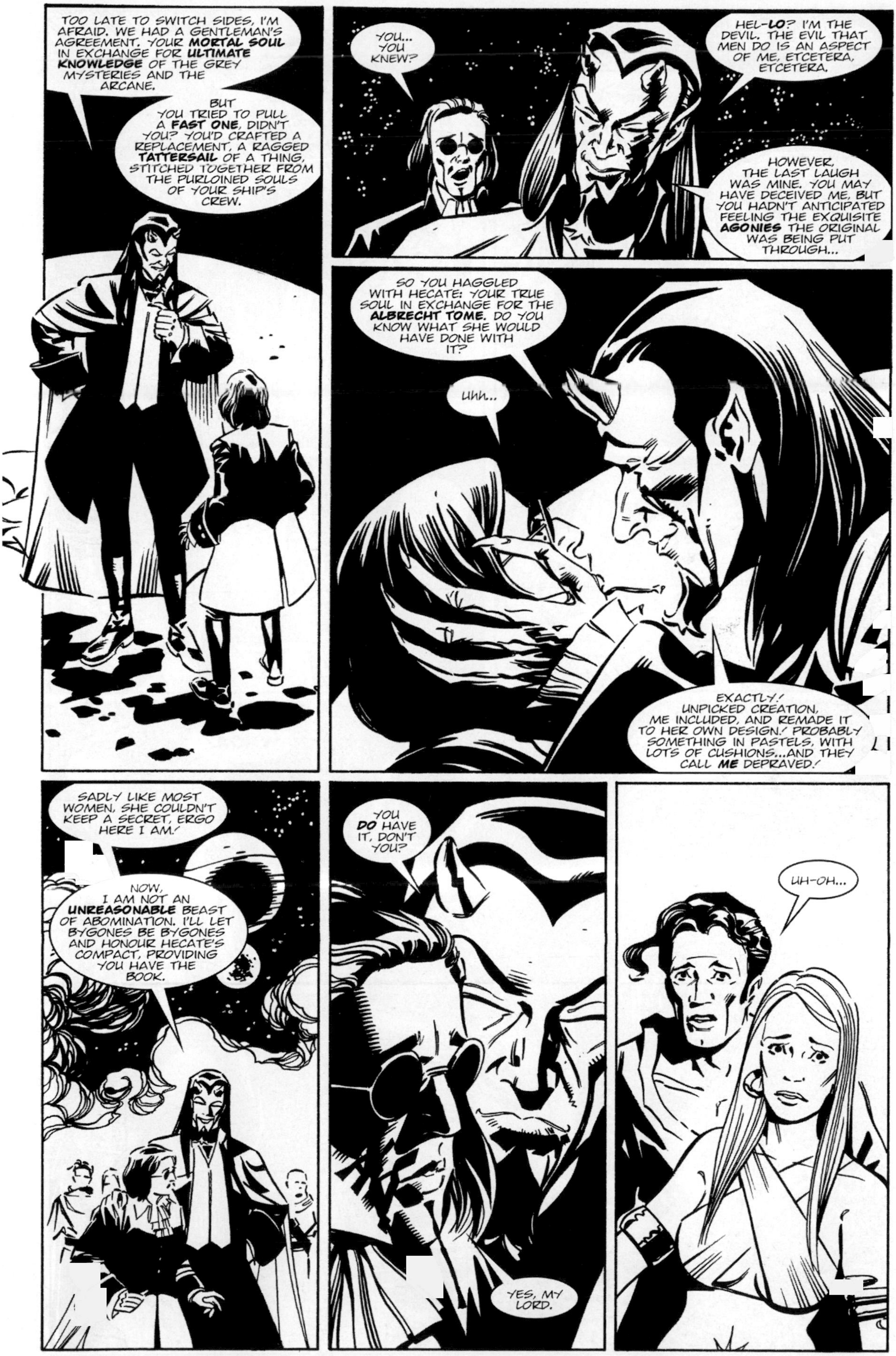
TOO LATE TO SWITCH SIDES, I'M AFRAID. WE HAD A GENTLEMAN'S AGREEMENT. YOUR **MORTAL SOUL** IN EXCHANGE FOR **ULTIMATE KNOWLEDGE** OF THE GREY MYSTERIES AND THE ARCANE.
BUT YOU TRIED TO PULL A **FAST ONE**, DIDN'T YOU? YOU'D CRAFTED A REPLACEMENT, A RAGGED **TATTERSAIL** OF A THING, STITCHED TOGETHER FROM THE PURLOINED SOULS OF YOUR SHIP'S CREW.
YOU... YOU KNEW?
HEL-**LO**? I'M THE DEVIL. THE EVIL THAT MEN DO IS AN ASPECT OF ME, ETCETERA, ETCETERA.
HOWEVER, THE LAST LAUGH WAS MINE. YOU MAY HAVE DECEIVED ME, BUT YOU HADN'T ANTICIPATED FEELING THE EXQUISITE **AGONIES** THE ORIGINAL WAS BEING PUT THROUGH...
SO YOU HAGGLED WITH HECATE: YOUR TRUE SOUL IN EXCHANGE FOR THE **ALBRECHT TOME**. DO YOU KNOW WHAT SHE WOULD HAVE DONE WITH IT?
UHH...
EXACTLY! UNPICKED CREATION, ME INCLUDED, AND REMADE IT TO HER OWN DESIGN! PROBABLY SOMETHING IN PASTELS, WITH LOTS OF CUSHIONS...AND THEY CALL **ME** DEPRAVED!
SADLY LIKE MOST WOMEN, SHE COULDN'T KEEP A SECRET, ERGO HERE I AM!
NOW, I AM NOT AN **UNREASONABLE** BEAST OF ABOMINATION. I'LL LET BYGONES BE BYGONES AND HONOUR HECATE'S COMPACT, PROVIDING YOU HAVE THE BOOK.
YOU **DO** HAVE IT, DON'T YOU?
YES, MY LORD.
UH-OH...

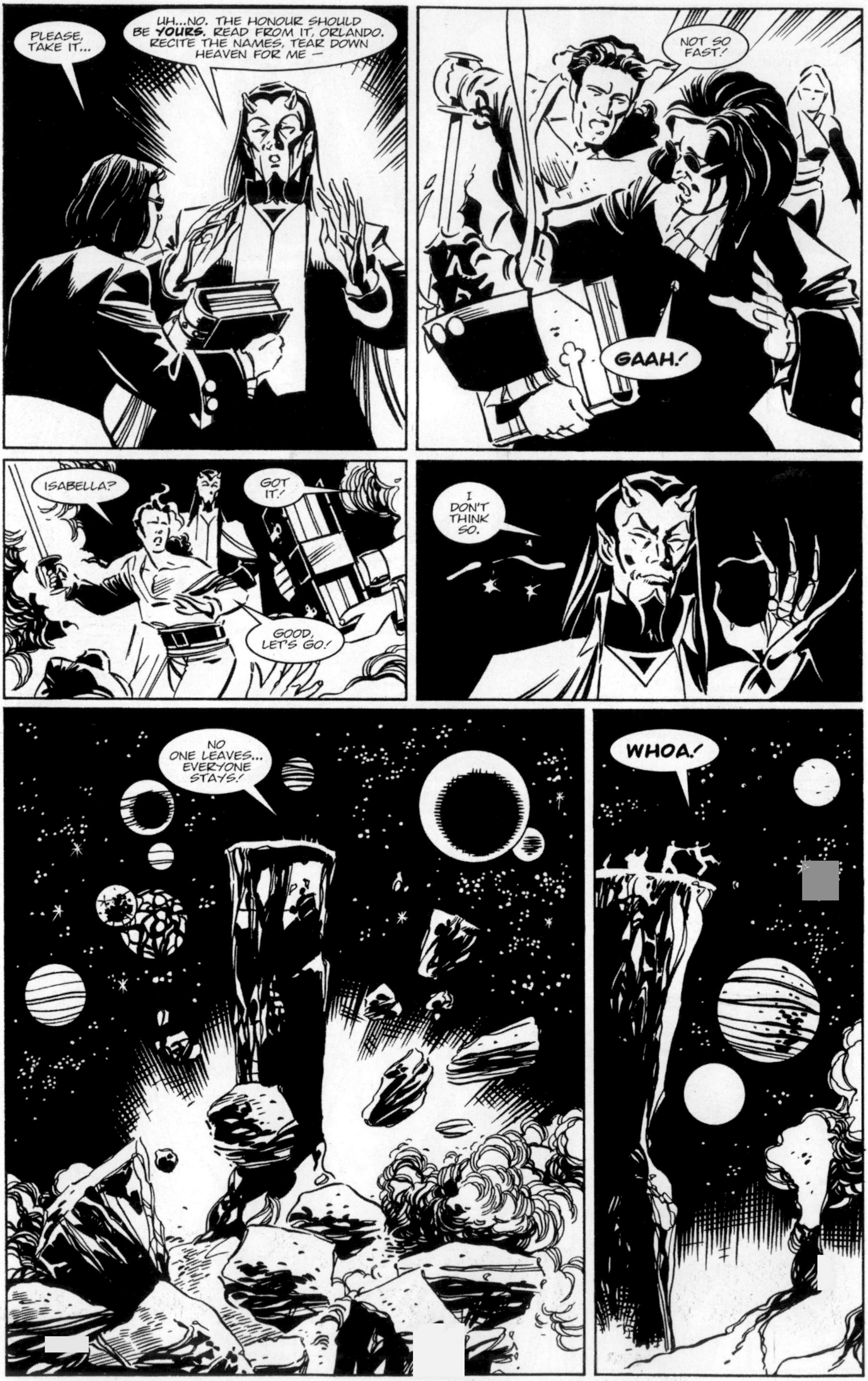
PLEASE, TAKE IT...
UH...NO. THE HONOUR SHOULD BE YOURS. READ FROM IT, ORLANDO. RECITE THE NAMES, TEAR DOWN HEAVEN FOR ME —
NOT SO FAST!
GAAH!
ISABELLA?
GOT IT!
GOOD, LET'S GO!
I DON'T THINK SO.
NO ONE LEAVES... EVERYONE STAYS!
WHOA!

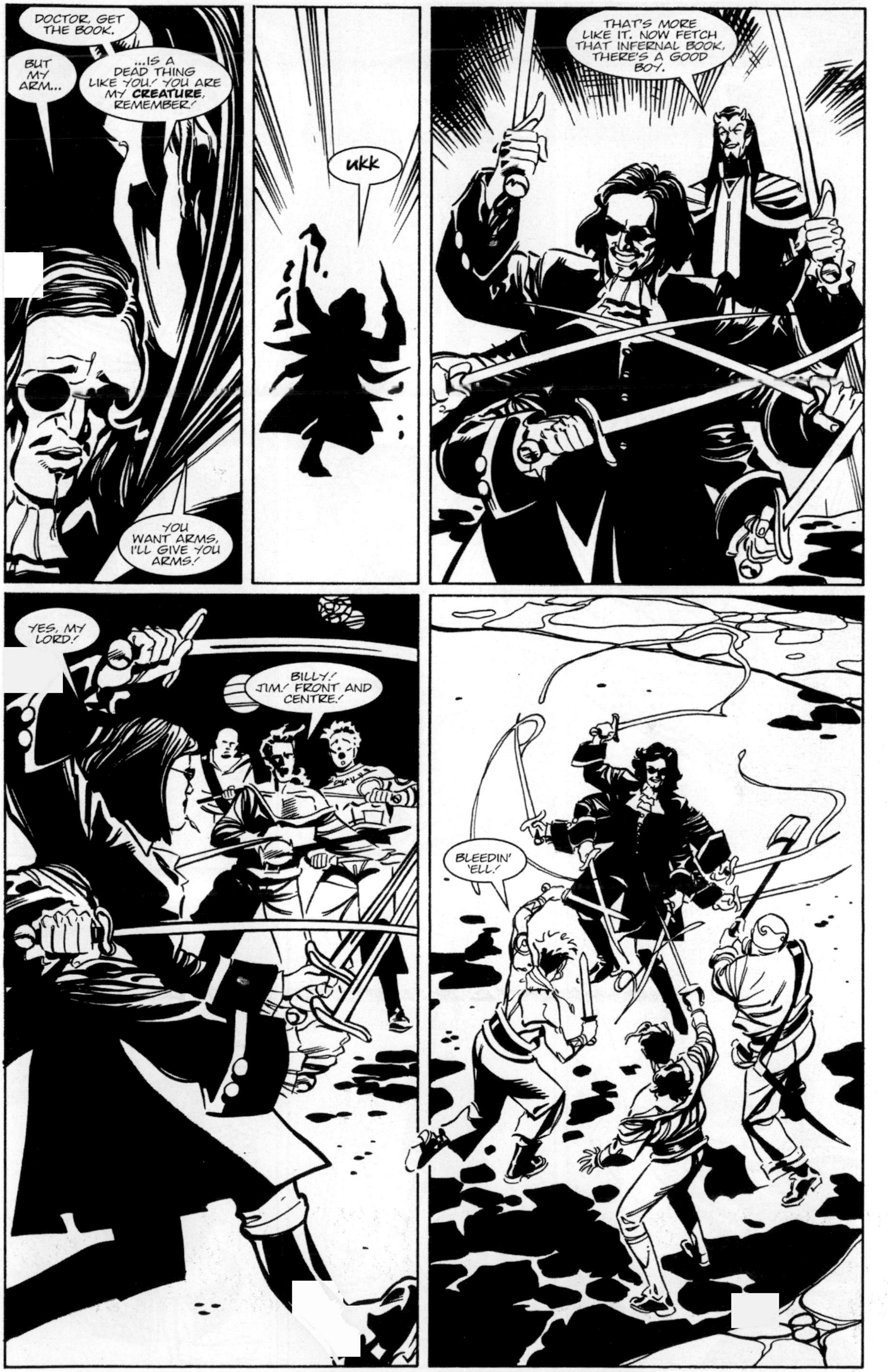
DOCTOR, GET THE BOOK.
BUT MY ARM...
...IS A DEAD THING LIKE YOU! YOU ARE MY CREATURE, REMEMBER!
YOU WANT ARMS, I'LL GIVE YOU ARMS!
UKK
THAT'S MORE LIKE IT. NOW FETCH THAT INFERNAL BOOK, THERE'S A GOOD BOY.
YES, MY LORD!
BILLY! JIM! FRONT AND CENTRE!
BLEEDIN' 'ELL!

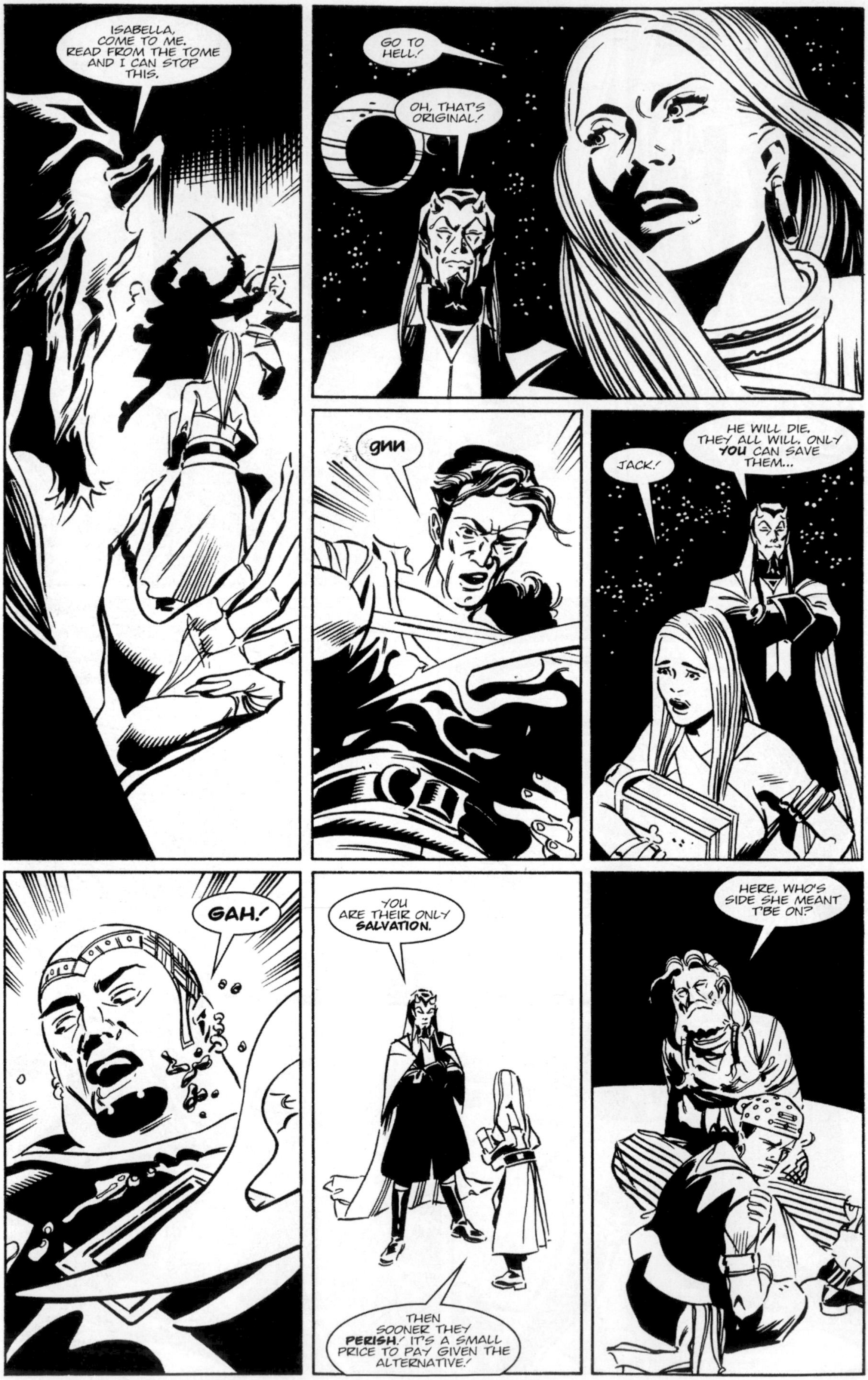
ISABELLA, COME TO ME. READ FROM THE TOME AND I CAN STOP THIS.
GO TO HELL!
OH, THAT'S ORIGINAL!
gnn
JACK!
HE WILL DIE, THEY ALL WILL. ONLY YOU CAN SAVE THEM...
GAH!
YOU ARE THEIR ONLY SALVATION.
THEN SOONER THEY PERISH! IT'S A SMALL PRICE TO PAY GIVEN THE ALTERNATIVE!
HERE, WHO'S SIDE SHE MEANT T'BE ON?

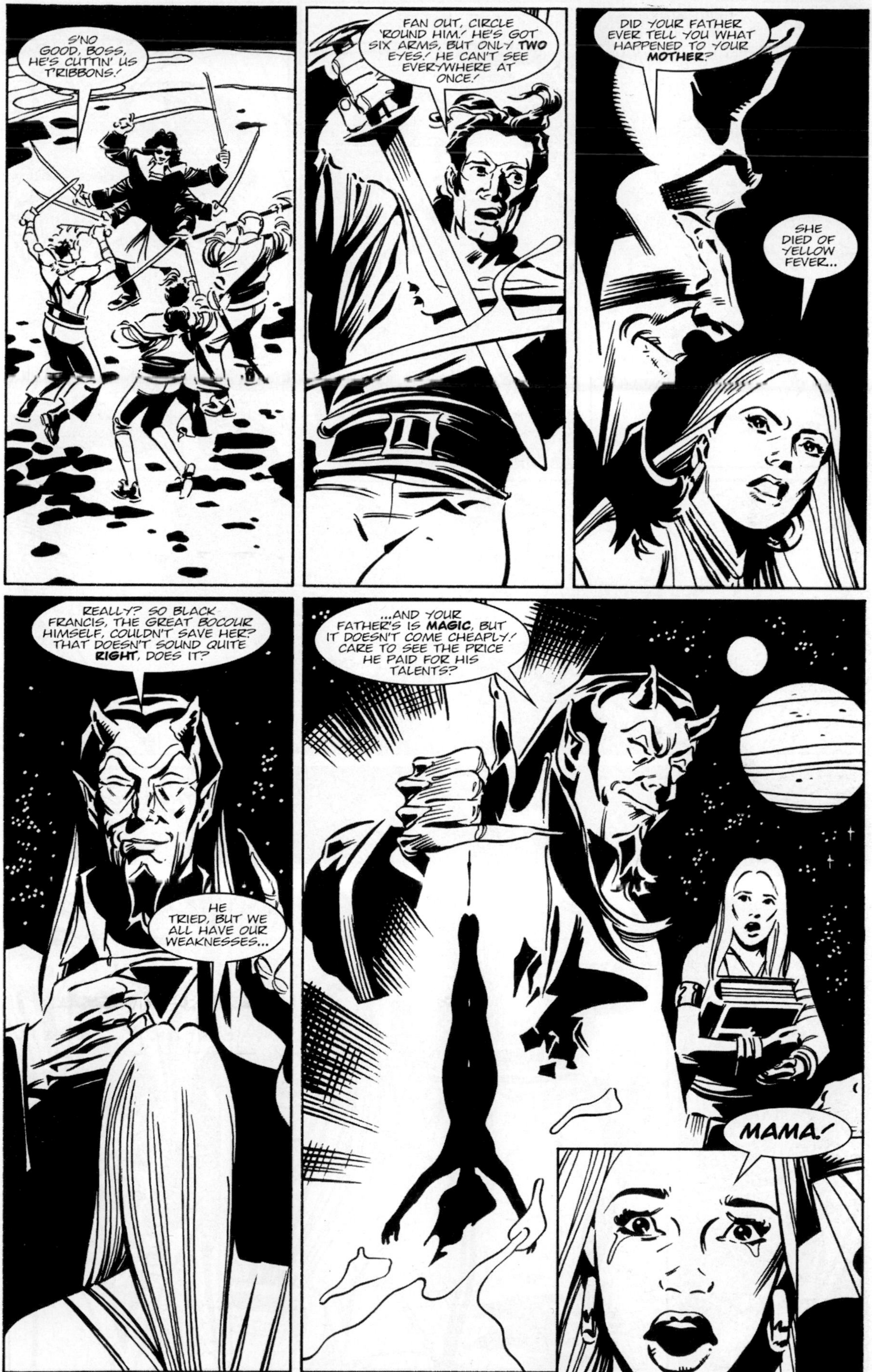
S'NO GOOD, BOSS, HE'S CUTTIN' US T'RIBBONS!
FAN OUT, CIRCLE 'ROUND HIM! HE'S GOT SIX ARMS, BUT ONLY **TWO** EYES! HE CAN'T SEE EVERYWHERE AT ONCE!
DID YOUR FATHER EVER TELL YOU WHAT HAPPENED TO YOUR **MOTHER**?
SHE DIED OF YELLOW FEVER...
REALLY? SO BLACK FRANCIS, THE GREAT BOCOUR HIMSELF, COULDN'T SAVE HER? THAT DOESN'T SOUND QUITE **RIGHT**, DOES IT?
HE TRIED, BUT WE ALL HAVE OUR WEAKNESSES...
...AND YOUR FATHER'S IS **MAGIC**, BUT IT DOESN'T COME CHEAPLY! CARE TO SEE THE PRICE HE PAID FOR HIS TALENTS?
MAMA!

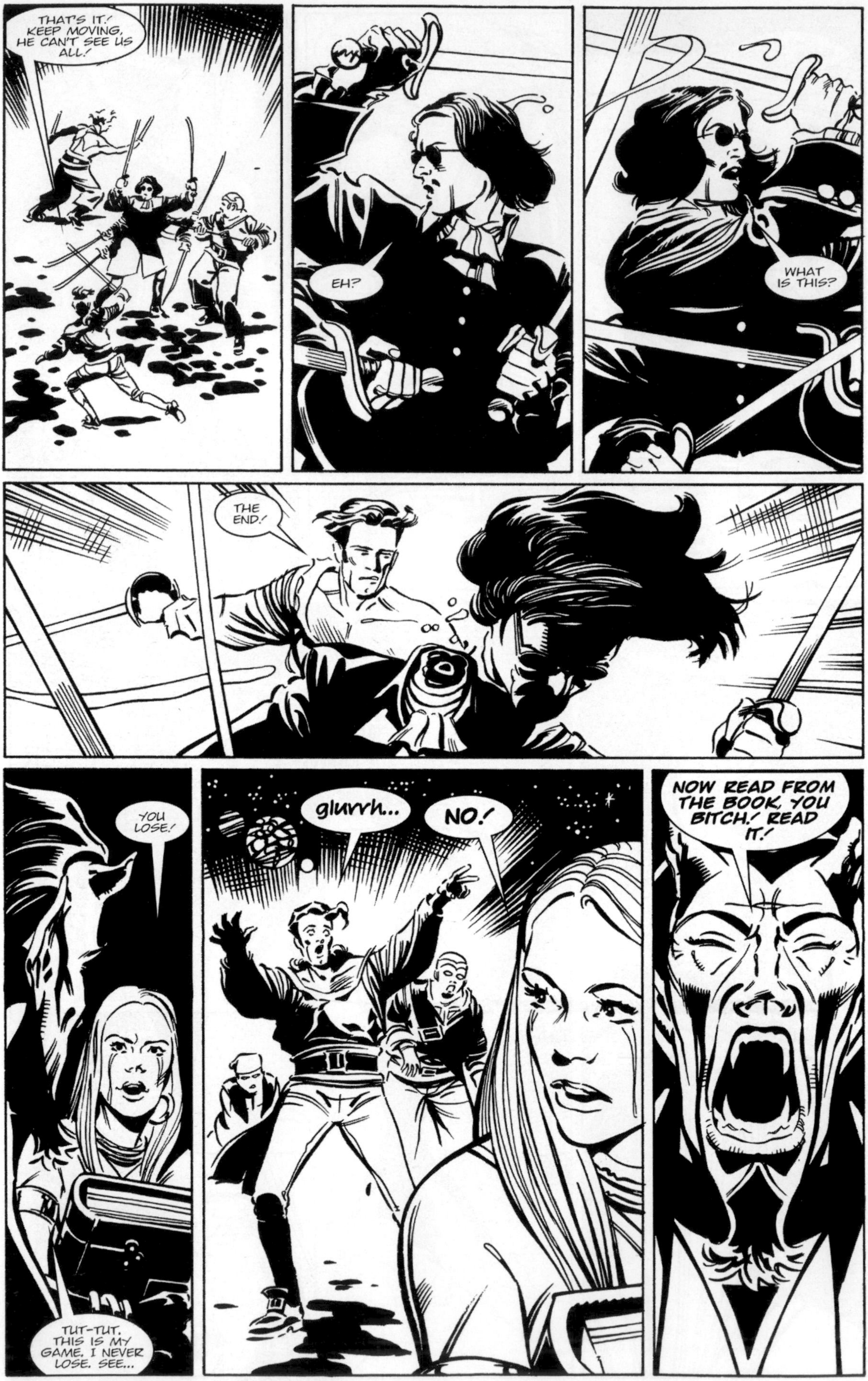
THAT'S IT! KEEP MOVING, HE CAN'T SEE US ALL!
EH?
WHAT IS THIS?
THE END!
YOU LOSE!
TUT-TUT. THIS IS MY GAME. I NEVER LOSE. SEE...
glurrh...
NO!
NOW READ FROM THE BOOK, YOU BITCH! READ IT!

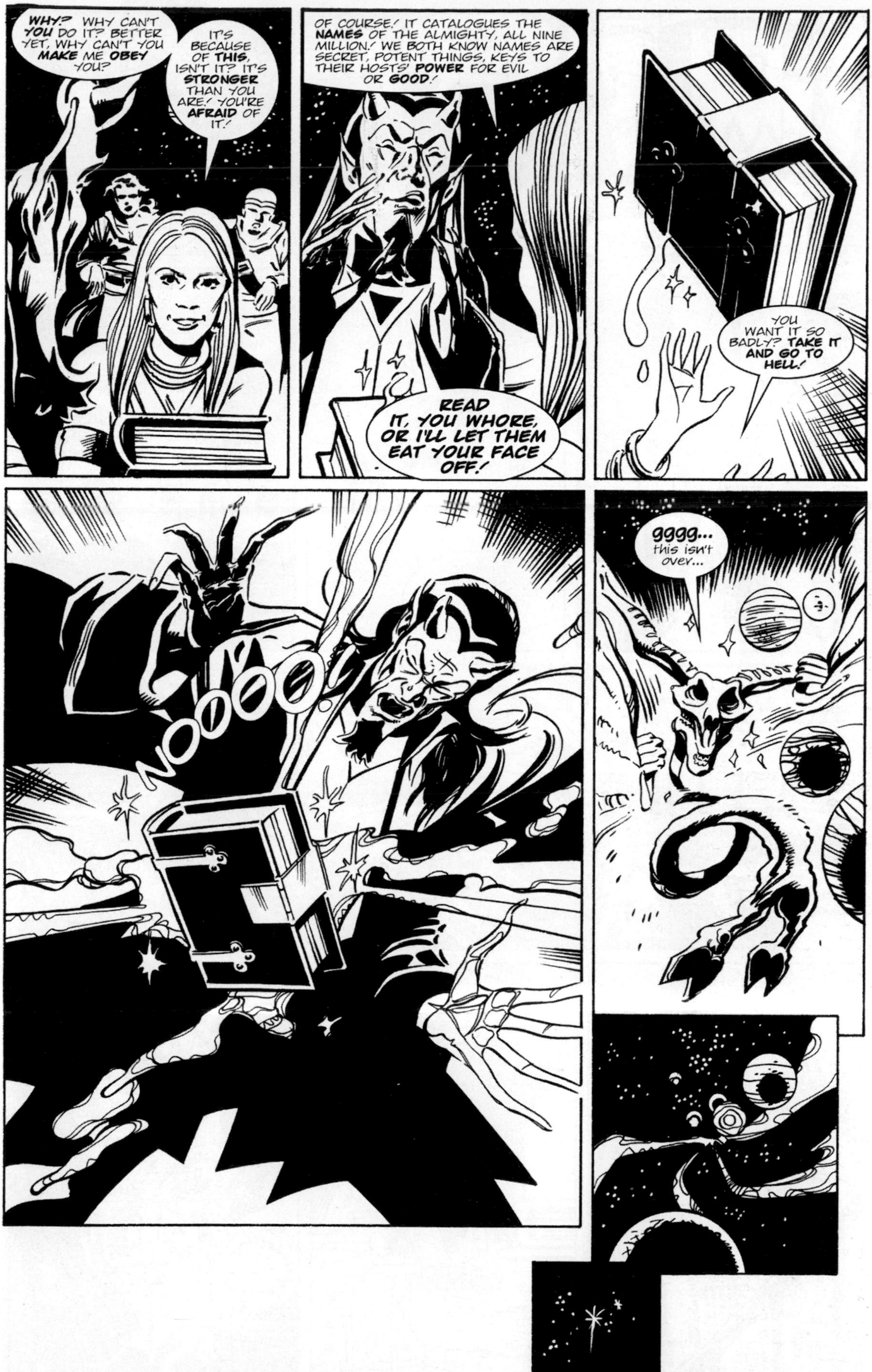
WHY? WHY CAN'T YOU DO IT? BETTER YET, WHY CAN'T YOU MAKE ME OBEY YOU?
IT'S BECAUSE OF THIS, ISN'T IT? IT'S STRONGER THAN YOU ARE! YOU'RE AFRAID OF IT!
OF COURSE! IT CATALOGUES THE NAMES OF THE ALMIGHTY, ALL NINE MILLION! WE BOTH KNOW NAMES ARE SECRET, POTENT THINGS, KEYS TO THEIR HOSTS' POWER FOR EVIL OR GOOD!
READ IT, YOU WHORE, OR I'LL LET THEM EAT YOUR FACE OFF!
YOU WANT IT SO BADLY? TAKE IT AND GO TO HELL!
NOOOOO!
gggg... this isn't over...

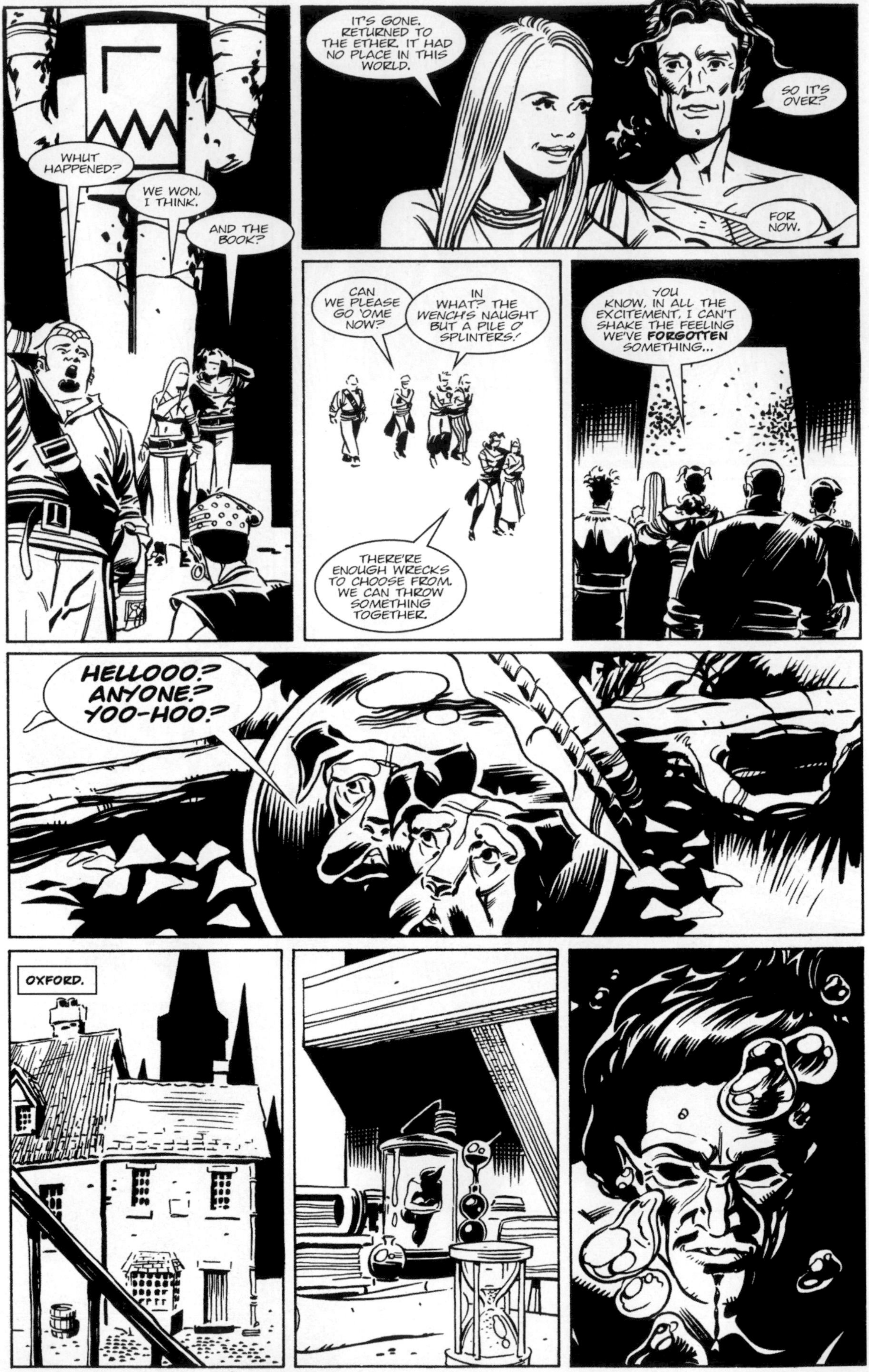
WHUT HAPPENED?
WE WON, I THINK.
AND THE BOOK?
IT'S GONE. RETURNED TO THE ETHER. IT HAD NO PLACE IN THIS WORLD.
SO IT'S OVER?
FOR NOW.
CAN WE PLEASE GO 'OME NOW?
IN WHAT? THE WENCH'S NAUGHT BUT A PILE O' SPLINTERS!
THERE'RE ENOUGH WRECKS TO CHOOSE FROM. WE CAN THROW SOMETHING TOGETHER.
YOU KNOW, IN ALL THE EXCITEMENT, I CAN'T SHAKE THE FEELING WE'VE **FORGOTTEN** SOMETHING...
HELLOOO? ANYONE? YOO-HOO?
OXFORD.

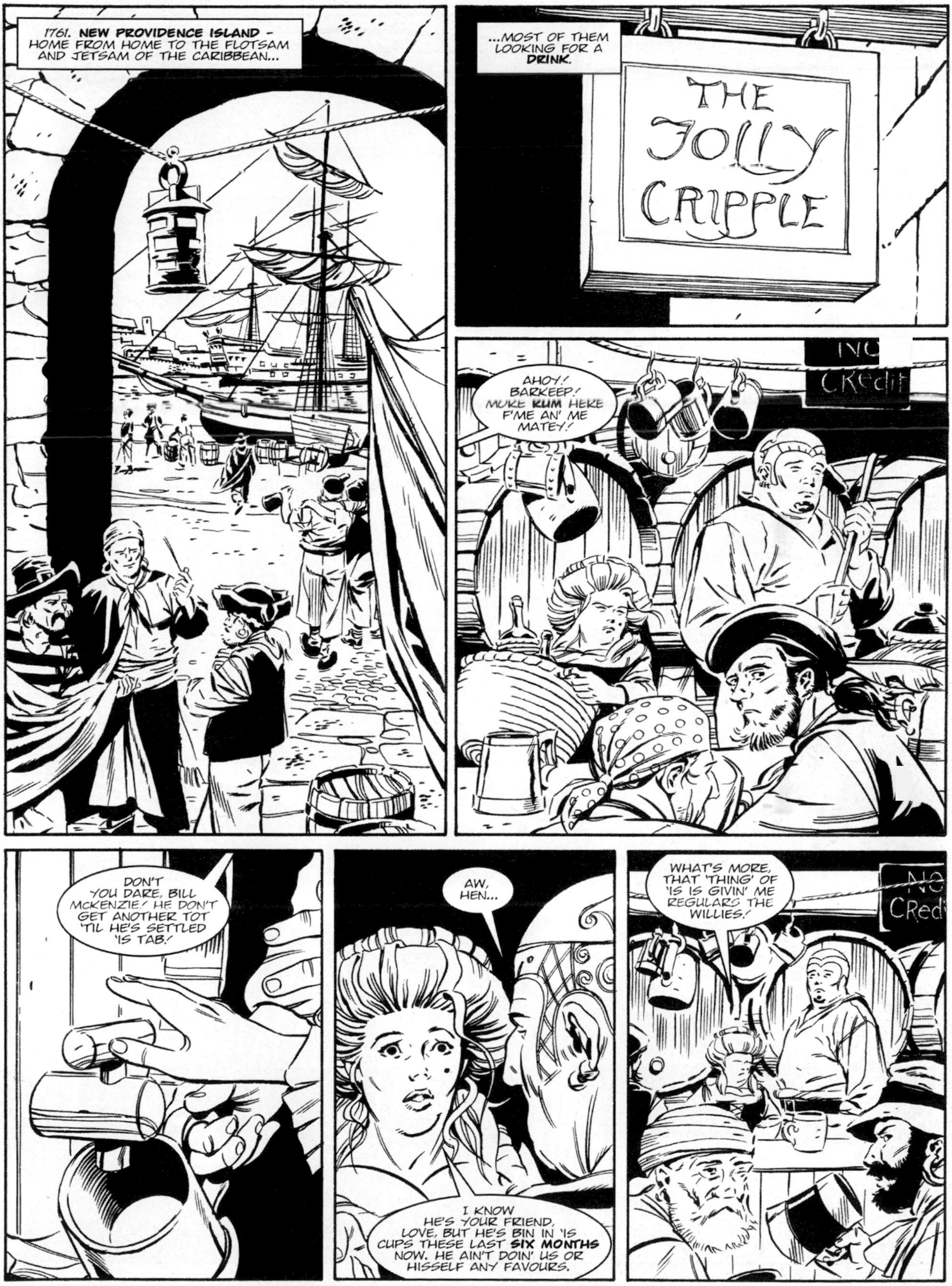
1761. NEW PROVIDENCE ISLAND - HOME FROM HOME TO THE FLOTSAM AND JETSAM OF THE CARIBBEAN...
...MOST OF THEM LOOKING FOR A DRINK.
THE JOLLY CRIPPLE
AHOY! BARKEEP! MORE RUM HERE F'ME AN' ME MATEY!
NO CREdit
DON'T YOU DARE, BILL McKENZIE! HE DON'T GET ANOTHER TOT 'TIL HE'S SETTLED 'IS TAB!
AW, HEN...
I KNOW HE'S YOUR FRIEND, LOVE, BUT HE'S BIN IN 'IS CUPS THESE LAST SIX MONTHS NOW. HE AIN'T DOIN' US OR HISSELF ANY FAVOURS.
WHAT'S MORE, THAT 'THING' OF 'IS IS GIVIN' ME REGULARS THE WILLIES!

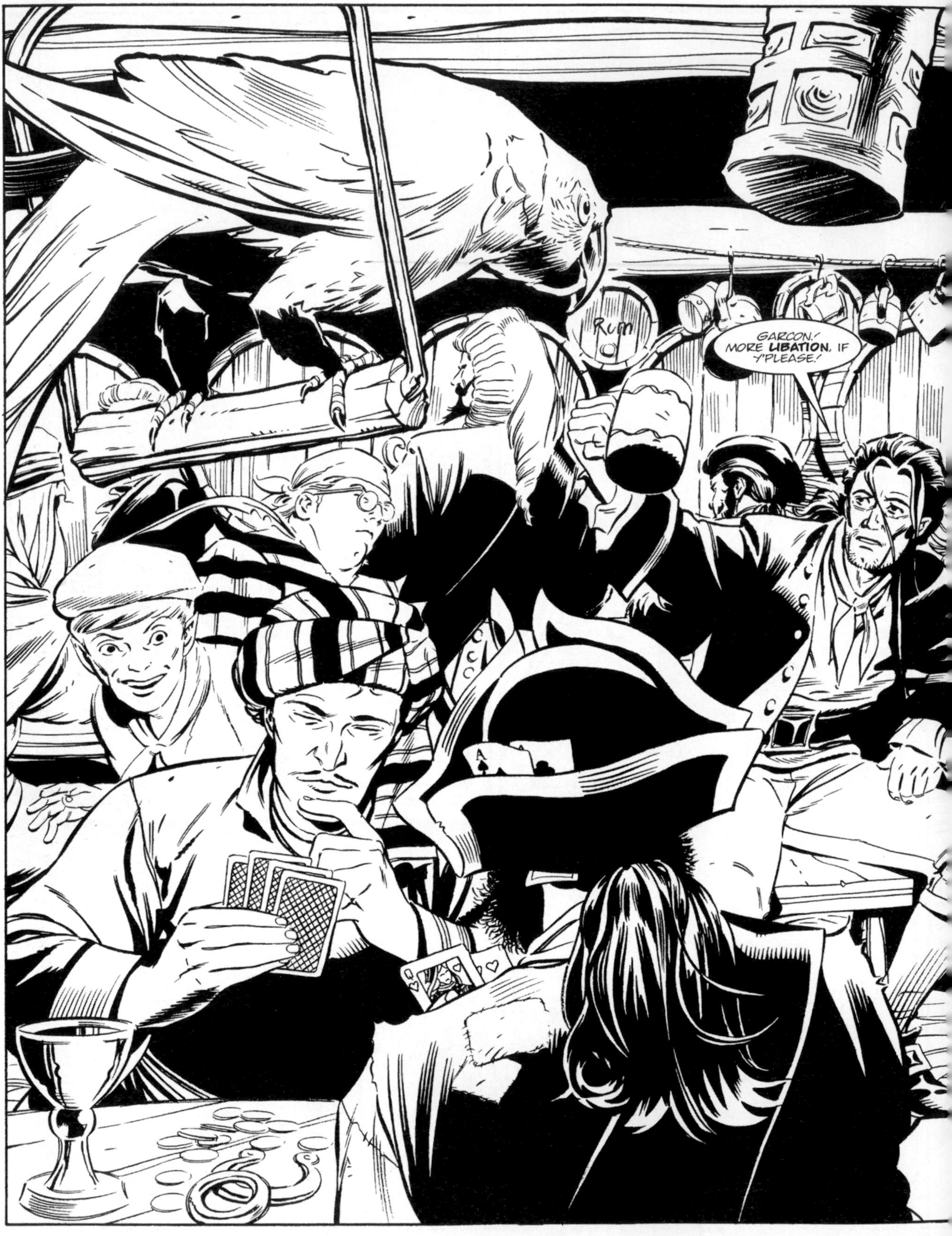
GARCON! MORE LIBATION, IF Y'PLEASE!
RUM

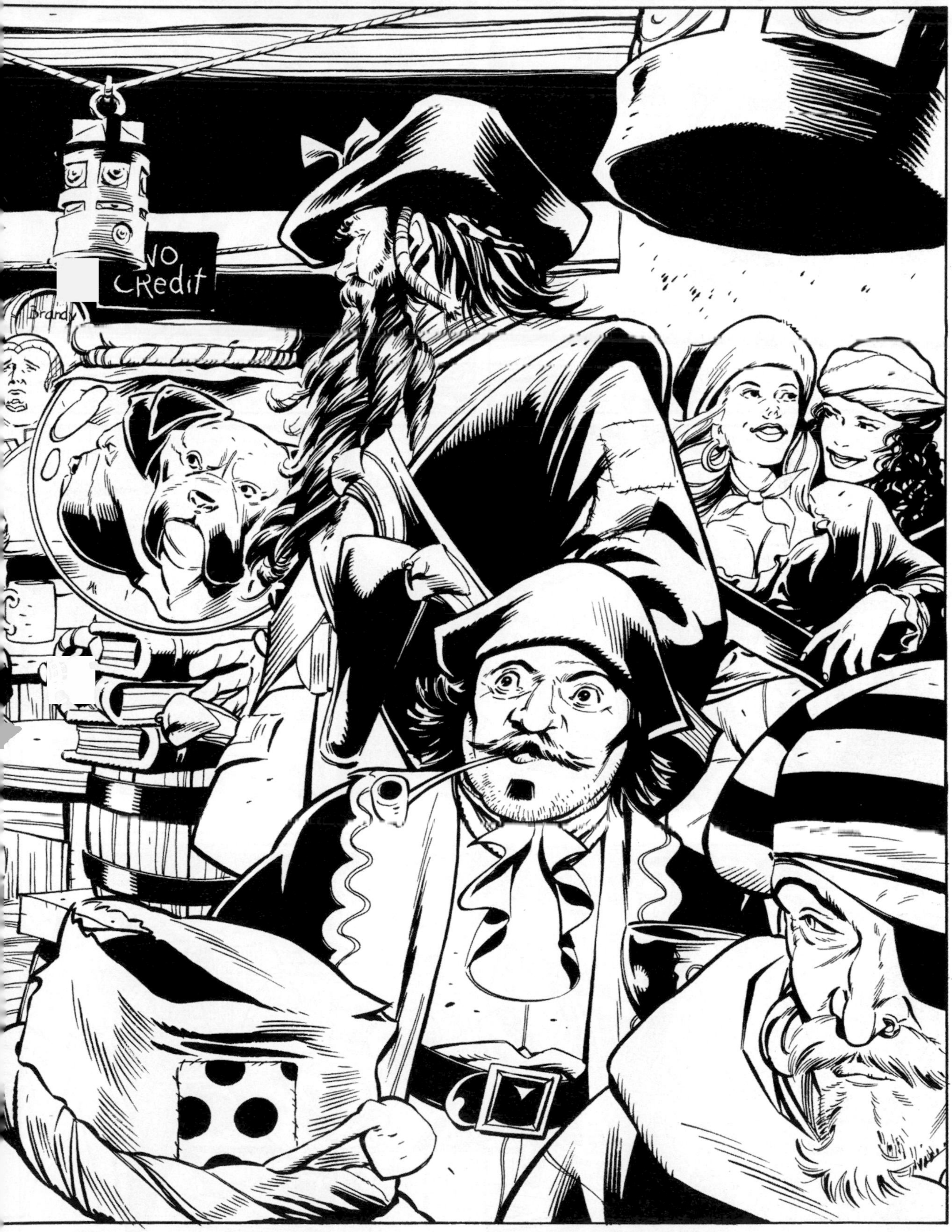
NO
CREdit
Brandy

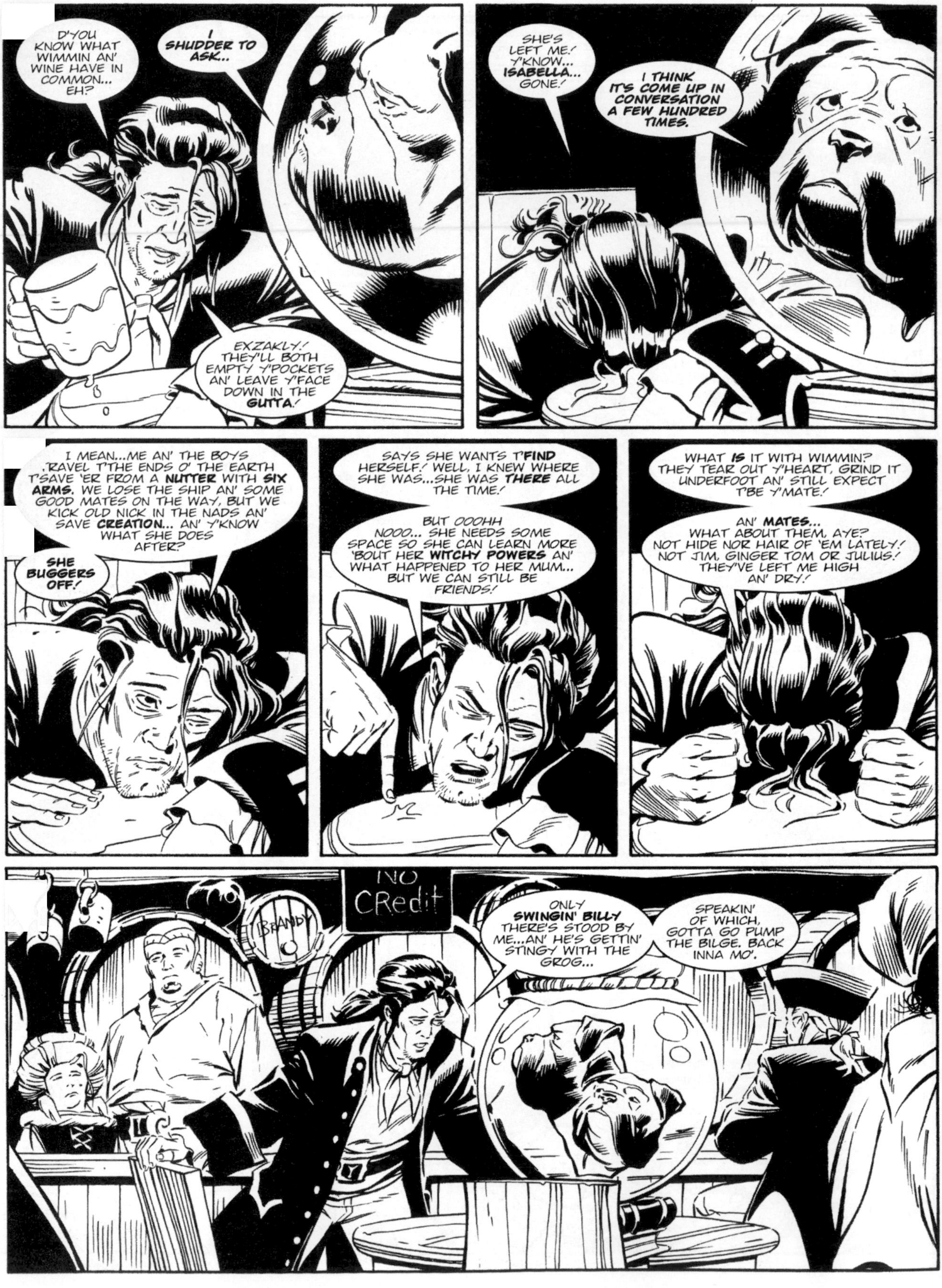
D'YOU KNOW WHAT WIMMIN AN' WINE HAVE IN COMMON... EH?
I SHUDDER TO ASK...
EXZAKLY! THEY'LL BOTH EMPTY Y'POCKETS AN' LEAVE Y'FACE DOWN IN THE GUTTA!
SHE'S LEFT ME! Y'KNOW... ISABELLA... GONE!
I THINK IT'S COME UP IN CONVERSATION A FEW HUNDRED TIMES.
I MEAN...ME AN' THE BOYS TRAVEL T'THE ENDS O' THE EARTH T'SAVE 'ER FROM A NUTTER WITH SIX ARMS. WE LOSE THE SHIP AN' SOME GOOD MATES ON THE WAY, BUT WE KICK OLD NICK IN THE NADS AN' SAVE CREATION... AN' Y'KNOW WHAT SHE DOES AFTER?
SHE BUGGERS OFF!
SAYS SHE WANTS T'FIND HERSELF! WELL, I KNEW WHERE SHE WAS...SHE WAS THERE ALL THE TIME!
BUT OOOHH NOOO... SHE NEEDS SOME SPACE SO SHE CAN LEARN MORE 'BOUT HER WITCHY POWERS AN' WHAT HAPPENED TO HER MUM... BUT WE CAN STILL BE FRIENDS!
WHAT IS IT WITH WIMMIN? THEY TEAR OUT Y'HEART, GRIND IT UNDERFOOT AN' STILL EXPECT T'BE Y'MATE!
AN' MATES... WHAT ABOUT THEM, AYE? NOT HIDE NOR HAIR OF 'EM LATELY! NOT JIM, GINGER TOM OR JULIUS! THEY'VE LEFT ME HIGH AN' DRY!
NO CRedit
BRANDY
ONLY SWINGIN' BILLY THERE'S STOOD BY ME...AN' HE'S GETTIN' STINGY WITH THE GROG...
SPEAKIN' OF WHICH, GOTTA GO PUMP THE BILGE. BACK INNA MO'.

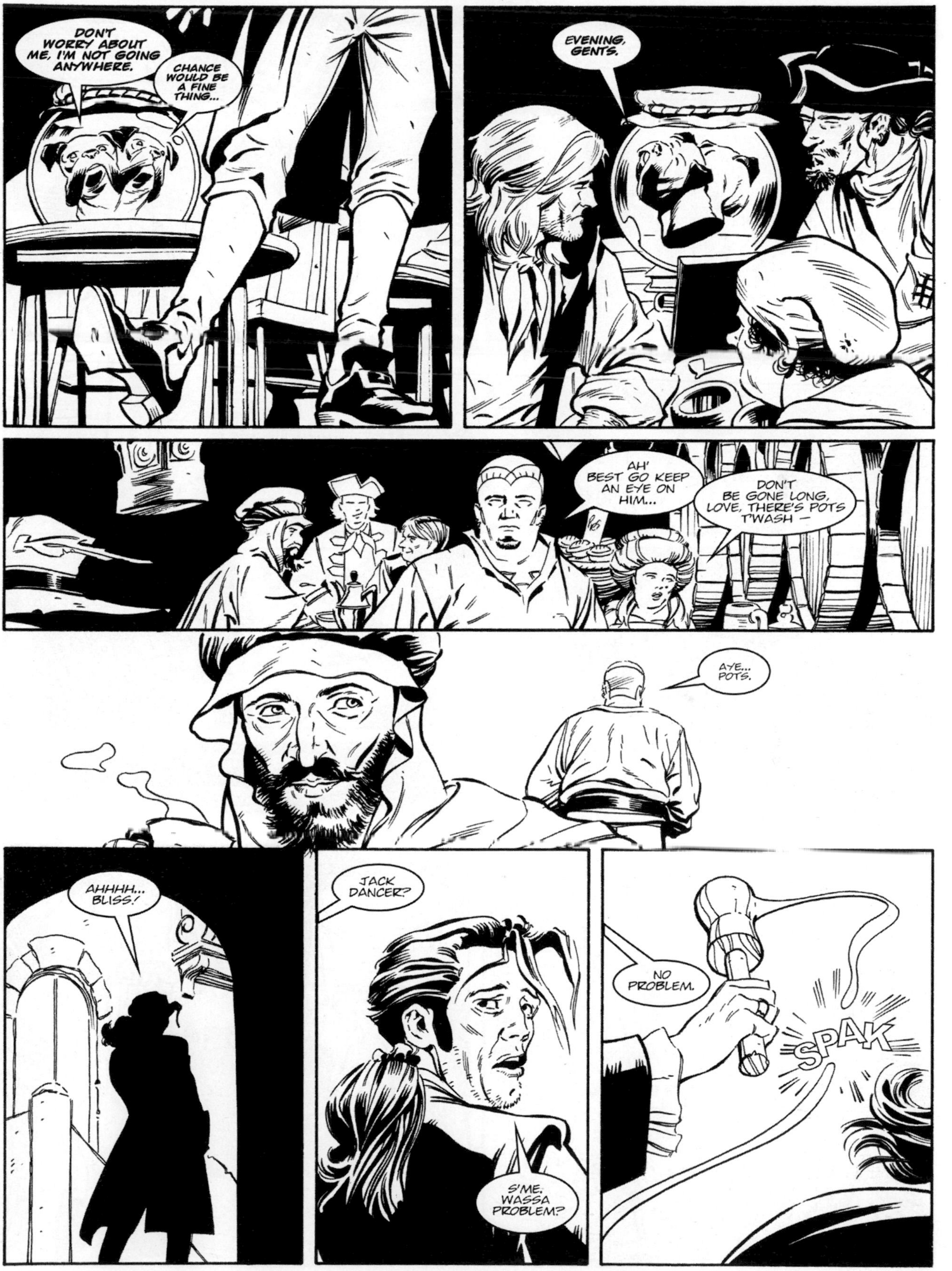
DON'T WORRY ABOUT ME, I'M NOT GOING ANYWHERE.
CHANCE WOULD BE A FINE THING...
EVENING, GENTS.
AH' BEST GO KEEP AN EYE ON HIM...
DON'T BE GONE LONG, LOVE, THERE'S POTS T'WASH –
AYE... POTS.
AHHHH... BLISS!
JACK DANCER?
S'ME. WASSA PROBLEM?
NO PROBLEM.
SPAK

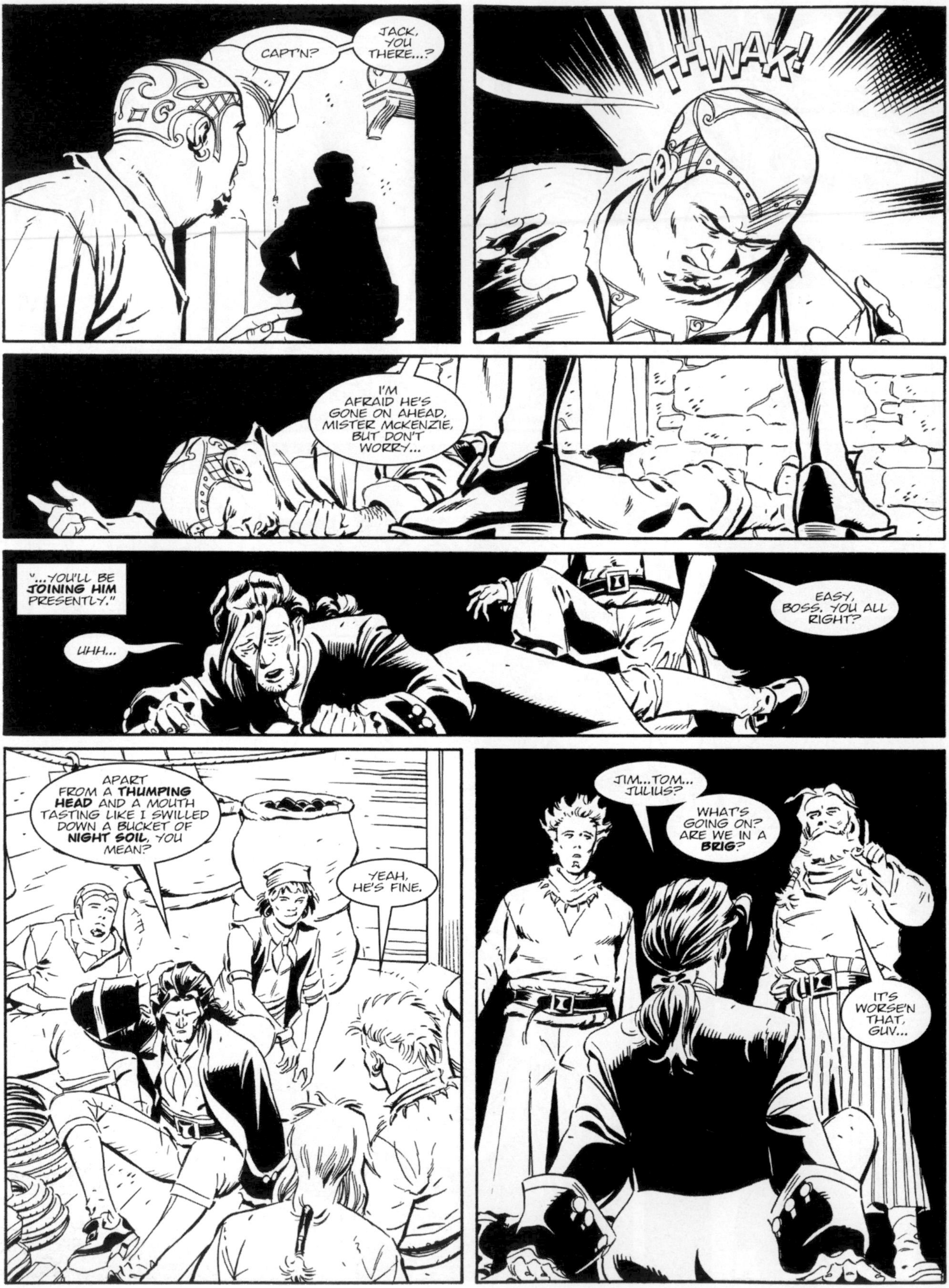
CAPT'N?
JACK, YOU THERE...?
THWAK!
I'M AFRAID HE'S GONE ON AHEAD, MISTER MCKENZIE, BUT DON'T WORRY...
"...YOU'LL BE JOINING HIM PRESENTLY."
UHH...
EASY, BOSS. YOU ALL RIGHT?
APART FROM A THUMPING HEAD AND A MOUTH TASTING LIKE I SWILLED DOWN A BUCKET OF NIGHT SOIL, YOU MEAN?
YEAH, HE'S FINE.
JIM...TOM... JULIUS?
WHAT'S GOING ON? ARE WE IN A BRIG?
IT'S WORSE'N THAT, GUV...

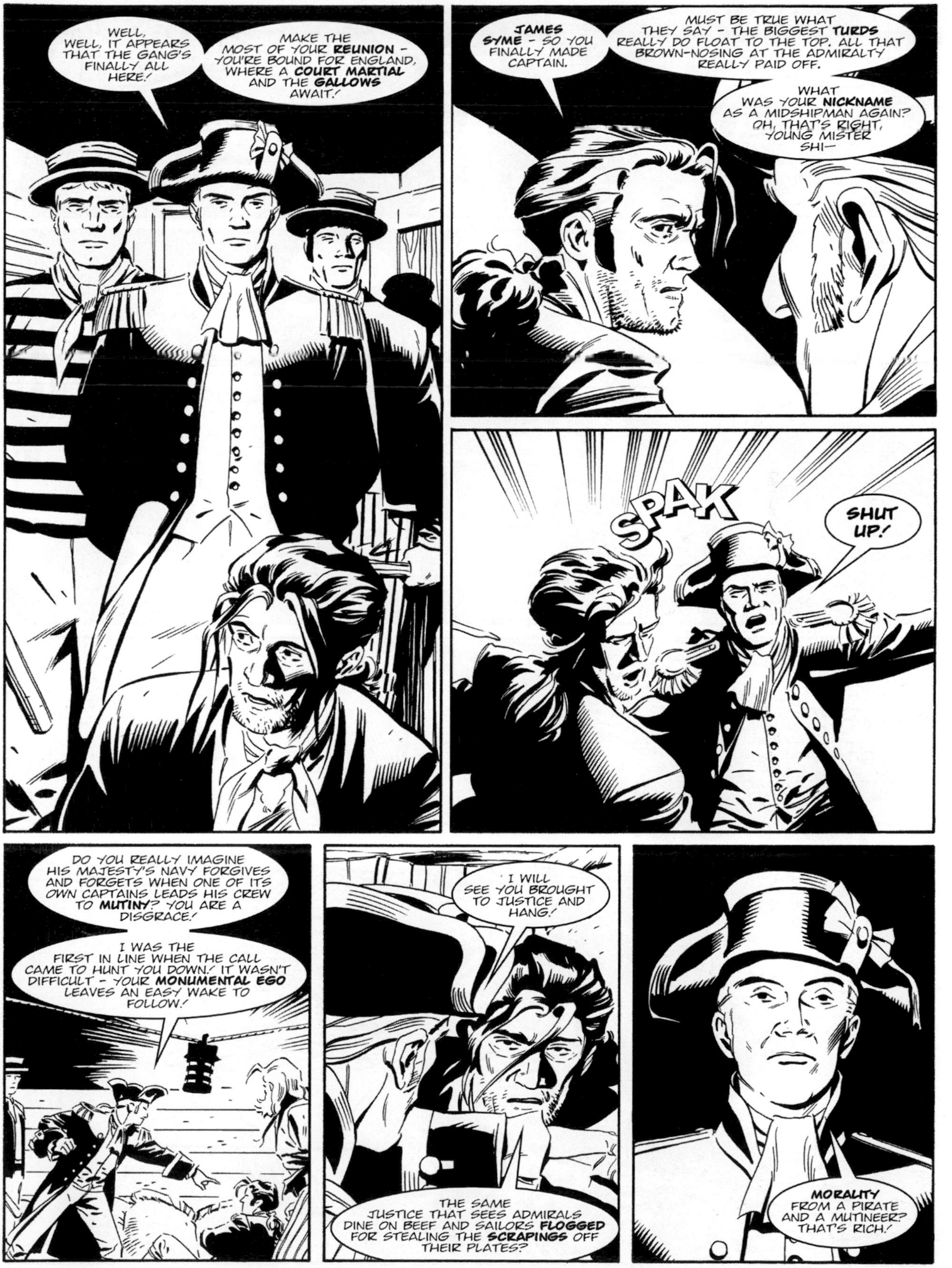

WELL, WELL, IT APPEARS THAT THE GANG'S FINALLY ALL HERE!
MAKE THE MOST OF YOUR REUNION - YOU'RE BOUND FOR ENGLAND, WHERE A COURT MARTIAL AND THE GALLOWS AWAIT!
JAMES SYME - SO YOU FINALLY MADE CAPTAIN.
MUST BE TRUE WHAT THEY SAY - THE BIGGEST TURDS REALLY DO FLOAT TO THE TOP. ALL THAT BROWN-NOSING AT THE ADMIRALTY REALLY PAID OFF.
WHAT WAS YOUR NICKNAME AS A MIDSHIPMAN AGAIN? OH, THAT'S RIGHT, YOUNG MISTER SHI—
SPAK
SHUT UP!
DO YOU REALLY IMAGINE HIS MAJESTY'S NAVY FORGIVES AND FORGETS WHEN ONE OF ITS OWN CAPTAINS LEADS HIS CREW TO MUTINY? YOU ARE A DISGRACE!
I WAS THE FIRST IN LINE WHEN THE CALL CAME TO HUNT YOU DOWN! IT WASN'T DIFFICULT - YOUR MONUMENTAL EGO LEAVES AN EASY WAKE TO FOLLOW!
I WILL SEE YOU BROUGHT TO JUSTICE AND HANG!
THE SAME JUSTICE THAT SEES ADMIRALS DINE ON BEEF AND SAILORS FLOGGED FOR STEALING THE SCRAPINGS OFF THEIR PLATES?
MORALITY FROM A PIRATE AND A MUTINEER? THAT'S RICH!

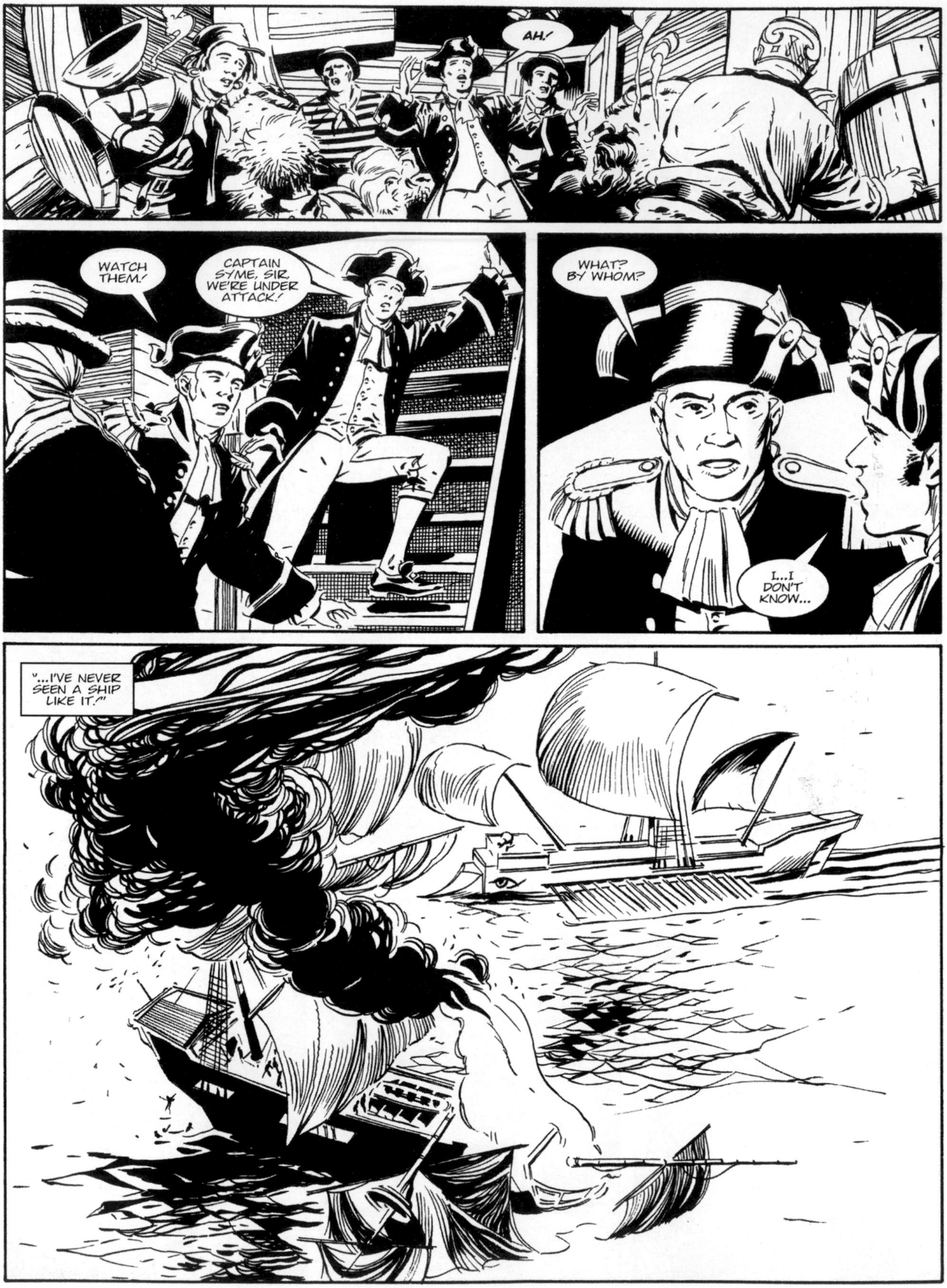
AH!
WATCH THEM!
CAPTAIN SYME, SIR, WE'RE UNDER ATTACK!
WHAT? BY WHOM?
I...I DON'T KNOW...
"...I'VE NEVER SEEN A SHIP LIKE IT."

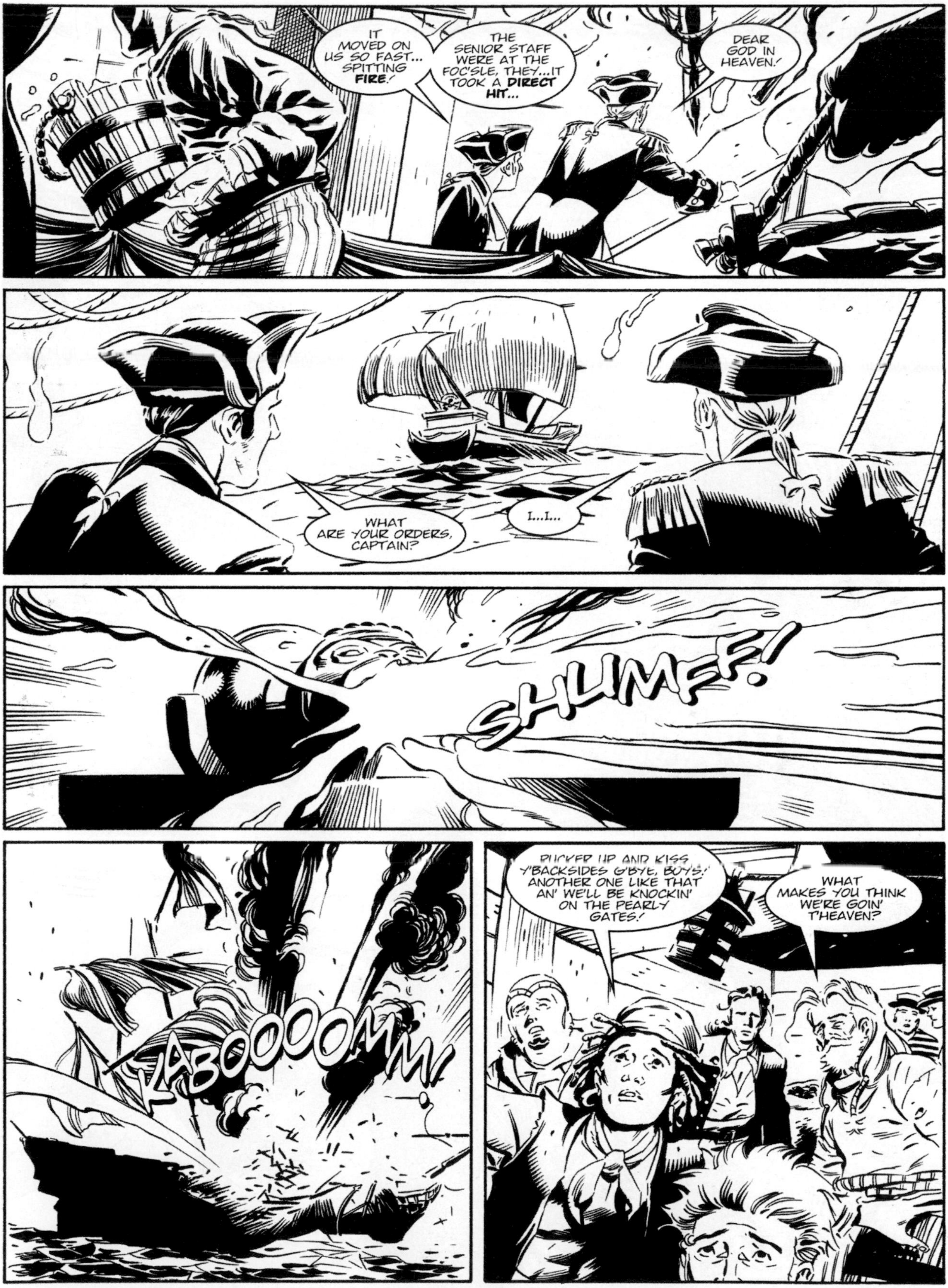
IT MOVED ON US SO FAST... SPITTING FIRE!
THE SENIOR STAFF WERE AT THE FOC'SLE, THEY...IT TOOK A DIRECT HIT...
DEAR GOD IN HEAVEN!
WHAT ARE YOUR ORDERS, CAPTAIN?
I...I...
SHLIMFF!
KABOOOOOMM!
PUCKER UP AND KISS Y'BACKSIDES G'BYE, BOYS! ANOTHER ONE LIKE THAT AN' WE'LL BE KNOCKIN' ON THE PEARLY GATES!
WHAT MAKES YOU THINK WE'RE GOIN' T'HEAVEN?

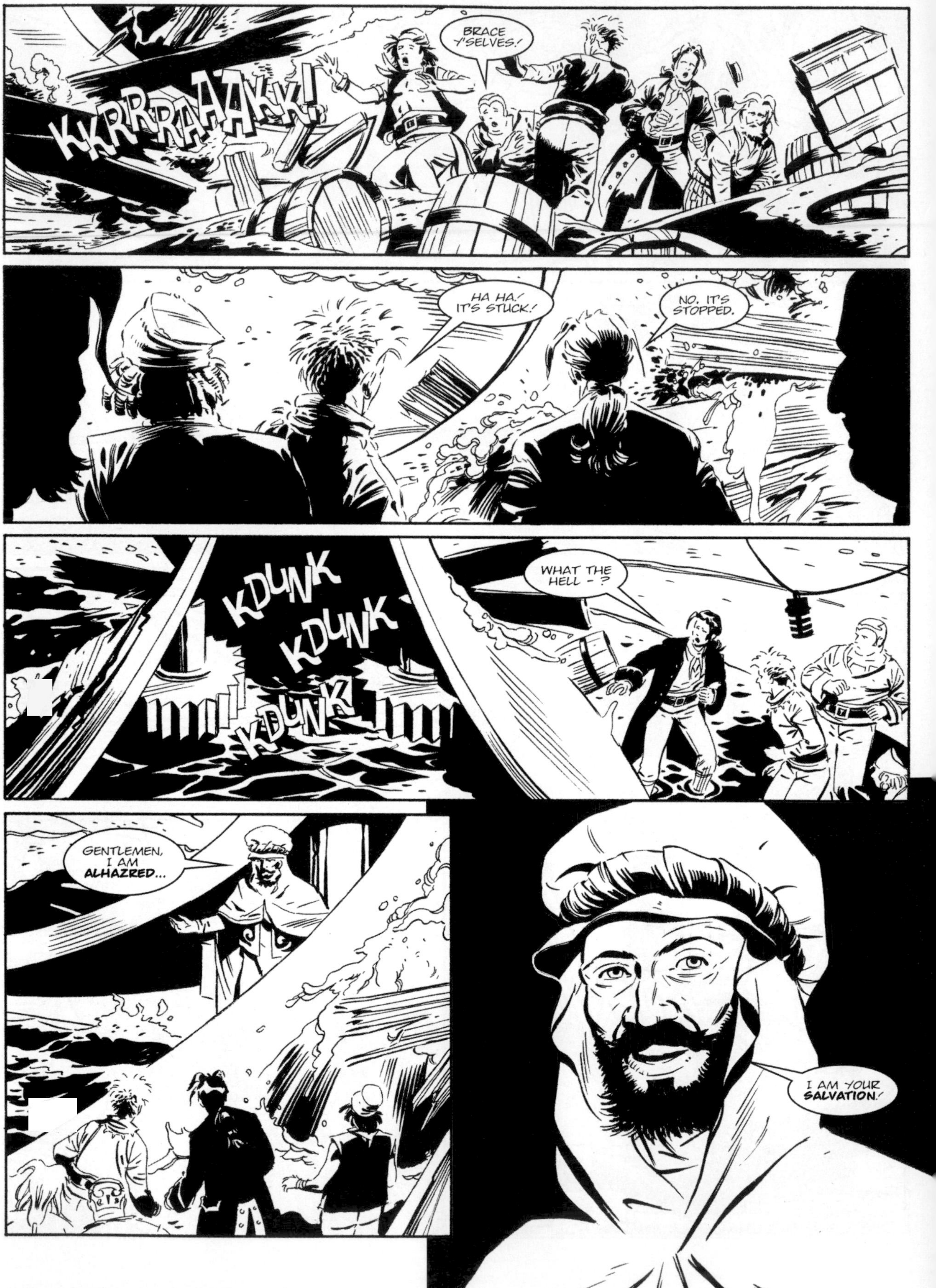
BRACE Y'SELVES!
KKRRRAAAKK!
HA HA! IT'S STUCK!
NO. IT'S STOPPED.
KDUNK
KDUNK
KDUNK
WHAT THE HELL - ?
GENTLEMEN, I AM **ALHAZRED**...
I AM YOUR **SALVATION**!

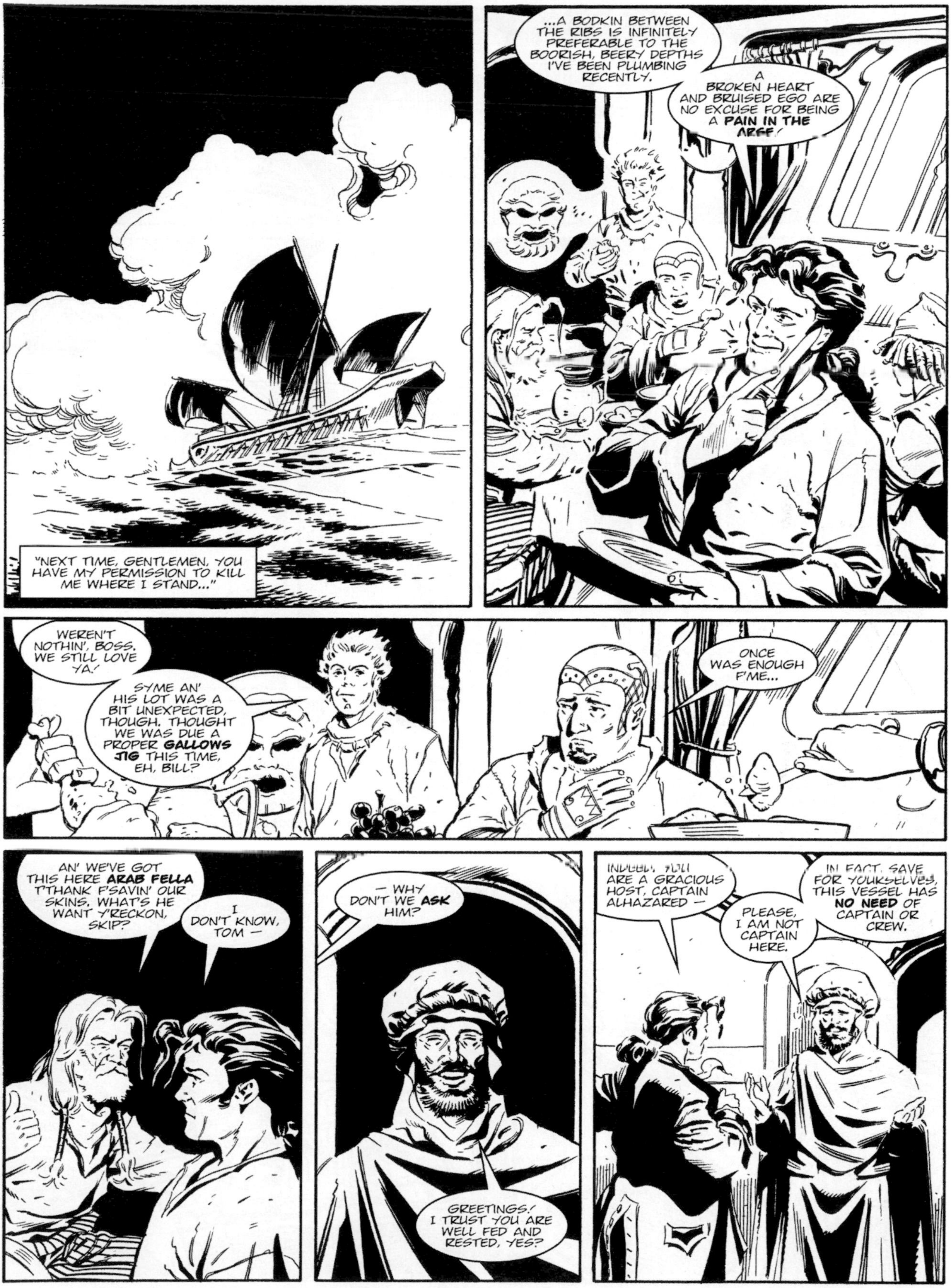

"NEXT TIME, GENTLEMEN, YOU HAVE MY PERMISSION TO KILL ME WHERE I STAND..."
...A BODKIN BETWEEN THE RIBS IS INFINITELY PREFERABLE TO THE BOORISH, BEERY DEPTHS I'VE BEEN PLUMBING RECENTLY.
A BROKEN HEART AND BRUISED EGO ARE NO EXCUSE FOR BEING A **PAIN IN THE ARSE!**
WEREN'T NOTHIN', BOSS. WE STILL LOVE YA!
SYME AN' HIS LOT WAS A BIT UNEXPECTED, THOUGH. THOUGHT WE WAS DUE A PROPER **GALLOWS JIG** THIS TIME, EH, BILL?
ONCE WAS ENOUGH F'ME...
AN' WE'VE GOT THIS HERE **ARAB FELLA** T'THANK F'SAVIN' OUR SKINS. WHAT'S HE WANT Y'RECKON, SKIP?
I DON'T KNOW, TOM —
— WHY DON'T WE **ASK** HIM?
GREETINGS! I TRUST YOU ARE WELL FED AND RESTED, YES?
ARE A GRACIOUS HOST, CAPTAIN ALHAZARED —
PLEASE, I AM NOT CAPTAIN HERE.
IN FACT, SAVE FOR YOURSELVES, THIS VESSEL HAS **NO NEED** OF CAPTAIN OR CREW.

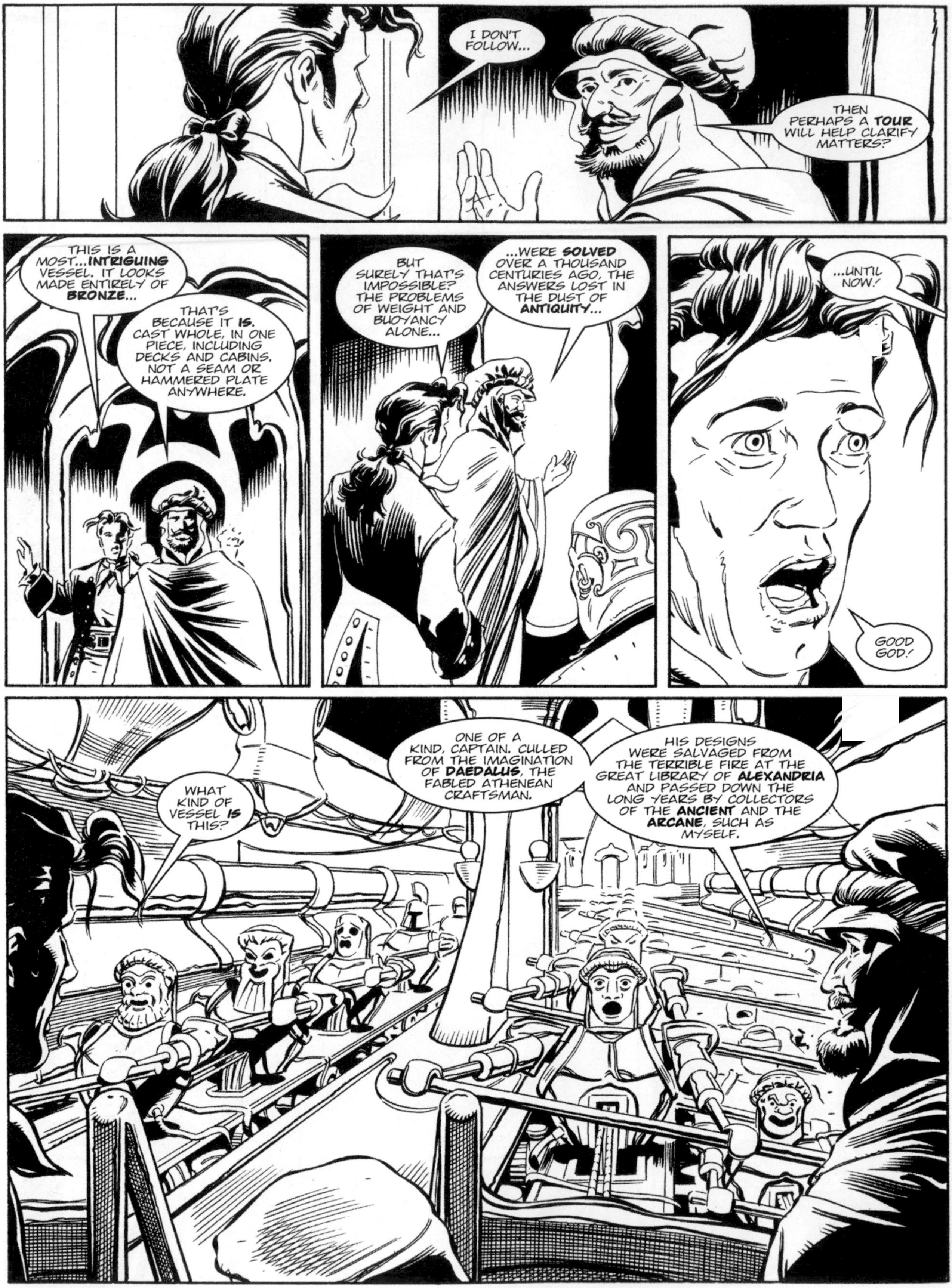
I DON'T FOLLOW...
THEN PERHAPS A **TOUR** WILL HELP CLARIFY MATTERS?
THIS IS A MOST... **INTRIGUING** VESSEL. IT LOOKS MADE ENTIRELY OF **BRONZE**...
THAT'S BECAUSE IT **IS**. CAST WHOLE, IN ONE PIECE, INCLUDING DECKS AND CABINS. NOT A SEAM OR HAMMERED PLATE ANYWHERE.
BUT SURELY THAT'S IMPOSSIBLE? THE PROBLEMS OF WEIGHT AND BUOYANCY ALONE...
...WERE **SOLVED** OVER A THOUSAND CENTURIES AGO, THE ANSWERS LOST IN THE DUST OF **ANTIQUITY**...
...UNTIL NOW.!
GOOD GOD.!
WHAT KIND OF VESSEL **IS** THIS?
ONE OF A KIND, CAPTAIN. CULLED FROM THE IMAGINATION OF **DAEDALUS**, THE FABLED ATHENEAN CRAFTSMAN.
HIS DESIGNS WERE SALVAGED FROM THE TERRIBLE FIRE AT THE GREAT LIBRARY OF **ALEXANDRIA** AND PASSED DOWN THE LONG YEARS BY COLLECTORS OF THE **ANCIENT** AND THE **ARCANE**, SUCH AS MYSELF.

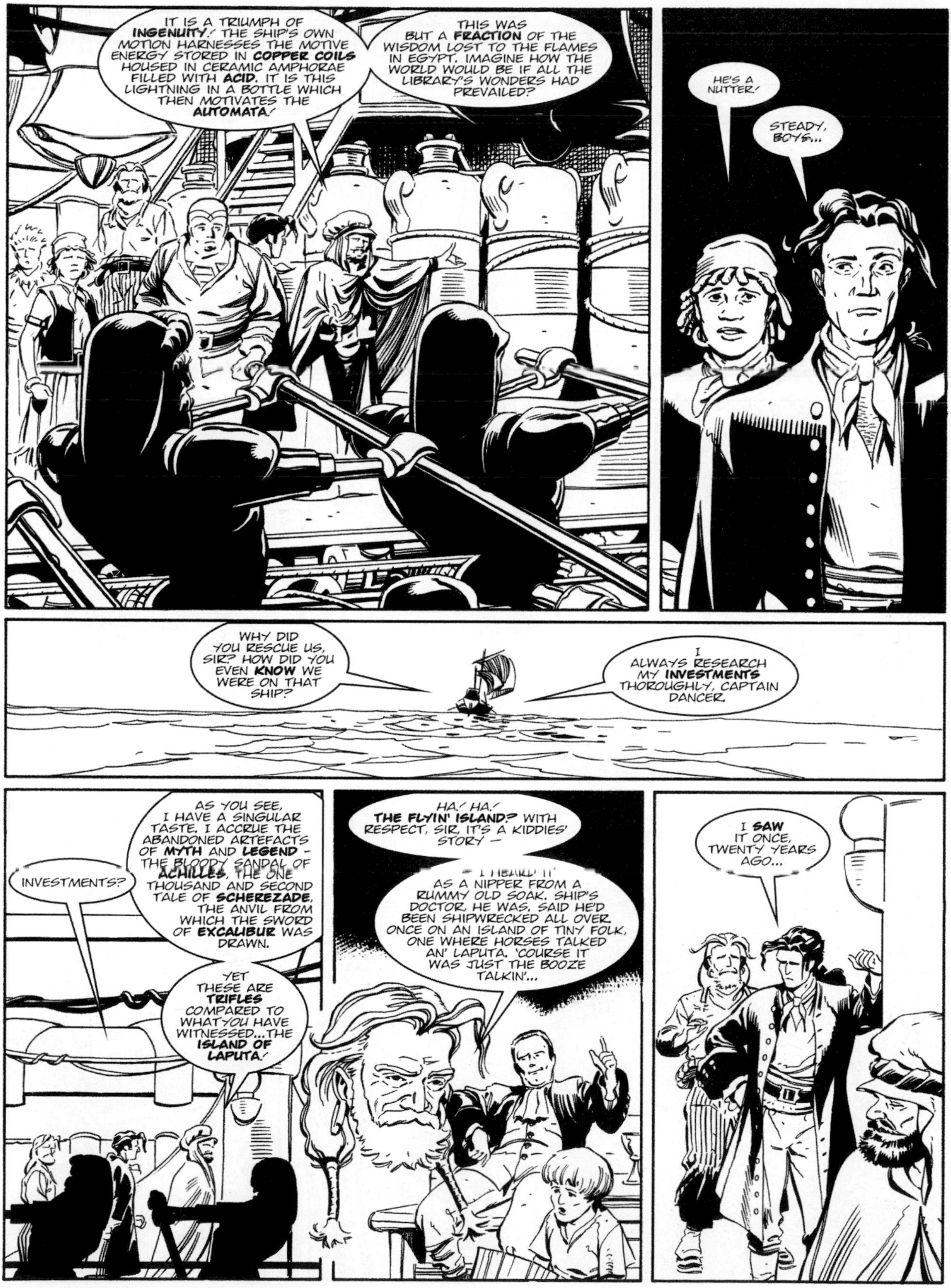
IT IS A TRIUMPH OF INGENUITY! THE SHIP'S OWN MOTION HARNESSES THE MOTIVE ENERGY STORED IN COPPER COILS HOUSED IN CERAMIC AMPHORAE FILLED WITH ACID. IT IS THIS LIGHTNING IN A BOTTLE WHICH THEN MOTIVATES THE AUTOMATA!
THIS WAS BUT A FRACTION OF THE WISDOM LOST TO THE FLAMES IN EGYPT. IMAGINE HOW THE WORLD WOULD BE IF ALL THE LIBRARY'S WONDERS HAD PREVAILED?
HE'S A NUTTER!
STEADY, BOYS...
WHY DID YOU RESCUE US, SIR? HOW DID YOU EVEN KNOW WE WERE ON THAT SHIP?
I ALWAYS RESEARCH MY INVESTMENTS THOROUGHLY, CAPTAIN DANCER.
INVESTMENTS?
AS YOU SEE, I HAVE A SINGULAR TASTE. I ACCRUE THE ABANDONED ARTEFACTS OF MYTH AND LEGEND – THE BLOODY SANDAL OF ACHILLES, THE ONE THOUSAND AND SECOND TALE OF SCHEREZADE, THE ANVIL FROM WHICH THE SWORD OF EXCALIBUR WAS DRAWN.
YET THESE ARE TRIFLES COMPARED TO WHAT YOU HAVE WITNESSED... THE ISLAND OF LAPUTA!
HA! HA! THE FLYIN' ISLAND? WITH RESPECT, SIR, IT'S A KIDDIES' STORY –
I HEARD IT AS A NIPPER FROM A RUMMY OLD SOAK. SHIP'S DOCTOR, HE WAS. SAID HE'D BEEN SHIPWRECKED ALL OVER. ONCE ON AN ISLAND OF TINY FOLK, ONE WHERE HORSES TALKED AN' LAPUTA. 'COURSE IT WAS JUST THE BOOZE TALKIN'...
I SAW IT ONCE, TWENTY YEARS AGO...

"I WAS A MIDSHIPMAN ON THE *VULCAN*. I'D JUST FINISHED THE NIGHTWATCH WHEN SOMETHING CAUGHT MY EYE..."

"...AND THERE IT **WAS**, BATHED IN DAWN SUNLIGHT. I WAS TRANSFIXED BY THE **WONDER** OF IT...THEN IT WAS GONE, SWALLOWED BY THE CLOUDS.

"I TOLD NO ONE, FEARFUL OF BEING MOCKED OR THAT I'D DREAMED IT, BUT THE VISION OF IT HAUNTS ME TO THIS DAY..."

AND I ASSURE YOU, GENTLEMEN, I HADN'T TOUCHED A DROP.'

"YOU WERE INDEED BLESSED, CAPTAIN. THE ISLAND IS A THING OF RARE MAGIC, INVISIBLE TO MOST.

"I AM NOT SO FORTUNATE AND SO SEEK OUT THE HALVES OF A **GOLDEN MAP** THAT SHOWS THE ISLAND'S SECRET ORBIT OF THE WORLD."

I KNOW THEIR **LOCATION**, BUT CANNOT OBTAIN THEM ALONE. I NEED YOUR UNIQUE VISION AND MEN OF DARING AND GUILE TO AID ME.

WE'VE TRUCKED WI' MAGIC BEFORE AN' IT'S COST US DEAR! AH'LL NO WALK THAT ROAD AGIN'.'

NAME YOUR PRICE.' YOUR WEIGHT IN GOLD? DIAMONDS? RUBIES?

ENOUGH TO BUY YOU **SANCTUARY** FROM THE BOUNTY THE **BRITISH NAVY** HAS UNDOUBTEDLY PUT ON YOUR HEADS.'

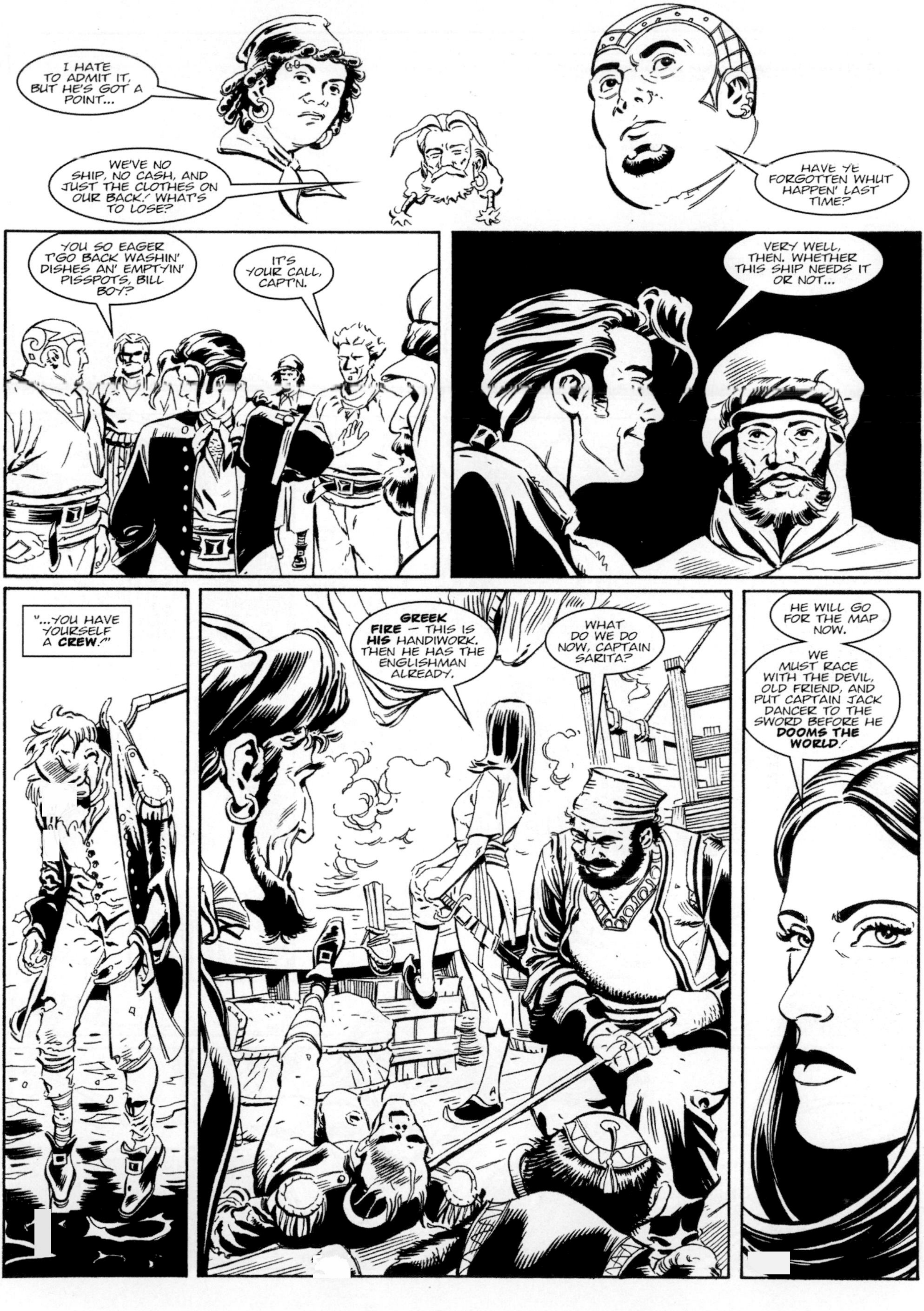

I HATE TO ADMIT IT, BUT HE'S GOT A POINT...
WE'VE NO SHIP, NO CASH, AND JUST THE CLOTHES ON OUR BACK! WHAT'S TO LOSE?
HAVE YE FORGOTTEN WHUT HAPPEN' LAST TIME?
YOU SO EAGER T'GO BACK WASHIN' DISHES AN' EMPTYIN' PISSPOTS, BILL BOY?
IT'S YOUR CALL, CAPT'N.
VERY WELL, THEN. WHETHER THIS SHIP NEEDS IT OR NOT...
"...YOU HAVE YOURSELF A **CREW**!"
**GREEK FIRE** — THIS IS **HIS** HANDIWORK. THEN HE HAS THE ENGLISHMAN ALREADY.
WHAT DO WE DO NOW, CAPTAIN SARITA?
HE WILL GO FOR THE MAP NOW.
WE MUST RACE WITH THE DEVIL, OLD FRIEND, AND PUT CAPTAIN JACK DANCER TO THE SWORD BEFORE HE **DOOMS THE WORLD**!

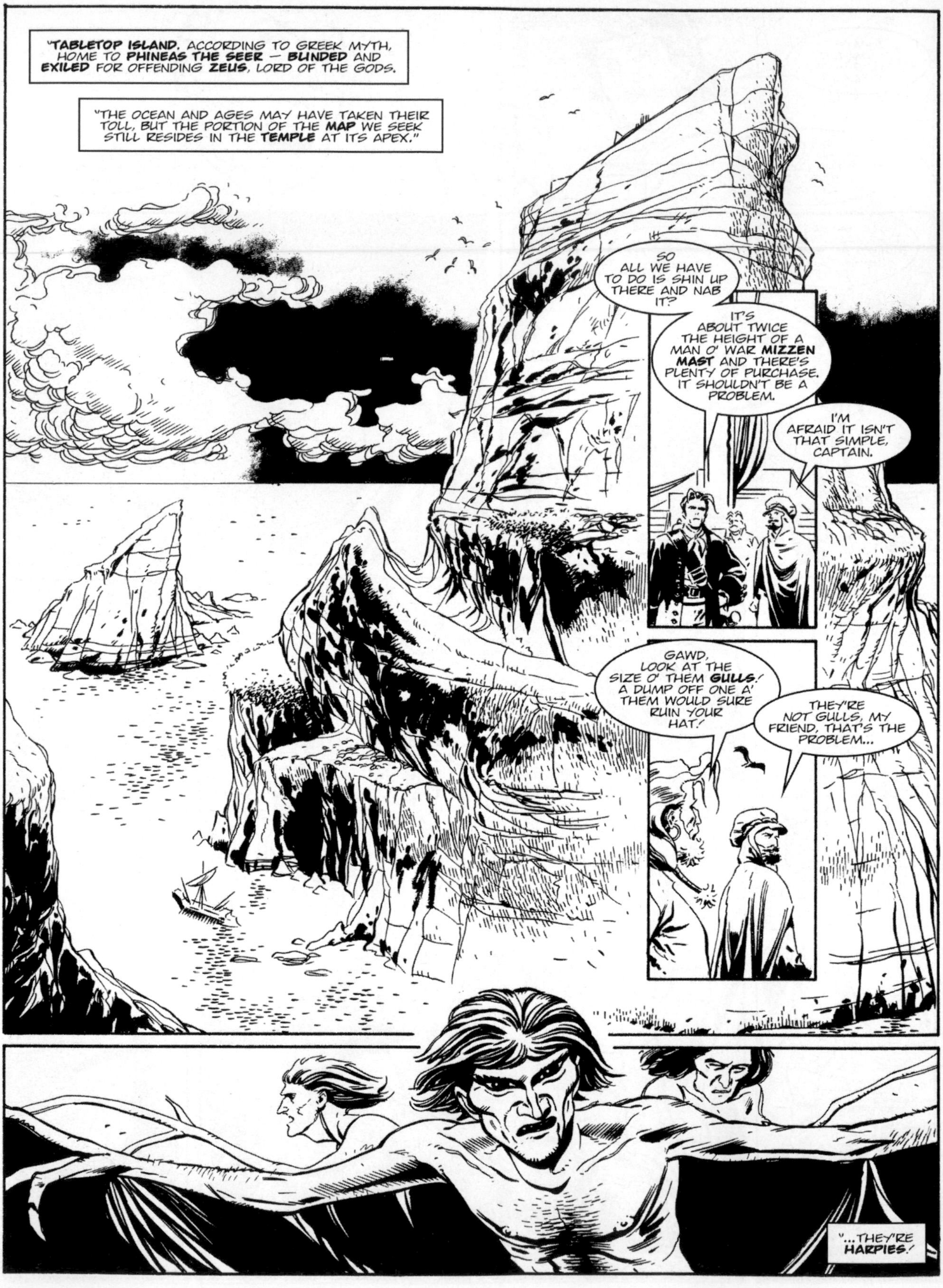
"TABLETOP ISLAND. ACCORDING TO GREEK MYTH, HOME TO PHINEAS THE SEER — BLINDED AND EXILED FOR OFFENDING ZEUS, LORD OF THE GODS.
"THE OCEAN AND AGES MAY HAVE TAKEN THEIR TOLL, BUT THE PORTION OF THE MAP WE SEEK STILL RESIDES IN THE TEMPLE AT ITS APEX."
SO ALL WE HAVE TO DO IS SHIN UP THERE AND NAB IT?
IT'S ABOUT TWICE THE HEIGHT OF A MAN O' WAR MIZZEN MAST AND THERE'S PLENTY OF PURCHASE. IT SHOULDN'T BE A PROBLEM.
I'M AFRAID IT ISN'T THAT SIMPLE, CAPTAIN.
GAWD, LOOK AT THE SIZE O' THEM GULLS! A DUMP OFF ONE A' THEM WOULD SURE RUIN YOUR HAT!
THEY'RE NOT GULLS, MY FRIEND, THAT'S THE PROBLEM...
"...THEY'RE HARPIES!

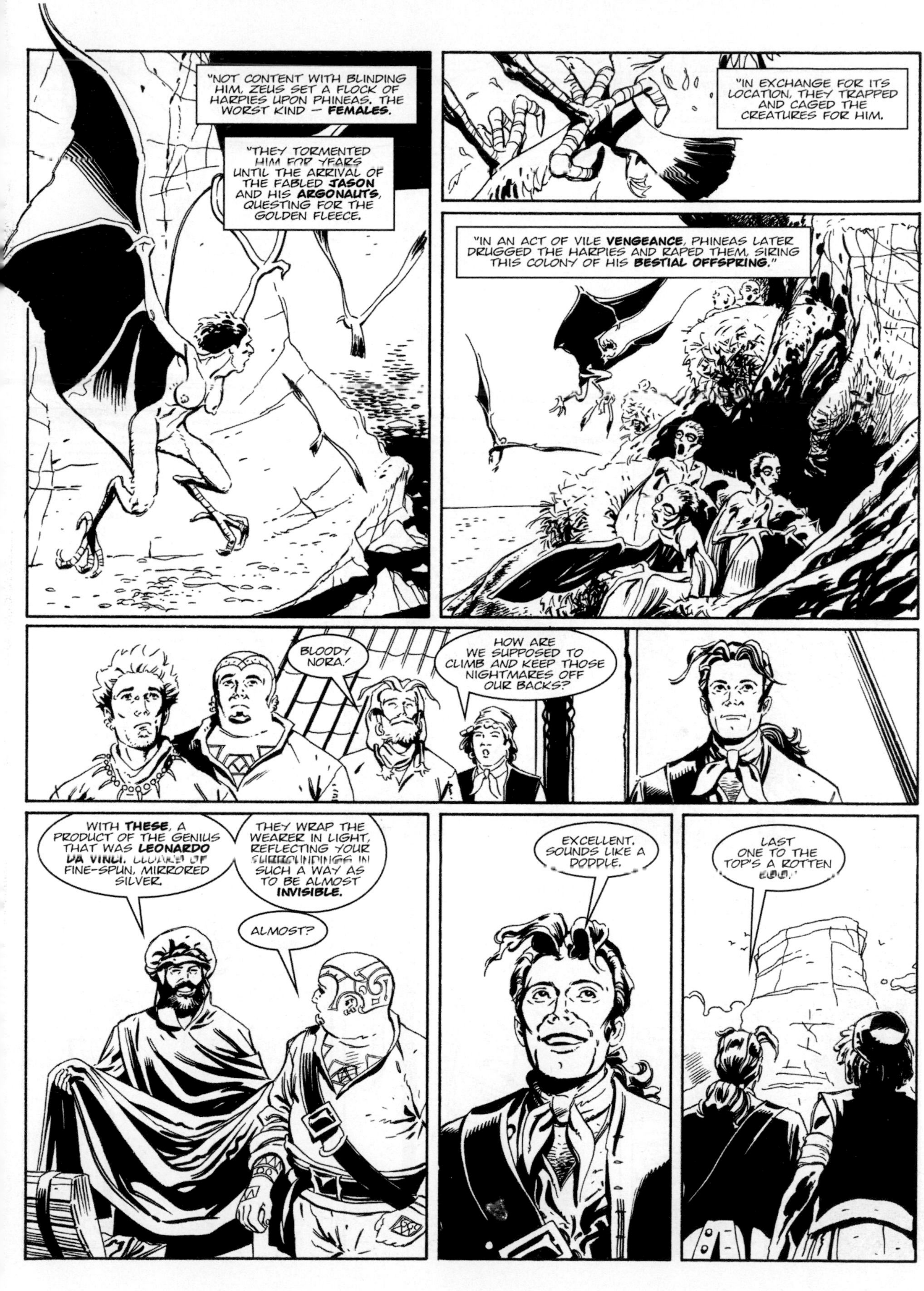
"NOT CONTENT WITH BLINDING HIM, ZEUS SET A FLOCK OF HARPIES UPON PHINEAS. THE WORST KIND — **FEMALES.**
"THEY TORMENTED HIM FOR YEARS UNTIL THE ARRIVAL OF THE FABLED **JASON** AND HIS **ARGONAUTS**, QUESTING FOR THE GOLDEN FLEECE.
"IN EXCHANGE FOR ITS LOCATION, THEY TRAPPED AND CAGED THE CREATURES FOR HIM.
"IN AN ACT OF VILE **VENGEANCE**, PHINEAS LATER DRUGGED THE HARPIES AND RAPED THEM, SIRING THIS COLONY OF HIS **BESTIAL OFFSPRING.**"
BLOODY NORA!
HOW ARE WE SUPPOSED TO CLIMB AND KEEP THOSE NIGHTMARES OFF OUR BACKS?
WITH **THESE**, A PRODUCT OF THE GENIUS THAT WAS **LEONARDO DA VINCI.** FINE-SPUN, MIRRORED SILVER.
THEY WRAP THE WEARER IN LIGHT, REFLECTING YOUR SURROUNDINGS IN SUCH A WAY AS TO BE ALMOST **INVISIBLE.**
ALMOST?
EXCELLENT. SOUNDS LIKE A DODDLE.
LAST ONE TO THE TOP'S A ROTTEN

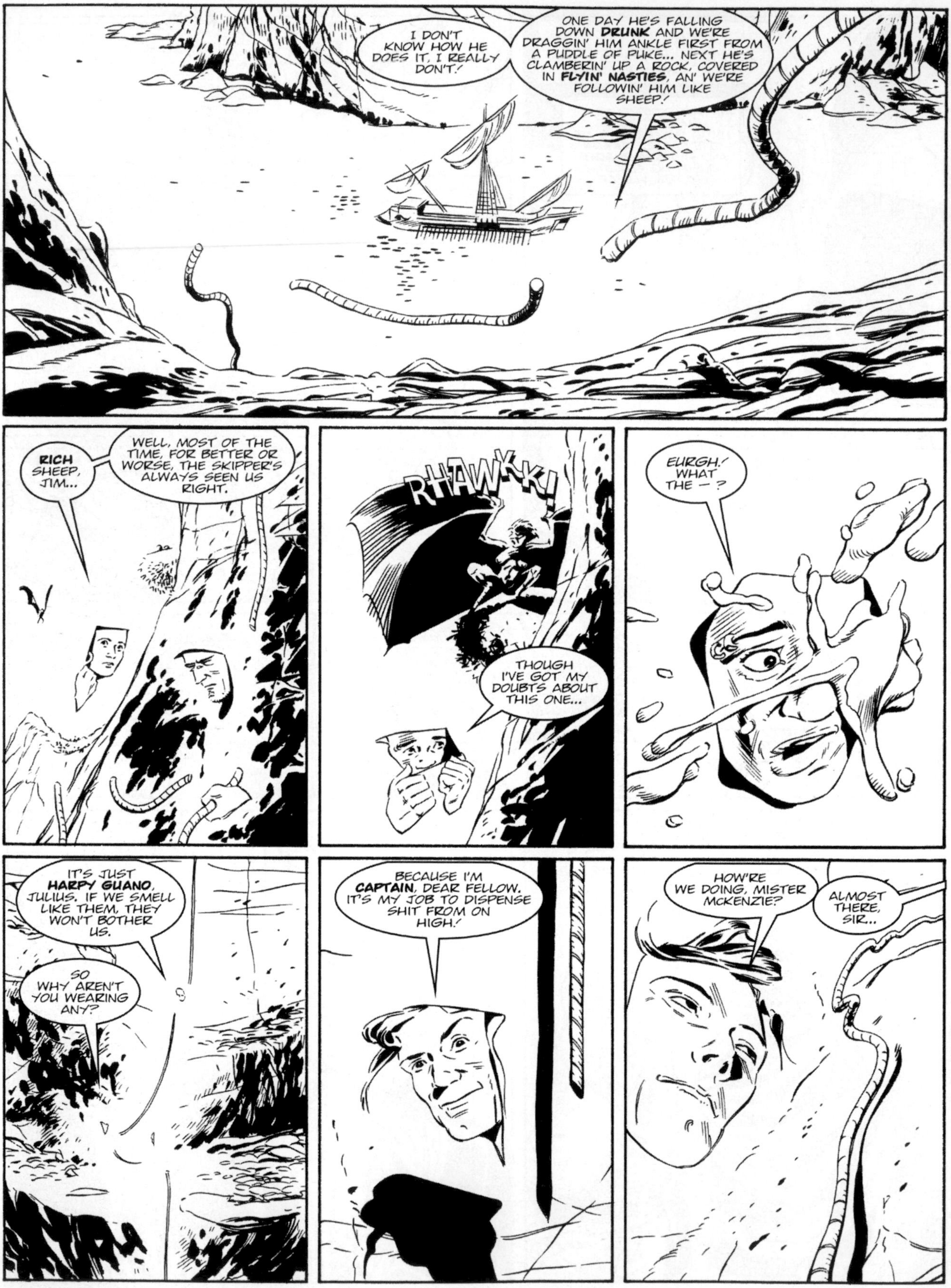
I DON'T KNOW HOW HE DOES IT, I REALLY DON'T!
ONE DAY HE'S FALLING DOWN **DRUNK** AND WE'RE DRAGGIN' HIM ANKLE FIRST FROM A PUDDLE OF PUKE... NEXT HE'S CLAMBERIN' UP A ROCK, COVERED IN **FLYIN' NASTIES**, AN' WE'RE FOLLOWIN' HIM LIKE SHEEP!
**RICH** SHEEP, JIM...
WELL, MOST OF THE TIME, FOR BETTER OR WORSE, THE SKIPPER'S ALWAYS SEEN US RIGHT.
RHAWKKK!
THOUGH I'VE GOT MY DOUBTS ABOUT THIS ONE...
EURGH! WHAT THE — ?
IT'S JUST **HARPY GUANO**, JULIUS. IF WE SMELL LIKE THEM, THEY WON'T BOTHER US.
SO WHY AREN'T YOU WEARING ANY?
BECAUSE I'M **CAPTAIN**, DEAR FELLOW. IT'S MY JOB TO DISPENSE SHIT FROM ON HIGH!
HOW'RE WE DOING, MISTER MCKENZIE?
ALMOST THERE, SIR...

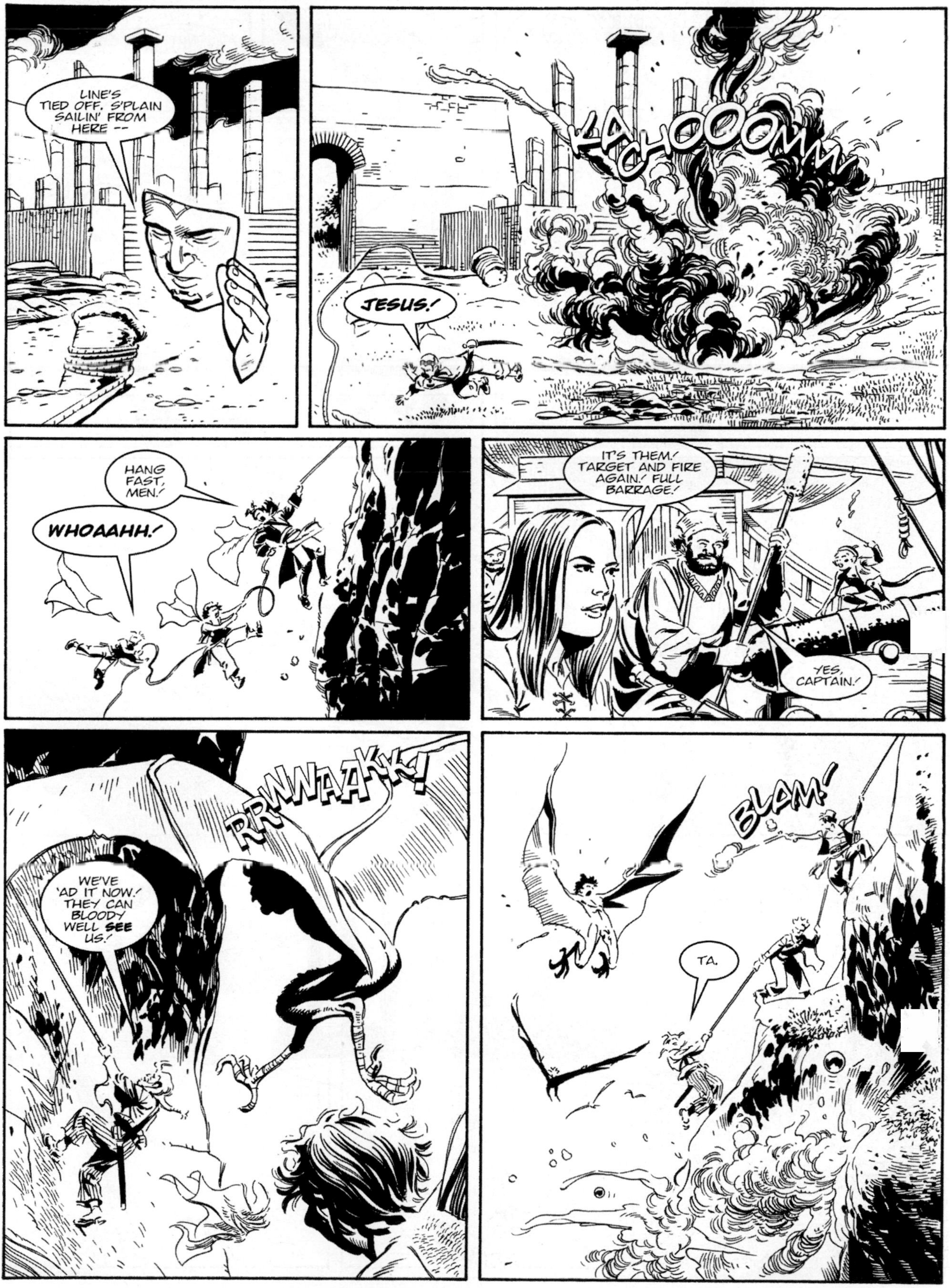
LINE'S TIED OFF. S'PLAIN SAILIN' FROM HERE --
KACHOOOOMM!
JESUS!
HANG FAST, MEN!
WHOAAHH!
IT'S THEM! TARGET AND FIRE AGAIN! FULL BARRAGE!
YES, CAPTAIN!
RRNNAAKK!
WE'VE 'AD IT NOW! THEY CAN BLOODY WELL SEE US!
BLAM!
TA.

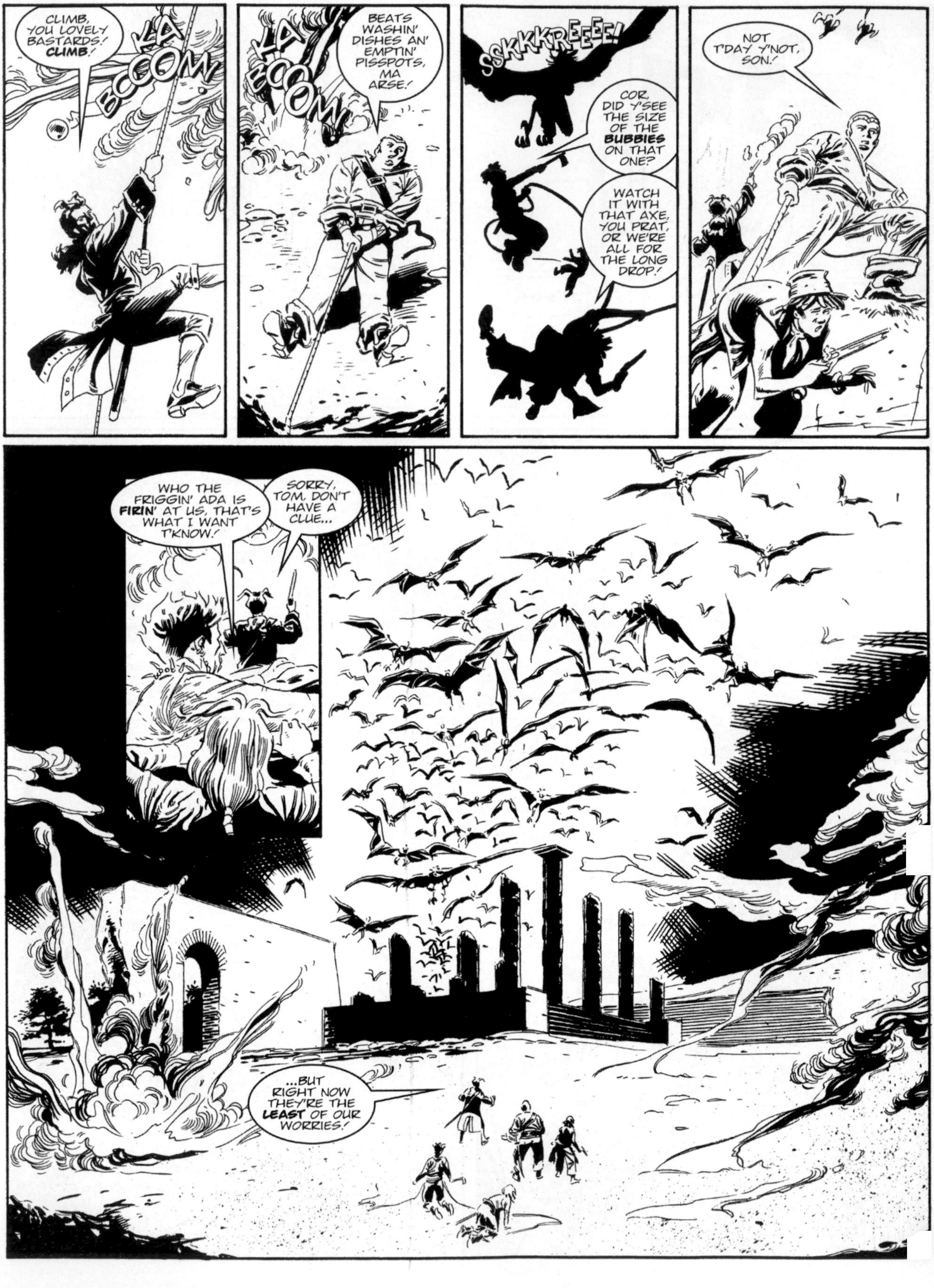
CLIMB, YOU LOVELY BASTARDS! CLIMB!
KA BOOOM!
KA BOOOM!
BEATS WASHIN' DISHES AN' EMPTIN' PISSPOTS, MA ARSE!
SSKKKREEEEE!
COR, DID Y'SEE THE SIZE OF THE BUBBIES ON THAT ONE?
WATCH IT WITH THAT AXE, YOU PRAT, OR WE'RE ALL FOR THE LONG DROP!
NOT T'DAY Y'NOT, SON!
WHO THE FRIGGIN' ADA IS FIRIN' AT US, THAT'S WHAT I WANT T'KNOW!
SORRY, TOM, DON'T HAVE A CLUE...
...BUT RIGHT NOW THEY'RE THE LEAST OF OUR WORRIES!

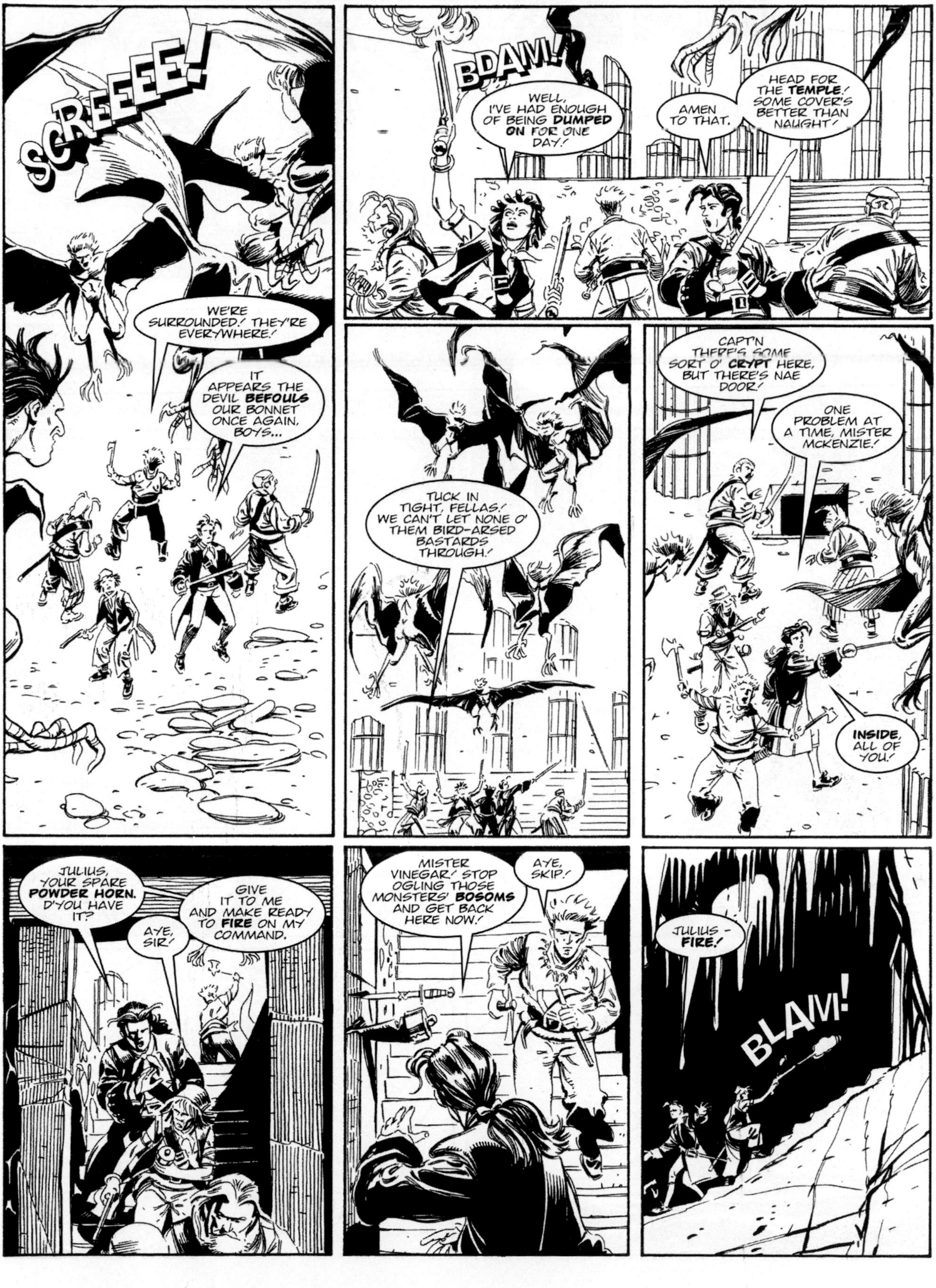
SCREEEE!
WE'RE SURROUNDED! THEY'RE EVERYWHERE!
IT APPEARS THE DEVIL BEFOULS OUR BONNET ONCE AGAIN, BOYS...
BDAM!
WELL, I'VE HAD ENOUGH OF BEING DUMPED ON FOR ONE DAY!
AMEN TO THAT.
HEAD FOR THE TEMPLE! SOME COVER'S BETTER THAN NAUGHT!
TUCK IN TIGHT, FELLAS! WE CAN'T LET NONE O' THEM BIRD-ARSED BASTARDS THROUGH!
CAPT'N THERE'S SOME SORT O' CRYPT HERE, BUT THERE'S NAE DOOR!
ONE PROBLEM AT A TIME, MISTER MCKENZIE!
INSIDE, ALL OF YOU!
JULIUS, YOUR SPARE POWDER HORN. D'YOU HAVE IT?
AYE, SIR!
GIVE IT TO ME AND MAKE READY TO FIRE ON MY COMMAND.
MISTER VINEGAR! STOP OGLING THOSE MONSTERS' BOSOMS AND GET BACK HERE NOW!
AYE, SKIP!
JULIUS - FIRE!
BLAM!

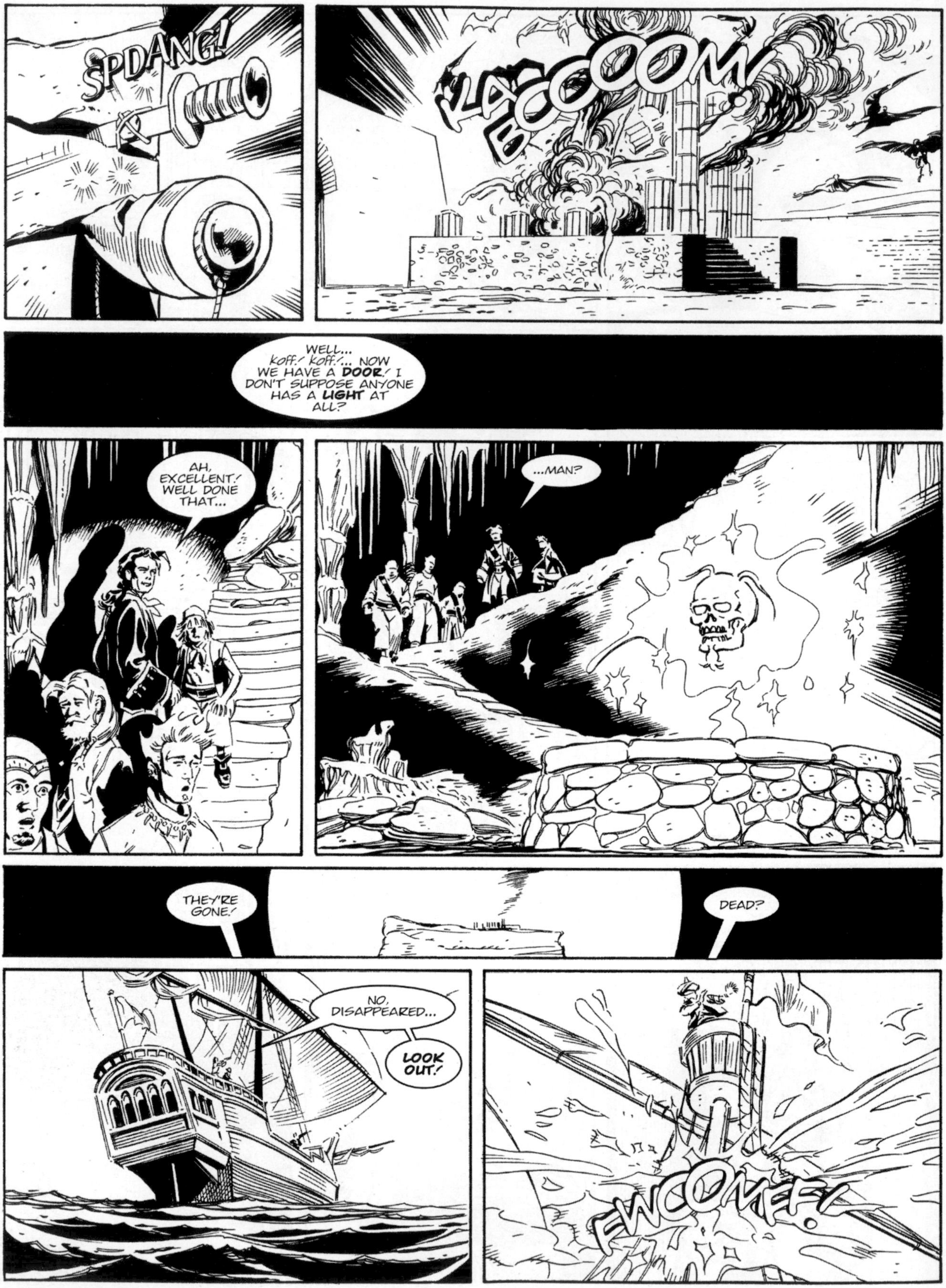
SPDANG!
KA BOOOOM!
WELL... KOFF! KOFF!... NOW WE HAVE A DOOR! I DON'T SUPPOSE ANYONE HAS A LIGHT AT ALL?
AH, EXCELLENT! WELL DONE THAT...
...MAN?
THEY'RE GONE!
DEAD?
NO, DISAPPEARED...
LOOK OUT!
FWOMF!

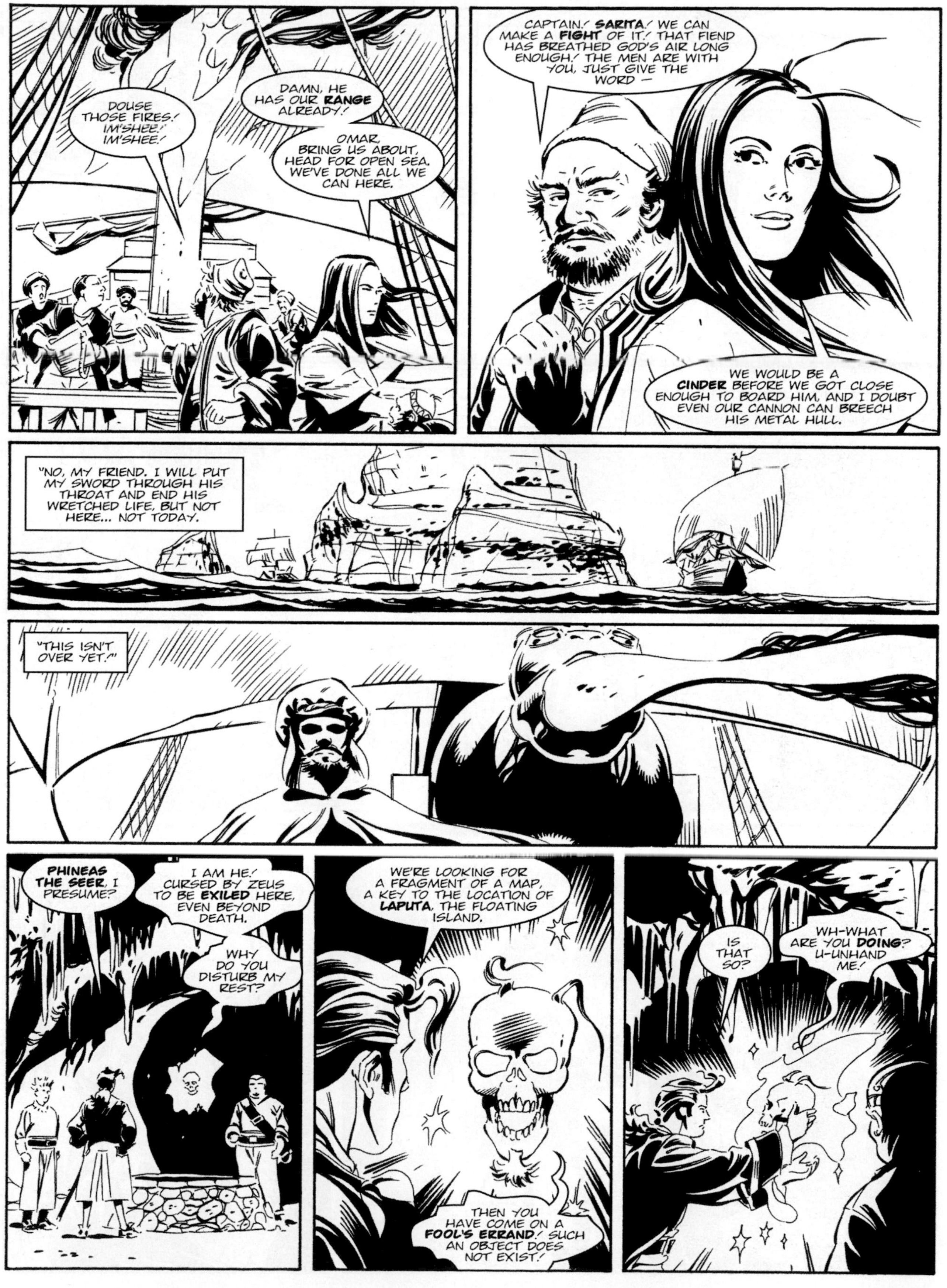
DOUSE THOSE FIRES! IM'SHEE! IM'SHEE!
DAMN, HE HAS OUR RANGE ALREADY!
OMAR, BRING US ABOUT, HEAD FOR OPEN SEA. WE'VE DONE ALL WE CAN HERE.
CAPTAIN! SARITA! WE CAN MAKE A FIGHT OF IT! THAT FIEND HAS BREATHED GOD'S AIR LONG ENOUGH! THE MEN ARE WITH YOU, JUST GIVE THE WORD –
WE WOULD BE A CINDER BEFORE WE GOT CLOSE ENOUGH TO BOARD HIM, AND I DOUBT EVEN OUR CANNON CAN BREECH HIS METAL HULL.
"NO, MY FRIEND. I WILL PUT MY SWORD THROUGH HIS THROAT AND END HIS WRETCHED LIFE, BUT NOT HERE... NOT TODAY.
"THIS ISN'T OVER YET."
PHINEAS THE SEER, I PRESUME?
I AM HE! CURSED BY ZEUS TO BE EXILED HERE, EVEN BEYOND DEATH.
WHY DO YOU DISTURB MY REST?
WE'RE LOOKING FOR A FRAGMENT OF A MAP, A KEY TO THE LOCATION OF LAPUTA, THE FLOATING ISLAND.
THEN YOU HAVE COME ON A FOOL'S ERRAND! SUCH AN OBJECT DOES NOT EXIST!
IS THAT SO?
WH-WHAT ARE YOU DOING? U-UNHAND ME!

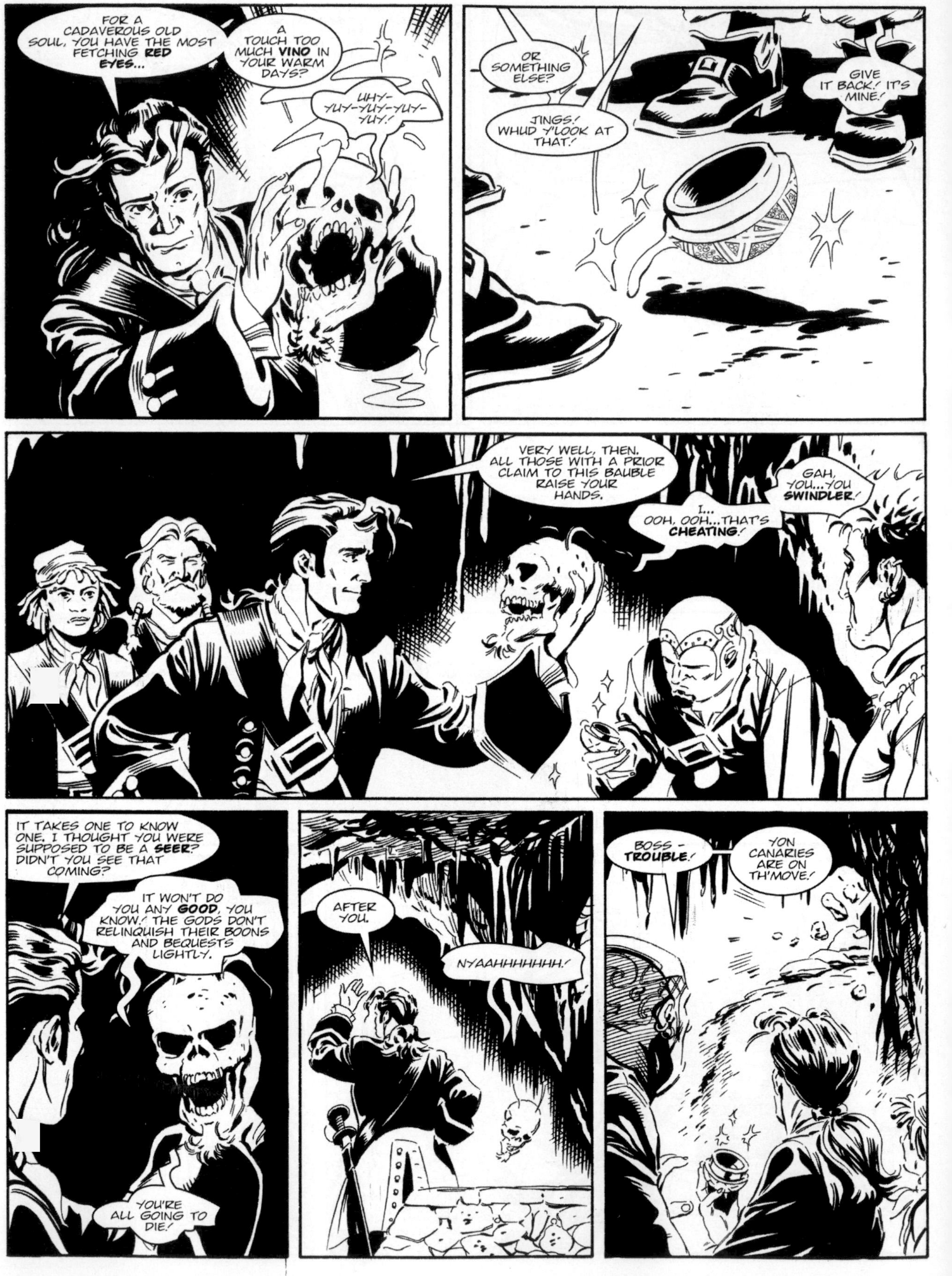
FOR A CADAVEROUS OLD SOUL, YOU HAVE THE MOST FETCHING **RED EYES**...
A TOUCH TOO MUCH **VINO** IN YOUR WARM DAYS?
UHY-YUY-YUY-YUY-YUY-YUY!
OR SOMETHING ELSE?
JINGS! WHUD Y'LOOK AT THAT!
GIVE IT BACK! IT'S MINE!
VERY WELL, THEN. ALL THOSE WITH A PRIOR CLAIM TO THIS BAUBLE RAISE YOUR HANDS.
I... OOH, OOH...THAT'S **CHEATING**!
GAH, YOU...YOU **SWINDLER**!
IT TAKES ONE TO KNOW ONE. I THOUGHT YOU WERE SUPPOSED TO BE A **SEER**? DIDN'T YOU SEE THAT COMING?
IT WON'T DO YOU ANY **GOOD**, YOU KNOW! THE GODS DON'T RELINQUISH THEIR BOONS AND BEQUESTS LIGHTLY.
YOU'RE ALL GOING TO DIE!
AFTER YOU.
NYAAHHHHHHH!
BOSS - **TROUBLE**!
YON CANARIES ARE ON TH'MOVE!

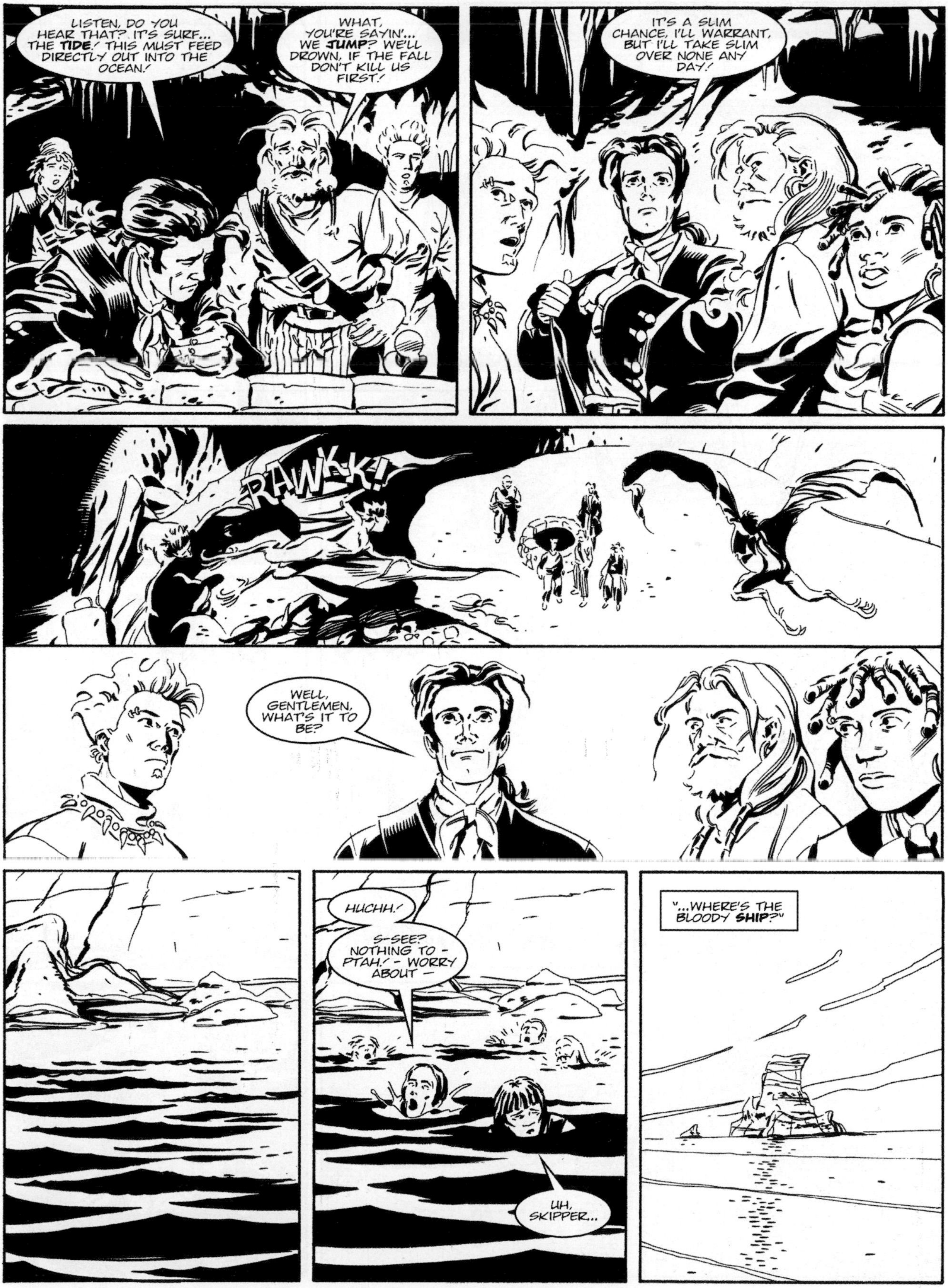
LISTEN, DO YOU HEAR THAT? IT'S SURF... THE **TIDE**! THIS MUST FEED DIRECTLY OUT INTO THE OCEAN!
WHAT, YOU'RE SAYIN'... WE **JUMP**? WE'LL DROWN, IF THE FALL DON'T KILL US FIRST!
IT'S A SLIM CHANCE, I'LL WARRANT, BUT I'LL TAKE SLIM OVER NONE ANY DAY!
RAWKKK!
WELL, GENTLEMEN, WHAT'S IT TO BE?
HUCHH!
S-SEE? NOTHING TO - PTAH! - WORRY ABOUT -
UH, SKIPPER...
"...WHERE'S THE BLOODY **SHIP**?"

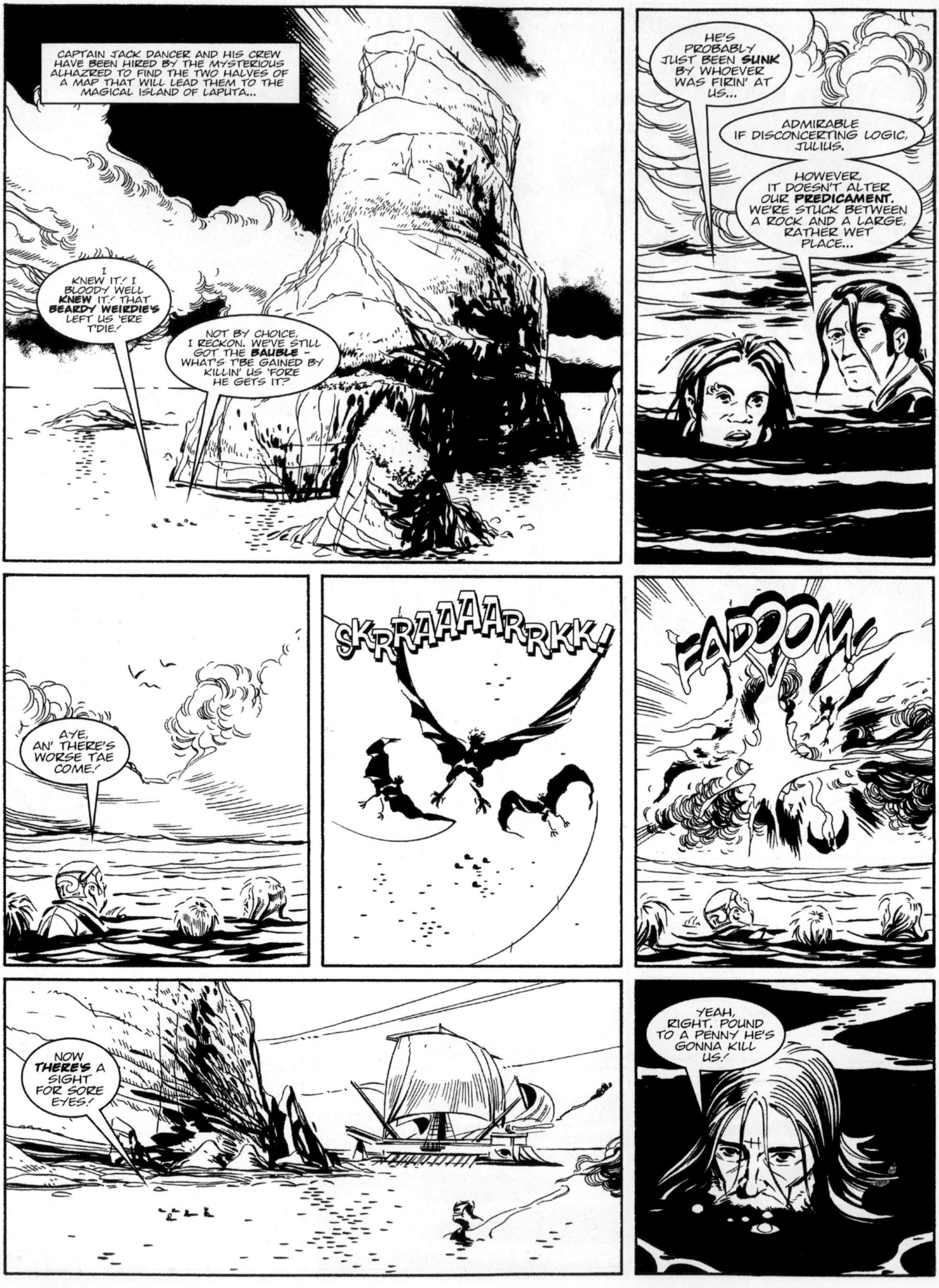
CAPTAIN JACK DANCER AND HIS CREW HAVE BEEN HIRED BY THE MYSTERIOUS ALHAZRED TO FIND THE TWO HALVES OF A MAP THAT WILL LEAD THEM TO THE MAGICAL ISLAND OF LAPUTA...
I KNEW IT! I BLOODY WELL KNEW IT! THAT BEARDY WEIRDIE'S LEFT US 'ERE T'DIE!
NOT BY CHOICE, I RECKON. WE'VE STILL GOT THE BAUBLE - WHAT'S T'BE GAINED BY KILLIN' US 'FORE HE GETS IT?
HE'S PROBABLY JUST BEEN SUNK BY WHOEVER WAS FIRIN' AT US...
ADMIRABLE IF DISCONCERTING LOGIC, JULIUS.
HOWEVER, IT DOESN'T ALTER OUR PREDICAMENT. WE'RE STUCK BETWEEN A ROCK AND A LARGE, RATHER WET PLACE...
AYE, AN' THERE'S WORSE TAE COME!
SKRRAAAAARRRKK!
FADOOM!
NOW THERE'S A SIGHT FOR SORE EYES!
YEAH, RIGHT. POUND TO A PENNY HE'S GONNA KILL US!

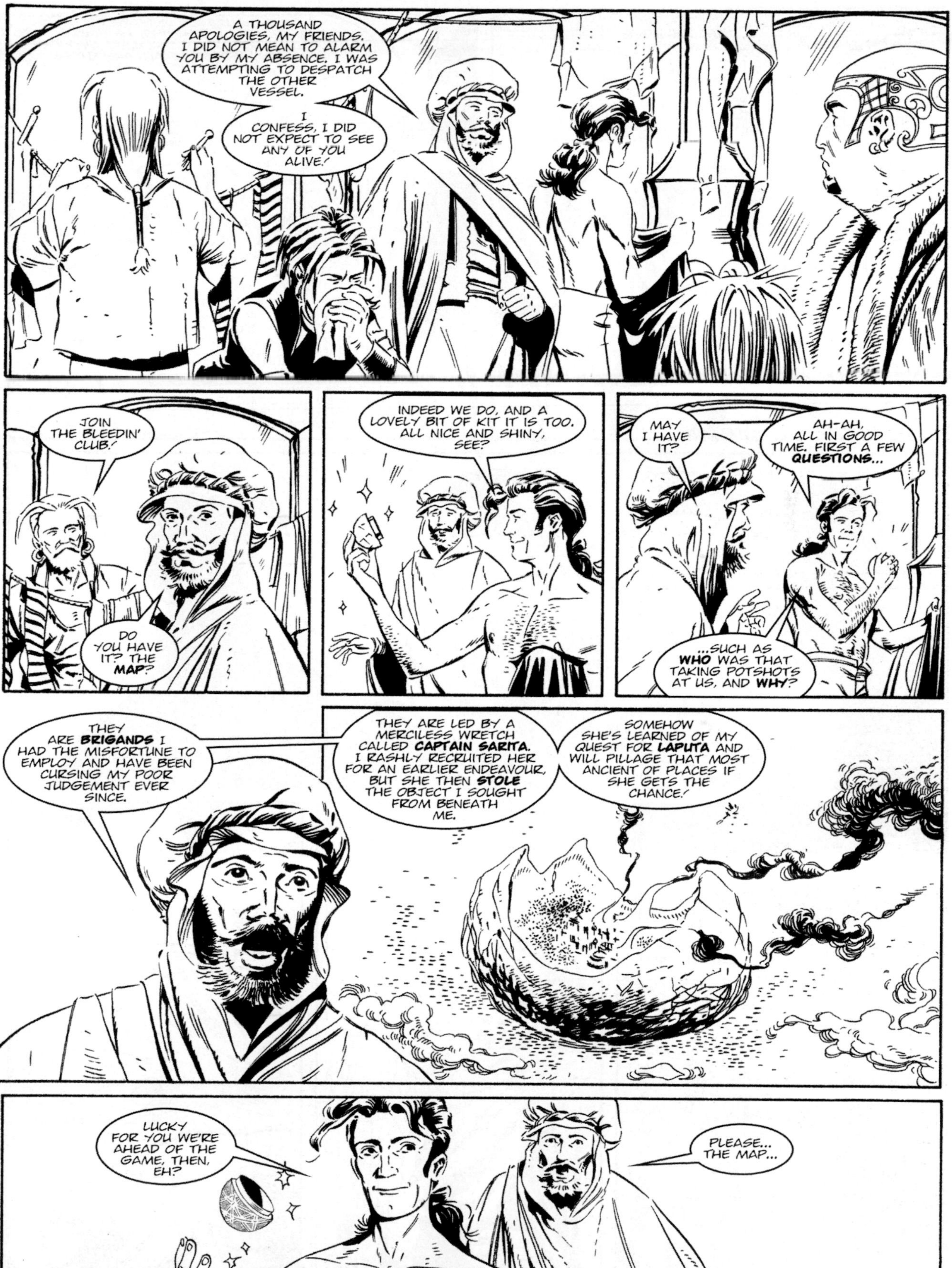
A THOUSAND APOLOGIES, MY FRIENDS. I DID NOT MEAN TO ALARM YOU BY MY ABSENCE. I WAS ATTEMPTING TO DESPATCH THE OTHER VESSEL.
I CONFESS, I DID NOT EXPECT TO SEE ANY OF YOU ALIVE!
JOIN THE BLEEDIN' CLUB!
DO YOU HAVE IT? THE **MAP**?
INDEED WE DO, AND A LOVELY BIT OF KIT IT IS TOO. ALL NICE AND SHINY, SEE?
MAY I HAVE IT?
AH-AH, ALL IN GOOD TIME. FIRST A FEW **QUESTIONS**...
...SUCH AS **WHO** WAS THAT TAKING POTSHOTS AT US, AND **WHY**?
THEY ARE **BRIGANDS** I HAD THE MISFORTUNE TO EMPLOY AND HAVE BEEN CURSING MY POOR JUDGEMENT EVER SINCE.
THEY ARE LED BY A MERCILESS WRETCH CALLED **CAPTAIN SARITA**. I RASHLY RECRUITED HER FOR AN EARLIER ENDEAVOUR, BUT SHE THEN **STOLE** THE OBJECT I SOUGHT FROM BENEATH ME.
SOMEHOW SHE'S LEARNED OF MY QUEST FOR **LAPUTA** AND WILL PILLAGE THAT MOST ANCIENT OF PLACES IF SHE GETS THE CHANCE!
LUCKY FOR YOU WE'RE AHEAD OF THE GAME, THEN, EH?
PLEASE... THE MAP...

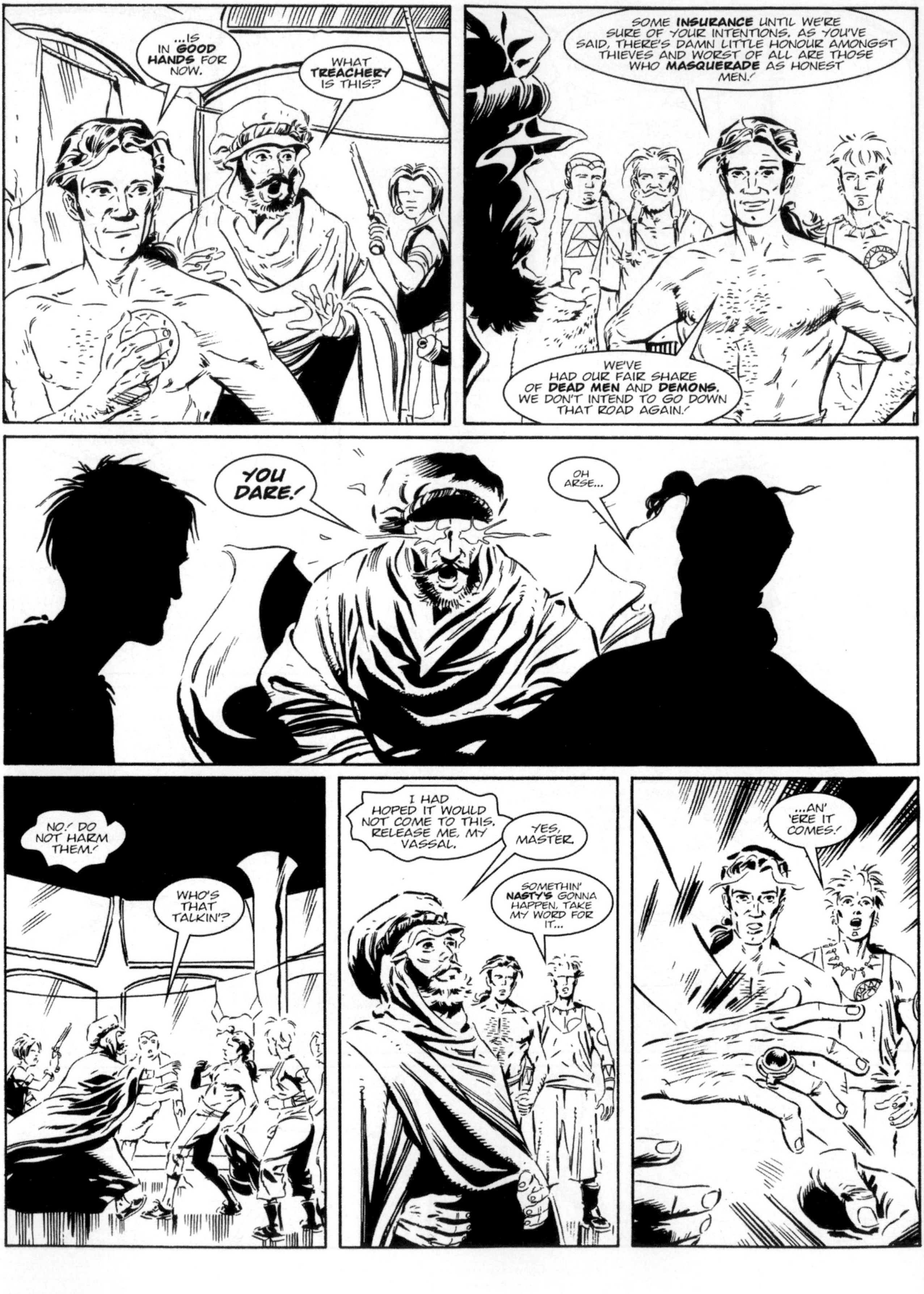
...IS IN GOOD HANDS FOR NOW.
WHAT TREACHERY IS THIS?
SOME INSURANCE UNTIL WE'RE SURE OF YOUR INTENTIONS. AS YOU'VE SAID, THERE'S DAMN LITTLE HONOUR AMONGST THIEVES AND WORST OF ALL ARE THOSE WHO MASQUERADE AS HONEST MEN!
WE'VE HAD OUR FAIR SHARE OF DEAD MEN AND DEMONS. WE DON'T INTEND TO GO DOWN THAT ROAD AGAIN!
YOU DARE!
OH ARSE...
NO! DO NOT HARM THEM!
WHO'S THAT TALKIN'?
I HAD HOPED IT WOULD NOT COME TO THIS. RELEASE ME, MY VASSAL.
YES, MASTER.
SOMETHIN' NASTY'S GONNA HAPPEN, TAKE MY WORD FOR IT...
...AN' 'ERE IT COMES!

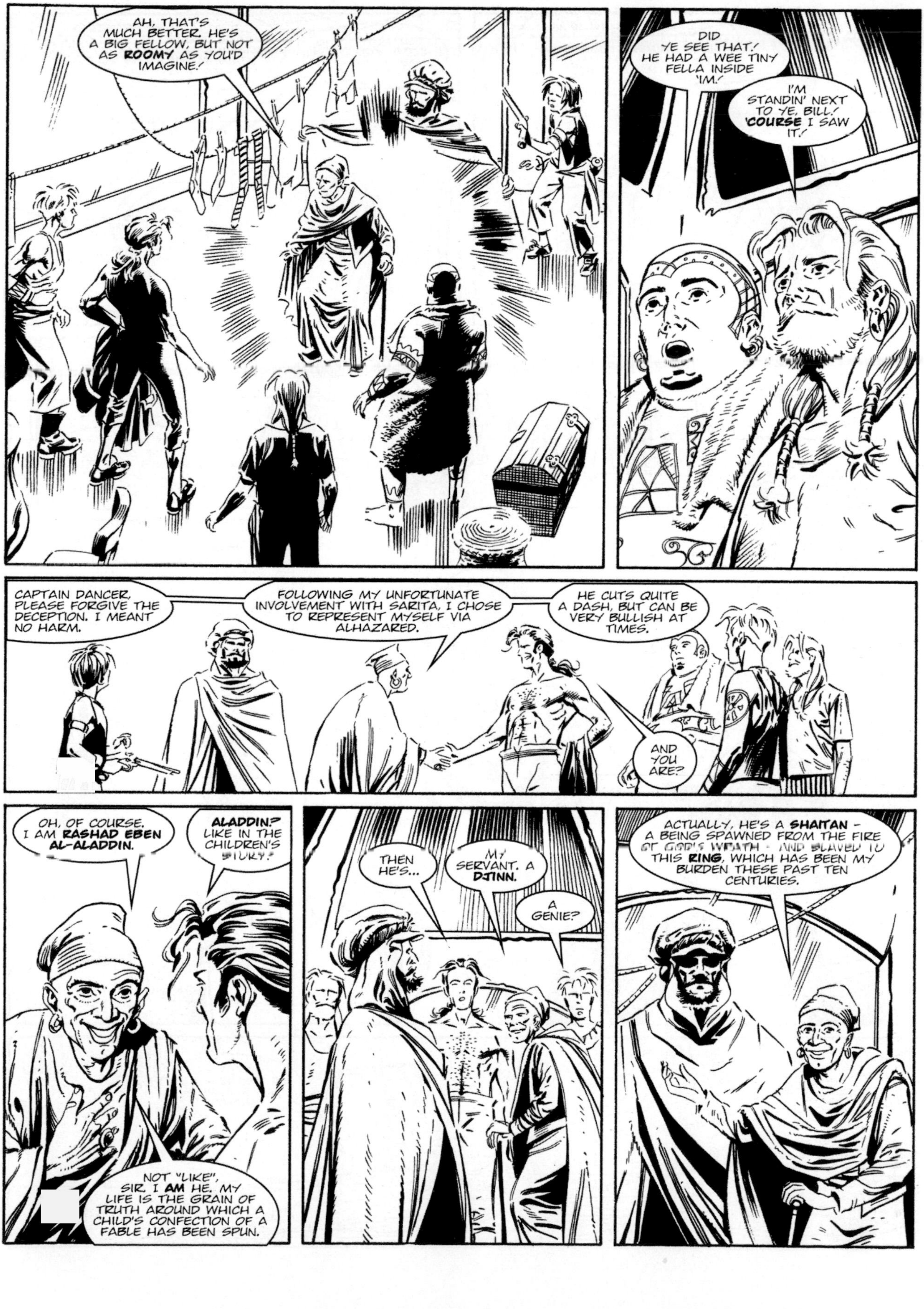

AH, THAT'S MUCH BETTER. HE'S A BIG FELLOW, BUT NOT AS **ROOMY** AS YOU'D IMAGINE!
DID YE SEE THAT! HE HAD A WEE TINY FELLA INSIDE 'IM!
I'M STANDIN' NEXT TO YE, BILL! '**COURSE** I SAW IT!
CAPTAIN DANCER, PLEASE FORGIVE THE DECEPTION. I MEANT NO HARM.
FOLLOWING MY UNFORTUNATE INVOLVEMENT WITH SARITA, I CHOSE TO REPRESENT MYSELF VIA ALHAZARED.
HE CUTS QUITE A DASH, BUT CAN BE VERY BULLISH AT TIMES.
AND YOU ARE?
OH, OF COURSE. I AM **RASHAD EBEN AL-ALADDIN.**
**ALADDIN?** LIKE IN THE CHILDREN'S STORY?
NOT "LIKE", SIR. I **AM** HE. MY LIFE IS THE GRAIN OF TRUTH AROUND WHICH A CHILD'S CONFECTION OF A FABLE HAS BEEN SPUN.
THEN HE'S...
MY SERVANT. A **DJINN.**
A GENIE?
ACTUALLY, HE'S A **SHAITAN** - A BEING SPAWNED FROM THE FIRE OF GOD'S WRATH - AND SLAVED TO THIS **RING**, WHICH HAS BEEN MY BURDEN THESE PAST TEN CENTURIES.

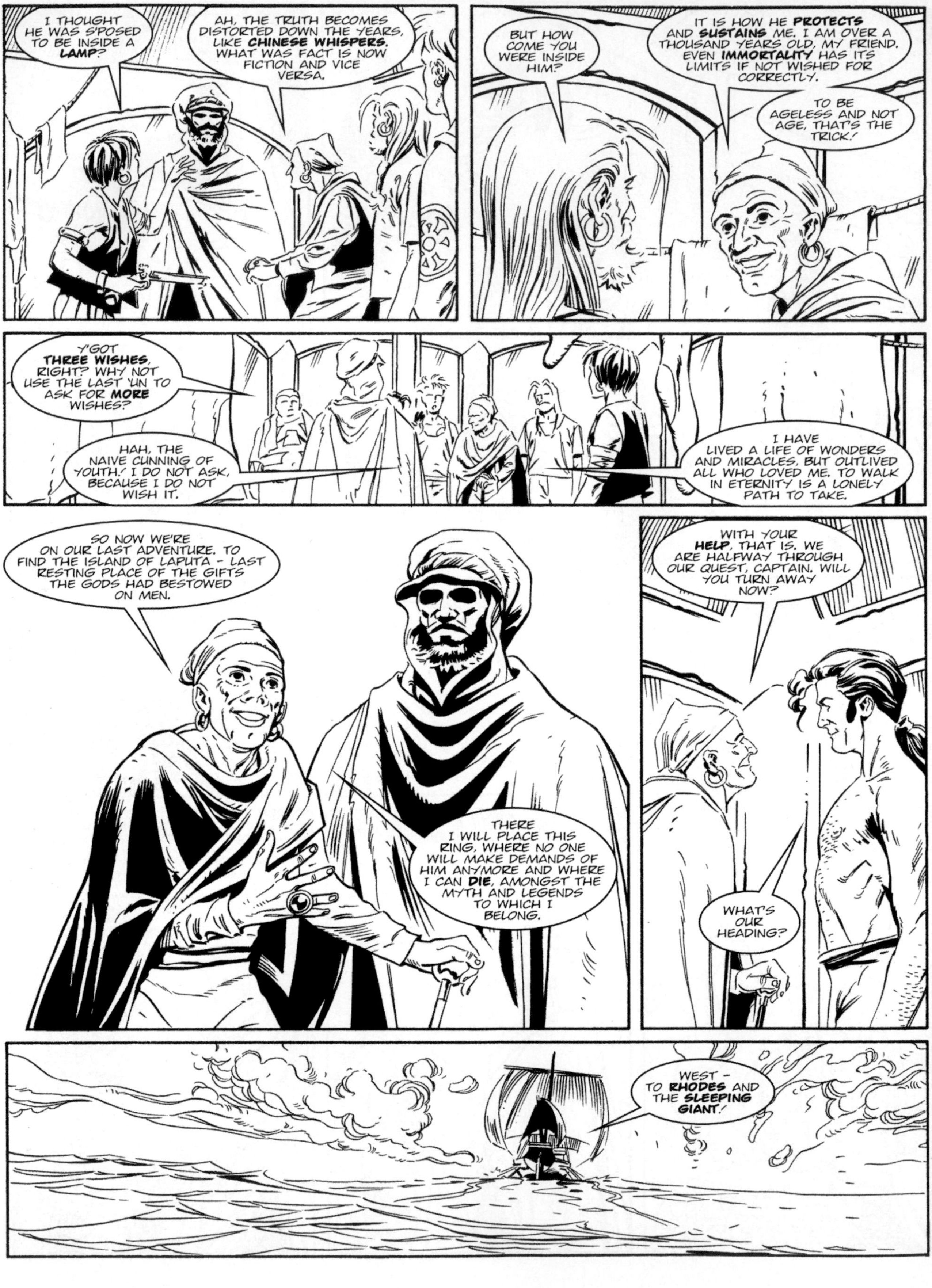
I THOUGHT HE WAS S'POSED TO BE INSIDE A LAMP?
AH, THE TRUTH BECOMES DISTORTED DOWN THE YEARS, LIKE CHINESE WHISPERS. WHAT WAS FACT IS NOW FICTION AND VICE VERSA.
BUT HOW COME YOU WERE INSIDE HIM?
IT IS HOW HE PROTECTS AND SUSTAINS ME. I AM OVER A THOUSAND YEARS OLD, MY FRIEND. EVEN IMMORTALITY HAS ITS LIMITS IF NOT WISHED FOR CORRECTLY.
TO BE AGELESS AND NOT AGE, THAT'S THE TRICK!
Y'GOT THREE WISHES, RIGHT? WHY NOT USE THE LAST 'UN TO ASK FOR MORE WISHES?
HAH, THE NAIVE CUNNING OF YOUTH! I DO NOT ASK, BECAUSE I DO NOT WISH IT.
I HAVE LIVED A LIFE OF WONDERS AND MIRACLES, BUT OUTLIVED ALL WHO LOVED ME. TO WALK IN ETERNITY IS A LONELY PATH TO TAKE.
SO NOW WE'RE ON OUR LAST ADVENTURE. TO FIND THE ISLAND OF LAPUTA – LAST RESTING PLACE OF THE GIFTS THE GODS HAD BESTOWED ON MEN.
THERE I WILL PLACE THIS RING, WHERE NO ONE WILL MAKE DEMANDS OF HIM ANYMORE AND WHERE I CAN DIE, AMONGST THE MYTH AND LEGENDS TO WHICH I BELONG.
WITH YOUR HELP, THAT IS. WE ARE HALFWAY THROUGH OUR QUEST, CAPTAIN. WILL YOU TURN AWAY NOW?
WHAT'S OUR HEADING?
WEST – TO RHODES AND THE SLEEPING GIANT!

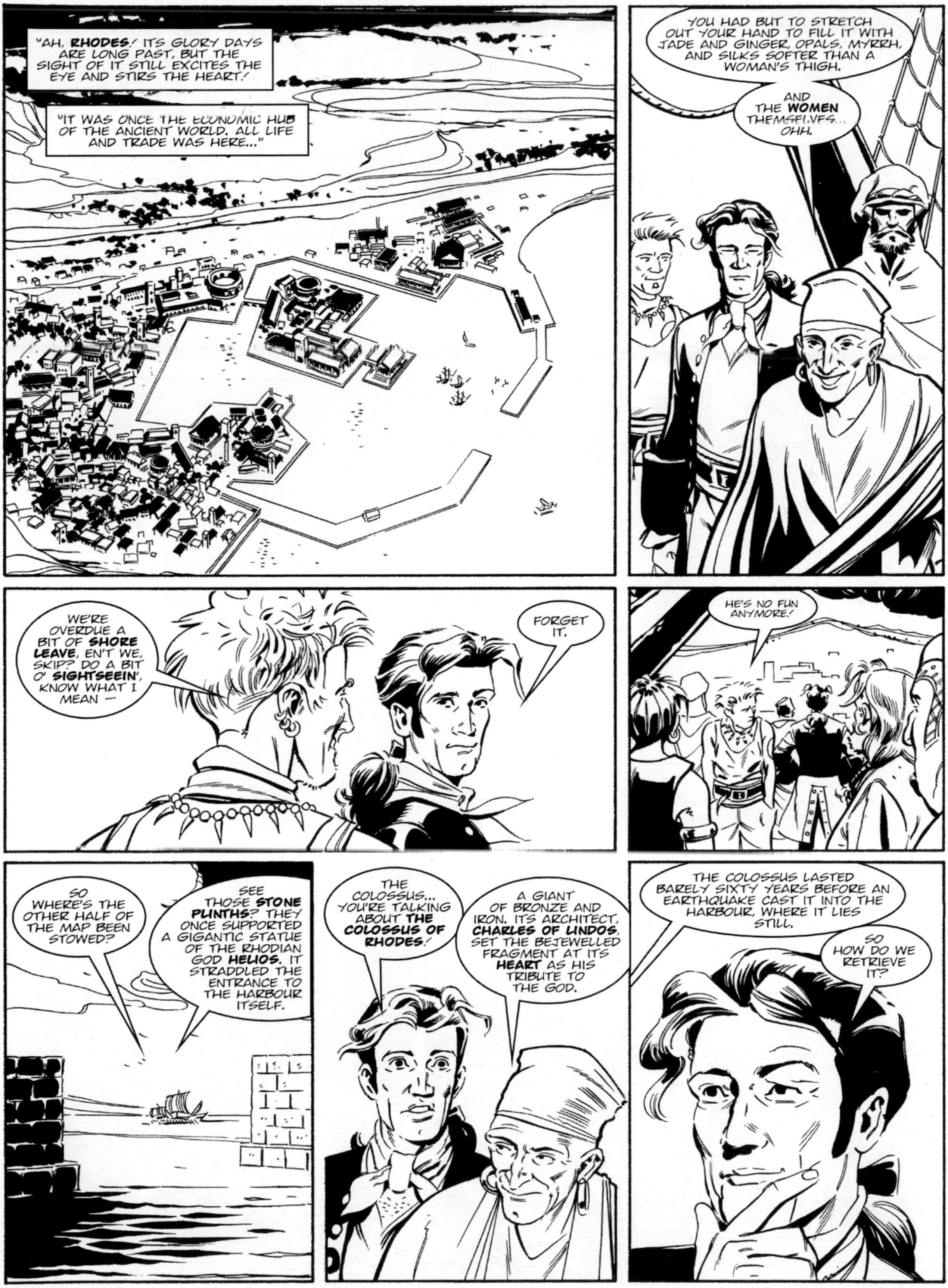
"AH, RHODES! ITS GLORY DAYS ARE LONG PAST, BUT THE SIGHT OF IT STILL EXCITES THE EYE AND STIRS THE HEART!
"IT WAS ONCE THE ECONOMIC HUB OF THE ANCIENT WORLD. ALL LIFE AND TRADE WAS HERE..."
YOU HAD BUT TO STRETCH OUT YOUR HAND TO FILL IT WITH JADE AND GINGER, OPALS, MYRRH, AND SILKS SOFTER THAN A WOMAN'S THIGH.
AND THE WOMEN THEMSELVES... OHH.
WE'RE OVERDUE A BIT OF SHORE LEAVE, EN'T WE, SKIP? DO A BIT O' SIGHTSEEIN', KNOW WHAT I MEAN —
FORGET IT.
HE'S NO FUN ANYMORE!
SO WHERE'S THE OTHER HALF OF THE MAP BEEN STOWED?
SEE THOSE STONE PLINTHS? THEY ONCE SUPPORTED A GIGANTIC STATUE OF THE RHODIAN GOD HELIOS. IT STRADDLED THE ENTRANCE TO THE HARBOUR ITSELF.
THE COLOSSUS... YOU'RE TALKING ABOUT THE COLOSSUS OF RHODES!
A GIANT OF BRONZE AND IRON. ITS ARCHITECT, CHARLES OF LINDOS, SET THE BEJEWELLED FRAGMENT AT ITS HEART AS HIS TRIBUTE TO THE GOD.
THE COLOSSUS LASTED BARELY SIXTY YEARS BEFORE AN EARTHQUAKE CAST IT INTO THE HARBOUR, WHERE IT LIES STILL.
SO HOW DO WE RETRIEVE IT?

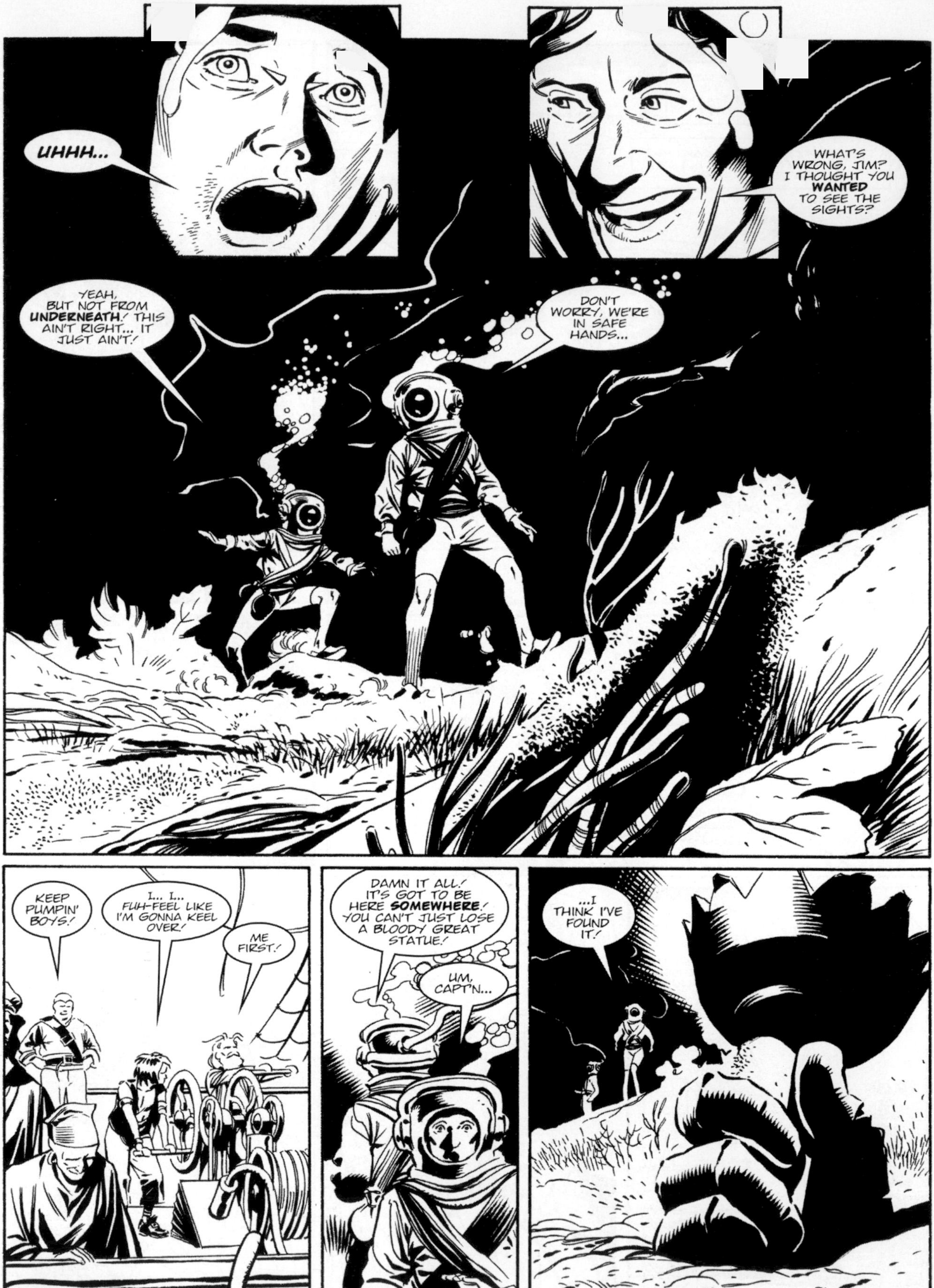
UHHH...
WHAT'S WRONG, JIM? I THOUGHT YOU **WANTED** TO SEE THE SIGHTS?
YEAH, BUT NOT FROM **UNDERNEATH**! THIS AIN'T RIGHT... IT JUST AIN'T!
DON'T WORRY, WE'RE IN SAFE HANDS...
KEEP PUMPIN' BOYS!
I... I... FUH-FEEL LIKE I'M GONNA KEEL OVER!
ME FIRST!
DAMN IT ALL! IT'S GOT TO BE HERE **SOMEWHERE**! YOU CAN'T JUST LOSE A BLOODY GREAT STATUE!
UM, CAPT'N...
...I THINK I'VE FOUND IT!

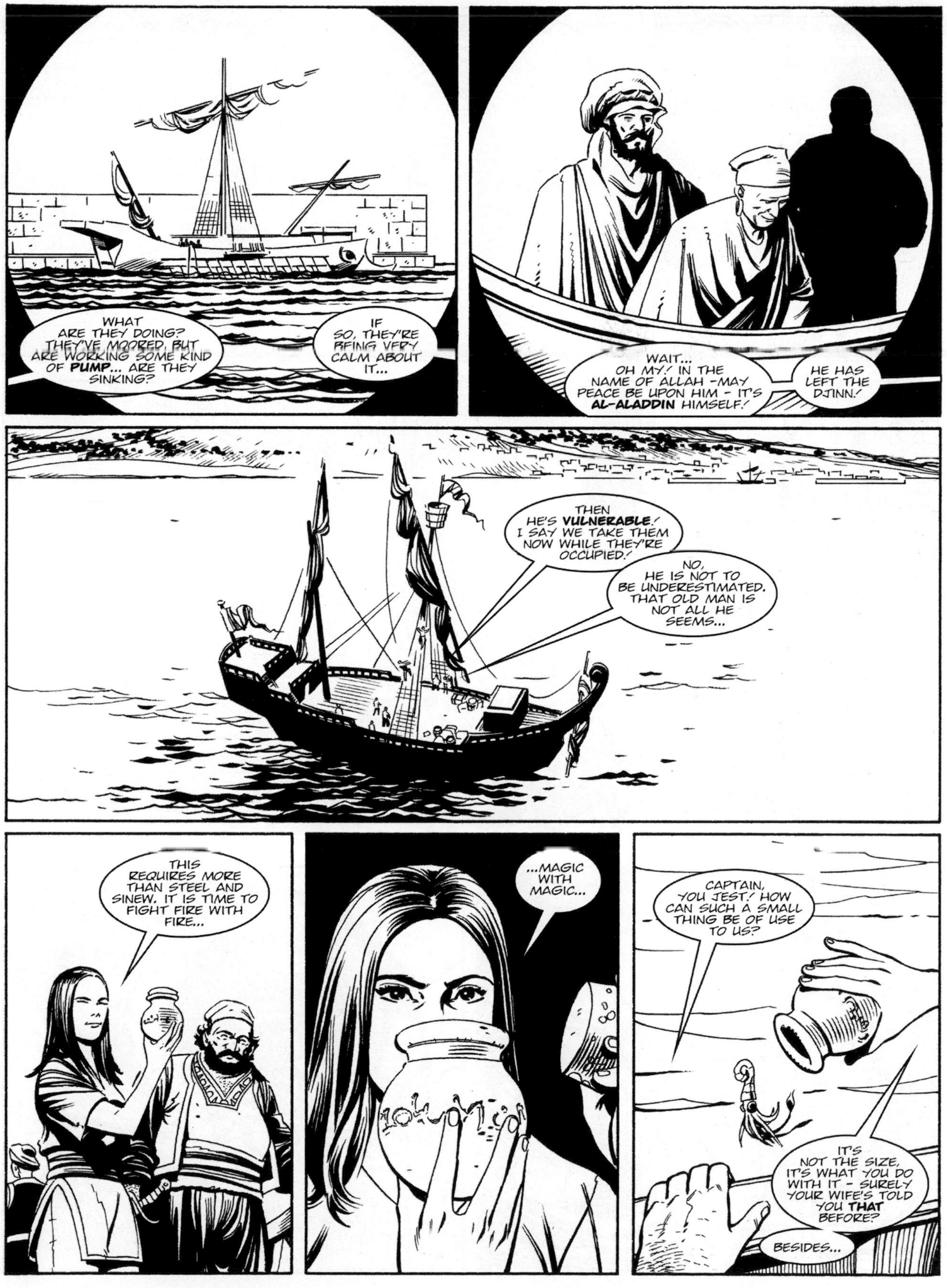
WHAT ARE THEY DOING? THEY'VE MOORED, BUT ARE WORKING SOME KIND OF PUMP... ARE THEY SINKING?
IF SO, THEY'RE BEING VERY CALM ABOUT IT...
WAIT... OH MY! IN THE NAME OF ALLAH -MAY PEACE BE UPON HIM - IT'S AL-ALADDIN HIMSELF!
HE HAS LEFT THE DJINN!
THEN HE'S VULNERABLE! I SAY WE TAKE THEM NOW WHILE THEY'RE OCCUPIED!
NO, HE IS NOT TO BE UNDERESTIMATED. THAT OLD MAN IS NOT ALL HE SEEMS...
THIS REQUIRES MORE THAN STEEL AND SINEW. IT IS TIME TO FIGHT FIRE WITH FIRE...
...MAGIC WITH MAGIC...
CAPTAIN, YOU JEST! HOW CAN SUCH A SMALL THING BE OF USE TO US?
IT'S NOT THE SIZE, IT'S WHAT YOU DO WITH IT - SURELY YOUR WIFE'S TOLD YOU THAT BEFORE?
BESIDES...

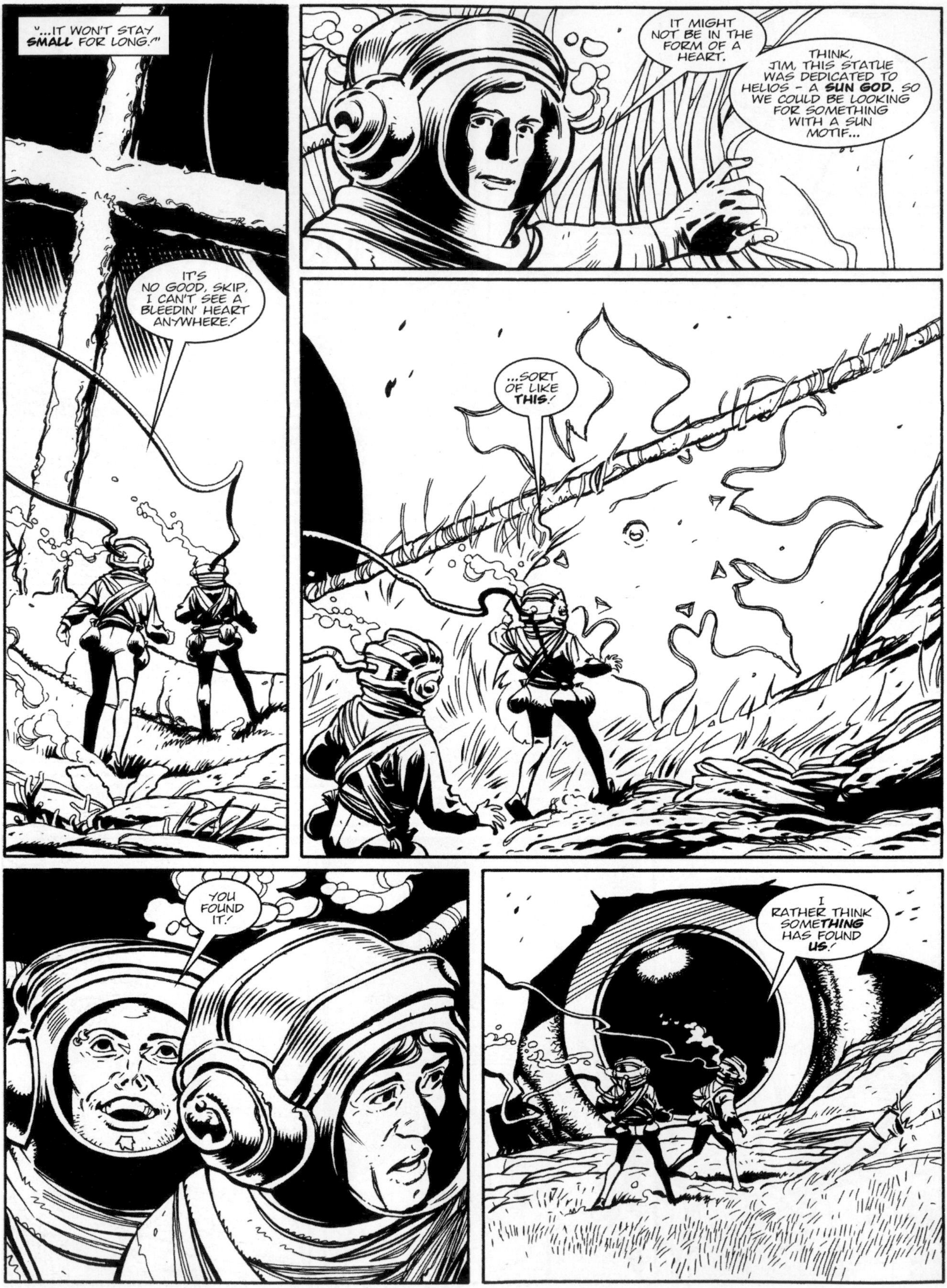

"...IT WON'T STAY SMALL FOR LONG."
IT MIGHT NOT BE IN THE FORM OF A HEART.
THINK, JIM, THIS STATUE WAS DEDICATED TO HELIOS - A SUN GOD. SO WE COULD BE LOOKING FOR SOMETHING WITH A SUN MOTIF...
IT'S NO GOOD, SKIP, I CAN'T SEE A BLEEDIN' HEART ANYWHERE!
...SORT OF LIKE THIS!
YOU FOUND IT!
I RATHER THINK SOMETHING HAS FOUND US!

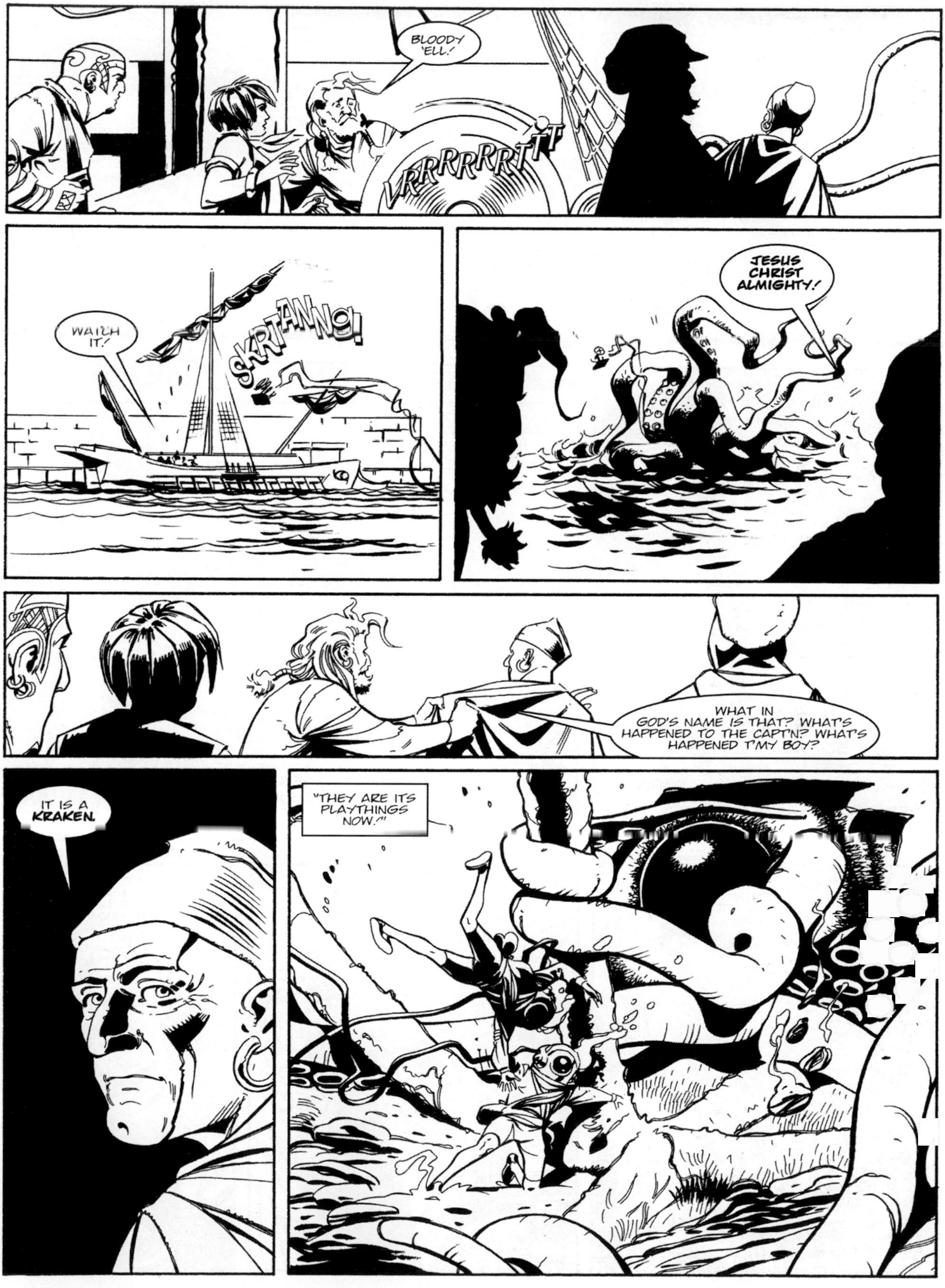
BLOODY 'ELL!
VRRRRRRRRTTT
WATCH IT!
SKRTANNG!
JESUS CHRIST ALMIGHTY!
WHAT IN GOD'S NAME IS THAT? WHAT'S HAPPENED TO THE CAPT'N? WHAT'S HAPPENED T'MY BOY?
IT IS A **KRAKEN.**
"THEY ARE ITS PLAYTHINGS NOW."

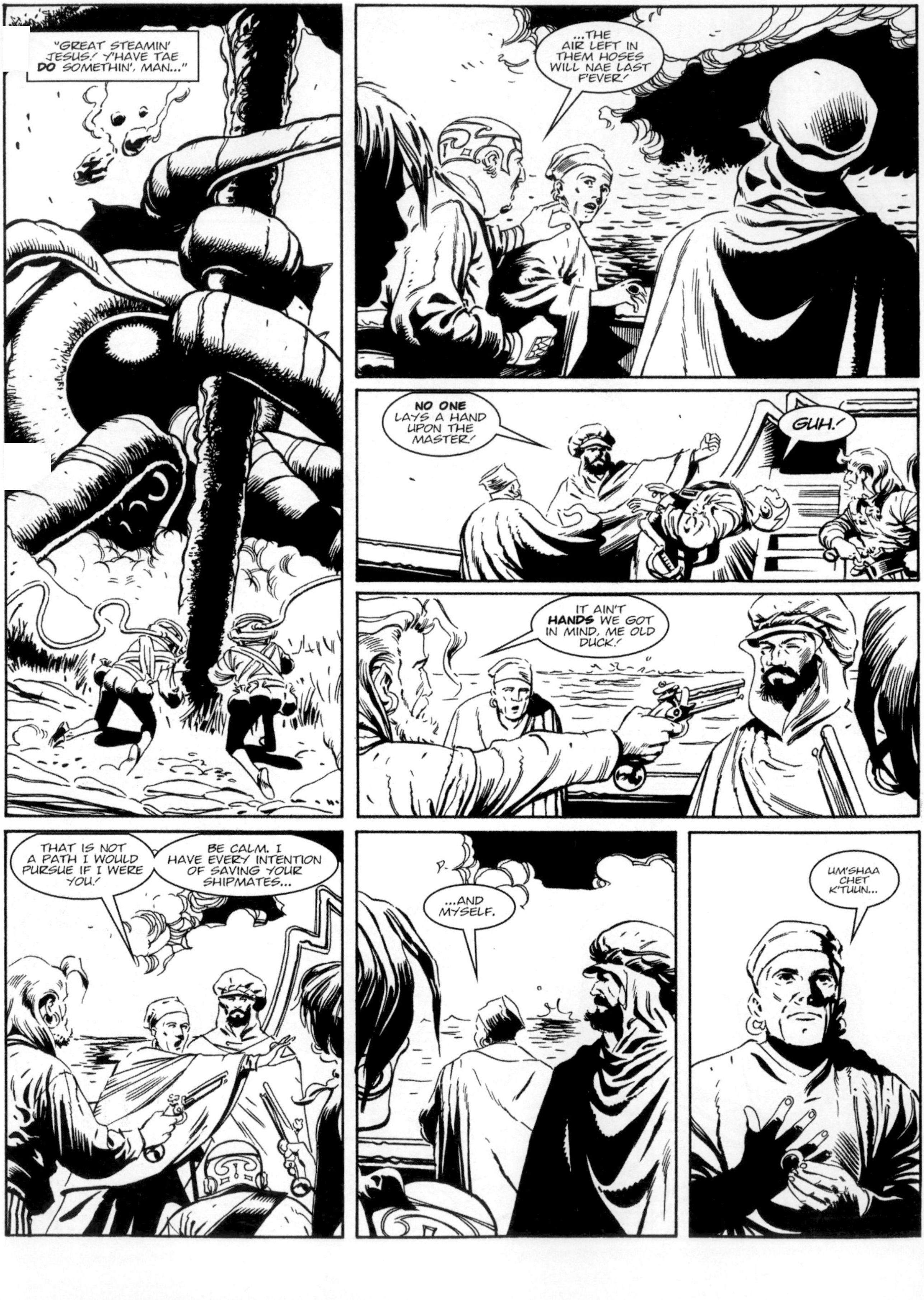
"GREAT STEAMIN' JESUS! Y'HAVE TAE DO SOMETHIN', MAN..."
...THE AIR LEFT IN THEM HOSES WILL NAE LAST F'EVER!
NO ONE LAYS A HAND UPON THE MASTER!
GUH!
IT AIN'T HANDS WE GOT IN MIND, ME OLD DUCK!
THAT IS NOT A PATH I WOULD PURSUE IF I WERE YOU!
BE CALM. I HAVE EVERY INTENTION OF SAVING YOUR SHIPMATES...
...AND MYSELF.
UM'SHAA CHET K'TUUN...

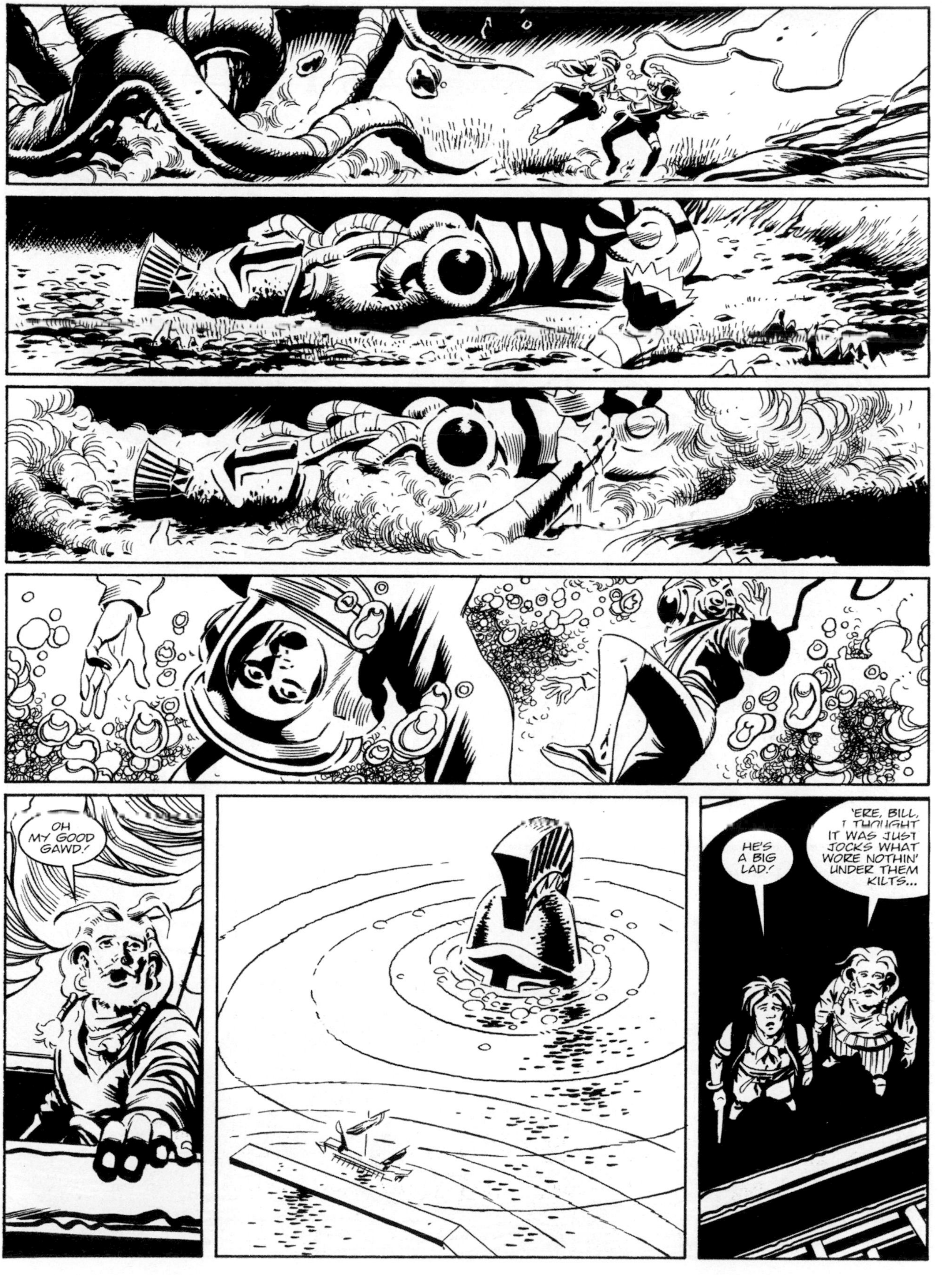
OH MY GOOD GAWD!
HE'S A BIG LAD!
'ERE, BILL, I THOUGHT IT WAS JUST JOCKS WHAT WORE NOTHIN' UNDER THEM KILTS...

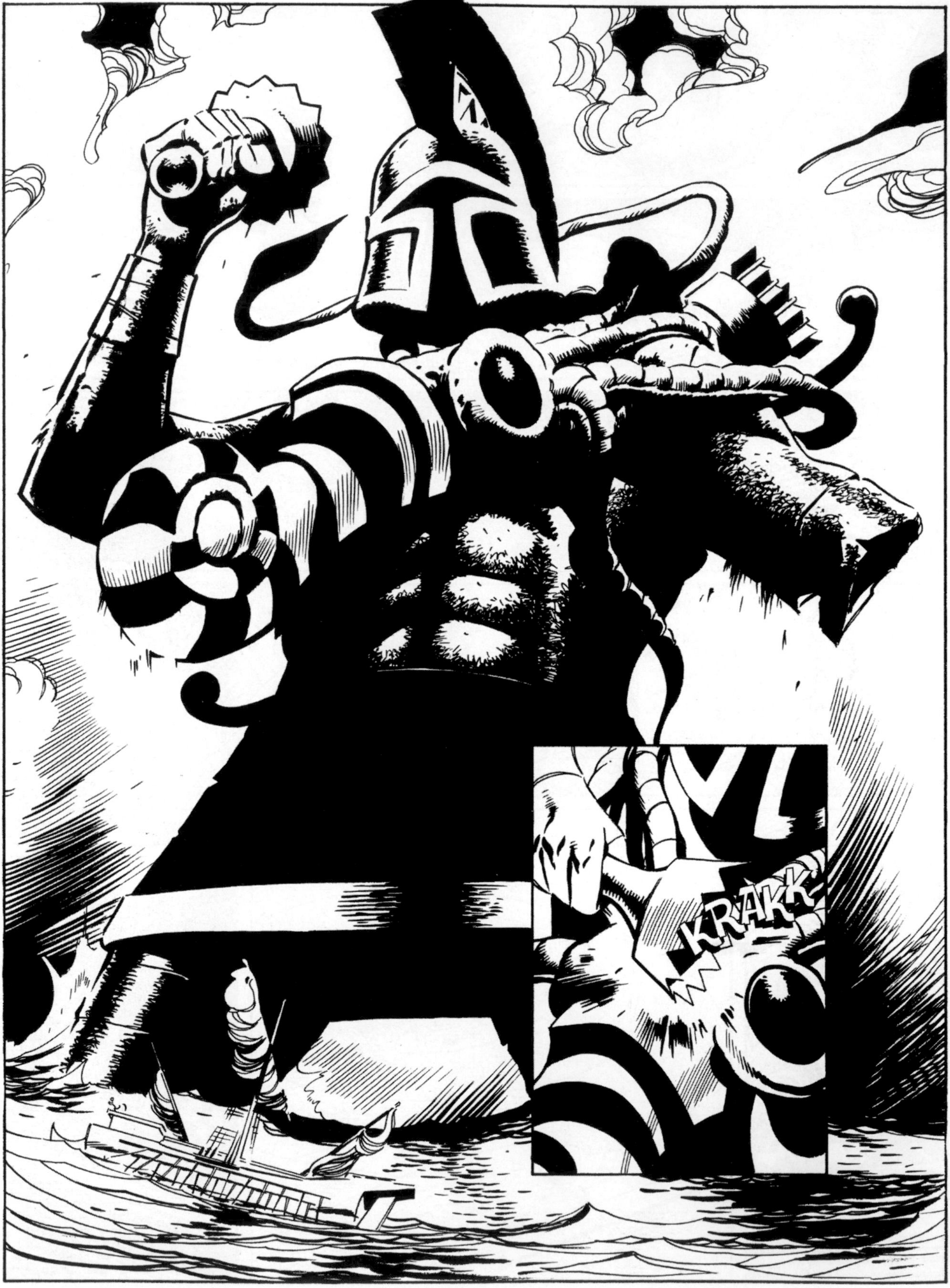
KRAKK-

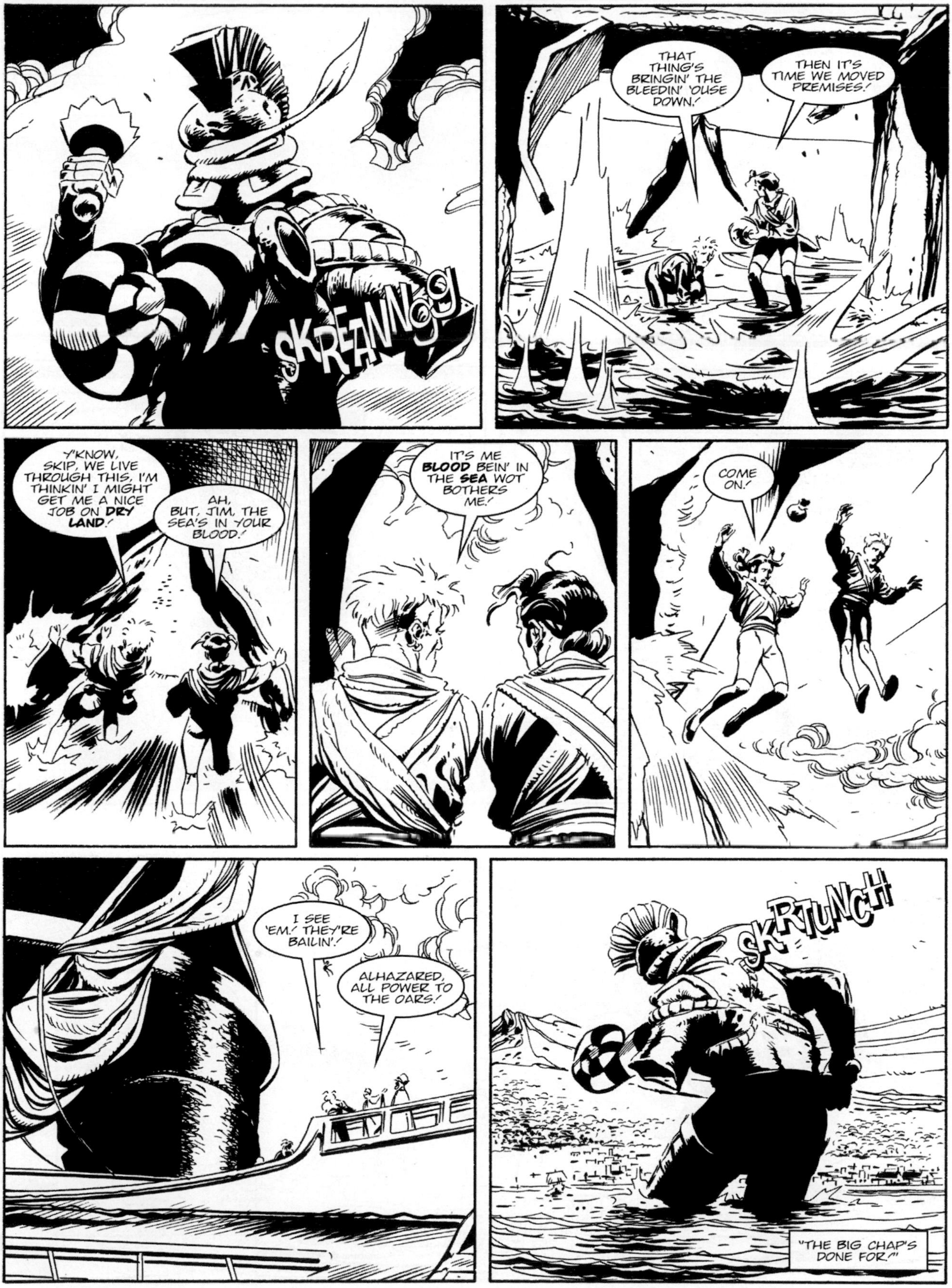
SKREANNGG
THAT THING'S BRINGIN' THE BLEEDIN' 'OUSE DOWN.
THEN IT'S TIME WE MOVED PREMISES.
Y'KNOW, SKIP, WE LIVE THROUGH THIS, I'M THINKIN' I MIGHT GET ME A NICE JOB ON DRY LAND.
AH, BUT, JIM, THE SEA'S IN YOUR BLOOD.
IT'S ME BLOOD BEIN' IN THE SEA WOT BOTHERS ME.
COME ON.
I SEE 'EM. THEY'RE BAILIN'.
ALHAZARED, ALL POWER TO THE OARS.
SKRTUNCH
"THE BIG CHAP'S DONE FOR."

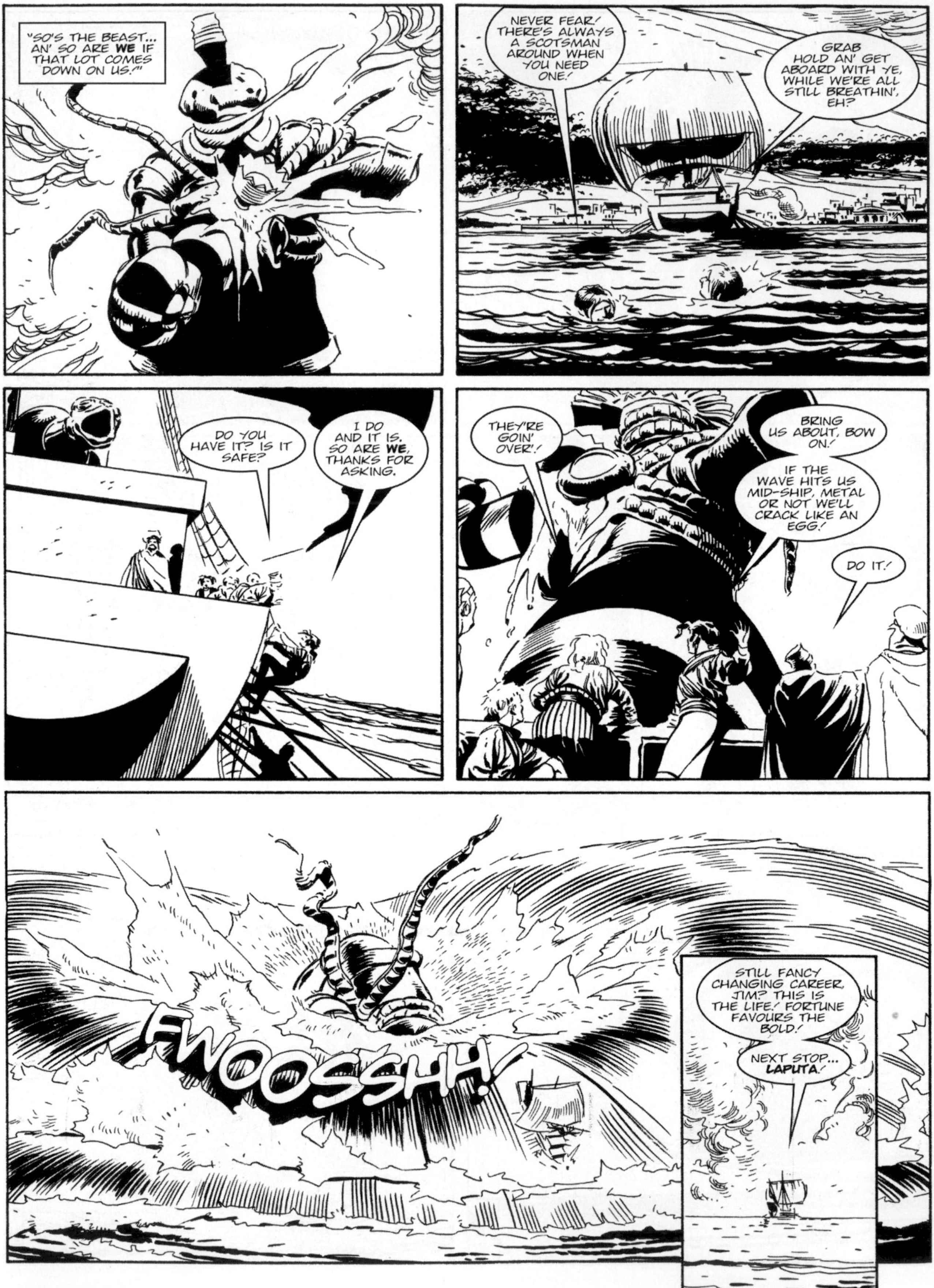
"SO'S THE BEAST... AN' SO ARE WE IF THAT LOT COMES DOWN ON US."
NEVER FEAR! THERE'S ALWAYS A SCOTSMAN AROUND WHEN YOU NEED ONE!
GRAB HOLD AN' GET ABOARD WITH YE, WHILE WE'RE ALL STILL BREATHIN', EH?
DO YOU HAVE IT? IS IT SAFE?
I DO AND IT IS. SO ARE WE, THANKS FOR ASKING.
THEY'RE GOIN' OVER'!
BRING US ABOUT, BOW ON!
IF THE WAVE HITS US MID-SHIP, METAL OR NOT WE'LL CRACK LIKE AN EGG!
DO IT!
FWOOSSHH!
STILL FANCY CHANGING CAREER, JIM? THIS IS THE LIFE! FORTUNE FAVOURS THE BOLD!
NEXT STOP... LAPUTA!

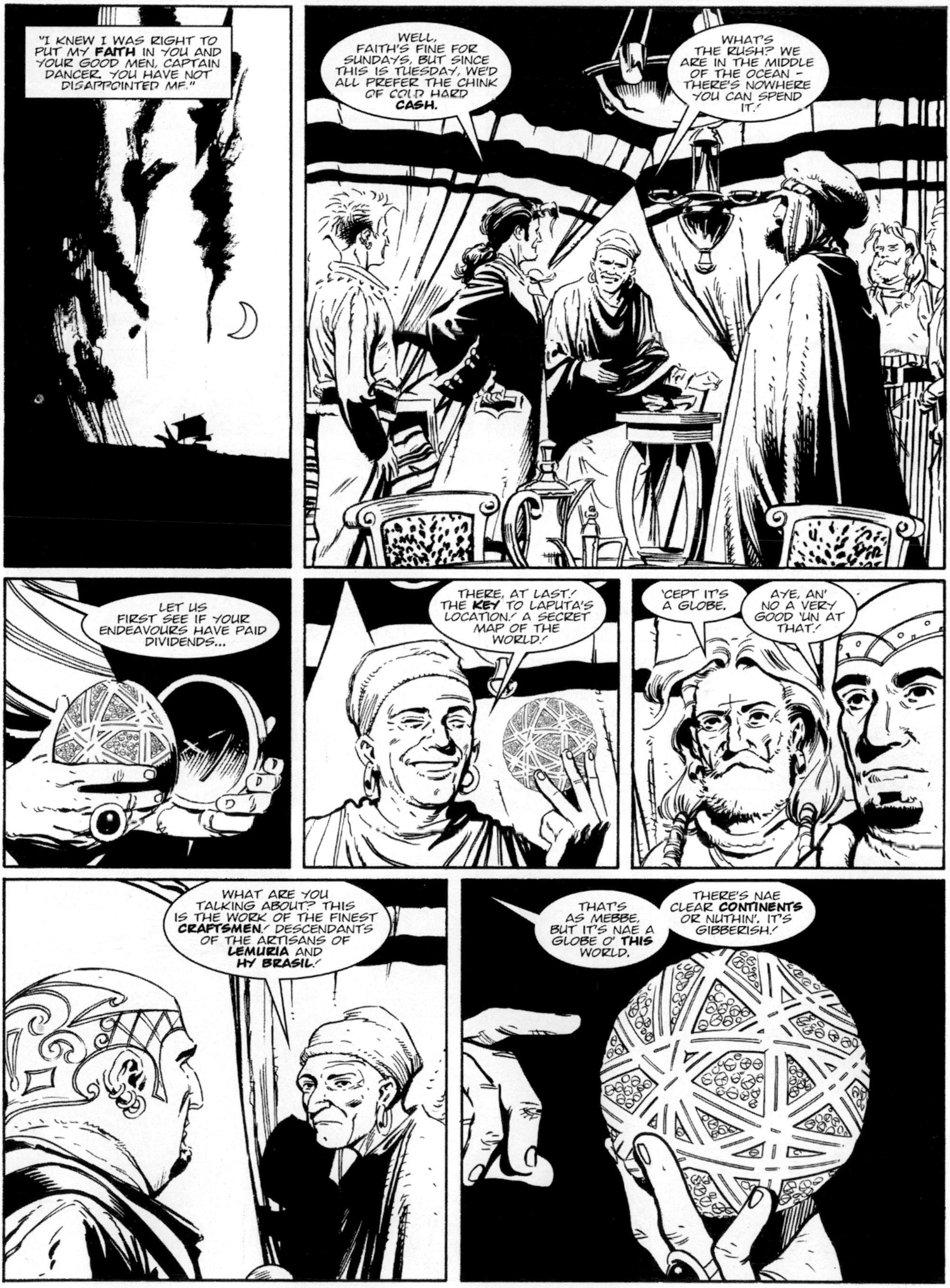
"I KNEW I WAS RIGHT TO PUT MY FAITH IN YOU AND YOUR GOOD MEN, CAPTAIN DANCER. YOU HAVE NOT DISAPPOINTED ME."
WELL, FAITH'S FINE FOR SUNDAYS, BUT SINCE THIS IS TUESDAY, WE'D ALL PREFER THE CHINK OF COLD HARD CASH.
WHAT'S THE RUSH? WE ARE IN THE MIDDLE OF THE OCEAN - THERE'S NOWHERE YOU CAN SPEND IT!
LET US FIRST SEE IF YOUR ENDEAVOURS HAVE PAID DIVIDENDS...
THERE, AT LAST! THE KEY TO LAPUTA'S LOCATION! A SECRET MAP OF THE WORLD!
'CEPT IT'S A GLOBE.
AYE, AN' NO A VERY GOOD 'UN AT THAT!
WHAT ARE YOU TALKING ABOUT? THIS IS THE WORK OF THE FINEST CRAFTSMEN! DESCENDANTS OF THE ARTISANS OF LEMURIA AND HY BRASIL!
THAT'S AS MEBBE, BUT IT'S NAE A GLOBE O' THIS WORLD.
THERE'S NAE CLEAR CONTINENTS OR NUTHIN'. IT'S GIBBERISH!

NO...
THAT CAN'T
BE!

ACTUALLY, GENTLEMEN,
YOU'RE BOTH RIGHT... AND
WRONG. IF YOU'LL DIM ALL THE
LIGHTS BUT ONE, I'LL
DEMONSTRATE.

MAY
I?

ALHAZARED.

YES,
MASTER.

YOU SEE, IT'S
ALL A MATTER OF
PERSPECTIVE...

...OF
LOOKING AT
THE PROBLEM IN
A DIFFERENT
LIGHT.

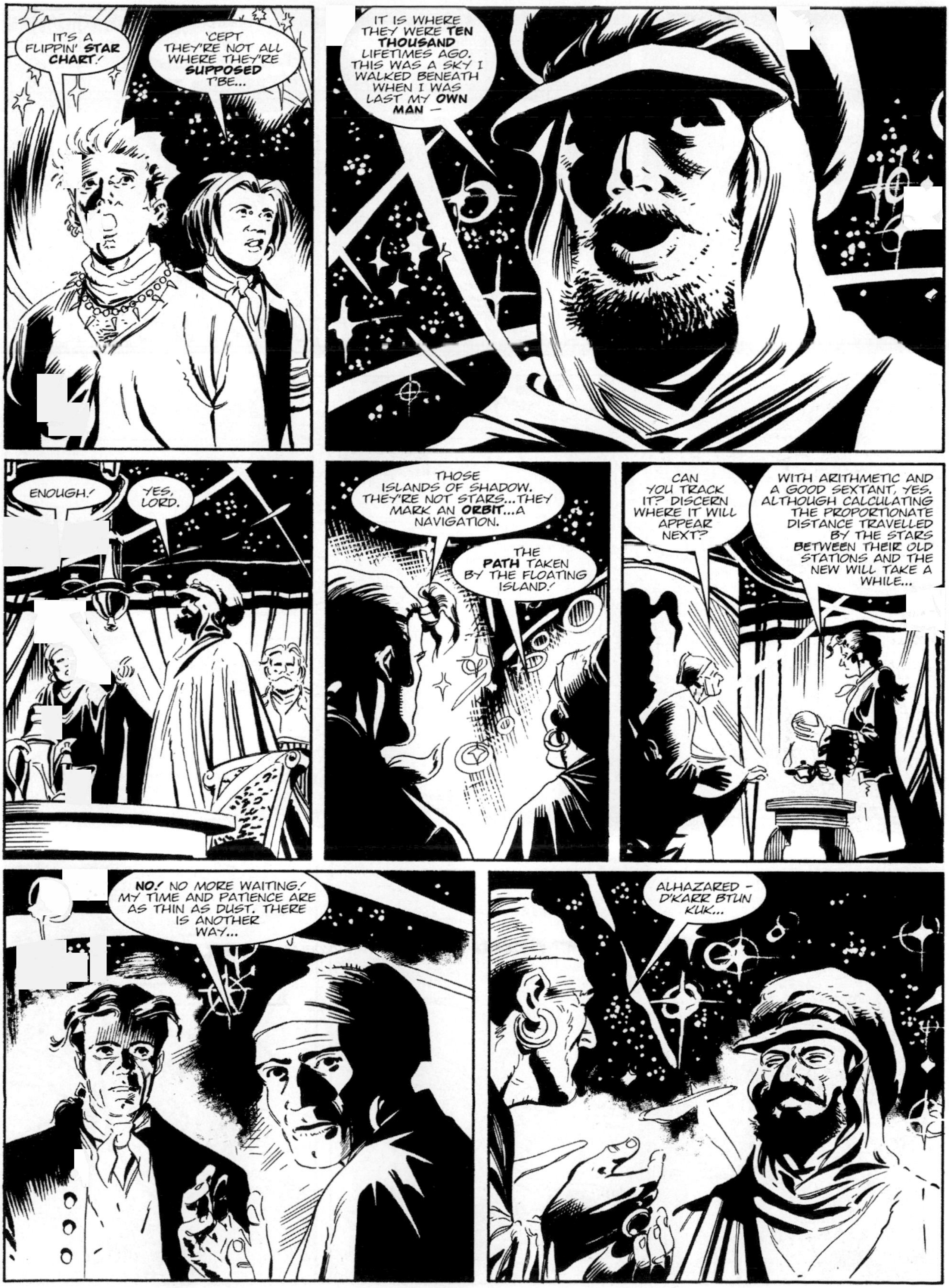
IT'S A FLIPPIN' **STAR CHART**!
'CEPT THEY'RE NOT ALL WHERE THEY'RE **SUPPOSED** T'BE...
IT IS WHERE THEY WERE **TEN THOUSAND** LIFETIMES AGO. THIS WAS A SKY I WALKED BENEATH WHEN I WAS LAST MY **OWN MAN** —
ENOUGH!
YES, LORD.
THOSE ISLANDS OF SHADOW. THEY'RE NOT STARS... THEY MARK AN **ORBIT**... A NAVIGATION.
THE **PATH** TAKEN BY THE FLOATING ISLAND!
CAN YOU TRACK IT? DISCERN WHERE IT WILL APPEAR NEXT?
WITH ARITHMETIC AND A GOOD SEXTANT, YES. ALTHOUGH CALCULATING THE PROPORTIONATE DISTANCE TRAVELLED BY THE STARS BETWEEN THEIR OLD STATIONS AND THE NEW WILL TAKE A WHILE...
**NO!** NO MORE WAITING! MY TIME AND PATIENCE ARE AS THIN AS DUST. THERE IS ANOTHER WAY...
ALHAZARED — D'KARR BTUN KUK...

WELL, THAT WAS EVENTFUL...

WHAT THE 'ECK...?

I SUGGEST WE TAKE A STROLL UP ON DECK, LADS...

THE NORTH POLE!

OH LOVELY, NOW WE GET T'FREEZE T'DEATH!

WHATEVER HAPPEN'D T'GOOD OLD ROBBIN' AN' PILLAGIN' THAT'S WHAT I WANT T'KNOW!

CEASE YOUR WHINING. THERE ARE ADEQUATE WINTER STORES ABOARD. I HAVE CATERED FOR EVERY EVENTUALITY.

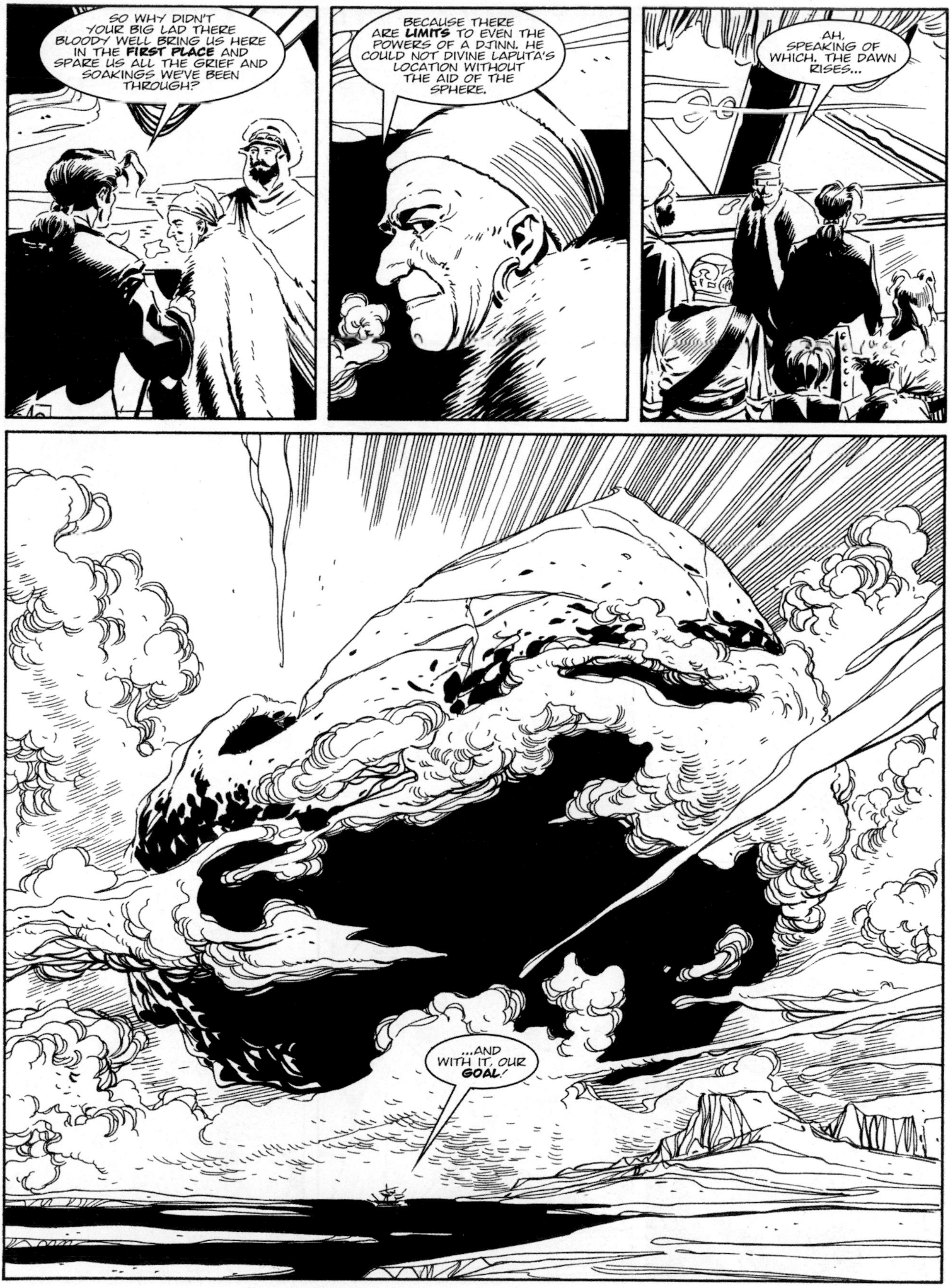
SO WHY DIDN'T YOUR BIG LAD THERE BLOODY WELL BRING US HERE IN THE FIRST PLACE AND SPARE US ALL THE GRIEF AND SOAKINGS WE'VE BEEN THROUGH?
BECAUSE THERE ARE LIMITS TO EVEN THE POWERS OF A DJINN. HE COULD NOT DIVINE LAPUTA'S LOCATION WITHOUT THE AID OF THE SPHERE.
AH, SPEAKING OF WHICH. THE DAWN RISES...
...AND WITH IT, OUR GOAL!

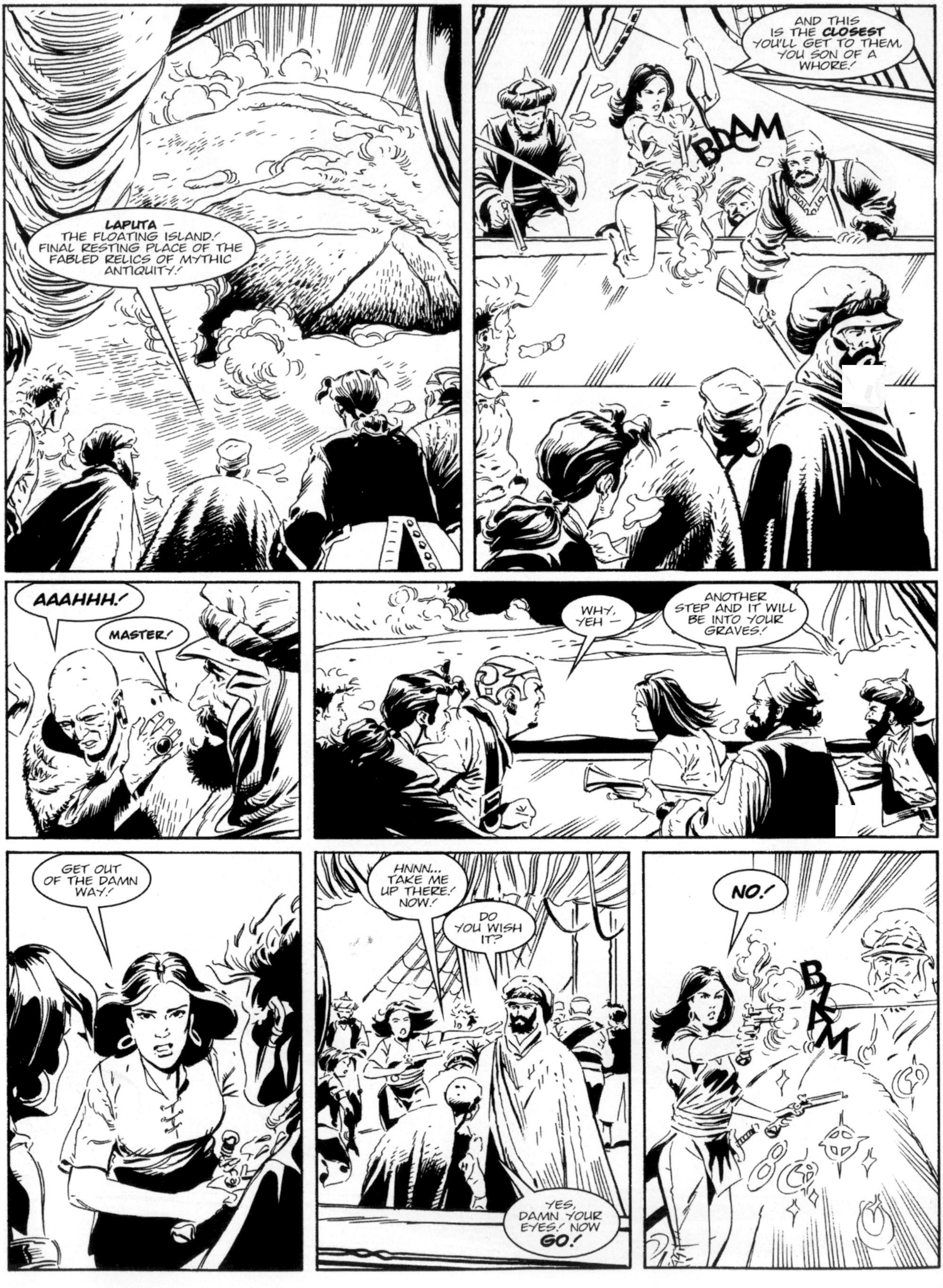
LAPUTA — THE FLOATING ISLAND! FINAL RESTING PLACE OF THE FABLED RELICS OF MYTHIC ANTIQUITY!
AND THIS IS THE CLOSEST YOU'LL GET TO THEM, YOU SON OF A WHORE!
BDAM
AAAHHH!
MASTER!
WHY, YEH —
ANOTHER STEP AND IT WILL BE INTO YOUR GRAVES!
GET OUT OF THE DAMN WAY!
HNNN... TAKE ME UP THERE! NOW!
DO YOU WISH IT?
YES, DAMN YOUR EYES! NOW GO!
NO!
BLAM

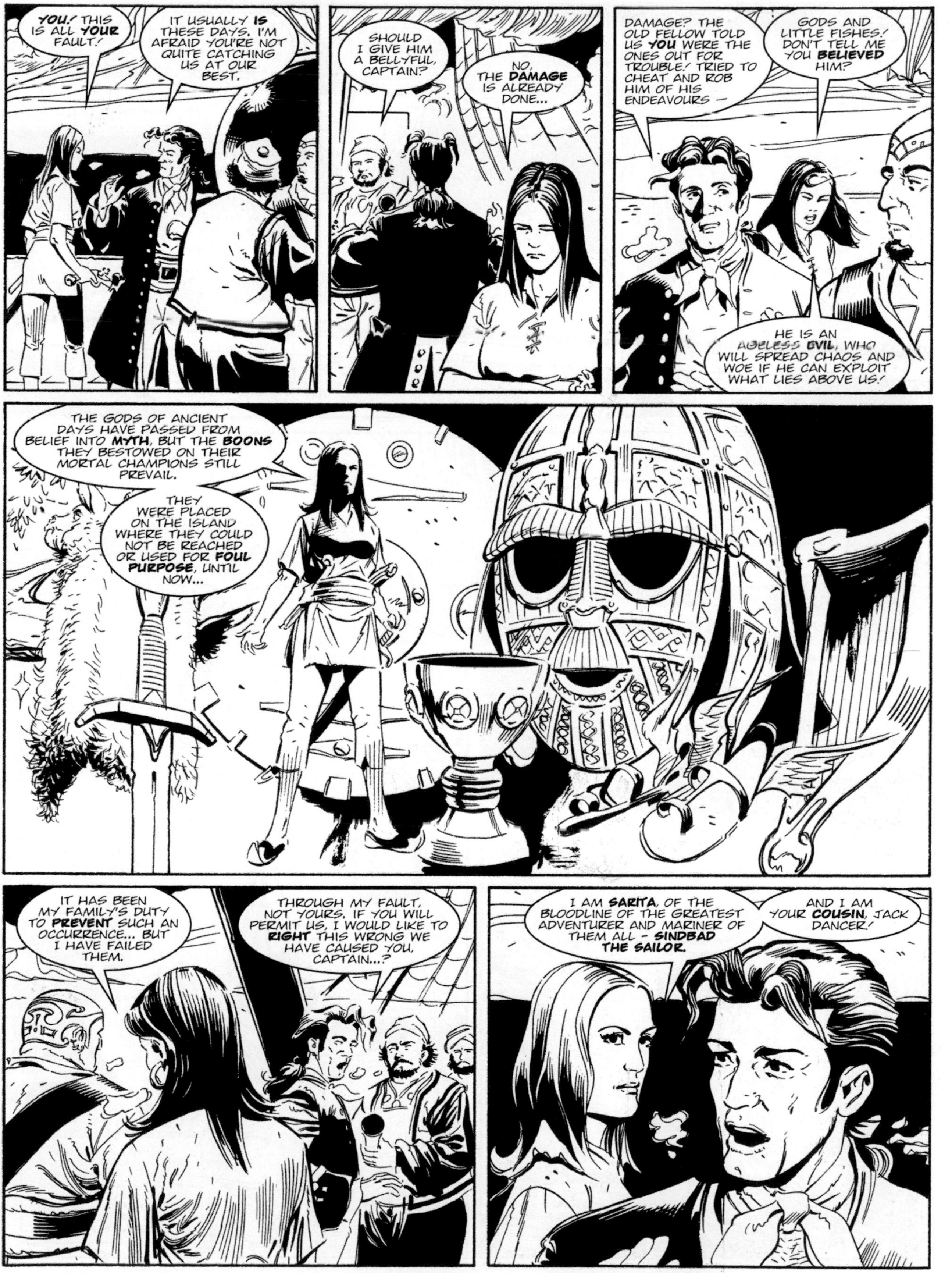
YOU! THIS IS ALL YOUR FAULT!
IT USUALLY IS THESE DAYS. I'M AFRAID YOU'RE NOT QUITE CATCHING US AT OUR BEST.
SHOULD I GIVE HIM A BELLYFUL, CAPTAIN?
NO, THE DAMAGE IS ALREADY DONE...
DAMAGE? THE OLD FELLOW TOLD US YOU WERE THE ONES OUT FOR TROUBLE! TRIED TO CHEAT AND ROB HIM OF HIS ENDEAVOURS —
GODS AND LITTLE FISHES! DON'T TELL ME YOU BELIEVED HIM?
HE IS AN AGELESS EVIL, WHO WILL SPREAD CHAOS AND WOE IF HE CAN EXPLOIT WHAT LIES ABOVE US!
THE GODS OF ANCIENT DAYS HAVE PASSED FROM BELIEF INTO MYTH, BUT THE BOONS THEY BESTOWED ON THEIR MORTAL CHAMPIONS STILL PREVAIL.
THEY WERE PLACED ON THE ISLAND WHERE THEY COULD NOT BE REACHED OR USED FOR FOUL PURPOSE, UNTIL NOW...
IT HAS BEEN MY FAMILY'S DUTY TO PREVENT SUCH AN OCCURRENCE... BUT I HAVE FAILED THEM.
THROUGH MY FAULT, NOT YOURS. IF YOU WILL PERMIT US, I WOULD LIKE TO RIGHT THIS WRONG WE HAVE CAUSED YOU, CAPTAIN...?
I AM SARITA, OF THE BLOODLINE OF THE GREATEST ADVENTURER AND MARINER OF THEM ALL - SINDBAD THE SAILOR.
AND I AM YOUR COUSIN, JACK DANCER!

AND THE THREE LITTLE PIGS ARE MY NEPHEWS AND MY GREAT AUNT NELLY IS REALLY OLD MOTHER HUBBARD?

MOCK ALL YOU WILL, BUT WE ARE DISTANT KIN.

OF ALL THE ROGUES AND RAKES, WHY DO YOU THINK AL-ALADDIN CHOSE *YOU*? BECAUSE ONLY THOSE OF SINDBAD'S BLOOD COULD SAFELY RETRIEVE THE HALVES OF THE MAP.

BUT THE OLD GEEZER KNEW WHERE THEY WAS ALL ALONG. HE JUST GOT US T'FETCH 'EM FOR 'IM.

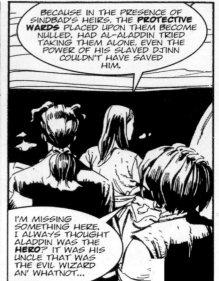

BECAUSE IN THE PRESENCE OF SINDBAD'S HEIRS, THE **PROTECTIVE WARDS** PLACED UPON THEM BECOME NULLED. HAD AL-ALADDIN TRIED TAKING THEM ALONE, EVEN THE POWER OF HIS SLAVED DJINN COULDN'T HAVE SAVED HIM.

I'M MISSING SOMETHING HERE. I ALWAYS THOUGHT ALADDIN WAS THE **HERO**? IT WAS HIS UNCLE THAT WAS THE EVIL WIZARD AN' WHATNOT...

THE **TRUTH** HAS BECOME TWISTED WITH TIME.

ABANAZAR WAS A GREAT SAGE AND SORCERER. AL-ALADDIN A WHORE, THIEF AND MURDERER. HE STOLE THE RING IN WHICH THE **WRAITH OF FIRE** WAS BOUND.

"BEING QUICK AND SLY, HE SOUGHT TO FOOL THE DJINN. WITH HIS FIRST WISH, HE DEMANDED AN **INFINITY** OF WISHES... BUT THERE IS A **REASON** YOU ARE ONLY PERMITTED THREE CHOICES.

"MAGIC IS **POISON** TO MEN. OVER TIME, IT BLACKENS THE HEART AND CANKERS THE SOUL.

"AL-ALADDIN HAS USED THOUSANDS OF WISHES, GNAWING HIM TO A HUSK. HIS ONLY SALVATION LIES IN USING THE RELICS OF LAPUTA TO **REJUVENATE** HIMSELF.

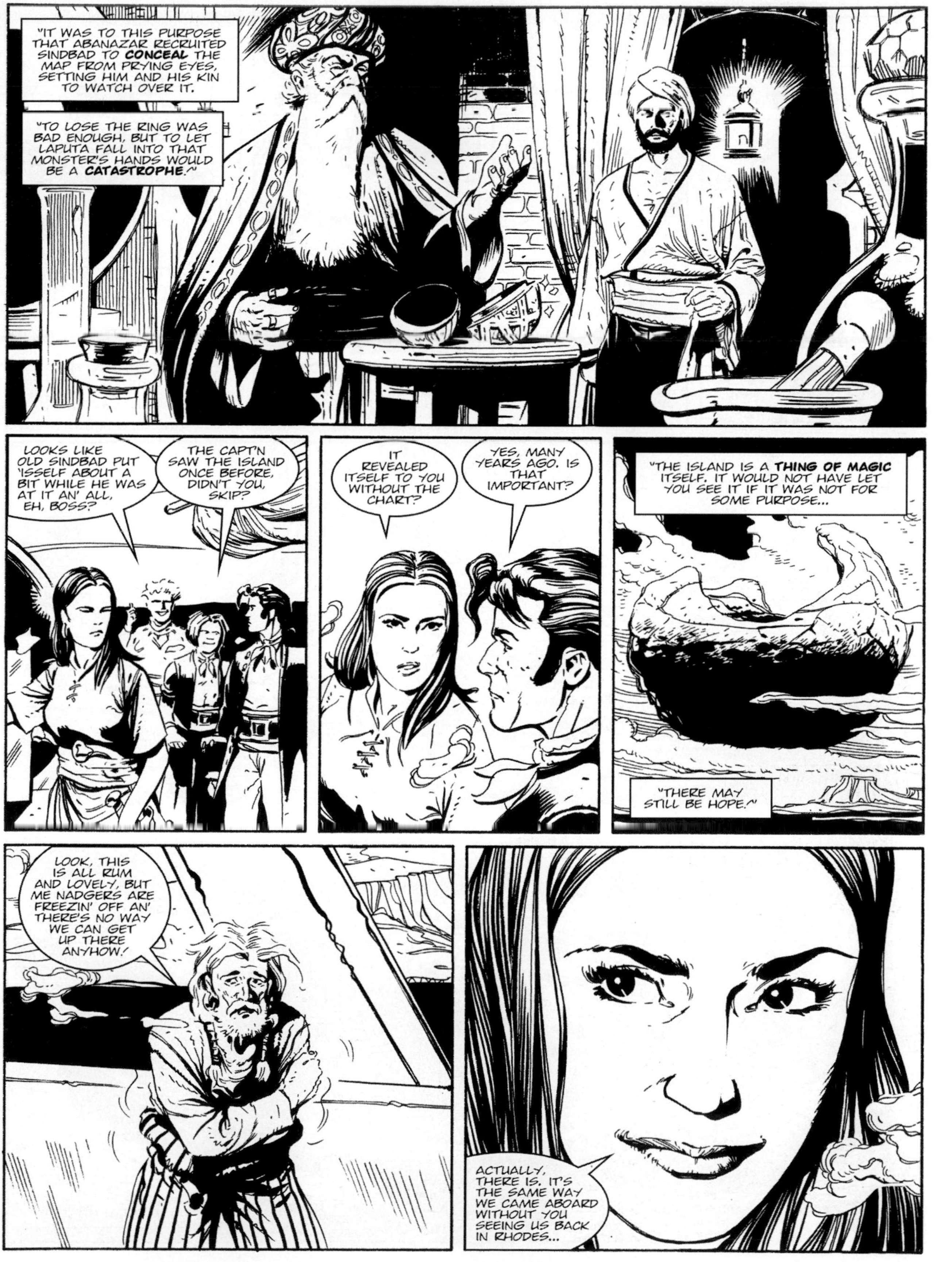
"IT WAS TO THIS PURPOSE THAT ABANAZAR RECRUITED SINDBAD TO **CONCEAL** THE MAP FROM PRYING EYES, SETTING HIM AND HIS KIN TO WATCH OVER IT.
"TO LOSE THE RING WAS BAD ENOUGH, BUT TO LET LAPUTA FALL INTO THAT MONSTER'S HANDS WOULD BE A **CATASTROPHE**."
LOOKS LIKE OLD SINDBAD PUT 'ISSELF ABOUT A BIT WHILE HE WAS AT IT AN' ALL, EH, BOSS?
THE CAPT'N SAW THE ISLAND ONCE BEFORE, DIDN'T YOU, SKIP?
IT REVEALED ITSELF TO YOU WITHOUT THE CHART?
YES, MANY YEARS AGO. IS THAT IMPORTANT?
"THE ISLAND IS A **THING OF MAGIC** ITSELF. IT WOULD NOT HAVE LET YOU SEE IT IF IT WAS NOT FOR SOME PURPOSE...
"THERE MAY STILL BE HOPE."
LOOK, THIS IS ALL RUM AND LOVELY, BUT ME NADGERS ARE FREEZIN' OFF AN' THERE'S NO WAY WE CAN GET UP THERE ANYHOW!
ACTUALLY, THERE IS. IT'S THE SAME WAY WE CAME ABOARD WITHOUT YOU SEEING US BACK IN RHODES...

"HOWEVER, IT MIGHT BE A TIGHT SQUEEZE..."

UHH...

STOP PUSHIN', WILL YEH?

I'M NOT PUSHIN', I'M BREATHIN' OUT!

THEN STOP BLOODY BREATHIN'!

SO DOES THIS MEAN WE'RE ALLIES NOW, CAPTAIN?

NEED MUST WHEN THE DEVIL DRIVES.

AND THAT HAD BETTER BE JUST YOUR SWORD PRESSED AGAINST MY THIGH, OTHERWISE YOU'RE MAN OVERBOARD!

GREAT GOD ALMIGHTY! WHUD Y'LOOK AT THAT!

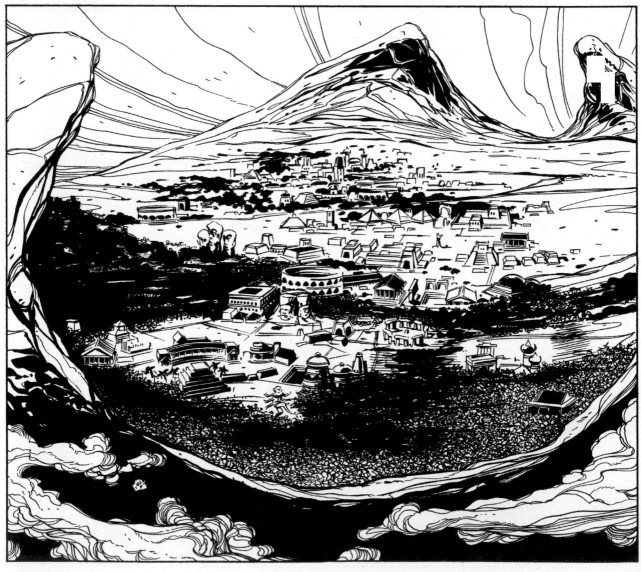

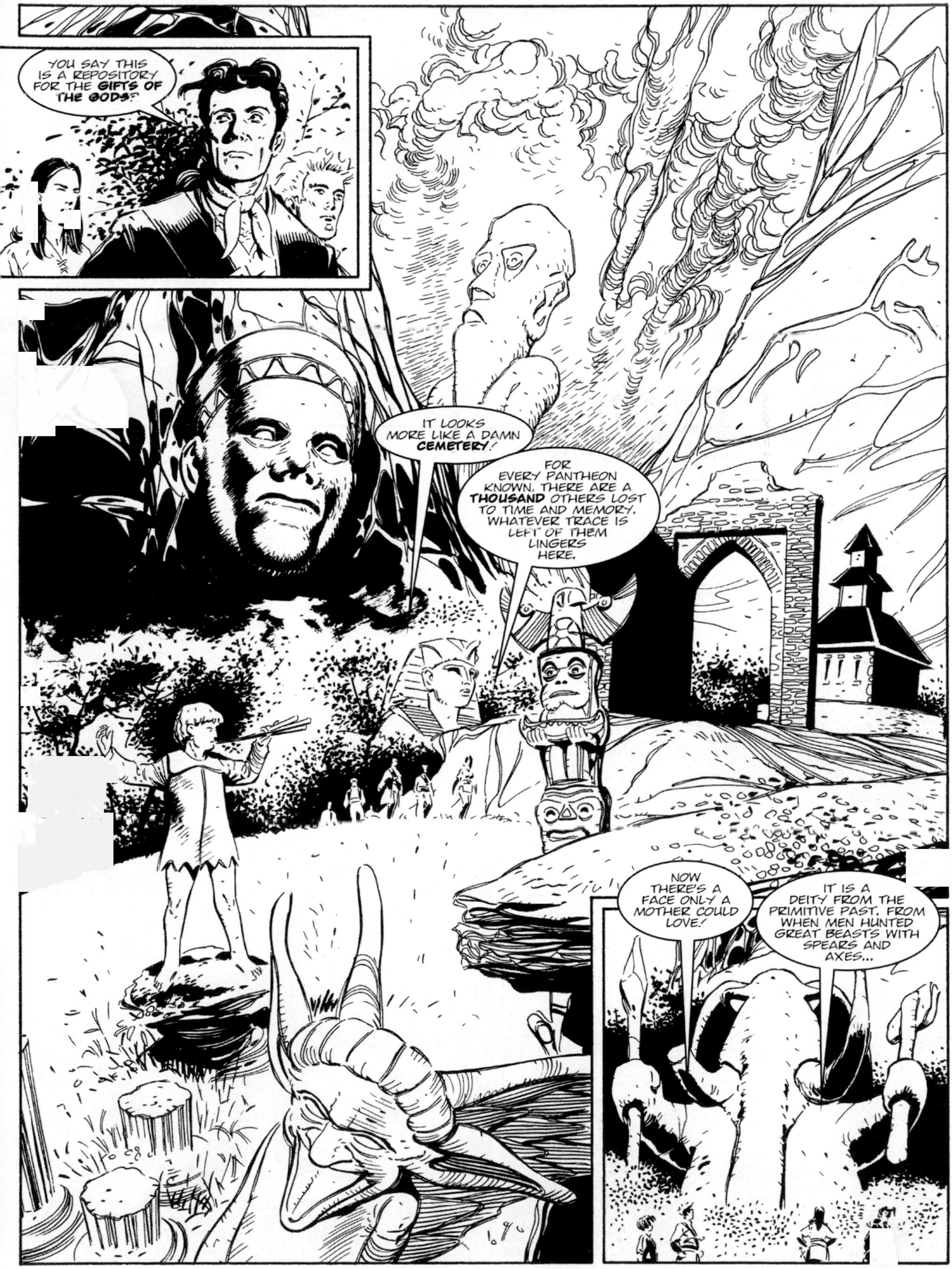
YOU SAY THIS IS A REPOSITORY FOR THE **GIFTS OF THE GODS**?
IT LOOKS MORE LIKE A DAMN **CEMETERY**!
FOR EVERY PANTHEON KNOWN, THERE ARE A **THOUSAND** OTHERS LOST TO TIME AND MEMORY. WHATEVER TRACE IS LEFT OF THEM LINGERS HERE.
NOW THERE'S A FACE ONLY A MOTHER COULD LOVE!
IT IS A DEITY FROM THE PRIMITIVE PAST, FROM WHEN MEN HUNTED GREAT BEASTS WITH SPEARS AND AXES...

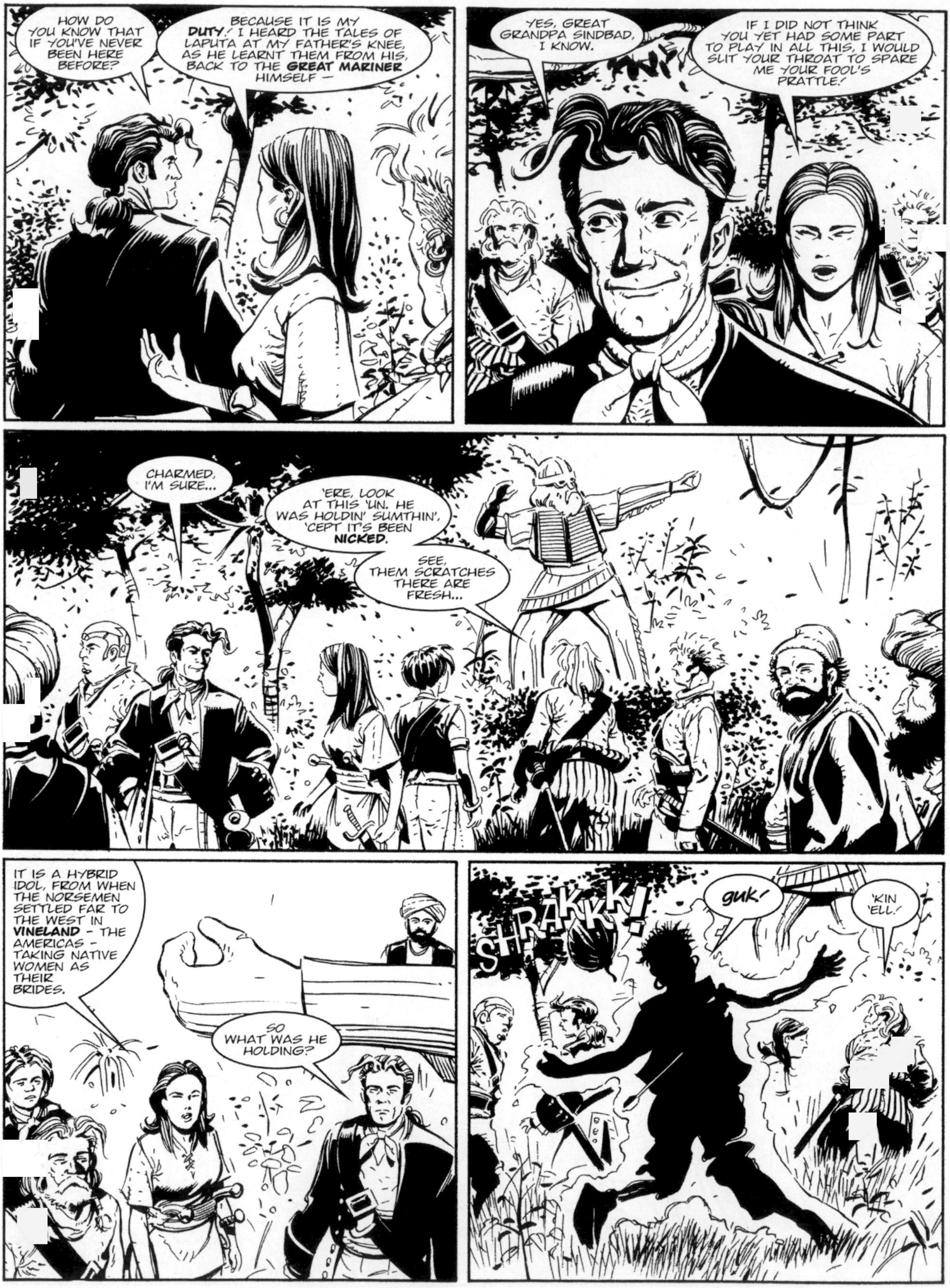
HOW DO YOU KNOW THAT IF YOU'VE NEVER BEEN HERE BEFORE?
BECAUSE IT IS MY DUTY! I HEARD THE TALES OF LAPUTA AT MY FATHER'S KNEE, AS HE LEARNT THEM FROM HIS, BACK TO THE GREAT MARINER HIMSELF —
YES, GREAT GRANDPA SINDBAD, I KNOW.
IF I DID NOT THINK YOU YET HAD SOME PART TO PLAY IN ALL THIS, I WOULD SLIT YOUR THROAT TO SPARE ME YOUR FOOL'S PRATTLE!
CHARMED, I'M SURE...
'ERE, LOOK AT THIS 'UN. HE WAS HOLDIN' SUMTHIN', 'CEPT IT'S BEEN NICKED.
SEE, THEM SCRATCHES THERE ARE FRESH...
IT IS A HYBRID IDOL, FROM WHEN THE NORSEMEN SETTLED FAR TO THE WEST IN VINELAND - THE AMERICAS - TAKING NATIVE WOMEN AS THEIR BRIDES.
SO WHAT WAS HE HOLDING?
SHRAKKK!
GUK!
'KIN 'ELL!

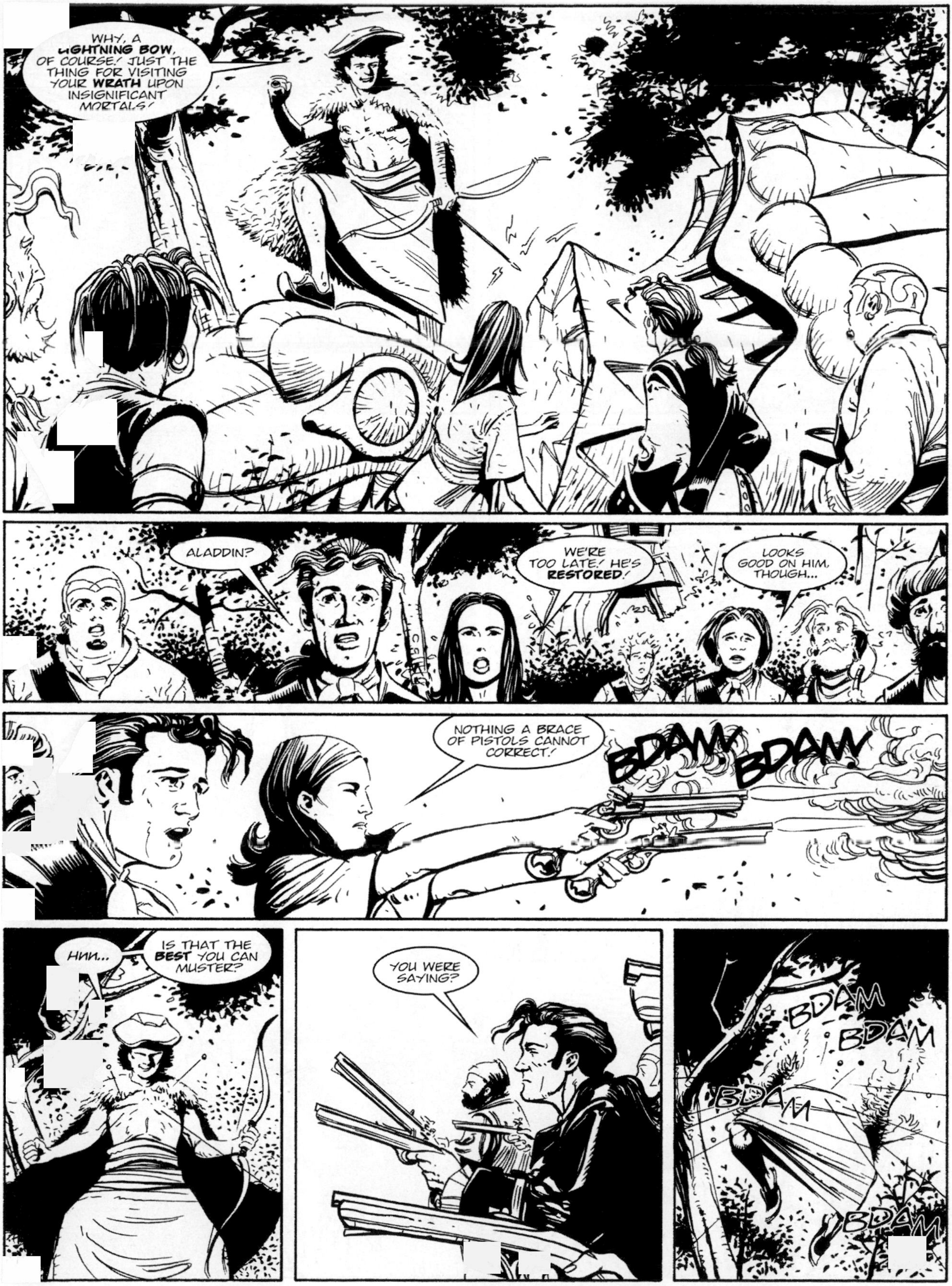
WHY, A LIGHTNING BOW, OF COURSE! JUST THE THING FOR VISITING YOUR WRATH UPON INSIGNIFICANT MORTALS!
ALADDIN?
WE'RE TOO LATE! HE'S RESTORED!
LOOKS GOOD ON HIM, THOUGH...
NOTHING A BRACE OF PISTOLS CANNOT CORRECT!
BDAM BDAM
HMM...
IS THAT THE BEST YOU CAN MUSTER?
YOU WERE SAYING?
BDAM
BDAM
BDAM
BDAM

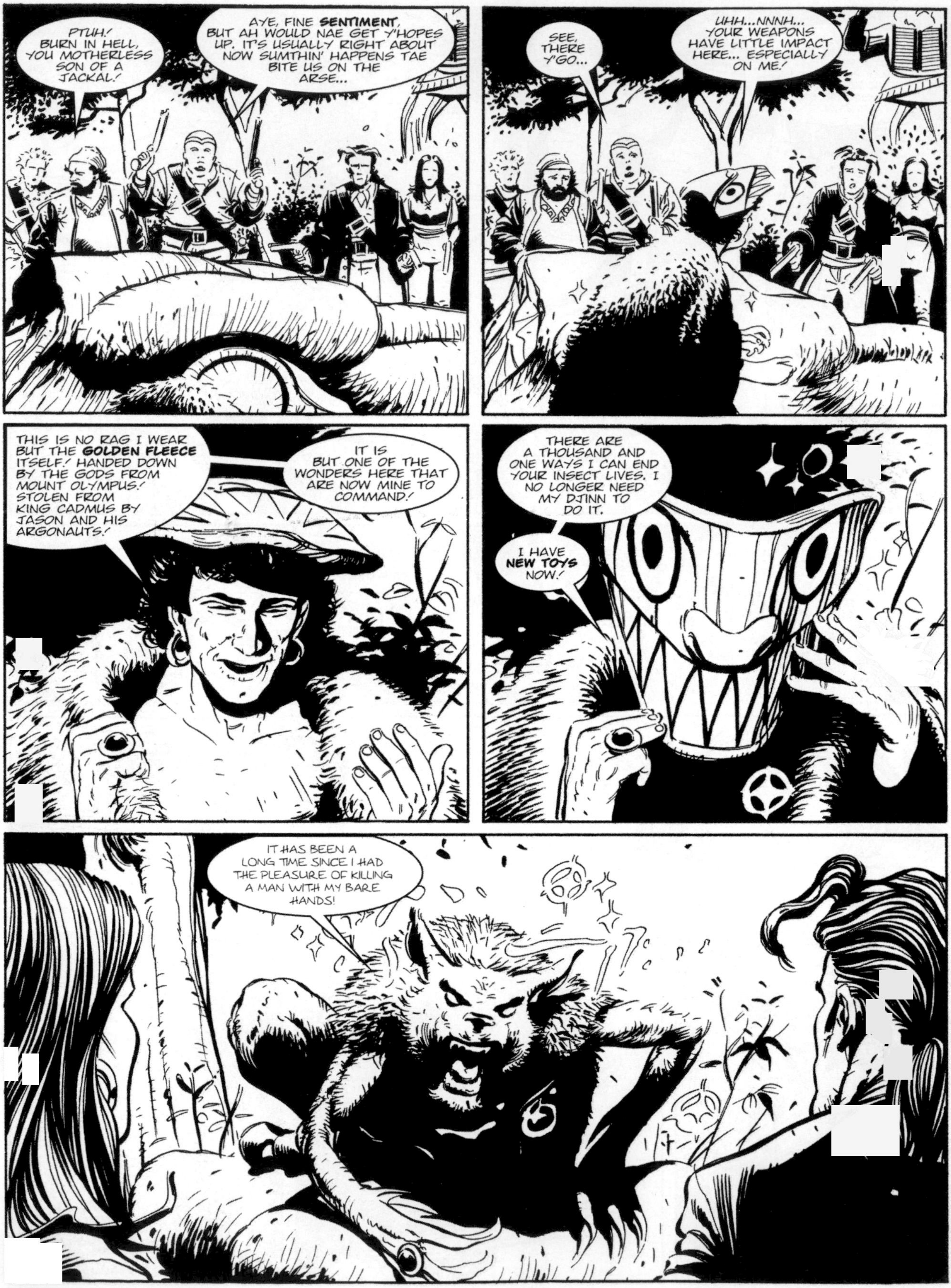
PTUH! BURN IN HELL, YOU MOTHERLESS SON OF A JACKAL!
AYE, FINE **SENTIMENT**, BUT AH WOULD NAE GET Y'HOPES UP. IT'S USUALLY RIGHT ABOUT NOW SUMTHIN' HAPPENS TAE BITE US ON THE ARSE...
SEE, THERE Y'GO...
UHH...NNNH... YOUR WEAPONS HAVE LITTLE IMPACT HERE... ESPECIALLY ON ME!
THIS IS NO RAG I WEAR BUT THE **GOLDEN FLEECE** ITSELF! HANDED DOWN BY THE GODS FROM MOUNT OLYMPUS! STOLEN FROM KING CADMUS BY JASON AND HIS ARGONAUTS!
IT IS BUT ONE OF THE WONDERS HERE THAT ARE NOW MINE TO COMMAND!
THERE ARE A THOUSAND AND ONE WAYS I CAN END YOUR INSECT LIVES. I NO LONGER NEED MY DJINN TO DO IT.
I HAVE **NEW TOYS** NOW!
IT HAS BEEN A LONG TIME SINCE I HAD THE PLEASURE OF KILLING A MAN WITH MY BARE HANDS!

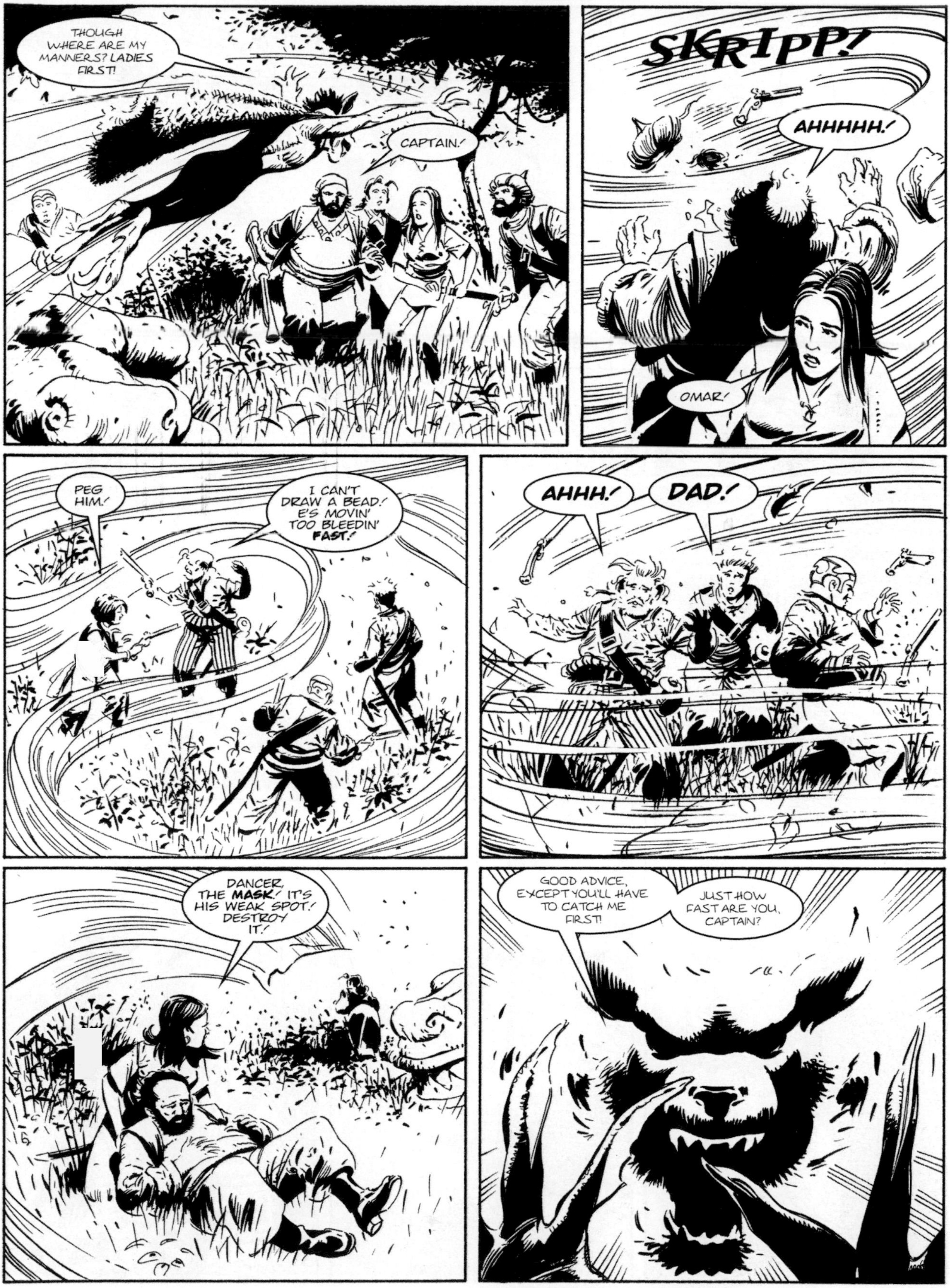
THOUGH WHERE ARE MY MANNERS? LADIES FIRST!
CAPTAIN!
SKRIPP!
AHHHHH!
OMAR!
PEG HIM!
I CAN'T DRAW A BEAD! E'S MOVIN' TOO BLEEDIN' FAST!
AHHH!
DAD!
DANCER, THE MASK! IT'S HIS WEAK SPOT! DESTROY IT!
GOOD ADVICE, EXCEPT YOU'LL HAVE TO CATCH ME FIRST!
JUST HOW FAST ARE YOU, CAPTAIN?

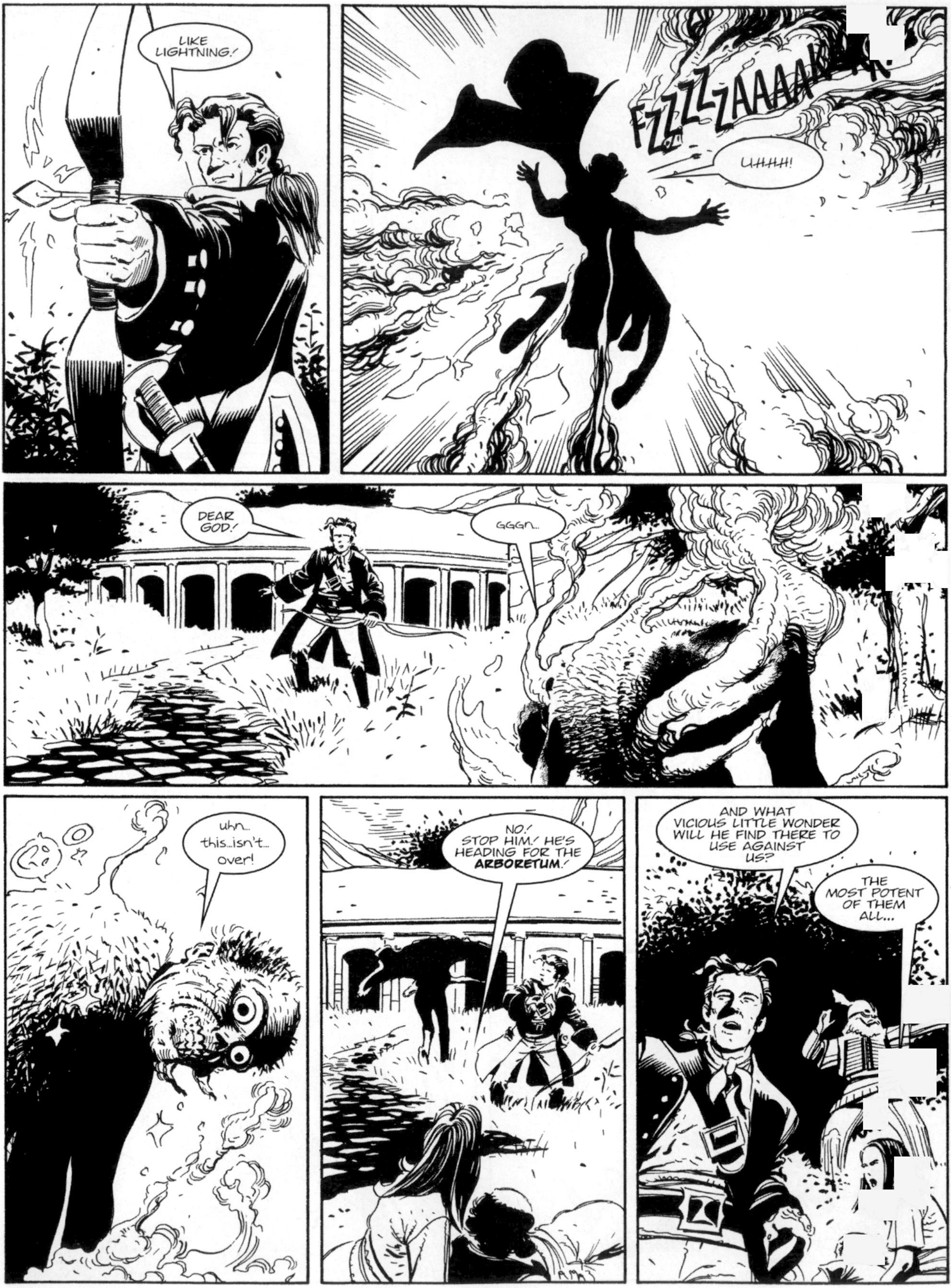
LIKE LIGHTNING!
FZZZZZAAAAK
UHHH!
DEAR GOD!
GGGN..
uhn... this...isn't... over!
NO! STOP HIM! HE'S HEADING FOR THE ARBORETUM!
AND WHAT VICIOUS LITTLE WONDER WILL HE FIND THERE TO USE AGAINST US?
THE MOST POTENT OF THEM ALL...

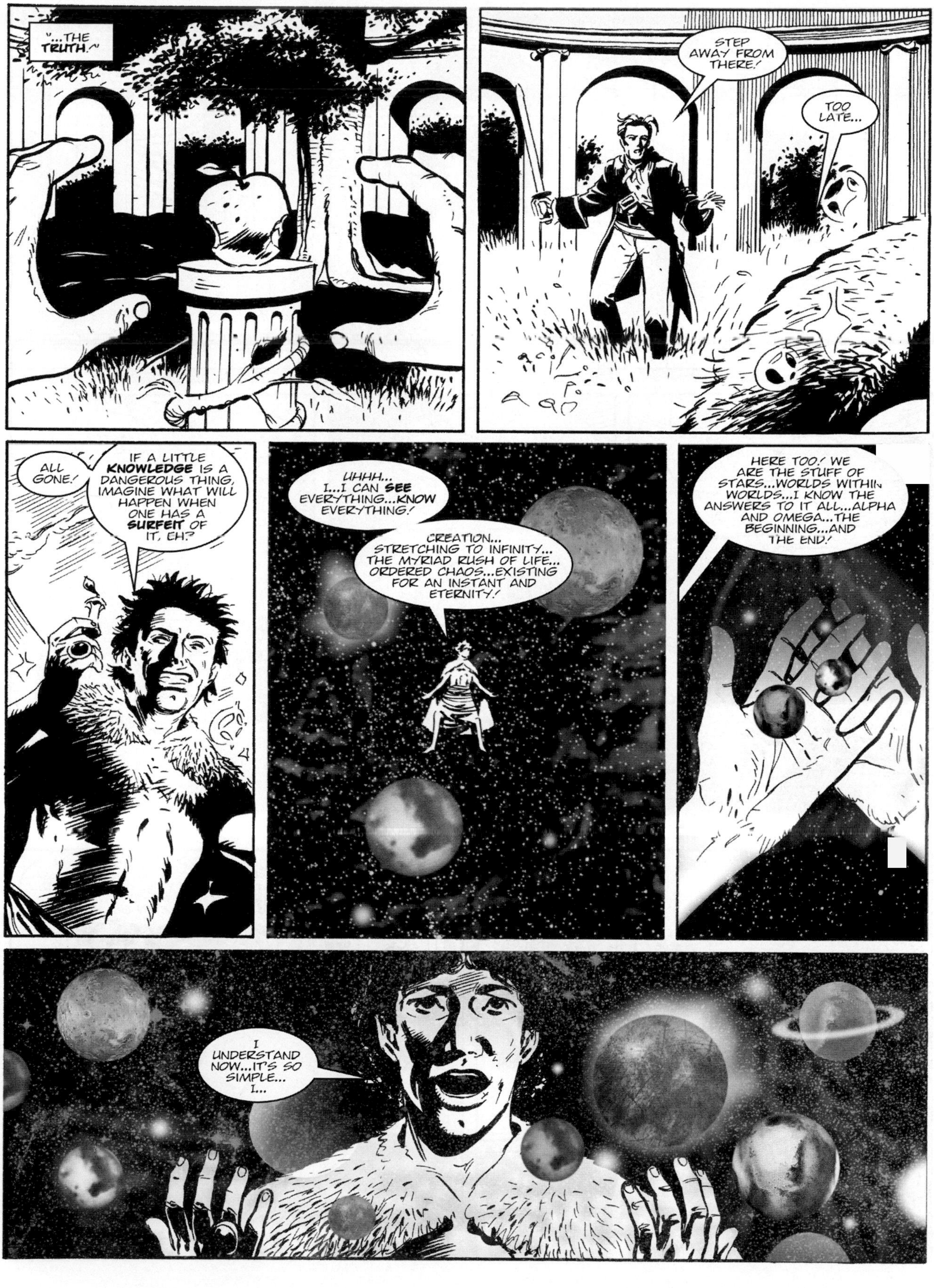
"...THE TRUTH."
STEP AWAY FROM THERE!
TOO LATE...
ALL GONE!
IF A LITTLE KNOWLEDGE IS A DANGEROUS THING, IMAGINE WHAT WILL HAPPEN WHEN ONE HAS A SURFEIT OF IT, EH?
UHHH... I...I CAN SEE EVERYTHING...KNOW EVERYTHING!
CREATION... STRETCHING TO INFINITY... THE MYRIAD RUSH OF LIFE... ORDERED CHAOS...EXISTING FOR AN INSTANT AND ETERNITY!
HERE TOO! WE ARE THE STUFF OF STARS...WORLDS WITHIN WORLDS...I KNOW THE ANSWERS TO IT ALL...ALPHA AND OMEGA...THE BEGINNING...AND THE END!
I UNDERSTAND NOW...IT'S SO SIMPLE... I...

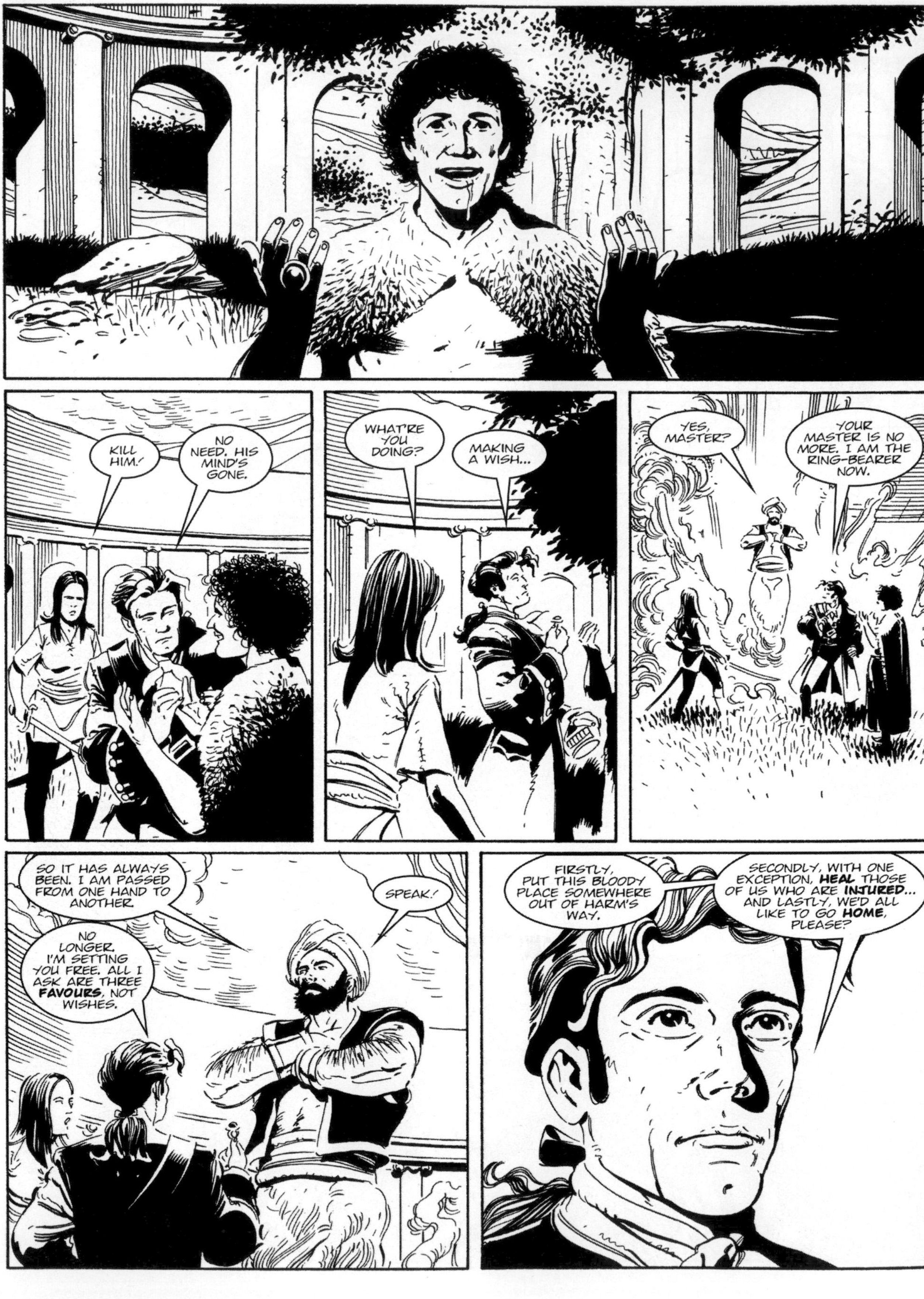
KILL HIM!
NO NEED. HIS MIND'S GONE.
WHAT'RE YOU DOING?
MAKING A WISH...
YES, MASTER?
YOUR MASTER IS NO MORE. I AM THE RING-BEARER NOW.
SO IT HAS ALWAYS BEEN. I AM PASSED FROM ONE HAND TO ANOTHER.
SPEAK!
NO LONGER. I'M SETTING YOU FREE. ALL I ASK ARE THREE FAVOURS, NOT WISHES.
FIRSTLY, PUT THIS BLOODY PLACE SOMEWHERE OUT OF HARM'S WAY.
SECONDLY, WITH ONE EXCEPTION, HEAL THOSE OF US WHO ARE INJURED... AND LASTLY, WE'D ALL LIKE TO GO HOME, PLEASE?

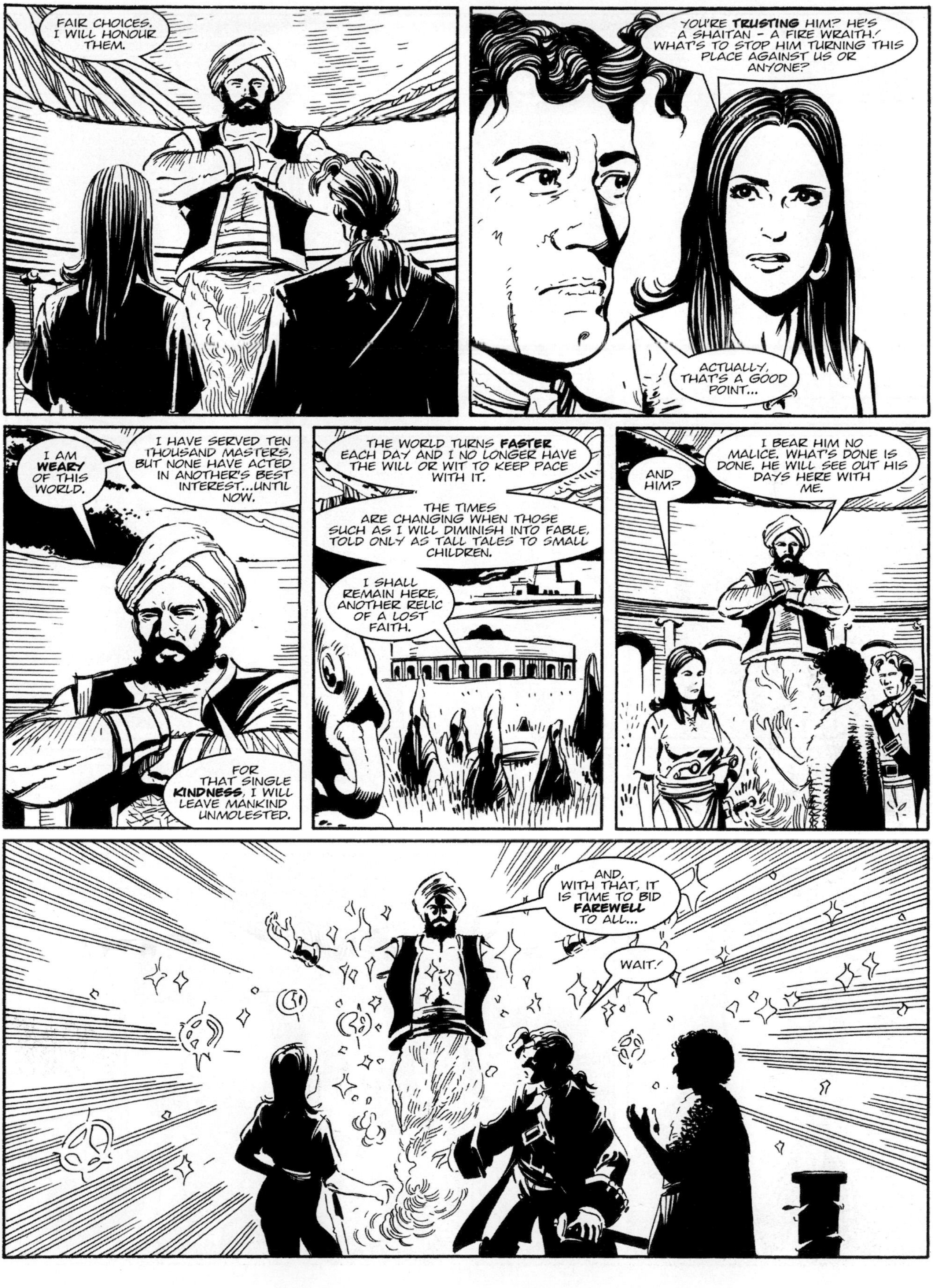
FAIR CHOICES. I WILL HONOUR THEM.
YOU'RE **TRUSTING** HIM? HE'S A SHAITAN - A FIRE WRAITH! WHAT'S TO STOP HIM TURNING THIS PLACE AGAINST US OR ANYONE?
ACTUALLY, THAT'S A GOOD POINT...
I AM **WEARY** OF THIS WORLD.
I HAVE SERVED TEN THOUSAND MASTERS, BUT NONE HAVE ACTED IN ANOTHER'S BEST INTEREST...UNTIL NOW.
FOR THAT SINGLE **KINDNESS**, I WILL LEAVE MANKIND UNMOLESTED.
THE WORLD TURNS **FASTER** EACH DAY AND I NO LONGER HAVE THE WILL OR WIT TO KEEP PACE WITH IT.
THE TIMES ARE CHANGING WHEN THOSE SUCH AS I WILL DIMINISH INTO FABLE, TOLD ONLY AS TALL TALES TO SMALL CHILDREN.
I SHALL REMAIN HERE, ANOTHER RELIC OF A LOST FAITH.
AND HIM?
I BEAR HIM NO MALICE. WHAT'S DONE IS DONE. HE WILL SEE OUT HIS DAYS HERE WITH ME.
AND, WITH THAT, IT IS TIME TO BID **FAREWELL** TO ALL...
WAIT!

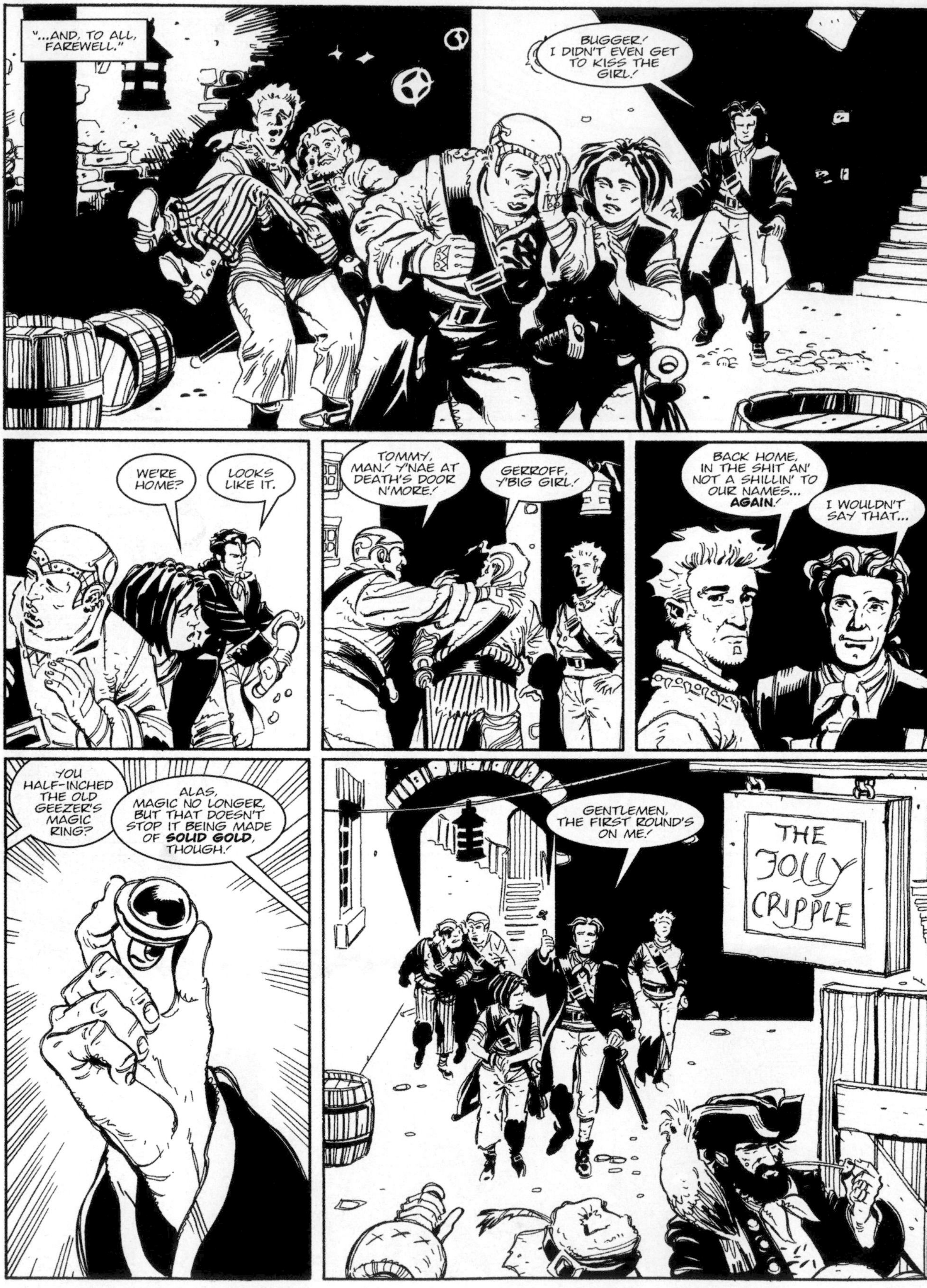
"...AND, TO ALL, FAREWELL."
BUGGER! I DIDN'T EVEN GET TO KISS THE GIRL!
WE'RE HOME?
LOOKS LIKE IT.
TOMMY, MAN! Y'NAE AT DEATH'S DOOR N'MORE!
GERROFF, Y'BIG GIRL!
BACK HOME, IN THE SHIT AN' NOT A SHILLIN' TO OUR NAMES... AGAIN!
I WOULDN'T SAY THAT...
YOU HALF-INCHED THE OLD GEEZER'S MAGIC RING?
ALAS, MAGIC NO LONGER, BUT THAT DOESN'T STOP IT BEING MADE OF SOLID GOLD, THOUGH!
GENTLEMEN, THE FIRST ROUND'S ON ME!
THE JOLLY CRIPPLE

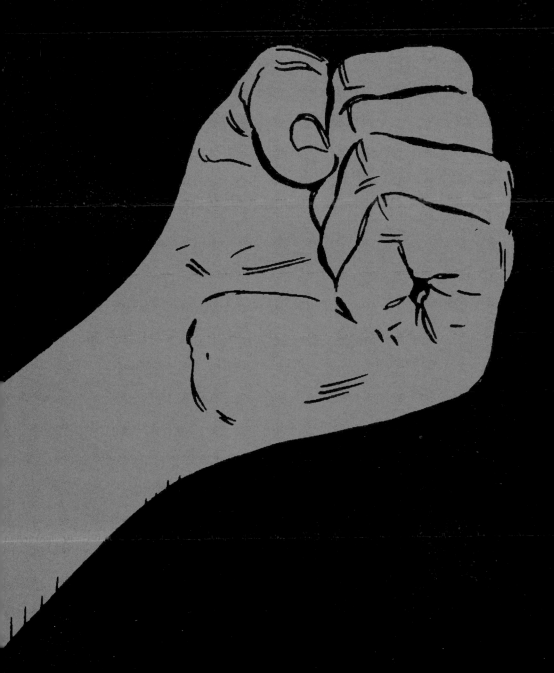

# MEANWHILE...

Script: Ian Edginton
Art: Steve Yeowell
Letters: Annie Parkhouse

Originally published in *2000 AD* Progs 1416 - 1419

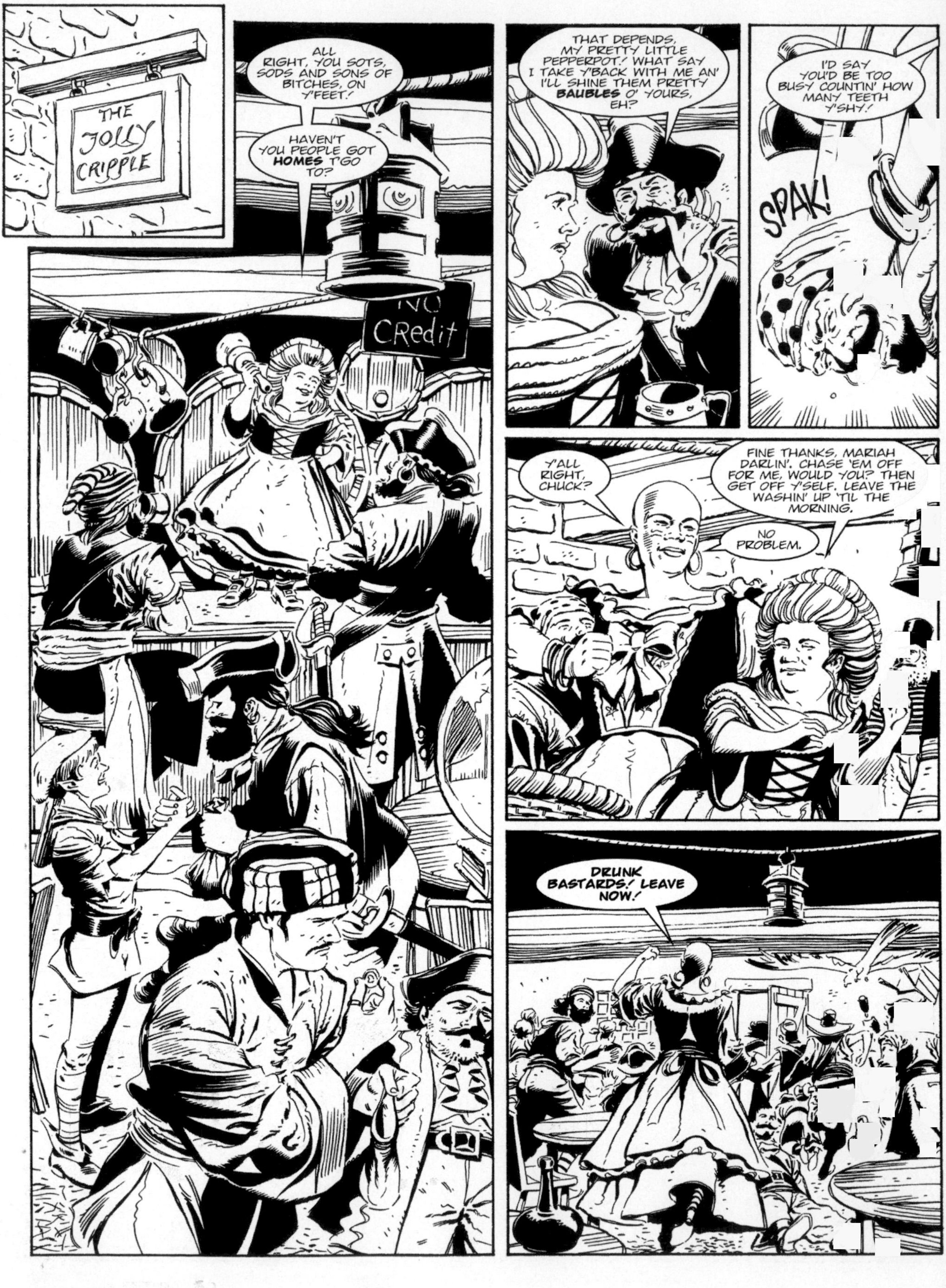
THE JOLLY CRIPPLE
ALL RIGHT, YOU SOTS, SODS AND SONS OF BITCHES, ON Y'FEET!
HAVEN'T YOU PEOPLE GOT **HOMES** T'GO TO?
NO CRedit
THAT DEPENDS, MY PRETTY LITTLE PEPPERPOT! WHAT SAY I TAKE Y'BACK WITH ME AN' I'LL SHINE THEM PRETTY **BAUBLES** O' YOURS, EH?
I'D SAY YOU'D BE TOO BUSY COUNTIN' HOW MANY TEETH Y'SHY!
SPAK!
Y'ALL RIGHT, CHUCK?
FINE THANKS, MARIAH DARLIN'. CHASE 'EM OFF FOR ME, WOULD YOU? THEN GET OFF Y'SELF. LEAVE THE WASHIN' UP 'TIL THE MORNING.
NO PROBLEM.
DRUNK BASTARDS! LEAVE NOW!

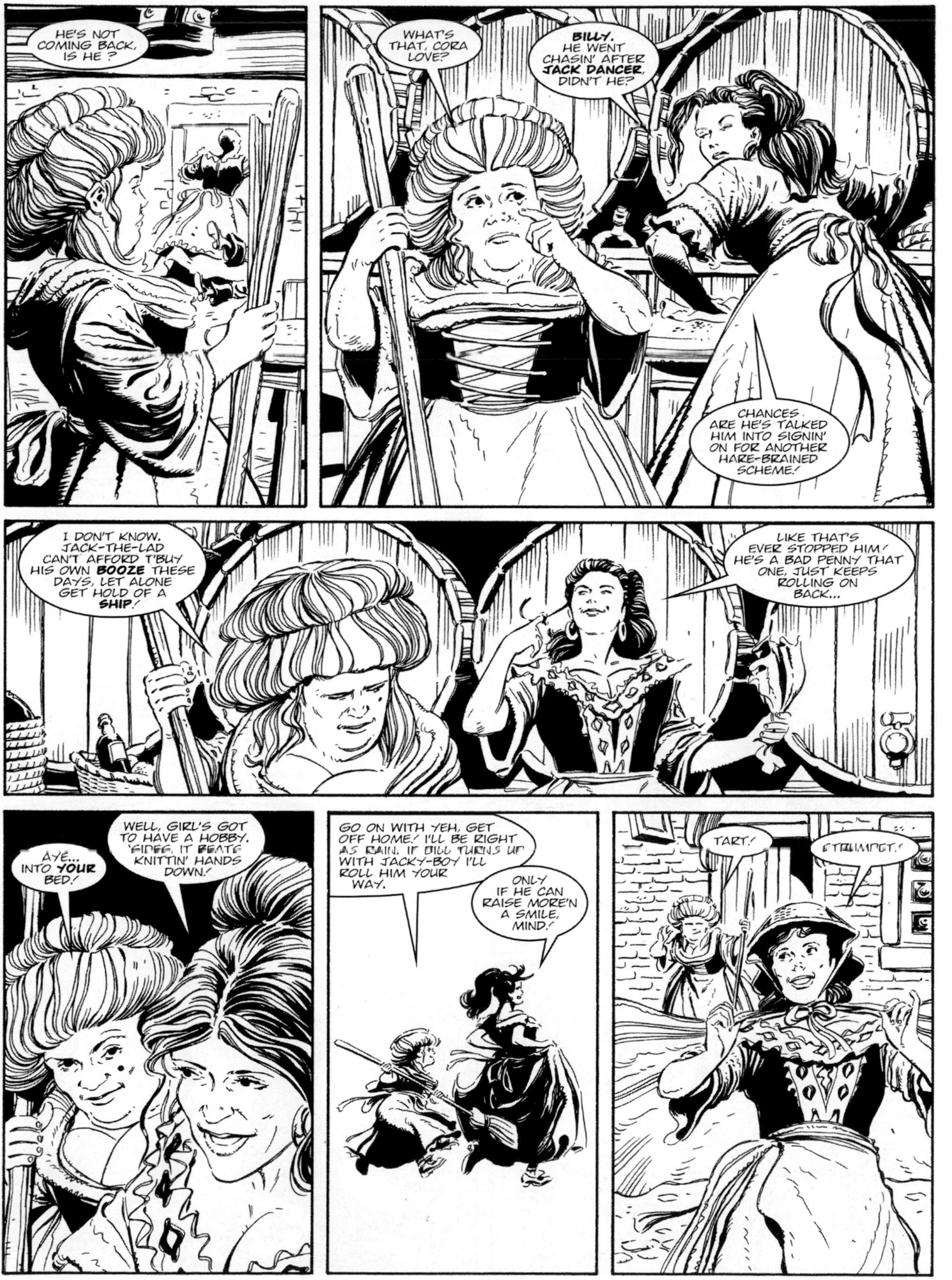
HE'S NOT COMING BACK, IS HE?
WHAT'S THAT, CORA LOVE?
**BILLY.** HE WENT CHASIN' AFTER **JACK DANCER**, DIDN'T HE?
CHANCES ARE HE'S TALKED HIM INTO SIGNIN' ON FOR ANOTHER HARE-BRAINED SCHEME!
I DON'T KNOW. JACK-THE-LAD CAN'T AFFORD T'BUY HIS OWN **BOOZE** THESE DAYS, LET ALONE GET HOLD OF A **SHIP**!
LIKE THAT'S EVER STOPPED HIM! HE'S A BAD PENNY THAT ONE, JUST KEEPS ROLLING ON BACK...
AYE... INTO **YOUR** BED!
WELL, GIRL'S GOT TO HAVE A HOBBY. 'SIDES, IT BEATS KNITTIN' HANDS DOWN!
GO ON WITH YEH, GET OFF HOME! I'LL BE RIGHT AS RAIN. IF BILL TURNS UP WITH JACKY-BOY I'LL ROLL HIM YOUR WAY.
ONLY IF HE CAN RAISE MORE'N A SMILE, MIND!
TART!
STRUMPET!

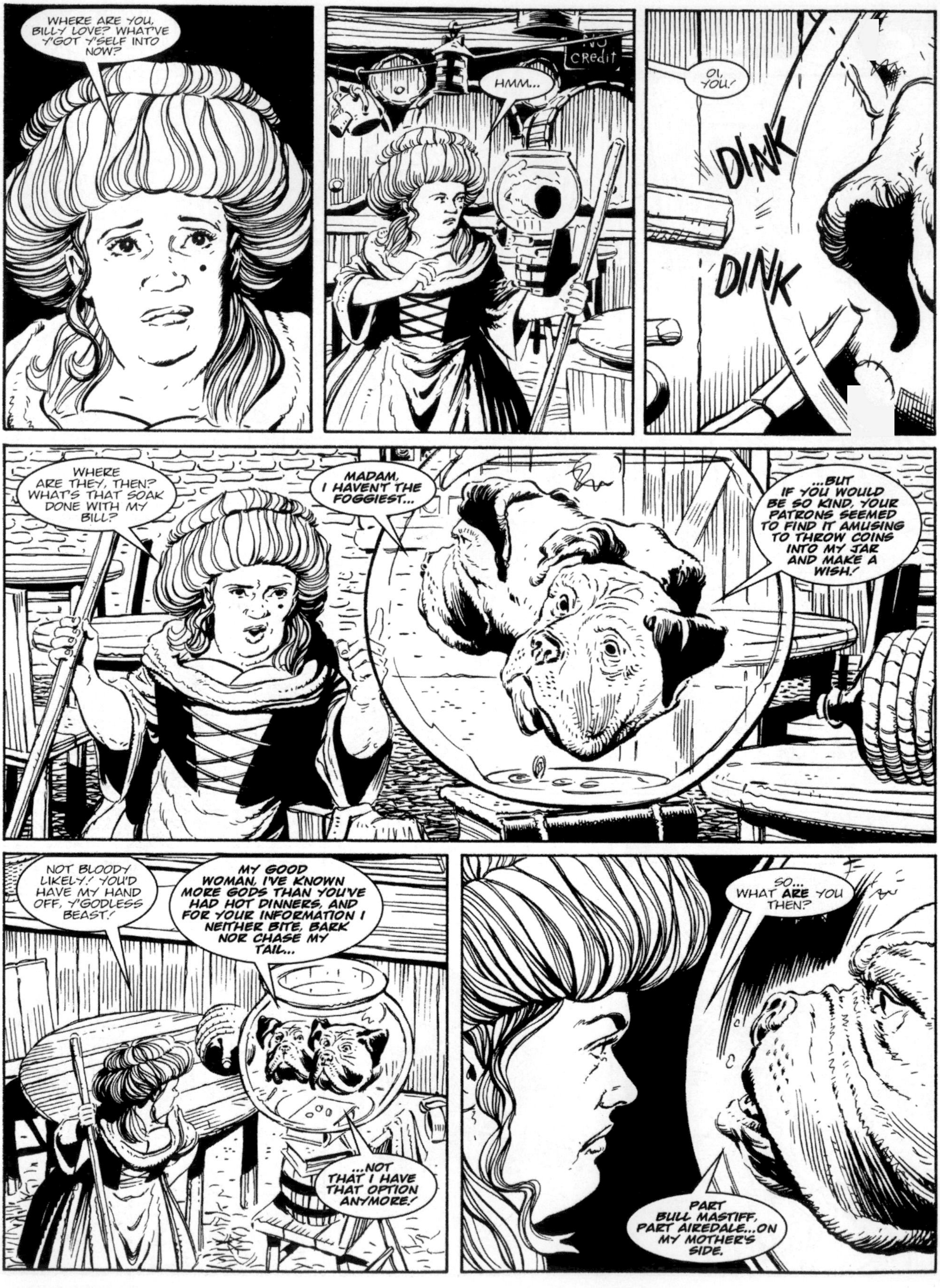
WHERE ARE YOU, BILLY LOVE? WHAT'VE Y'GOT Y'SELF INTO NOW?
NO Credit
HMM...
OI, YOU!
DINK
DINK
WHERE ARE THEY, THEN? WHAT'S THAT SOAK DONE WITH MY BILL?
MADAM, I HAVEN'T THE FOGGIEST...
...BUT IF YOU WOULD BE SO KIND, YOUR PATRONS SEEMED TO FIND IT AMUSING TO THROW COINS INTO MY JAR AND MAKE A WISH!
NOT BLOODY LIKELY! YOU'D HAVE MY HAND OFF, Y'GODLESS BEAST!
MY GOOD WOMAN, I'VE KNOWN MORE GODS THAN YOU'VE HAD HOT DINNERS, AND FOR YOUR INFORMATION I NEITHER BITE, BARK NOR CHASE MY TAIL...
...NOT THAT I HAVE THAT OPTION ANYMORE!
SO... WHAT ARE YOU THEN?
PART BULL MASTIFF, PART AIREDALE...ON MY MOTHER'S SIDE.

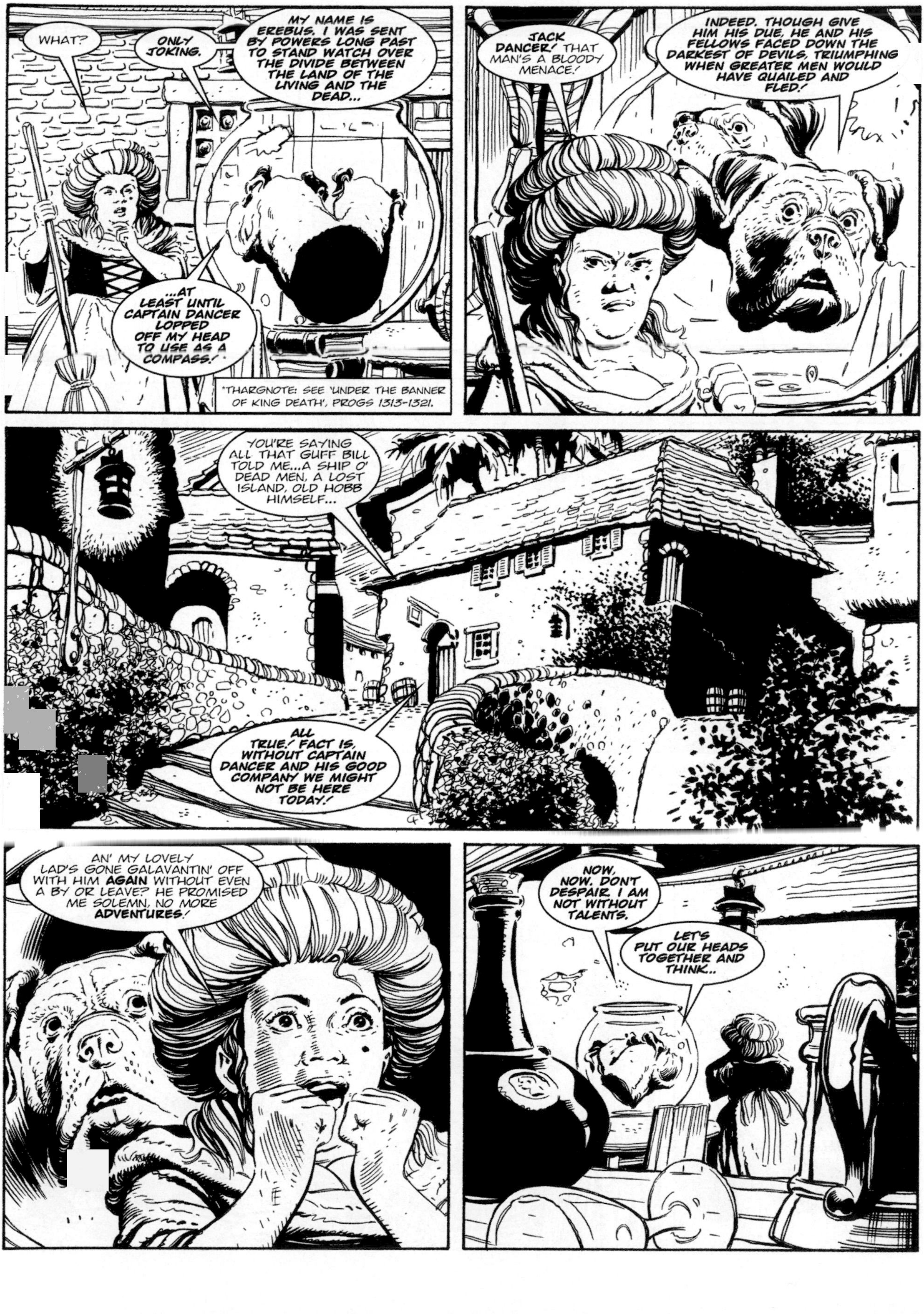
WHAT?
ONLY JOKING.
MY NAME IS EREBUS. I WAS SENT BY POWERS LONG PAST TO STAND WATCH OVER THE DIVIDE BETWEEN THE LAND OF THE LIVING AND THE DEAD...
...AT LEAST UNTIL CAPTAIN DANCER LOPPED OFF MY HEAD TO USE AS A COMPASS!
*THARGNOTE: SEE 'UNDER THE BANNER OF KING DEATH', PROGS 1313-1321.
JACK DANCER! THAT MAN'S A BLOODY MENACE!
INDEED. THOUGH GIVE HIM HIS DUE, HE AND HIS FELLOWS FACED DOWN THE DARKEST OF DEVILS, TRIUMPHING WHEN GREATER MEN WOULD HAVE QUAILED AND FLED!
YOU'RE SAYING ALL THAT GUFF BILL TOLD ME...A SHIP O' DEAD MEN, A LOST ISLAND, OLD HOBB HIMSELF...
ALL TRUE! FACT IS, WITHOUT CAPTAIN DANCER AND HIS GOOD COMPANY WE MIGHT NOT BE HERE TODAY!
AN' MY LOVELY LAD'S GONE GALAVANTIN' OFF WITH HIM AGAIN WITHOUT EVEN A BY OR LEAVE? HE PROMISED ME SOLEMN, NO MORE ADVENTURES!
NOW, NOW. DON'T DESPAIR. I AM NOT WITHOUT TALENTS.
LET'S PUT OUR HEADS TOGETHER AND THINK...

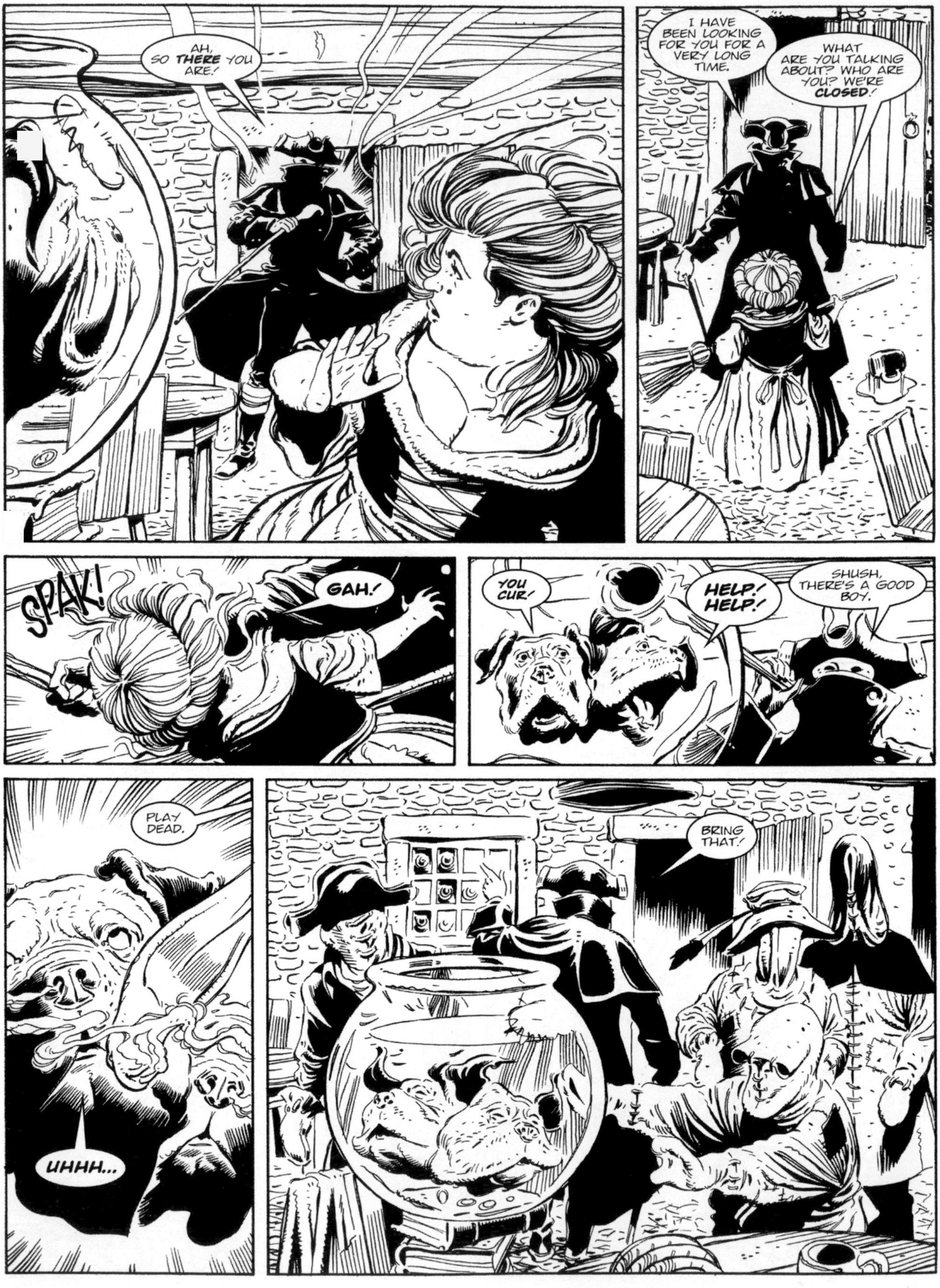
AH, SO THERE YOU ARE!
I HAVE BEEN LOOKING FOR YOU FOR A VERY LONG TIME.
WHAT ARE YOU TALKING ABOUT? WHO ARE YOU? WE'RE CLOSED!
SPAK!
GAH!
YOU CUR!
HELP! HELP!
SHUSH, THERE'S A GOOD BOY.
PLAY DEAD.
UHHH...
BRING THAT!

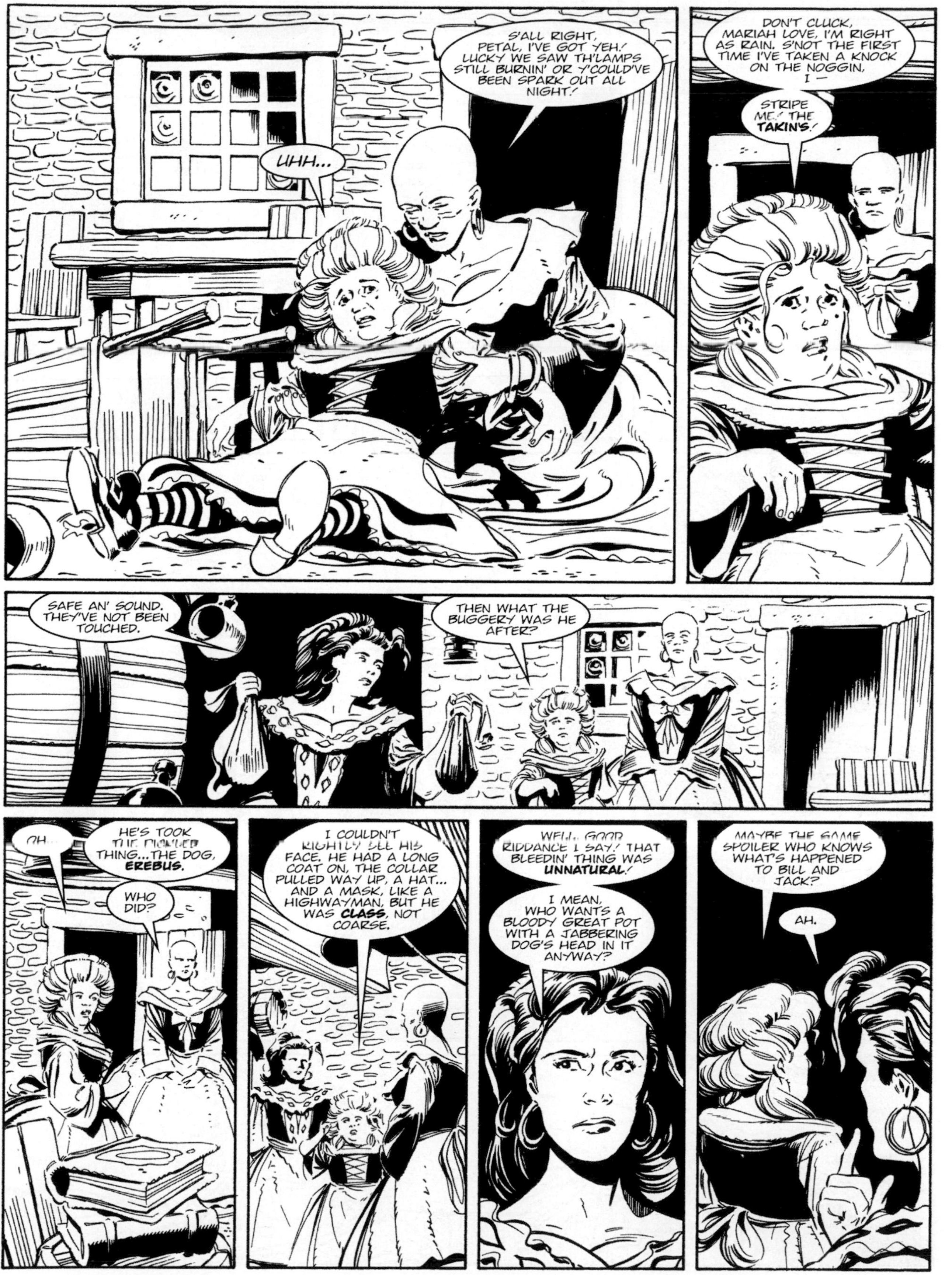
S'ALL RIGHT, PETAL, I'VE GOT YEH! LUCKY WE SAW TH'LAMPS STILL BURNIN' OR Y'COULD'VE BEEN SPARK OUT ALL NIGHT!
UHH...
DON'T CLUCK, MARIAH LOVE, I'M RIGHT AS RAIN. S'NOT THE FIRST TIME I'VE TAKEN A KNOCK ON THE NOGGIN, I —
STRIPE ME! THE TAKIN'S!
SAFE AN' SOUND. THEY'VE NOT BEEN TOUCHED.
THEN WHAT THE BUGGERY WAS HE AFTER?
OH...
HE'S TOOK THE PICKLED THING...THE DOG, EREBUS.
WHO DID?
I COULDN'T RIGHTLY SEE HIS FACE. HE HAD A LONG COAT ON, THE COLLAR PULLED WAY UP, A HAT... AND A MASK, LIKE A HIGHWAYMAN, BUT HE WAS CLASS, NOT COARSE.
WELL, GOOD RIDDANCE I SAY! THAT BLEEDIN' THING WAS UNNATURAL!
I MEAN, WHO WANTS A BLOODY GREAT POT WITH A JABBERING DOG'S HEAD IN IT ANYWAY?
MAYBE THE SAME SPOILER WHO KNOWS WHAT'S HAPPENED TO BILL AND JACK?
AH.

DOG'S 'EDS IN JARS, MEN IN MASKS WHO TAKE MONSTERS NOT MONEY, FOLK DISAPPEARIN' ...THERE'S DARK ARTS AT WORK 'ERE AN' NO MISTAKE!

WHO'D WE KNOW WHO DABBLES IN SUCH DOIN'S?

WHO'D WE DON'T? ORDINARILY I'D SAY **BLACK FRANCIS**. 'CEPT THERE'S BEEN NO SIGN OF HIM NOR HIS ISABELLA SINCE SHE UPPED AN' DUMPED JACK AFTER THEY GOT HOME.

AYE, HE MAY KEEP M'SHEETS SWEATY, BUT IT'S THAT MARDY COW HE'S STILL MOONIN' OVER! I RECKON SHE'S GOT HIM **BEWITCHED!**

NO, SWEETHEART, THAT'S JUST **MEN.** THEY ALWAYS WANT WHAT THEY CAN'T HAVE, AN' DON'T WANT WHAT THEY'VE **GOT!**

HANG ON A MO', THERE'S ALWAYS THAT NEW **FORTUNE TELLER** DOWN IN THE OLD TOWN —

"SHE MIGHT KNOW A THING OR TWO..."

Old Mother Delfi

Palms Read Fortunes Told

AHH, COME IN, M'DUCKS AN' DEARIOS. WHAT CAN I DO FOR THREE SUCH PRETTY CHICKS, EH?

SOMETHING WAS STOLEN FROM ME TONIGHT. SOMETHING... UNUSUAL.

I WAS HOPING YOU COULD GIVE US A **CLUE** WHERE T'FIND IT?

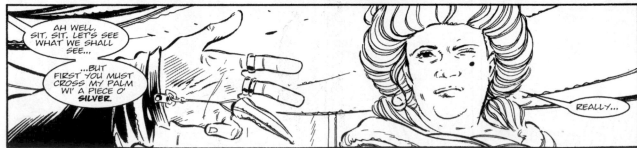

AH WELL, SIT, SIT. LET'S SEE WHAT WE SHALL SEE...

...BUT FIRST YOU MUST CROSS MY PALM WI' A PIECE O' **SILVER.**

REALLY...

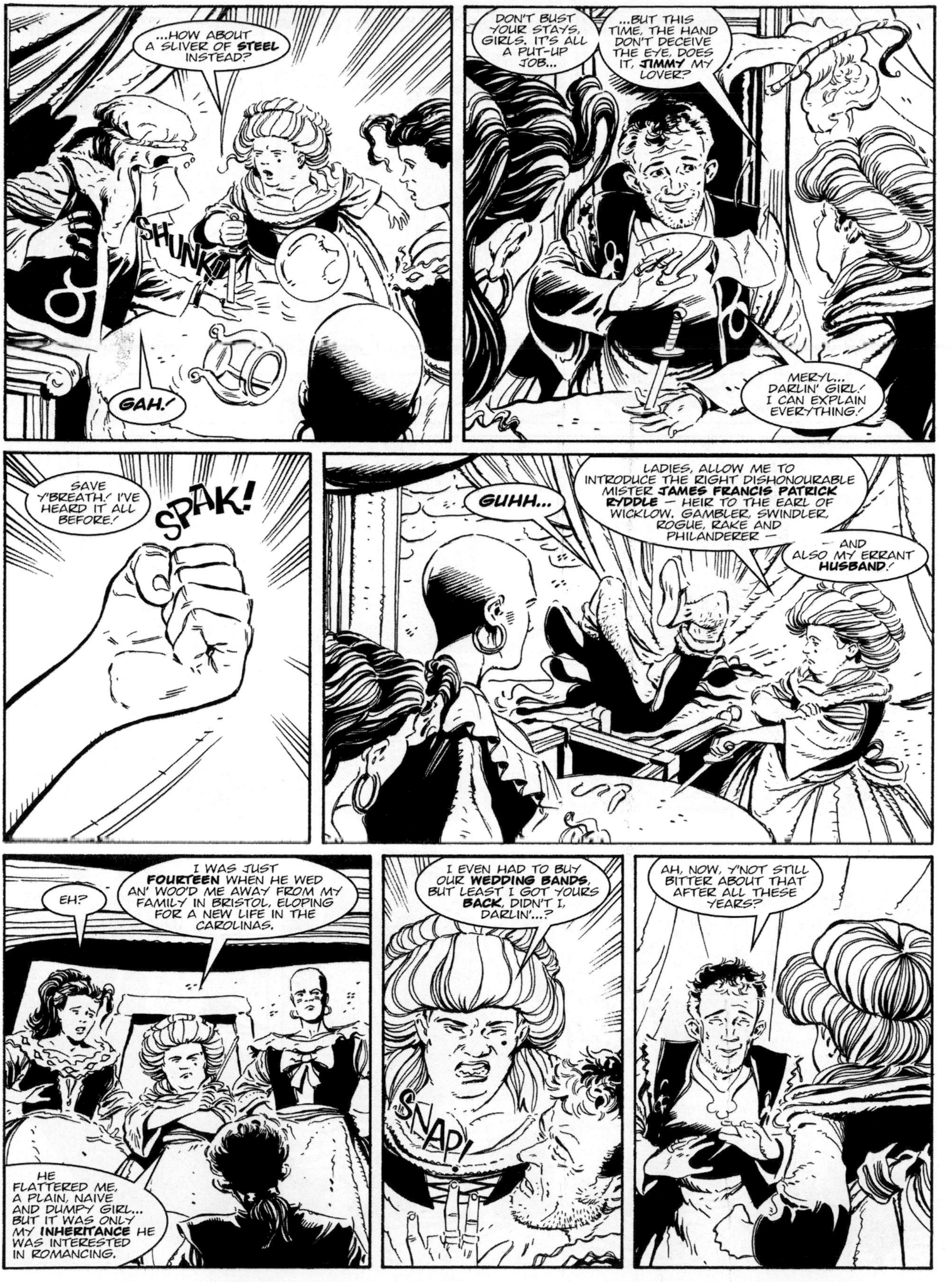
...HOW ABOUT A SLIVER OF STEEL INSTEAD?
SHUNK!
GAH!
DON'T BUST YOUR STAYS, GIRLS. IT'S ALL A PUT-UP JOB...
...BUT THIS TIME, THE HAND DON'T DECEIVE THE EYE, DOES IT, JIMMY MY LOVER?
MERYL... DARLIN' GIRL! I CAN EXPLAIN EVERYTHING!
SAVE Y'BREATH! I'VE HEARD IT ALL BEFORE!
SPAK!
GUHH...
LADIES, ALLOW ME TO INTRODUCE THE RIGHT DISHONOURABLE MISTER JAMES FRANCIS PATRICK RYDDLE — HEIR TO THE EARL OF WICKLOW, GAMBLER, SWINDLER, ROGUE, RAKE AND PHILANDERER —
— AND ALSO MY ERRANT HUSBAND!
EH?
I WAS JUST FOURTEEN WHEN HE WED AN' WOO'D ME AWAY FROM MY FAMILY IN BRISTOL, ELOPING FOR A NEW LIFE IN THE CAROLINAS.
HE FLATTERED ME, A PLAIN, NAIVE AND DUMPY GIRL... BUT IT WAS ONLY MY INHERITANCE HE WAS INTERESTED IN ROMANCING.
I EVEN HAD TO BUY OUR WEDDING BANDS, BUT LEAST I GOT YOURS BACK, DIDN'T I, DARLIN'...?
SNAP!
AH, NOW, Y'NOT STILL BITTER ABOUT THAT AFTER ALL THESE YEARS?

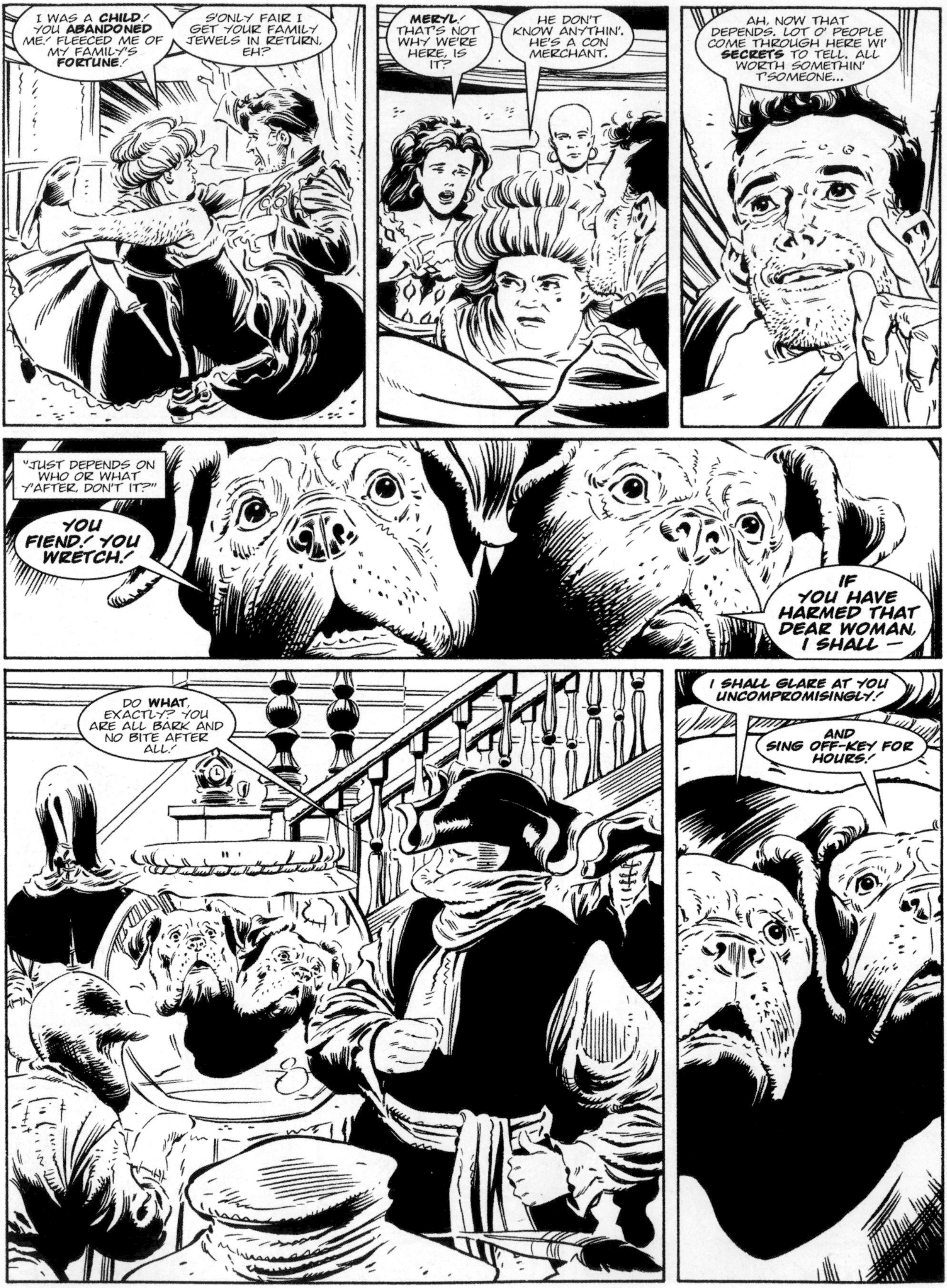
I WAS A CHILD! YOU ABANDONED ME! FLEECED ME OF MY FAMILY'S FORTUNE!
S'ONLY FAIR I GET YOUR FAMILY JEWELS IN RETURN, EH?
MERYL! THAT'S NOT WHY WE'RE HERE, IS IT?
HE DON'T KNOW ANYTHIN'. HE'S A CON MERCHANT.
AH, NOW THAT DEPENDS. LOT O' PEOPLE COME THROUGH HERE WI' SECRETS TO TELL. ALL WORTH SOMETHIN' T'SOMEONE...
"JUST DEPENDS ON WHO OR WHAT Y'AFTER, DON'T IT?"
YOU FIEND! YOU WRETCH!
IF YOU HAVE HARMED THAT DEAR WOMAN, I SHALL –
DO WHAT, EXACTLY? YOU ARE ALL BARK AND NO BITE AFTER ALL!
I SHALL GLARE AT YOU UNCOMPROMISINGLY!
AND SING OFF-KEY FOR HOURS!

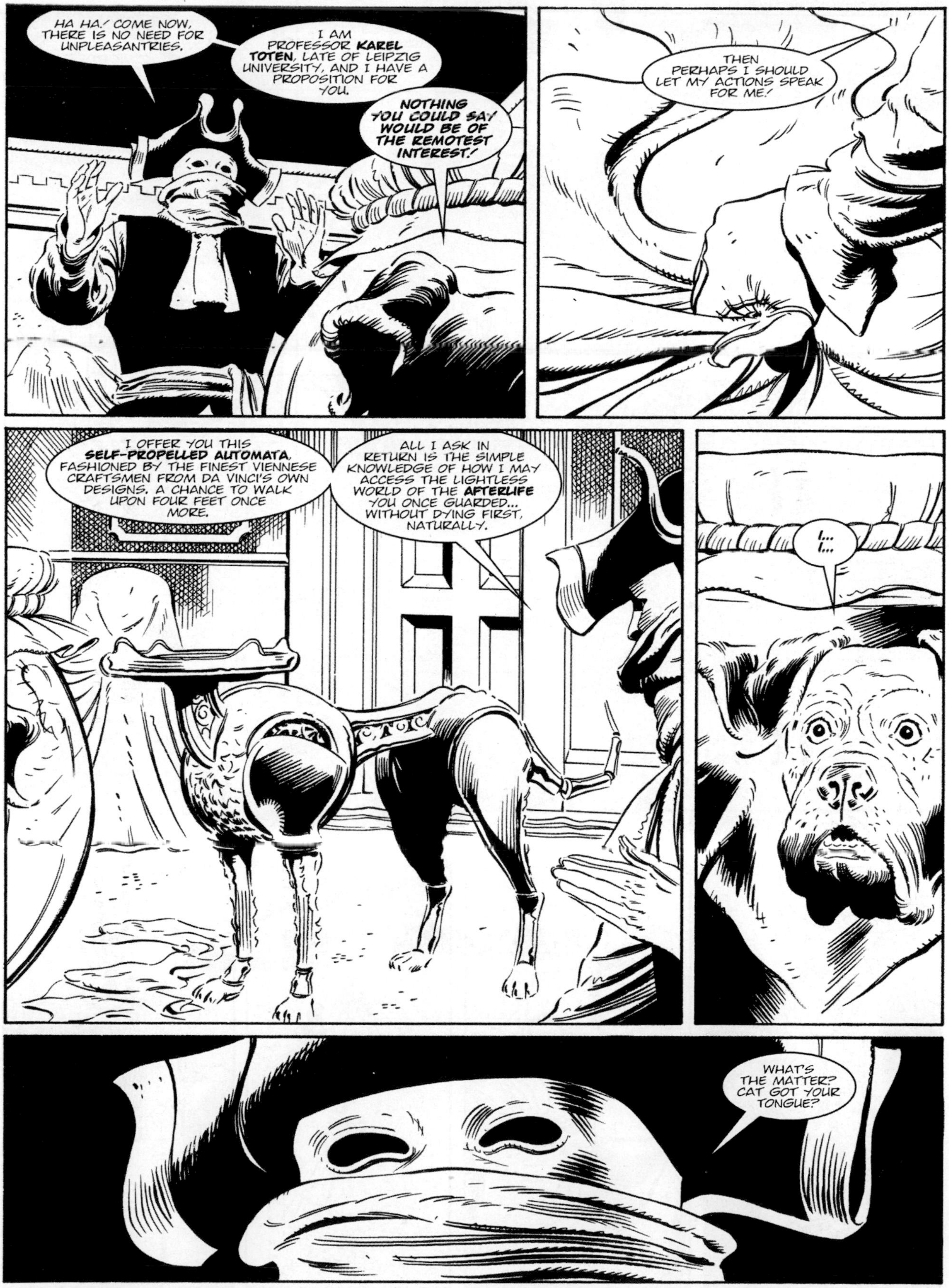
HA HA! COME NOW, THERE IS NO NEED FOR UNPLEASANTRIES.
I AM PROFESSOR KAREL TOTEN, LATE OF LEIPZIG UNIVERSITY, AND I HAVE A PROPOSITION FOR YOU.
NOTHING YOU COULD SAY WOULD BE OF THE REMOTEST INTEREST!
THEN PERHAPS I SHOULD LET MY ACTIONS SPEAK FOR ME!
I OFFER YOU THIS SELF-PROPELLED AUTOMATA, FASHIONED BY THE FINEST VIENNESE CRAFTSMEN FROM DA VINCI'S OWN DESIGNS. A CHANCE TO WALK UPON FOUR FEET ONCE MORE.
ALL I ASK IN RETURN IS THE SIMPLE KNOWLEDGE OF HOW I MAY ACCESS THE LIGHTLESS WORLD OF THE AFTERLIFE YOU ONCE GUARDED... WITHOUT DYING FIRST, NATURALLY.
I... I...
WHAT'S THE MATTER? CAT GOT YOUR TONGUE?

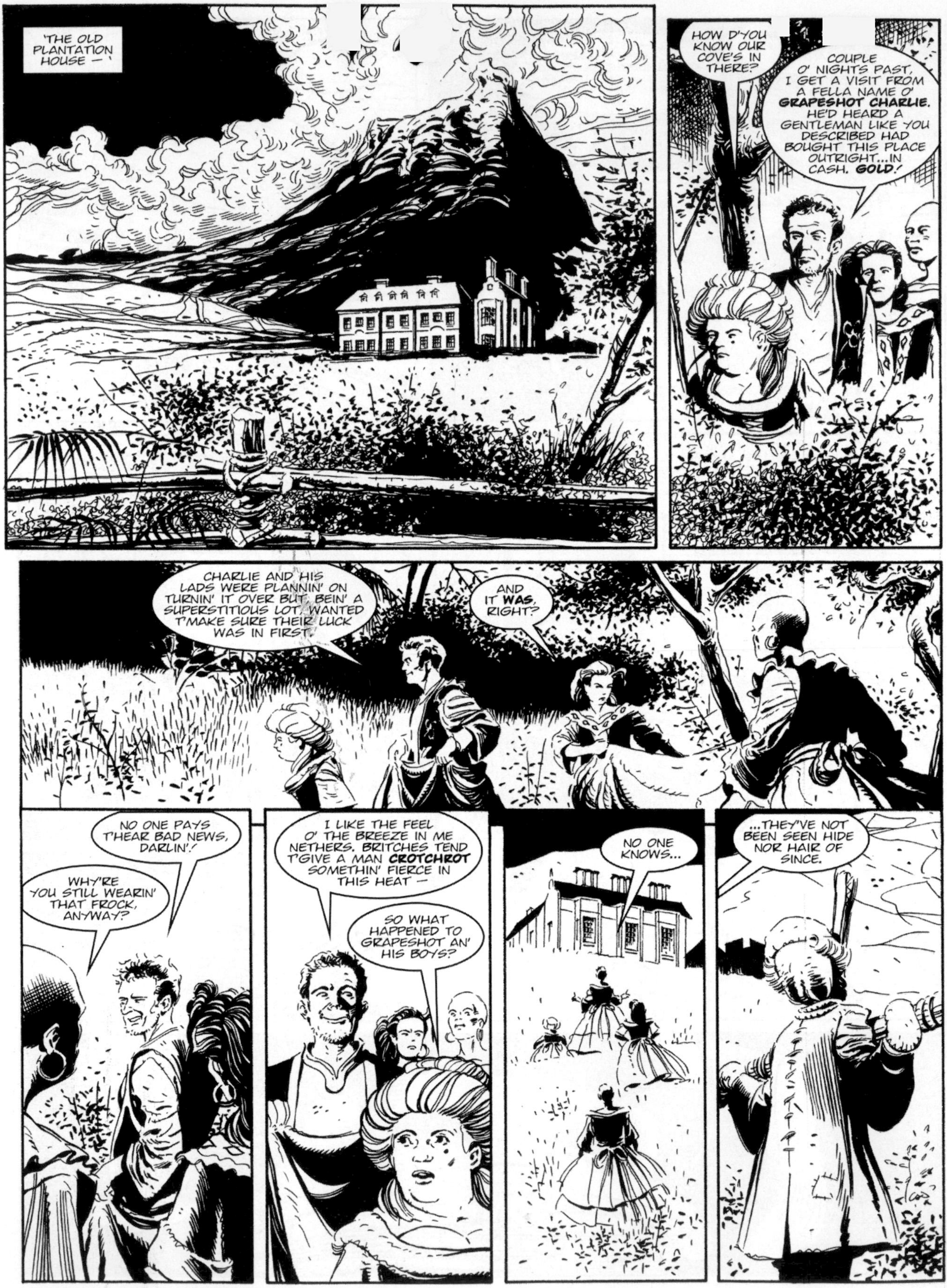
'THE OLD PLANTATION HOUSE —'
HOW D'YOU KNOW OUR COVE'S IN THERE?
COUPLE O' NIGHTS PAST, I GET A VISIT FROM A FELLA NAME O' **GRAPESHOT CHARLIE**. HE'D HEARD A GENTLEMAN LIKE YOU DESCRIBED HAD BOUGHT THIS PLACE OUTRIGHT...IN CASH. **GOLD**!
CHARLIE AND HIS LADS WERE PLANNIN' ON TURNIN' IT OVER BUT, BEIN' A SUPERSTITIOUS LOT, WANTED T'MAKE SURE THEIR LUCK WAS IN FIRST.
AND IT **WAS**, RIGHT?
NO ONE PAYS T'HEAR BAD NEWS, DARLIN'.
WHY'RE YOU STILL WEARIN' THAT FROCK, ANYWAY?
I LIKE THE FEEL O' THE BREEZE IN ME NETHERS. BRITCHES TEND T'GIVE A MAN **CROTCHROT** SOMETHIN' FIERCE IN THIS HEAT —
SO WHAT HAPPENED TO GRAPESHOT AN' HIS BOYS?
NO ONE KNOWS...
...THEY'VE NOT BEEN SEEN HIDE NOR HAIR OF SINCE.

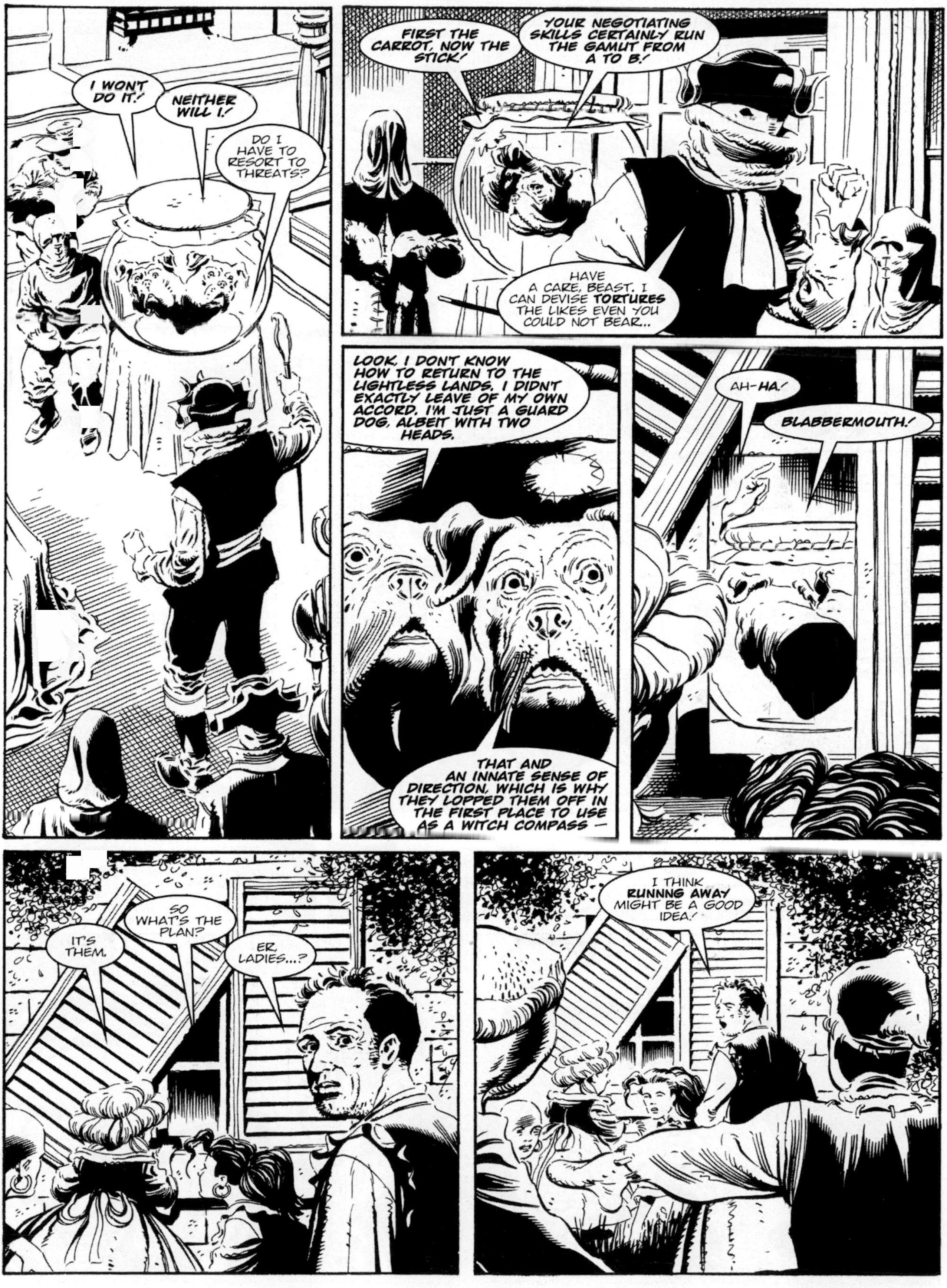
I WON'T DO IT!
NEITHER WILL I!
DO I HAVE TO RESORT TO THREATS?
FIRST THE CARROT, NOW THE STICK!
YOUR NEGOTIATING SKILLS CERTAINLY RUN THE GAMUT FROM A TO B!
HAVE A CARE, BEAST. I CAN DEVISE TORTURES THE LIKES EVEN YOU COULD NOT BEAR...
LOOK, I DON'T KNOW HOW TO RETURN TO THE LIGHTLESS LANDS. I DIDN'T EXACTLY LEAVE OF MY OWN ACCORD. I'M JUST A GUARD DOG, ALBEIT WITH TWO HEADS.
THAT AND AN INNATE SENSE OF DIRECTION, WHICH IS WHY THEY LOPPED THEM OFF IN THE FIRST PLACE TO USE AS A WITCH COMPASS —
AH-HA!
BLABBERMOUTH!
IT'S THEM.
SO WHAT'S THE PLAN?
ER, LADIES...?
I THINK RUNNNG AWAY MIGHT BE A GOOD IDEA!

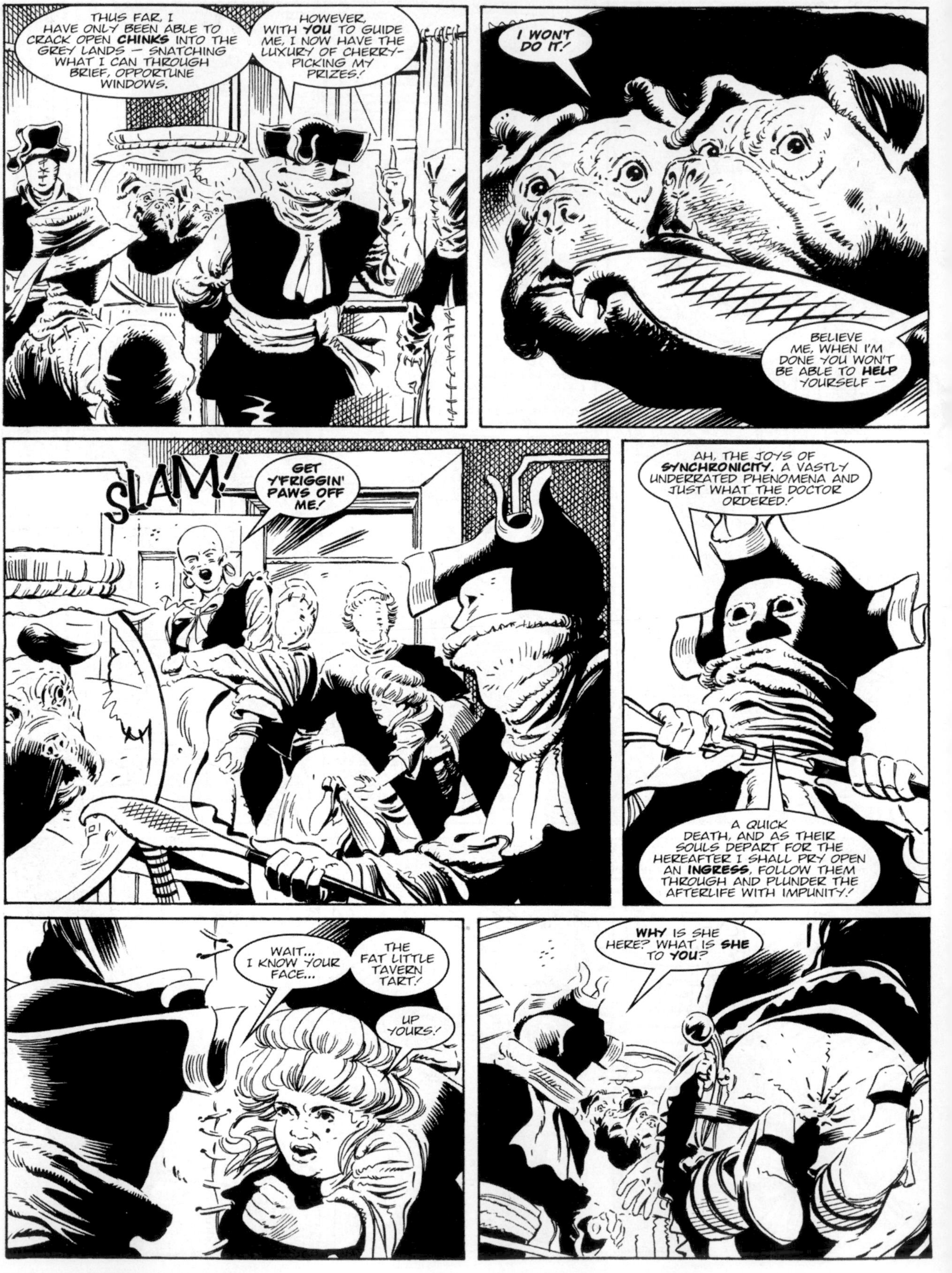
THUS FAR, I HAVE ONLY BEEN ABLE TO CRACK OPEN CHINKS INTO THE GREY LANDS — SNATCHING WHAT I CAN THROUGH BRIEF, OPPORTUNE WINDOWS.
HOWEVER, WITH YOU TO GUIDE ME, I NOW HAVE THE LUXURY OF CHERRY-PICKING MY PRIZES!
I WON'T DO IT!
BELIEVE ME, WHEN I'M DONE YOU WON'T BE ABLE TO HELP YOURSELF —
SLAM!
GET Y'FRIGGIN' PAWS OFF ME!
AH, THE JOYS OF SYNCHRONICITY. A VASTLY UNDERRATED PHENOMENA AND JUST WHAT THE DOCTOR ORDERED!
A QUICK DEATH, AND AS THEIR SOULS DEPART FOR THE HEREAFTER I SHALL PRY OPEN AN INGRESS, FOLLOW THEM THROUGH AND PLUNDER THE AFTERLIFE WITH IMPUNITY!
WAIT... I KNOW YOUR FACE...
THE FAT LITTLE TAVERN TART!
UP YOURS!
WHY IS SHE HERE? WHAT IS SHE TO YOU?

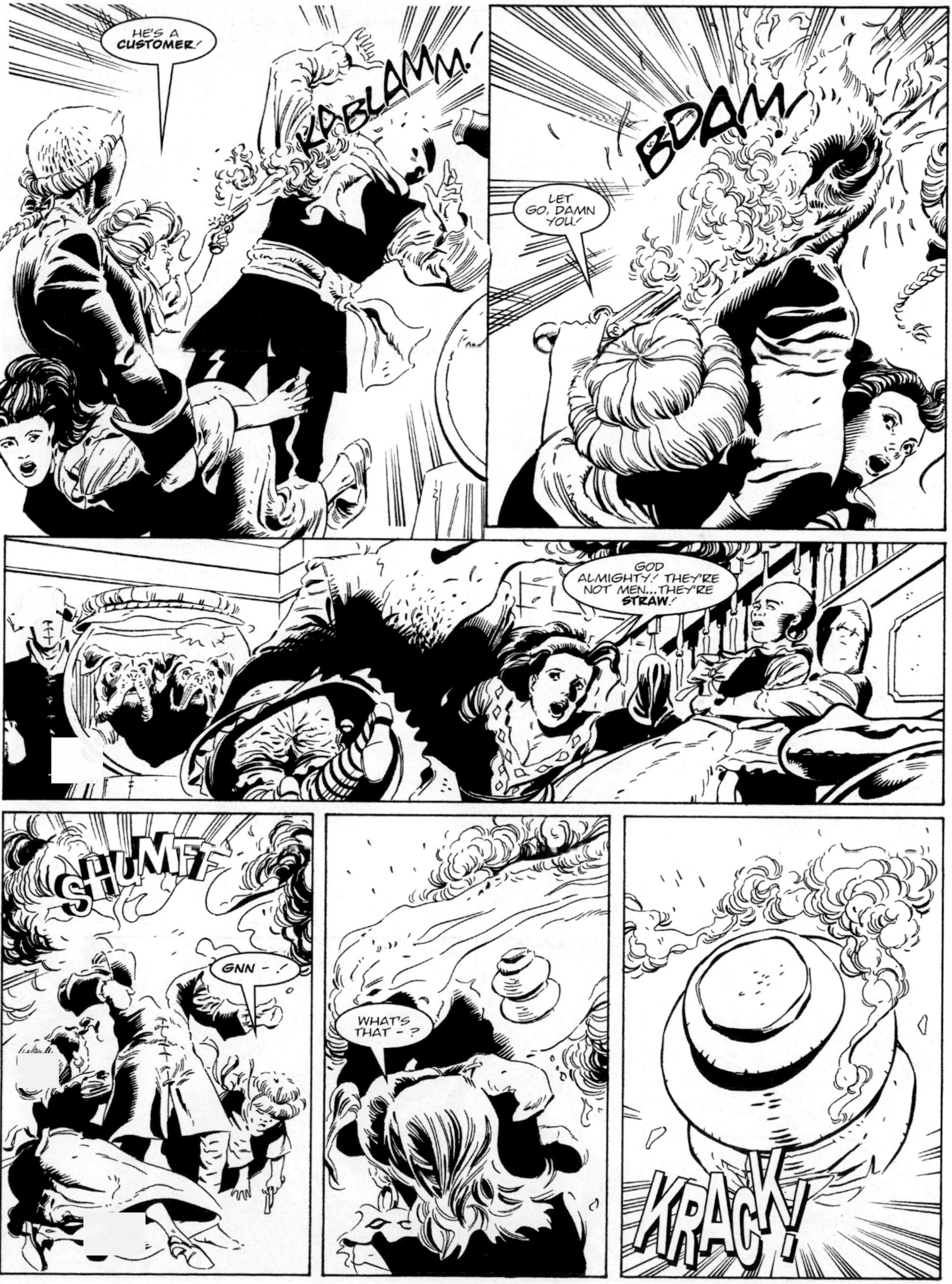
HE'S A CUSTOMER!
KA-BLAMM!
BDAM!
LET GO, DAMN YOU!
GOD ALMIGHTY! THEY'RE NOT MEN...THEY'RE STRAW!
SHUMFF
GNN --!
WHAT'S THAT --?
KRACK!

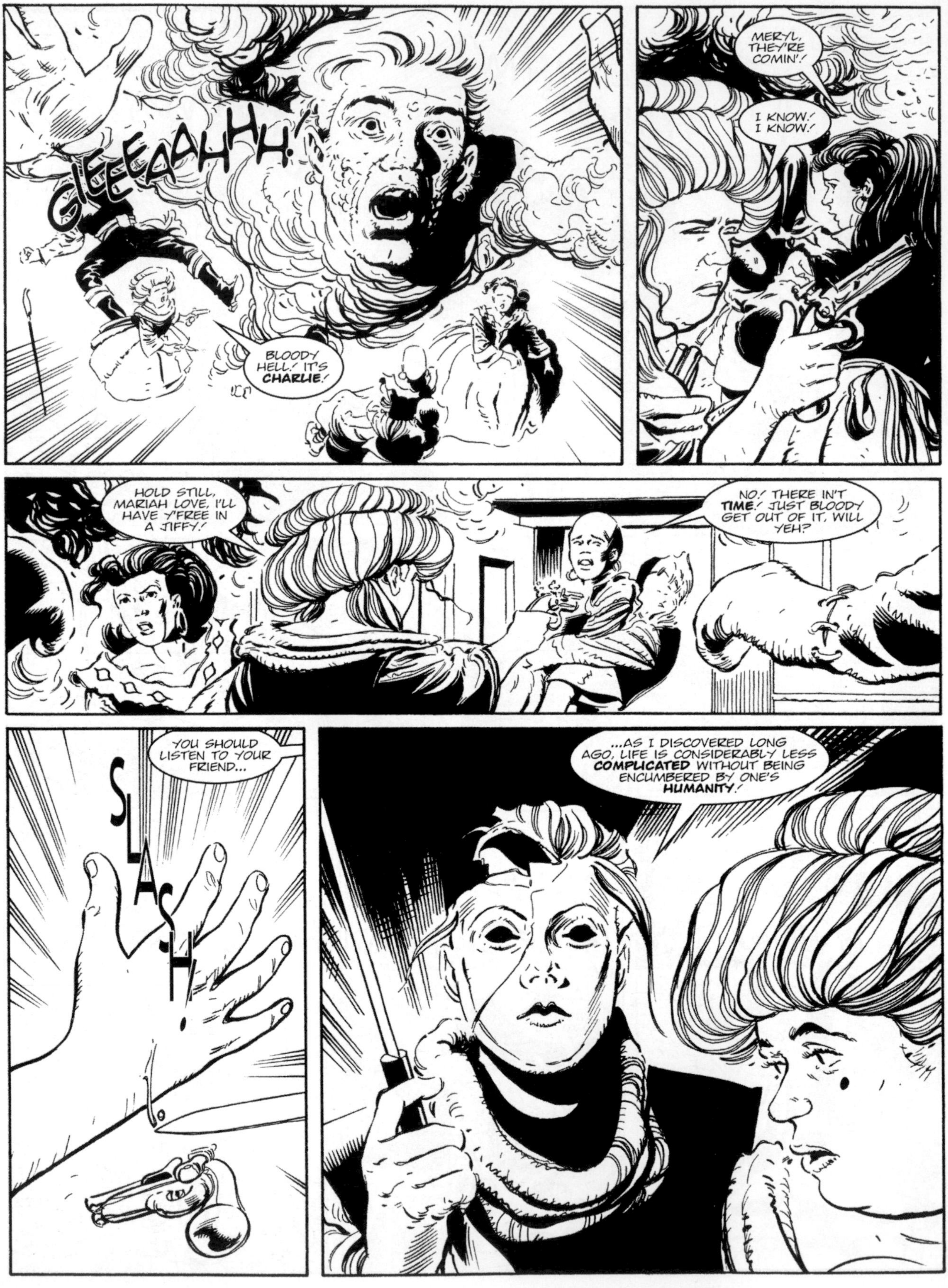
GIEEEAAHHH!
BLOODY HELL! IT'S **CHARLIE**!
MERYL, THEY'RE COMIN'!
I KNOW! I KNOW!
HOLD STILL, MARIAH LOVE, I'LL HAVE Y'FREE IN A JIFFY!
NO! THERE IN'T **TIME**! JUST BLOODY GET OUT OF IT, WILL YEH?
YOU SHOULD LISTEN TO YOUR FRIEND...
SLASH!
...AS I DISCOVERED LONG AGO, LIFE IS CONSIDERABLY LESS **COMPLICATED** WITHOUT BEING ENCUMBERED BY ONE'S **HUMANITY**!

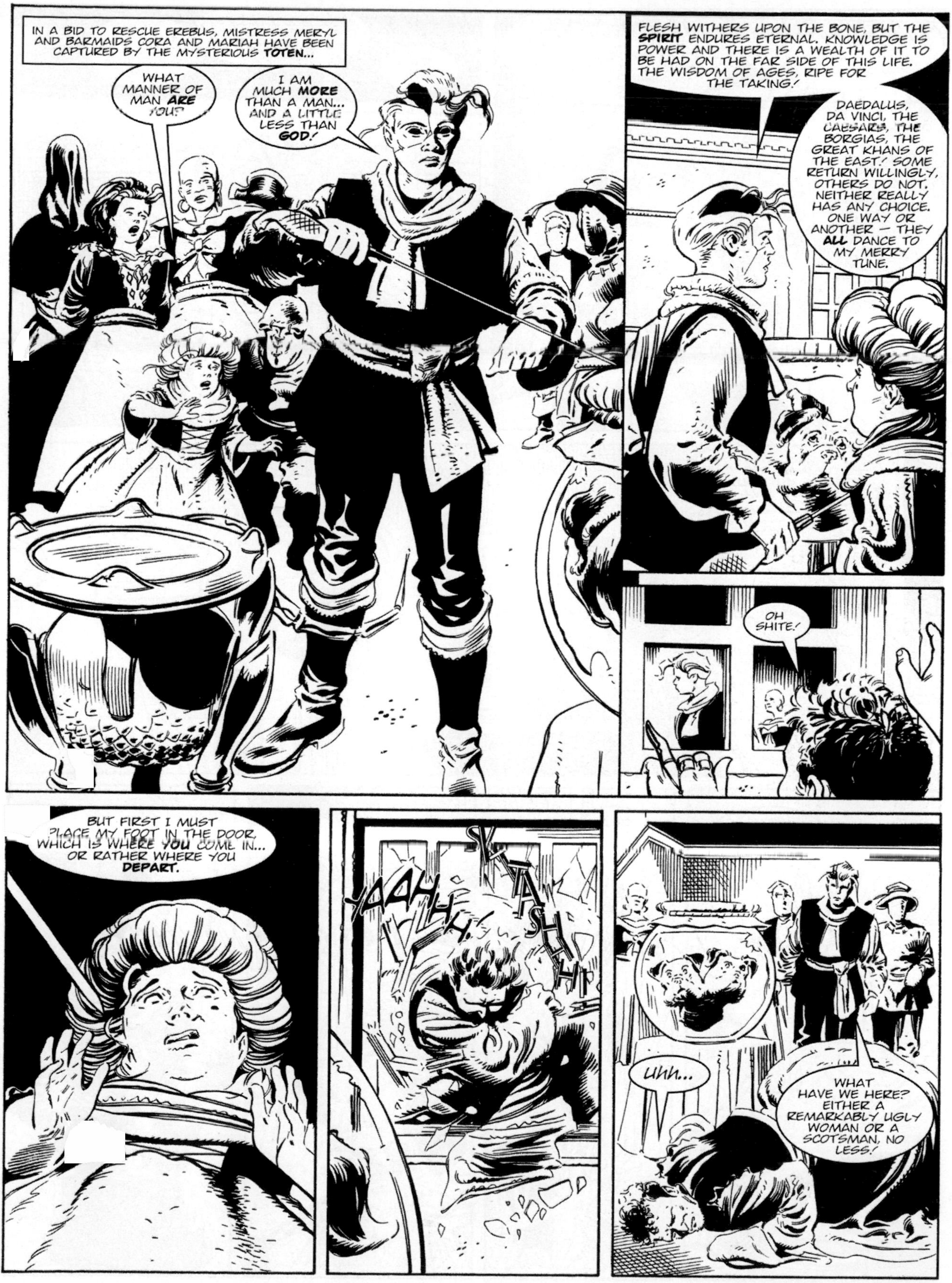

IN A BID TO RESCUE EREBUS, MISTRESS MERYL AND BARMAIDS CORA AND MARIAH HAVE BEEN CAPTURED BY THE MYSTERIOUS TOTEN...
WHAT MANNER OF MAN ARE YOU?
I AM MUCH MORE THAN A MAN... AND A LITTLE LESS THAN GOD!
FLESH WITHERS UPON THE BONE, BUT THE SPIRIT ENDURES ETERNAL. KNOWLEDGE IS POWER AND THERE IS A WEALTH OF IT TO BE HAD ON THE FAR SIDE OF THIS LIFE. THE WISDOM OF AGES, RIPE FOR THE TAKING!
DAEDALUS, DA VINCI, THE CAESARS, THE BORGIAS, THE GREAT KHANS OF THE EAST! SOME RETURN WILLINGLY, OTHERS DO NOT. NEITHER REALLY HAS ANY CHOICE. ONE WAY OR ANOTHER — THEY ALL DANCE TO MY MERRY TUNE.
OH SHITE!
BUT FIRST I MUST PLACE MY FOOT IN THE DOOR, WHICH IS WHERE YOU COME IN... OR RATHER WHERE YOU DEPART.
YAAHHH!
SKTASHH!
UHH...
WHAT HAVE WE HERE? EITHER A REMARKABLY UGLY WOMAN OR A SCOTSMAN, NO LESS!

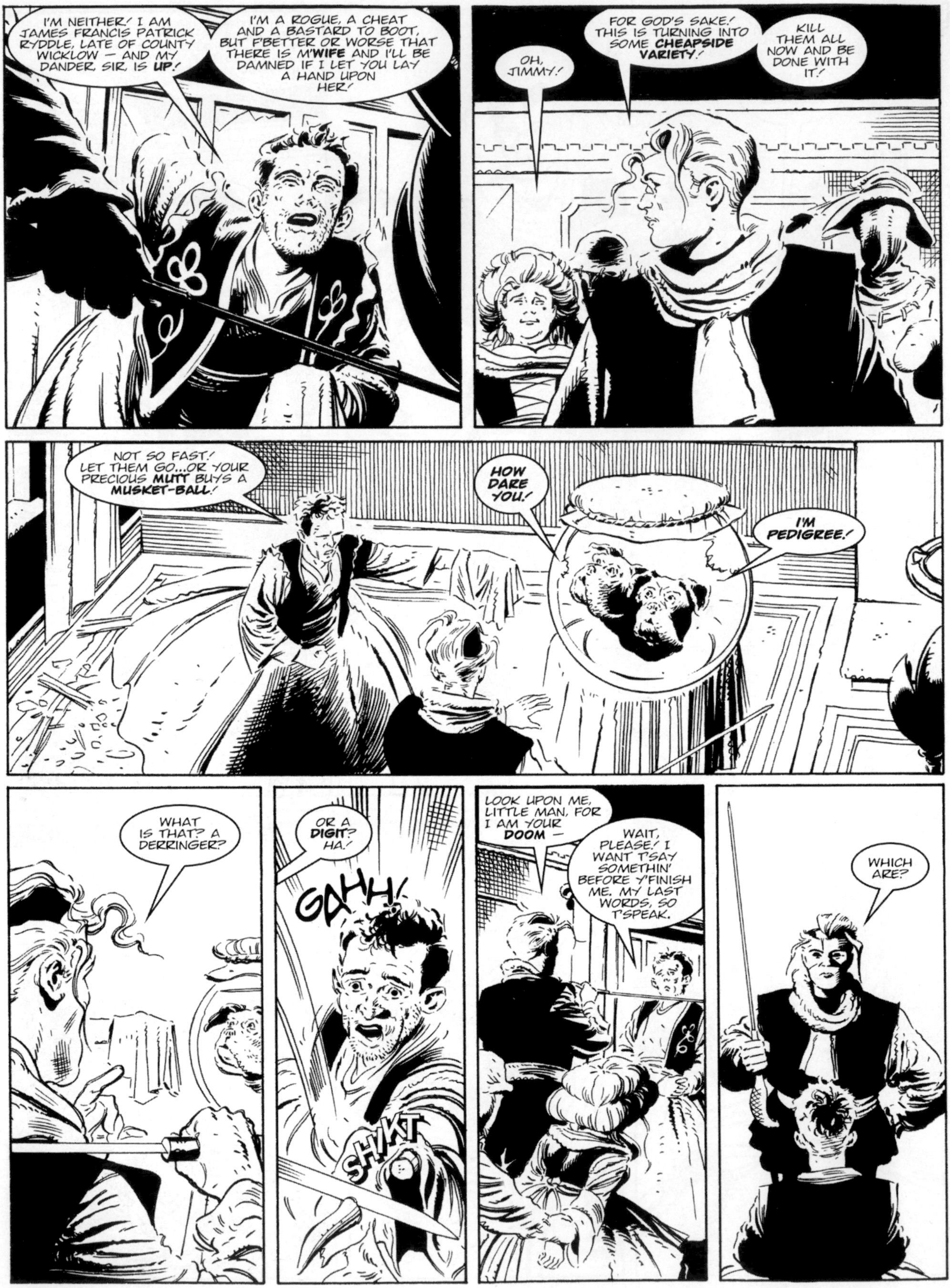
I'M NEITHER! I AM JAMES FRANCIS PATRICK RYDDLE, LATE OF COUNTY WICKLOW — AND MY DANDER, SIR, IS UP!
I'M A ROGUE, A CHEAT AND A BASTARD TO BOOT, BUT F'BETTER OR WORSE THAT THERE IS M'WIFE AND I'LL BE DAMNED IF I LET YOU LAY A HAND UPON HER!
OH, JIMMY!
FOR GOD'S SAKE! THIS IS TURNING INTO SOME CHEAPSIDE VARIETY!
KILL THEM ALL NOW AND BE DONE WITH IT!
NOT SO FAST! LET THEM GO...OR YOUR PRECIOUS MUTT BUYS A MUSKET-BALL!
HOW DARE YOU!
I'M PEDIGREE!
WHAT IS THAT? A DERRINGER?
OR A DIGIT? HA!
GAHH!
SHIKT
LOOK UPON ME, LITTLE MAN, FOR I AM YOUR DOOM —
WAIT, PLEASE! I WANT T'SAY SOMETHIN' BEFORE Y'FINISH ME. MY LAST WORDS, SO T'SPEAK.
WHICH ARE?

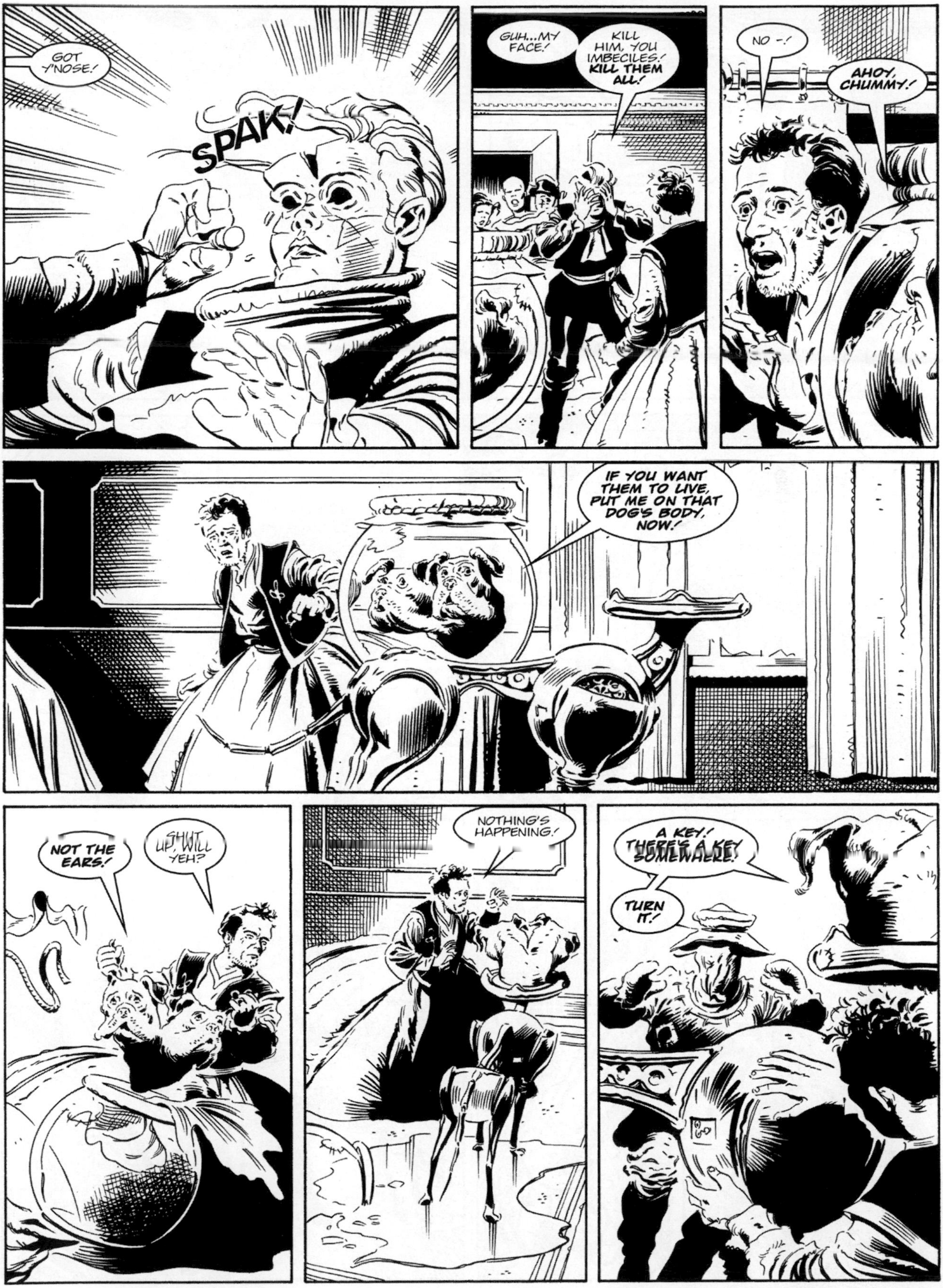
GOT Y'NOSE!
SPAK!
GUH... MY FACE!
KILL HIM, YOU IMBECILES! KILL THEM ALL!
NO -!
AHOY, CHUMMY!
IF YOU WANT THEM TO LIVE, PUT ME ON THAT DOG'S BODY, NOW!
NOT THE EARS!
SHUT UP, WILL YEH?
NOTHING'S HAPPENING!
A KEY! THERE'S A KEY SOMEWHERE!
TURN IT!

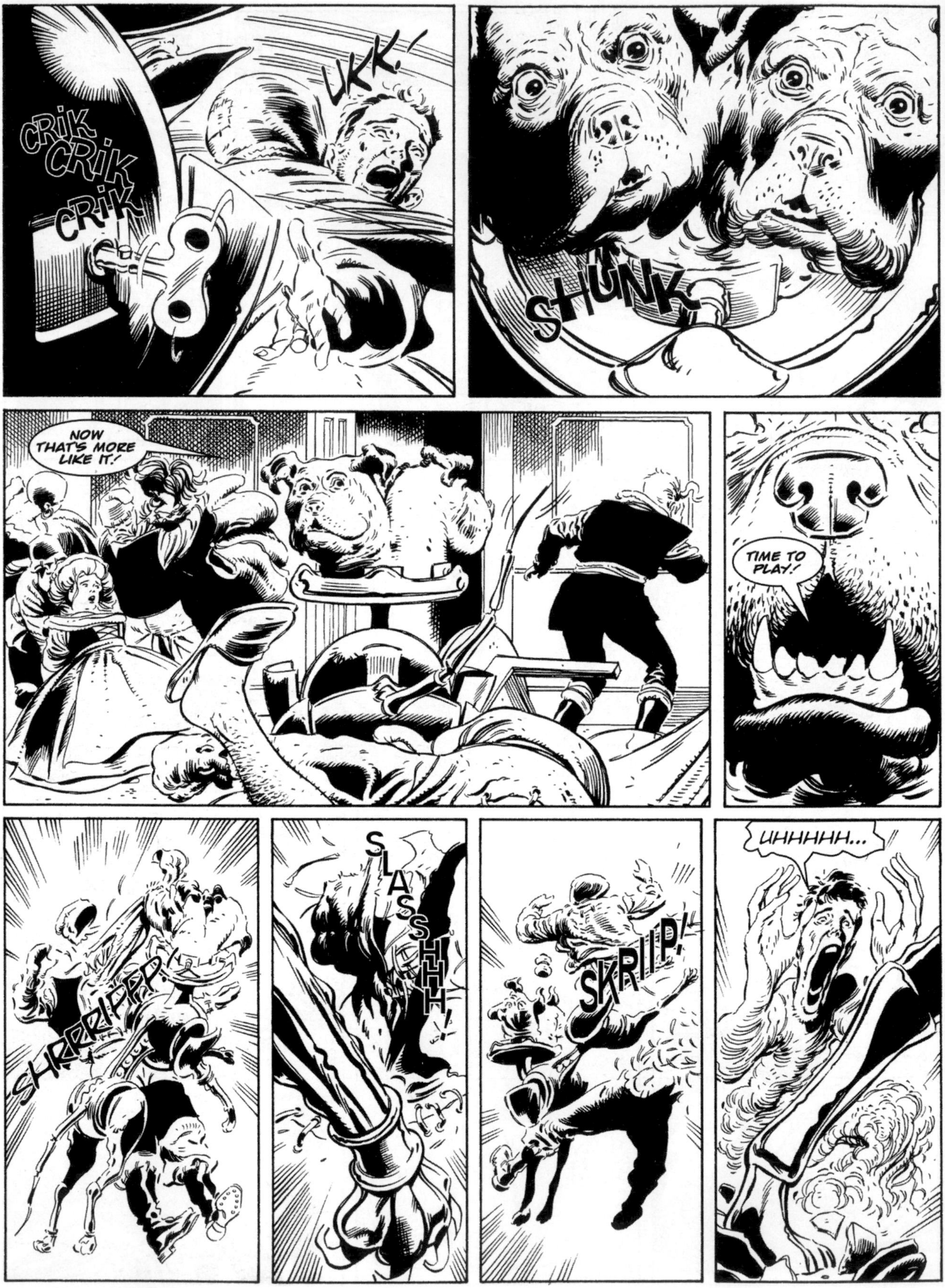
CRIK CRIK CRIK
UKK!
SHUNK
NOW THAT'S MORE LIKE IT!
TIME TO PLAY!
SHRRIPPP!
SLASSHHH!
SKRIIP!
UHHHHH...

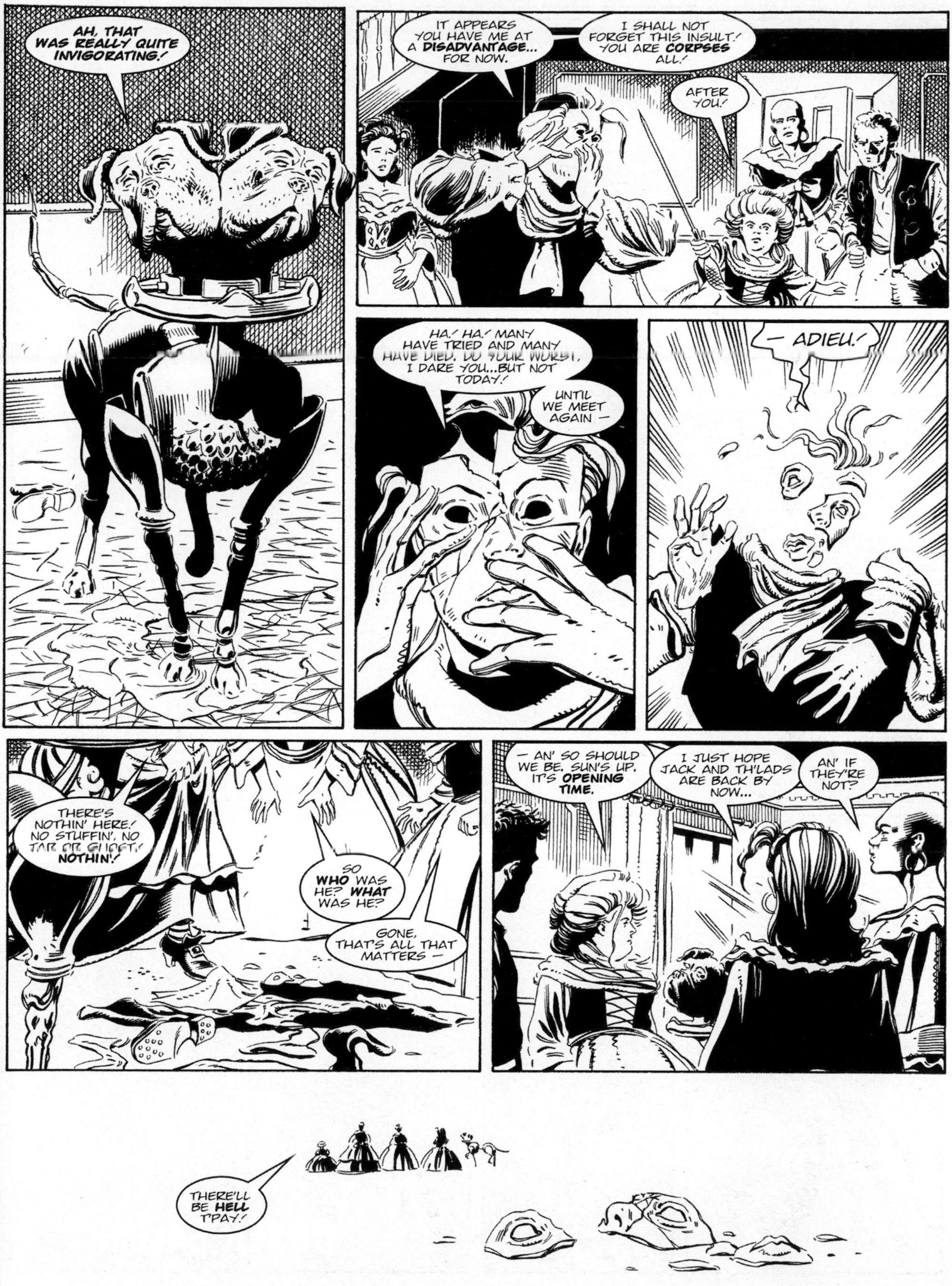
AH, THAT WAS REALLY QUITE INVIGORATING!
IT APPEARS YOU HAVE ME AT A DISADVANTAGE... FOR NOW.
I SHALL NOT FORGET THIS INSULT! YOU ARE CORPSES ALL!
AFTER YOU!
HA! HA! MANY HAVE TRIED AND MANY HAVE DIED. DO YOUR WORST, I DARE YOU...BUT NOT TODAY!
UNTIL WE MEET AGAIN —
— ADIEU!
THERE'S NOTHIN' HERE! NO STUFFIN', NO JAR OR GHOST! NOTHIN'!
SO WHO WAS HE? WHAT WAS HE?
GONE, THAT'S ALL THAT MATTERS —
— AN' SO SHOULD WE BE. SUN'S UP. IT'S OPENING TIME.
I JUST HOPE JACK AND TH'LADS ARE BACK BY NOW...
AN' IF THEY'RE NOT?
THERE'LL BE HELL T'PAY!

COVER GALLERY

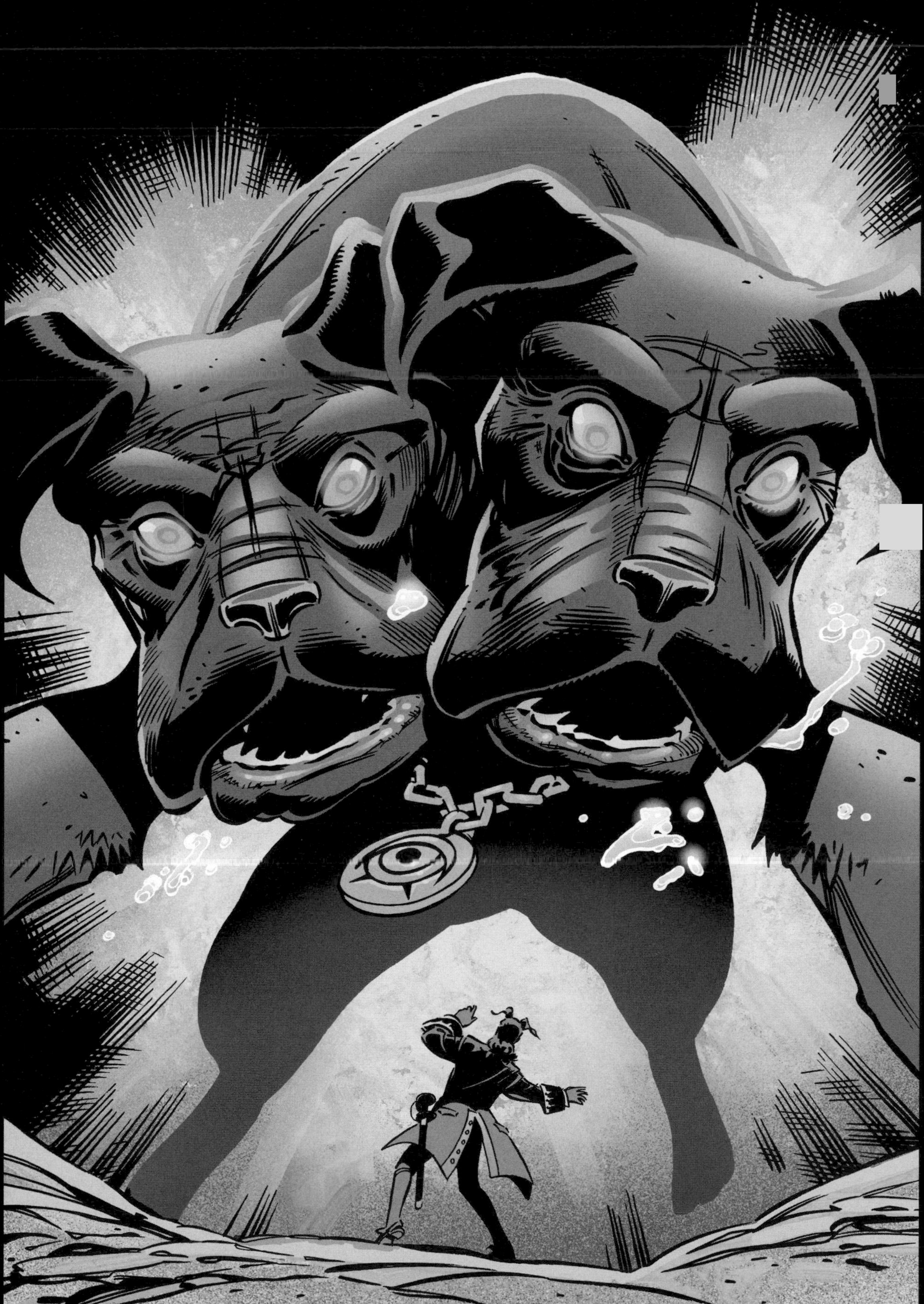

*2000 AD* Prog 1317: Cover by **Steve Yeowell**

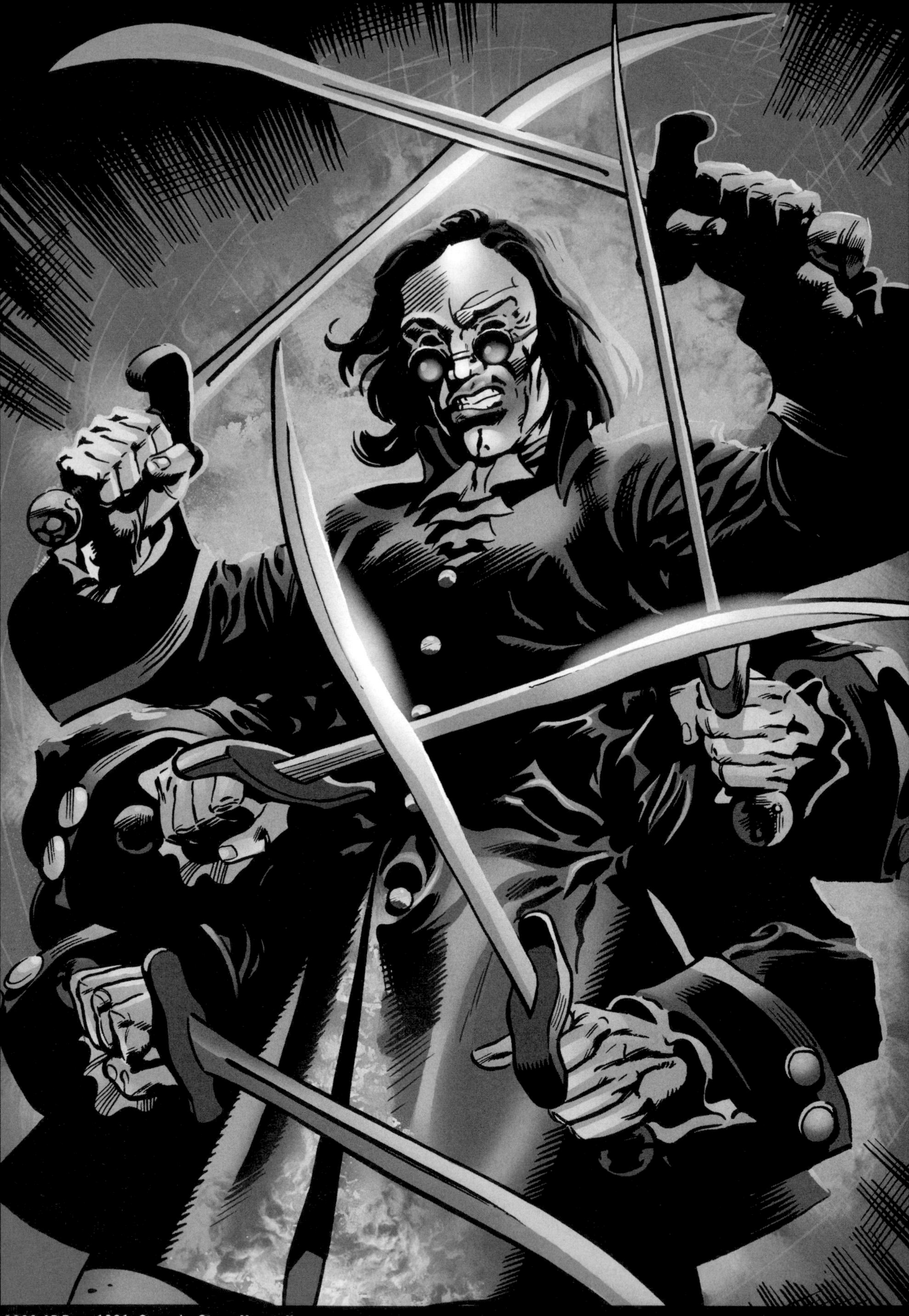

*2000 AD* Prog 1321: Cover by **Steve Yeowell**

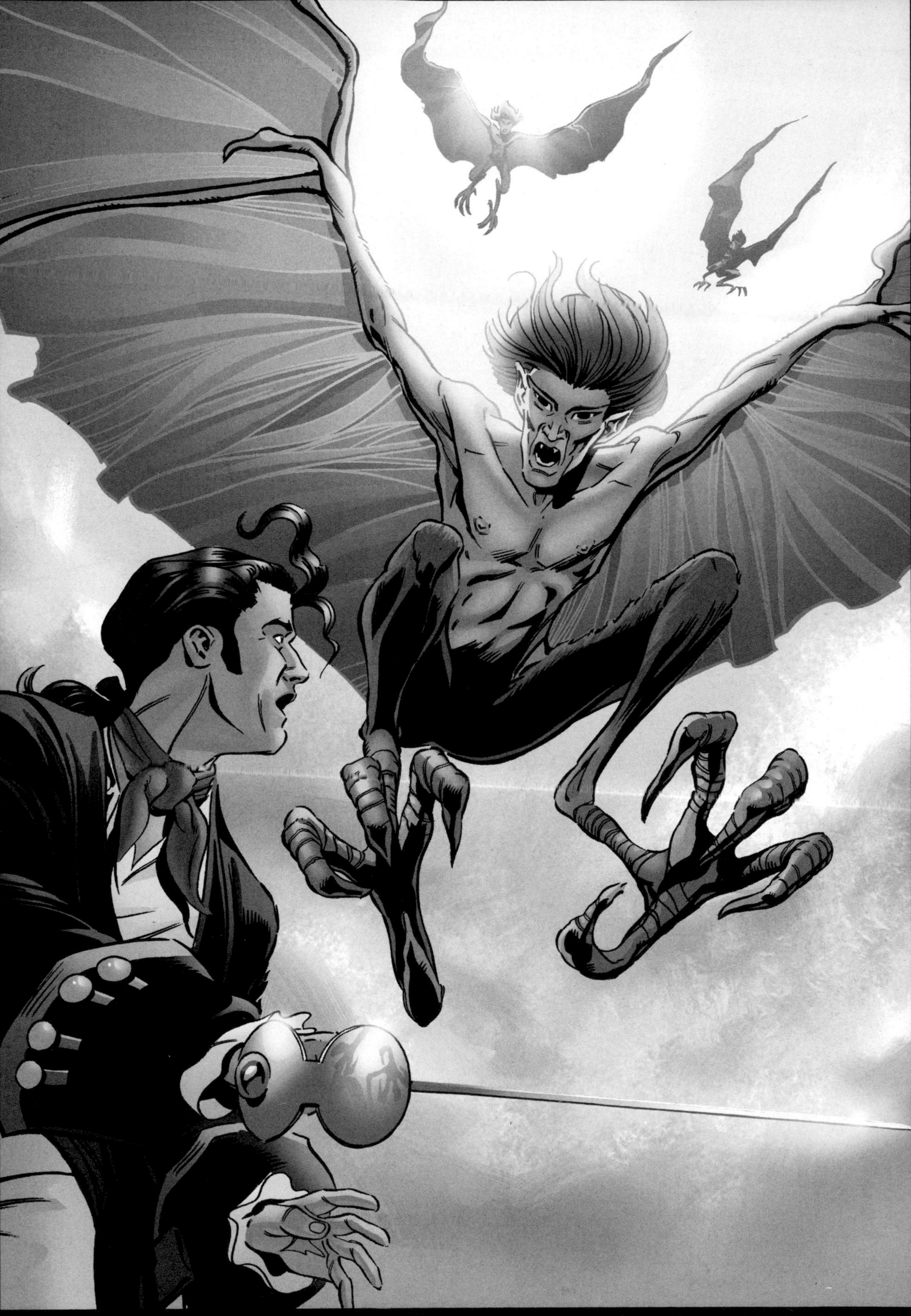

*2000 AD* Prog 1373: Cover by **Steve Yeowell**

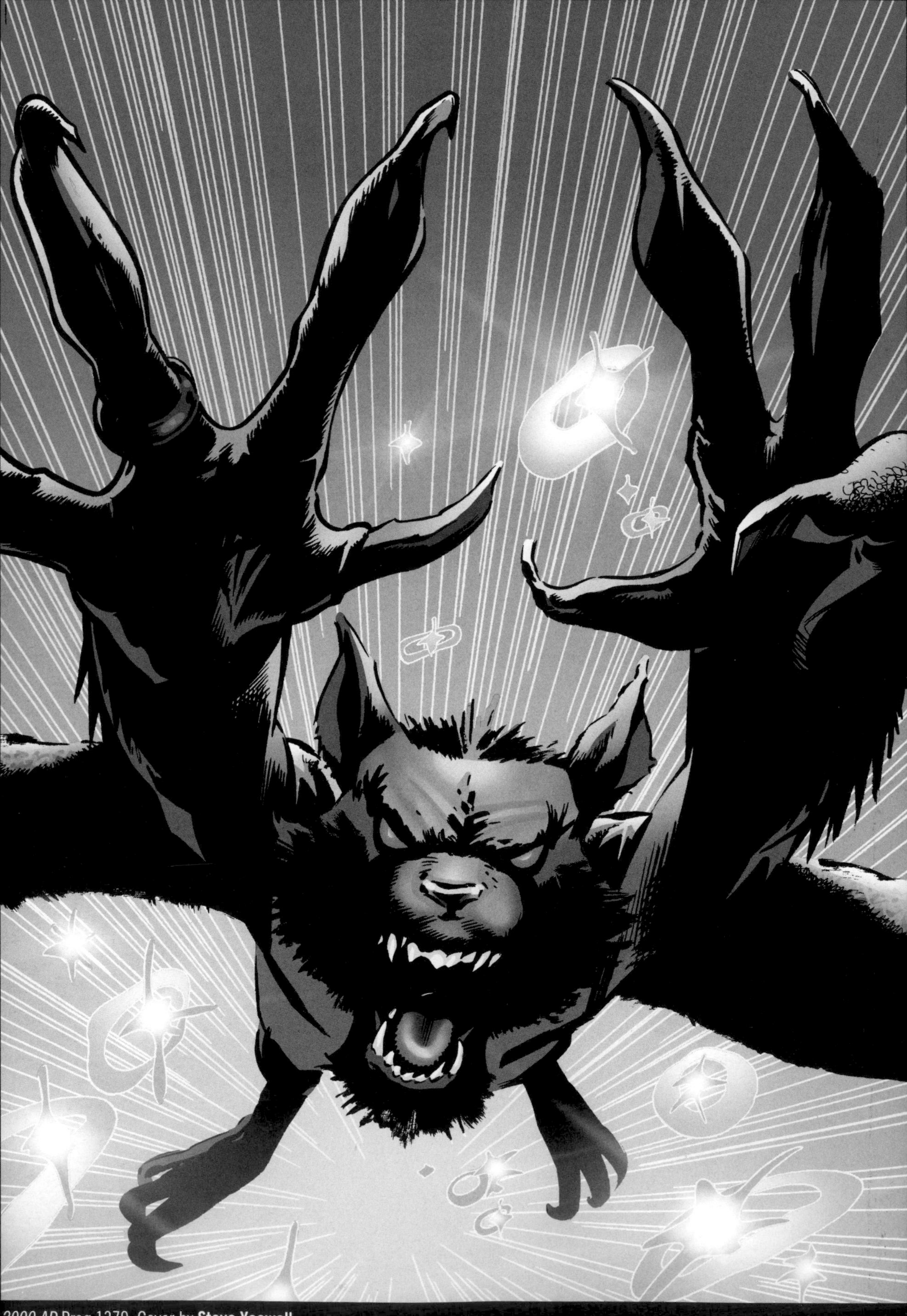

*2000 AD* Prog 1379: Cover by **Steve Yeowell**

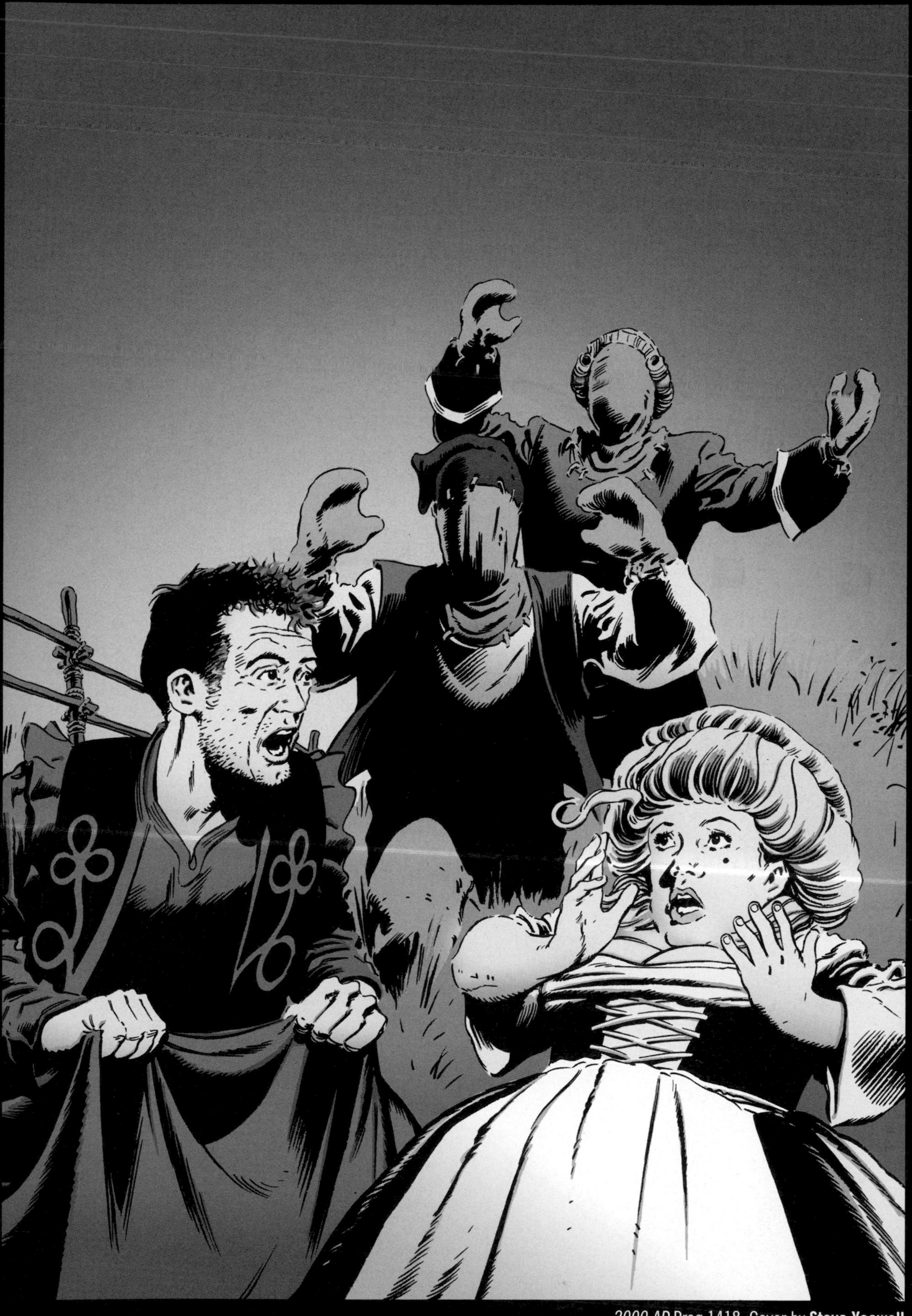

*2000 AD* Prog 1418: Cover by **Steve Yeowell**

BONUS MATERIAL

# ORIGINAL PITCH

*The following text details the original pitch for The Red Seas: Under The Banner of King Death.*

**The Red Seas**
*By Ian Edginton and Steve Yeowell*

A different spin on the sword and sorcery deal and not a hairy arsed barbarian in sight!

1760, the Caribbean. Deranged Oxford Don, Orlando Doyle captains a galleon crewed by zombies and guided by an occult compass, comprising the severed head of two headed dog floating in a bucket of vinegar. Doyle is hunting down pages from The Albrecht Tome; a legendary book from the dark ages purporting to list the nine million names of God. In magic, names hold power and to know the names of the Almighty would give one dominion over him as well as the ability to undo and remake Creation however you wanted.

The Byronesque Doyle seeks the book because, decades earlier, he sold his soul to one of the Devil's Dukes, Xipe Toltec "Our Lord the Flayed One", in exchange for ultimate enlightenment. However Doyle sought to trick the demon and using his occult talents, manufactured himself a new soul from remnants he had torn from his hapless victims. All went to plan except Doyle hadn't counted on being able to feel the terrible torment his original soul was enduring in Hell.

To retrieve it and cease his agonies (that had by now driven him insane), Doyle made another deal with the Duke, to gather the pages of the Tome and deliver them to him. To this end Doyle has travelled to the ends of the earth amassing the pages until there is just one left - amongst the cargo of a Spanish Man of War bound for Spain from South America which is where our story begins.

Unfortunately for Doyle, he's beaten to the punch by Captain Jack Dancer; late of his Majesty's Royal Navy now buccaneer and master of the ship The Red Wench. Along with his crew (including such luminaries as Swinging Billy and Ginger Tom) they plunder the galleon and take their booty back to one of the several pirate communities that flourished around the West Indies at that time.

Not to be thwarted, Doyle gives chase. Anchoring some way off shore, Doyle waits until nightfall before ordering his undead crew to jump over the side. They then walk along the seabed and wade ashore killing everyone they find. They take the page and Dancer's girlfriend, the Native American shamaness Isabella, back to Doyle.

Dancer and his much-depleted crew give chase and follow Doyle to the ruins of a lost city on a remote island where he plans to summon Xipe Toltec and make good on their deal. He requires a human sacrifice to summon the Demon Duke, which is why he took Isabella.

The two crews clash. Dancer faces off against Doyle and rescues Isabella but Doyle kills one of Dancer's men and summons the Duke.

The Demon appears and demands the book. Distracted, Doyle is killed by Dancer. The demon offers to strike a deal with Dancer but suddenly the Devil himself appears. It transpires that the Duke was going to use the book to remake not only Creation but also Heaven and Hell, setting himself up as the new boss of both. Needless to say Big Red doesn't like the idea of being deposed and eviscerates the Duke.

Now the Devil wants the book and he intends to take it. Using her own powers, Isabella destroys the Tome. Fiat Lux - Holy light pouring out and driving the Devil back to Hell. Dancer and his crew return home to lick their wounds and get pissed. Meanwhile in a huge glass vat somewhere in Oxford, a life sized homunculus of Orlando Doyle has almost finished growing. Don't forget, the Demon Duke gifted him with ultimate enlightenment, and knowledge is power. Doyle may have been thwarted this time but he's made ample provision for his return.

But that's another story…

# SERIES TWO PITCH

*The following text details the original pitch for The Red Seas: Twilight Of The Idols.*

**The Red Seas: Twilight of the Idols**
*By Ian Edginton and Steve Yeowell.*

**1)** Since we last saw him, Jack Dancer's fortunes have nosedived. Most of his crew are dead, he's broke, has no ship and his love, Isabella has returned to her father to find out exactly what happened to her mother in the light of the Devil's revelations.

Dancer spends his days getting drunk in the Jolly Cripple, pouring out his woes to Erebus. Even his crew have deserted him as Jim, Julius and Tom are no longer around. Billy's helping his missus, Mistress Meryl run the JC and keeping a weather eye on the downwardly mobile Dancer.

Things take a turn for the worse when, staggering home, he's grabbed by British Naval Intelligence. They already have Jim, Julius and Tom. Billy comes to his aid but he's overpowered too. They're to be shipped back to Blighty in irons where the gallows awaits them.

However, they're rescued by the enigmatic Arab, Abdul Alhazred who had been looking to hire Dancer anyway. With no time to loose and several Navy clippers breathing down their neck, they escape in Alhazred's ship – a galley made of bronze.

As the clippers cannons find their range, Alhazred pulls a lever and an array of cannon mechanically appear on deck. They let rip with blasts of flaming Greek fire, forcing the now blazing clippers to retreat.

Dancer and the boys are amazed at this, especially since there's no sign of a crew on the bronze ship. Alhazred shows them below, where rows of mechanical men full of cogs and gears work the oars. This ship is built from a sign of the great Greek inventor Daedelus, the father of the ill-fated Icarus. It is just one of the many marvels Alhazred has at his command.

What they are all unaware of though, is that they're being watched via telescope by a wily, cunning and stunningly beautiful adventurer. Her name is Sarita and she is the great-granddaughter of Sinbad the sailor.

**2)** Alhazred is servant of a collector of ancient artefacts.

His masters greatest goal is to locate a mysterious flying island which is believed to be the last resting place of many artefacts of myth and legend.

Now that the Gods of antiquity have left this plain of existence, these relics have been collected on the island but there's a catch. The island is a magical thing in itself and only appears in certain places at certain times.

Billy and the others scoff at this, they're use to sailors yarns but this is too incredible until Dancer declares he saw it once. As a young Midshipman in the Royal Navy, he was coming off last watch when he caught the briefest of glimpses of it in the dawn sea fog. Alhazred says this is why he wants Dancer. The island has only ever revealed itself to a handful of people. To locate the island Alhazred needs someone who can see it, which is where Dancer comes in.

The boys are unsure, they've had a nasty brush with things magical before, however Dancer agrees to go. He has no ties and nothing left to loose. Besides, he's always wanted to solve the mystery of the island ever since he first saw it. He also wryly adds that since the British Navy has undoubtedly put a price on all their heads, where are they going to go? Alhazred offers them a huge cache of gold and jewels if they'll sign on with him. With little to loose, they decide to sign on.

Alhazred needs their help in obtaining the two halves of a map that shows the ever changing location of the island. Unfortunately they are going to be difficult to obtain but he's sure men of their talents and resolve will find a way.

Their first port of call is a remote Greek island, now worn away by the sea, it's little more than a spire of rock with a temple on top of it. Thousands of years ago it was where Zeus had imprisoned Escalus, a seer who had offended him. Zeus blinded the seer and left him to the mercies of a flock of savage Harpies. However, in their quest to find the Golden Fleece, Jason and his Argonauts captured the Harpies in exchange for the seers knowledge of it's whereabouts.

The seer wasn't a particularly good man though. He later drugged the Harpies and had his wicked way with the

female creatures.
Over the years their successive off-spring gave rise to a colony of feral semi-human winged monsters.

The island is thick with creatures perching like gulls on the rock face but Alhazred has equipped Dancer and the rest with capes cut from magic cloth that renders them invisible. They successfully scale the hazardous cliff-face, when cannon shells burst against the rock, showering them with razor sharp shards, shredding the cloaks. The shot has come from Sarita's fast approaching ship. What's more, the Harpies can now see Dancer and his men!

3) The Harpies attack in droves. There's a running battle as the boys head for the cover of the ruined temple. They make it to a chamber beneath the temple and Billy tears a crumbling pillar sealing them in.

As the galley fires blasts of blazing Greek fire to ward off Sarita's ship, Alhazred reports events to his unseen Master who is also onboard. From their exchange it's clear they've tried this before, Dancer and the boys aren't the first.

Back in the chamber. The red eyed skull of the long dead seer rises up from a scrying pool and cryptically warns them that death walks at their heel. This they know already and Tom smashes the skull to reveal the red eyes are in fact rubies and half of the map they're after. It's made out of jewels and filigreed gold.

Suddenly the Harpies break through and it's all Hell let loose.

4) Outnumbered by the Harpies. Dancer realises the scrying pool is full of sea water and leads out into the ocean. Grabbing rocks for ballast, the boys leap into the pool and sink down and down.

With their last gasps of air they surface in the ocean and are picked up by a jubilant Alhazred. He explains that he isn't alone in his desire to find the island and that there is another who will go to any lengths to beat them to the map.

We cut to Sarita and her men dousing fires on their ship. Her crew are despondent but Sarita says that they can catch up with the bronze galley at their next port of call… the Island of Rhodes.

5) Cut to Rhodes and an unhappy Dancer and crew.

Alhazred explains that the final map segment lies beneath the ocean, actually inside the head of the long collapsed Colossus that once straddled the harbour.

He wants Dancer and Jim to use bronze diving suits/diving bells built from Daedalus' design and retrieve it. Dancer is quite intrigued by the idea and relents. Trusting to Dancers judgement, Jim reluctantly agrees to follow suit.

They dive and find themselves dwarfed by the massive stone body of the Colossus that's more or less intact. They make their way to the head and enter through a shattered eye.

Meanwhile Sarita's ship is moored someway off. Her first mate asks if they shouldn't be closer? Sarita shows him a small jar inscribed with runes and says they don't want to be anywhere near what's in it when it gets going. She whispers into the jar then tips it into the ocean and a tiny Cuttlefish/ Nautilus type creature swims out.

It doesn't stay tiny for long. It is a Kraken.

The now giant creature attacks the Colossus with our heroes still inside.

6) Back on the bronze galley. They all impotently stare in horror at the boiling ocean and thrashing waves. Even Alhazred appears ruffled.

He consults his mysterious master who, much to the boys surprise is on the ship but they don't get to see him. Stroking a gold ring on his finger, he tells Alhazred what to do.

The giant stone Colossus comes alive. It rises from the sea bed and grapples with the Kraken. Dancer and Jim shuck off their suits and leap into the ocean, tightly clutching the second map segment.

After killing the Kraken, the Colossus returns to it's inanimate state and tumbles back into the ocean.

7) They fit both halves of the map together to make an elaborate sphere but they're still none the wiser on how it works. It's like no map they've ever seen.

In a flash of inspiration. Dancer puts a candle inside. The shadows it throws on the walls creates a huge map using the constellations of the zodiac as reference points but even Dancer is perplexed as they're not where they should be.

At this point Alhazred's ancient and wizened master appears. He says the map is true for when it was made, it is an ancient thing and the stars where in different positions then. Dancer asks how he knows this? The old guy replies that he was alive then, as a boy he slept beneath them.

This is treated with incredulity by the boys but not Dancer. As Alhazred snaps at them to treat his master with respect, they see he's not human but a Djinn — a creature of fire and magic.

The genial old guy announces that he is Al Aladdin and that thanks to a magic ring and the Djinn bound to it, he is over five hundred years old.

**8)** A few minutes before dawn. Having  followed the coordinates on the map, Dancer and the rest wait for the sun to rise and the island to be revealed to them.  Al Aladdin says that he used the ring's wishes judiciously and now he wants to repay the Djinn by releasing him from his imprisonment within it so he can return to his race.

All Al Aladdin wants is to be young just once more, to live a normal life span, that is why he wanted to find the island. Amongst the relics is the Golden Fleece of Greek myth. It's regenerative powers will restore his youth and vigour.

The flying island duly appears and it's an awesome sight. The Djinn carries Dancer and Al Aladdin up to it, leaving the rest on the ship. The island is an incredible place, strewn with temples, shrines and statues to entire pantheons of gods long since forgotten.

While the boys are distracted, Sarita and several of her men mysteriously appear and waylay them. Once she realises that they don't genuinely know what's actually going on, she brings them up to speed.

Al Aladdin is a twisted, vile individual. Each time he's used the ring, he's used the last of the three wishes to create another three wishes and another and another. However, even wishing takes its toll and it has twisted and corrupted his mind and body. He's not satisfied with just the power of the ring anymore, once he has his youth back, he's going to use the ring and the Djinn to give him the means to exploit the power of all the abandoned relics on the island. The power of a hundred pantheons. God only knows what he'll do with it.

Billy asks how she knows all of this? Sarita replies that it was her great-great grandfather Sinbad who hid the halves of the map from Aladdin centuries ago. His descendants have been making sure he doesn't track them down ever since but it looks like she's failed. She unfurls the flying carpet she and her men used to sneak up on the bronze ship. She agrees to let the boys go with her. They have to get to the island before it's too late.

On the island, Al Aladdin's true nature is revealed as he dons the Golden Fleece and his youth is restored. He orders the Djinn to give him access to the power of all the relics on the island. There's nothing Dancer can do.

Sarita and the others watch impotently as the island vanishes before they can reach it.

**To be continued...**

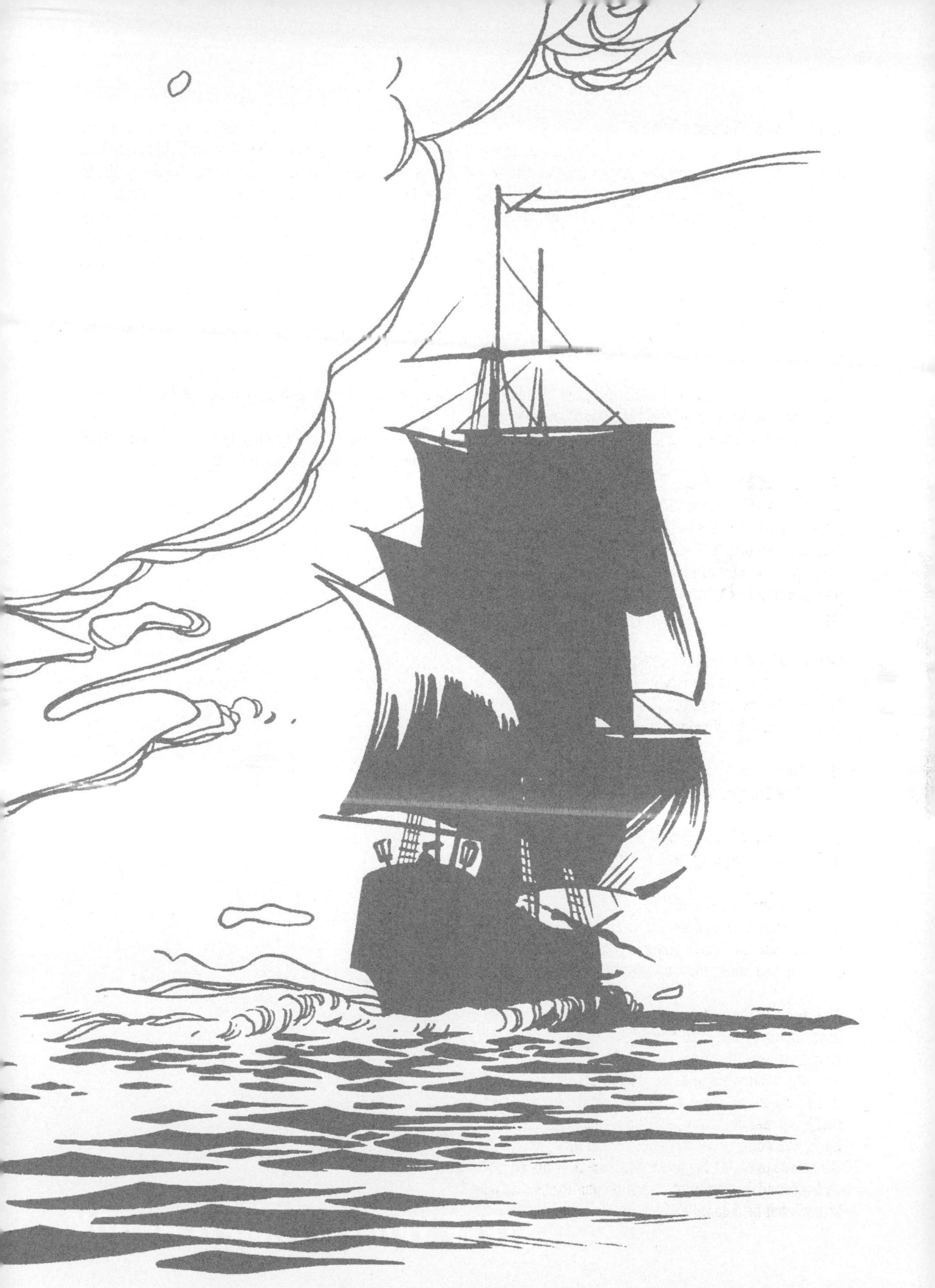

STEVE YEOWELL SKETCHBOOK

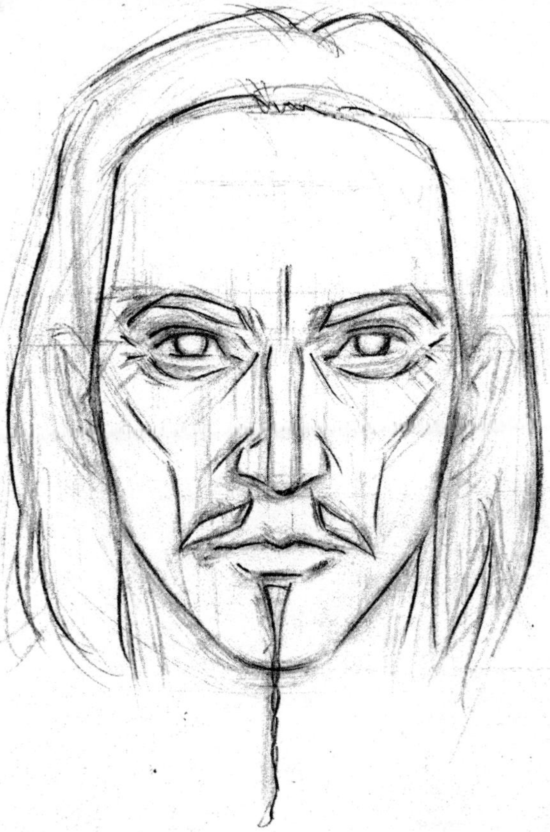
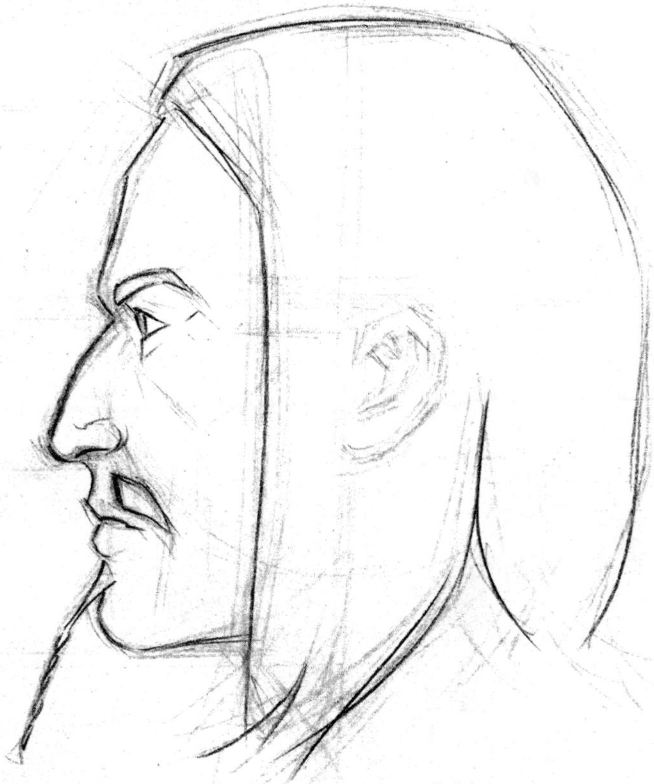
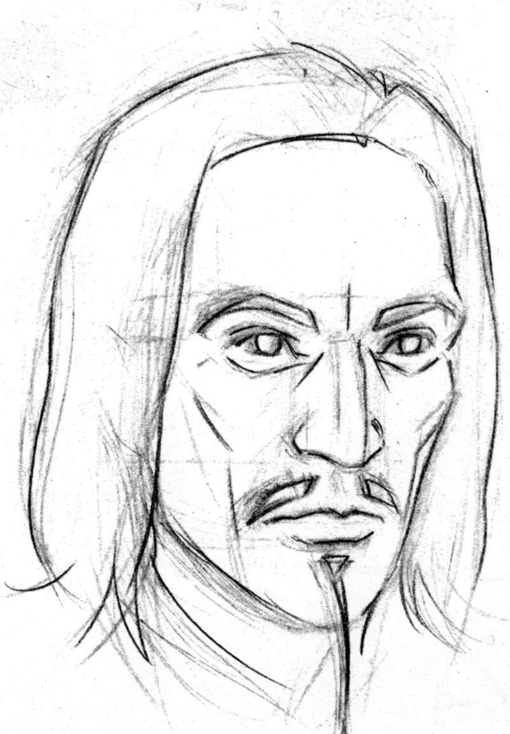

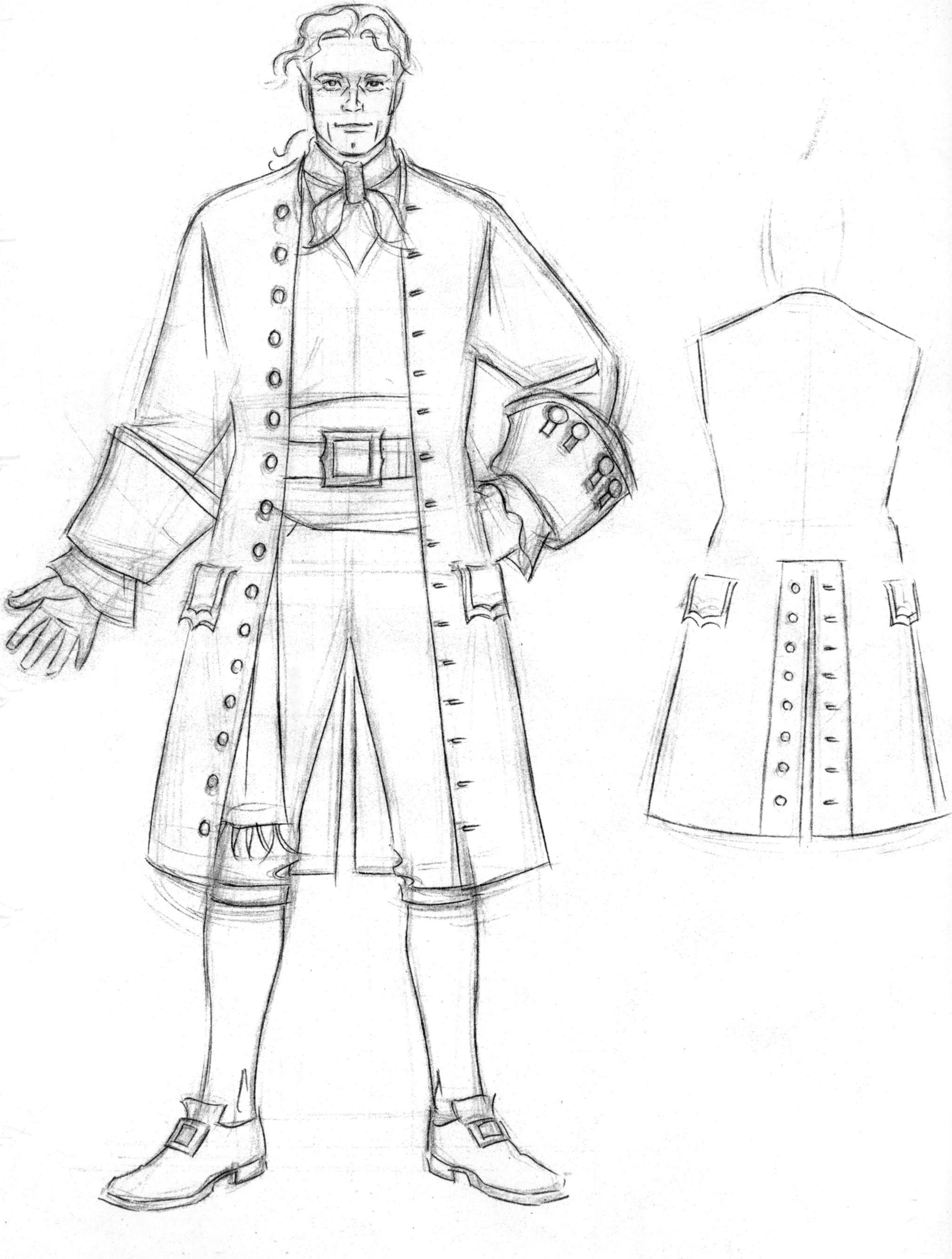

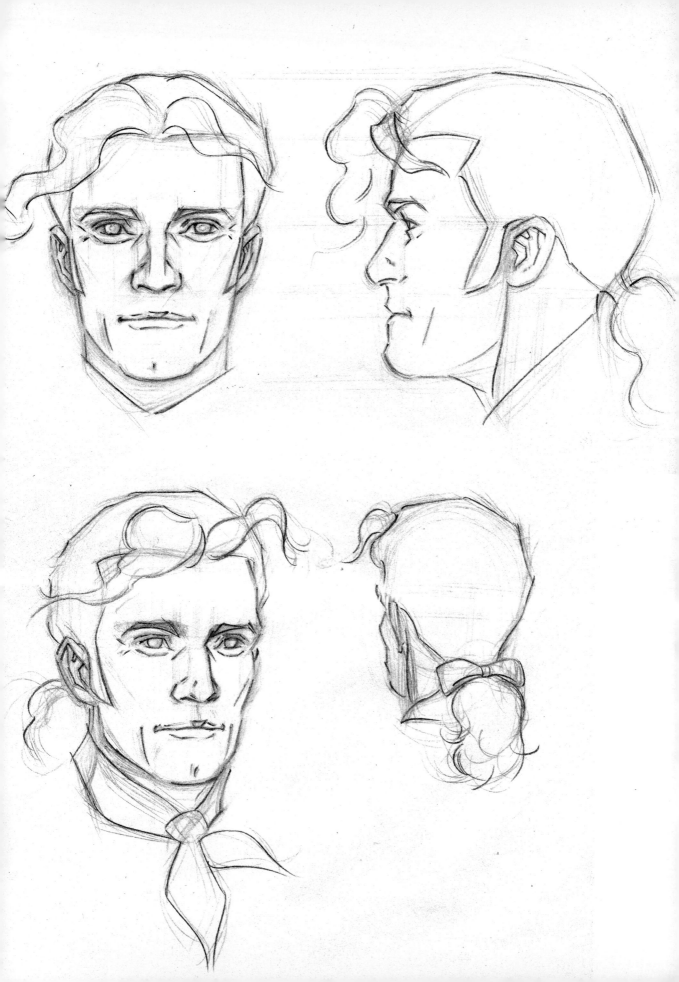

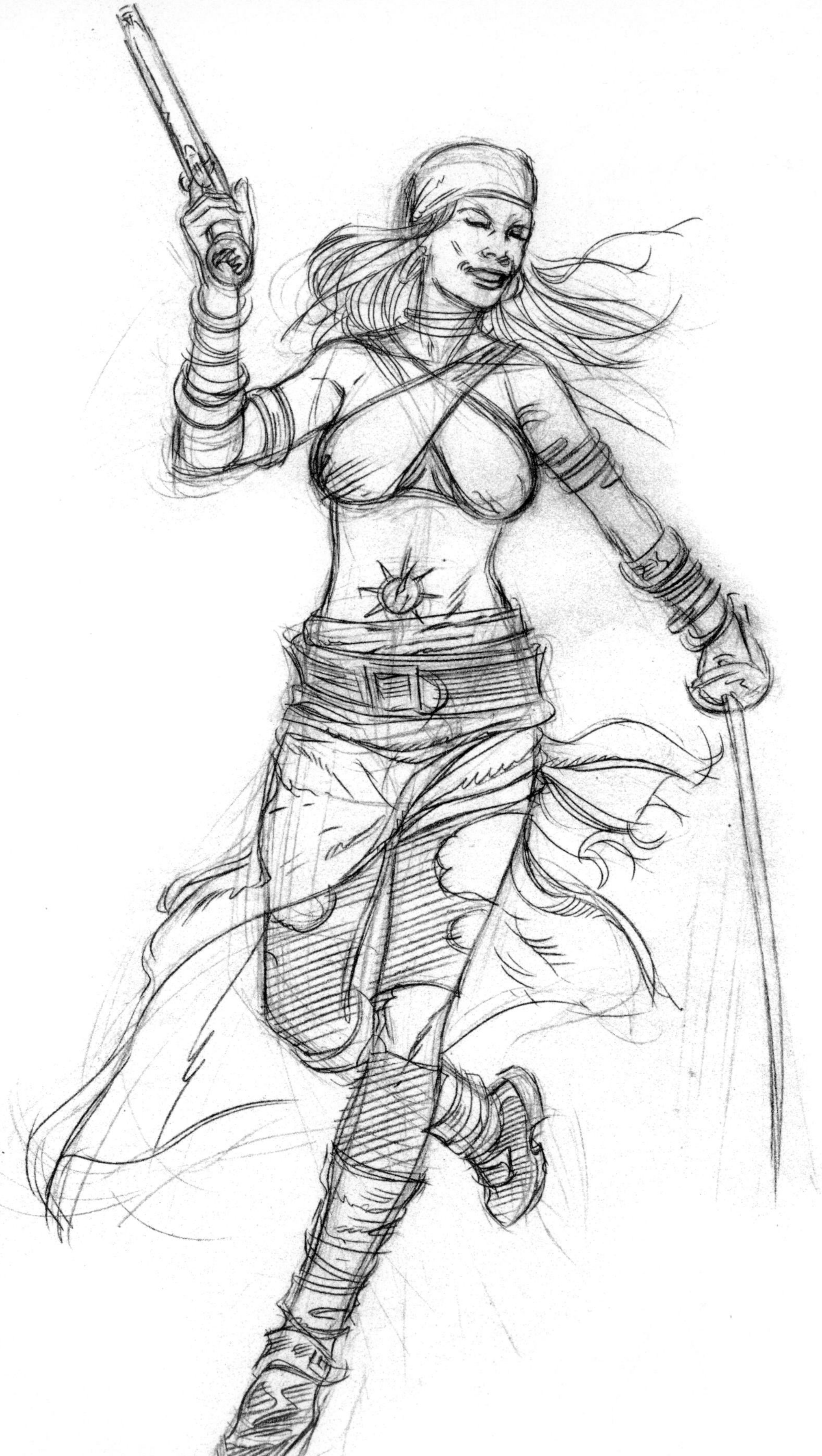

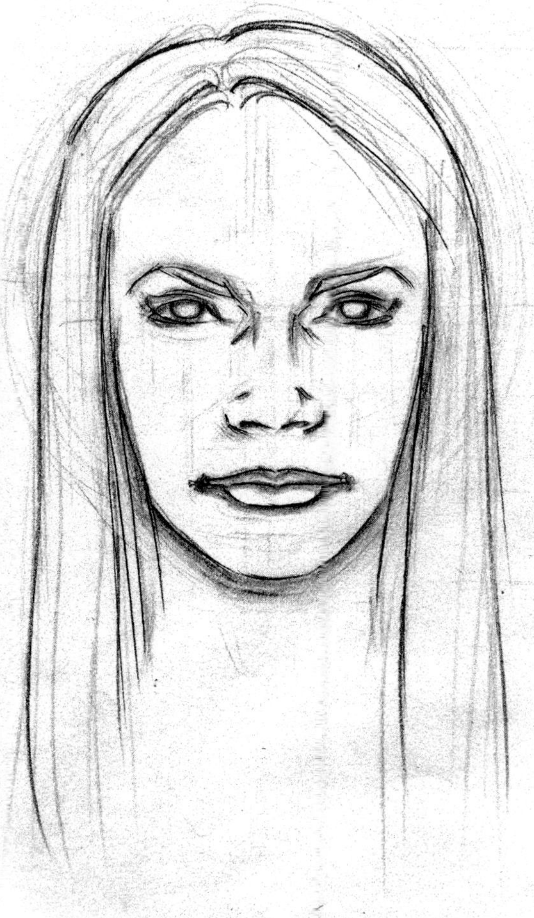

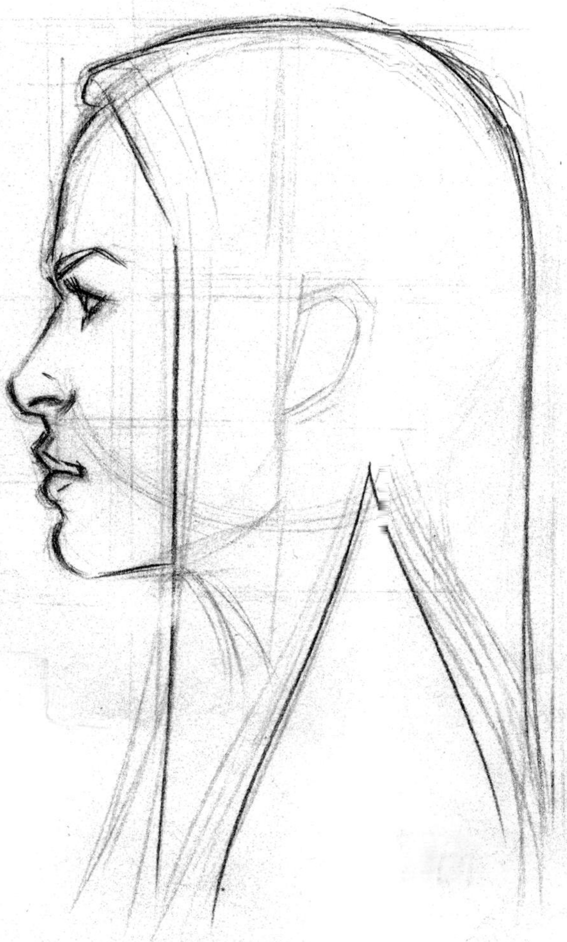

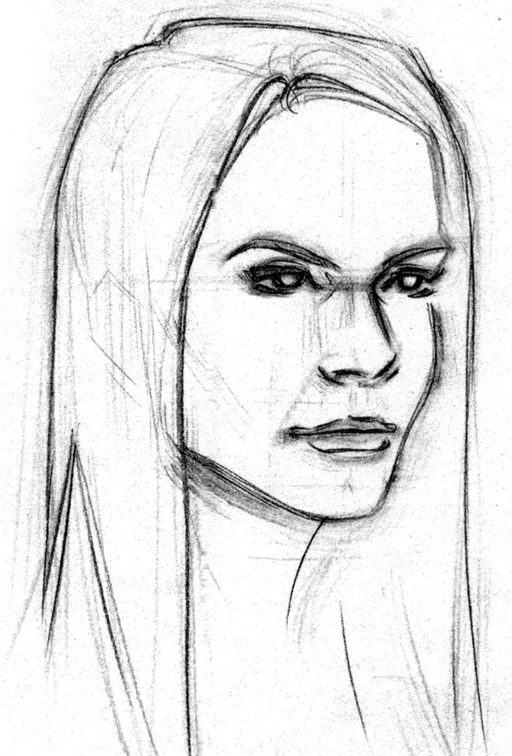

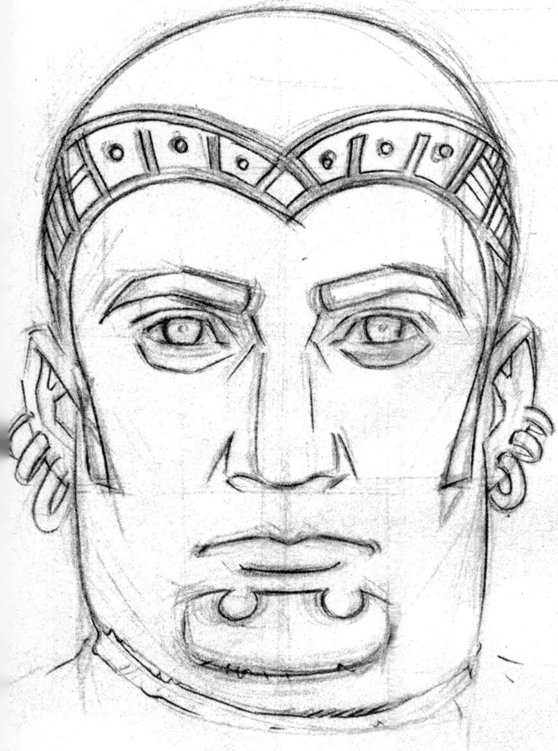
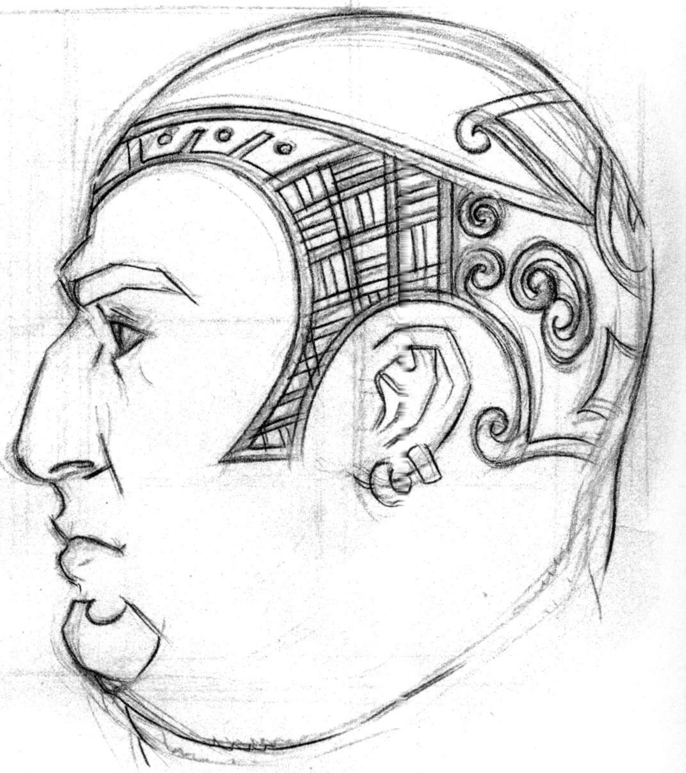
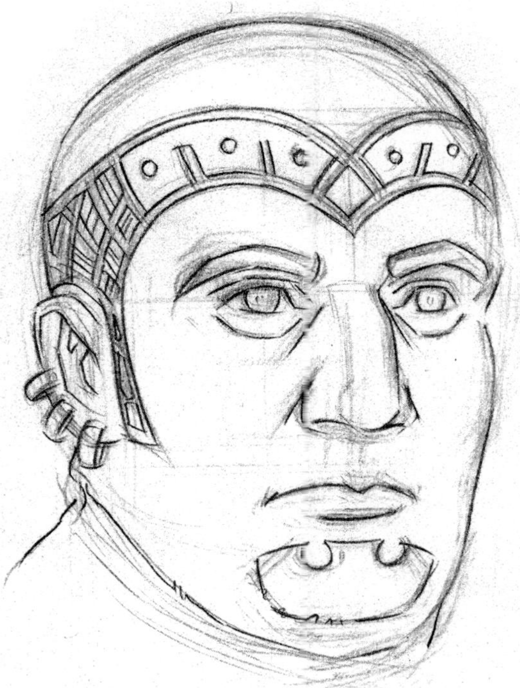
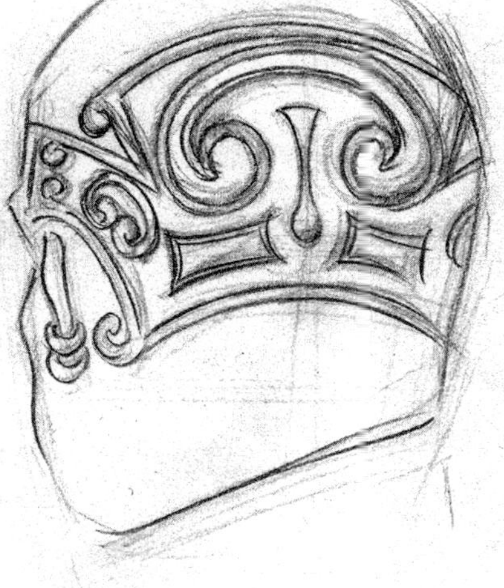

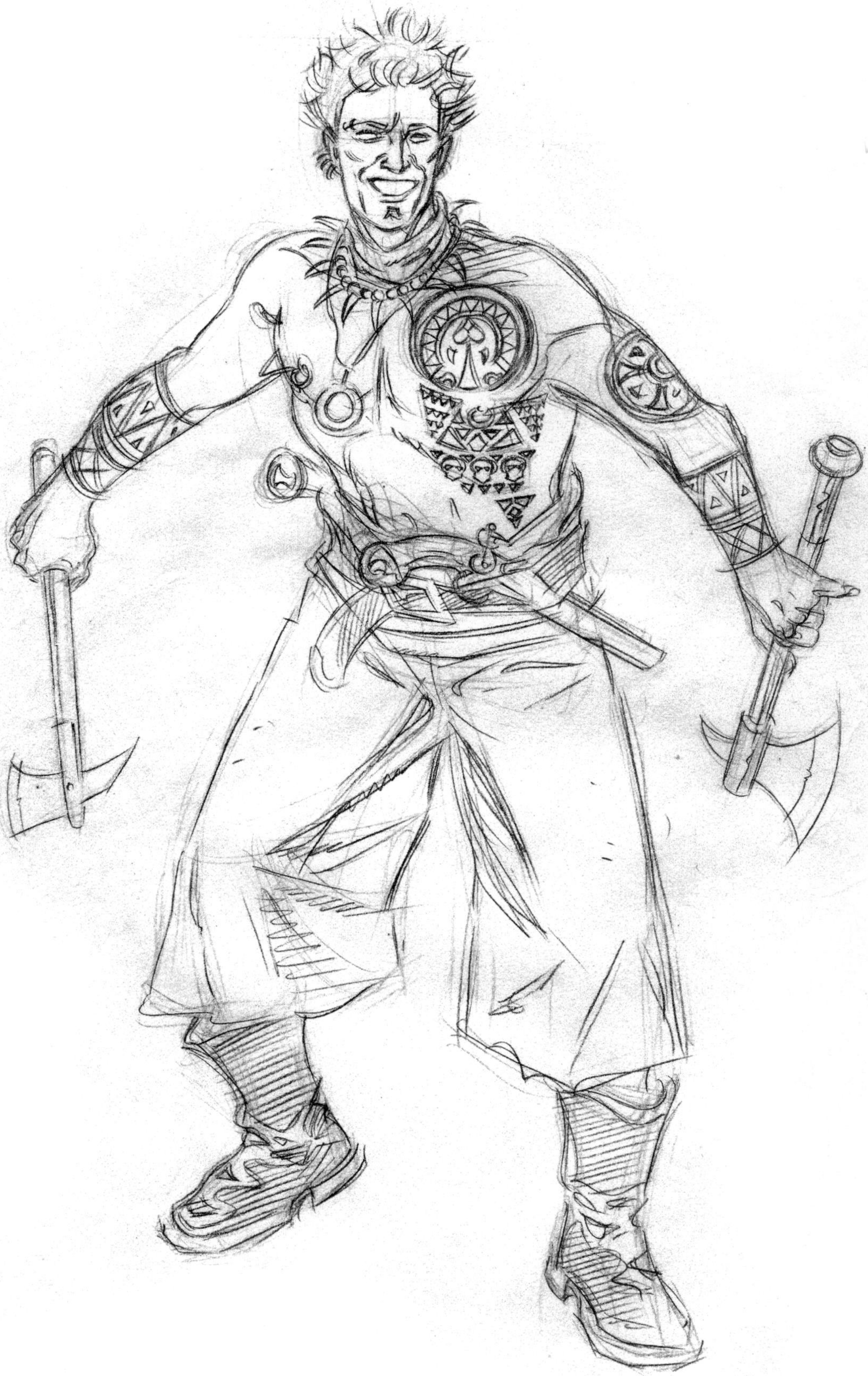

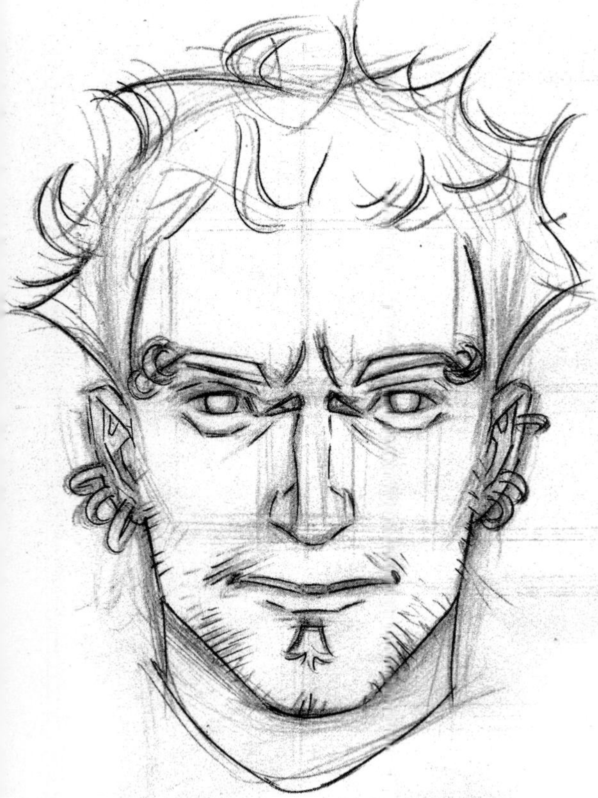
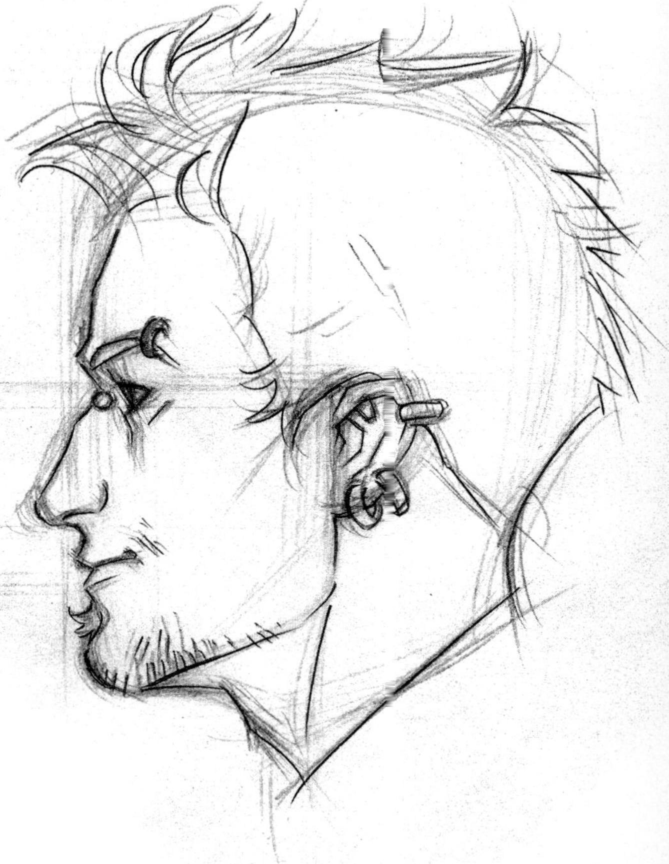
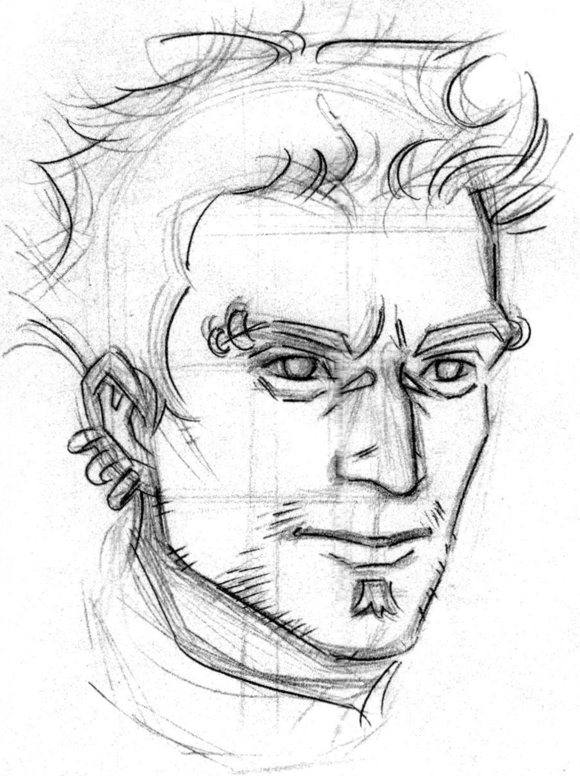

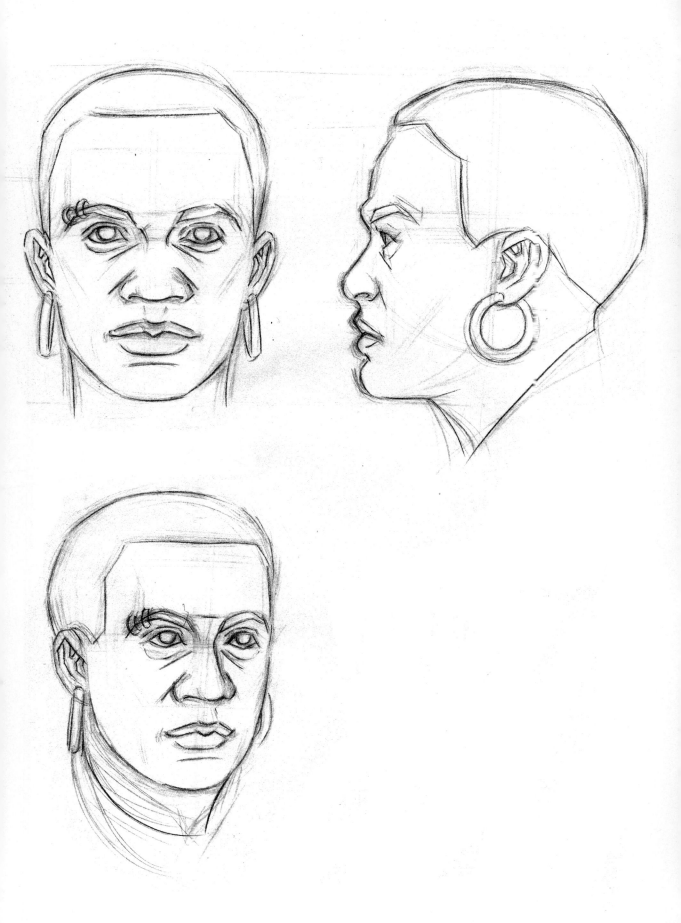

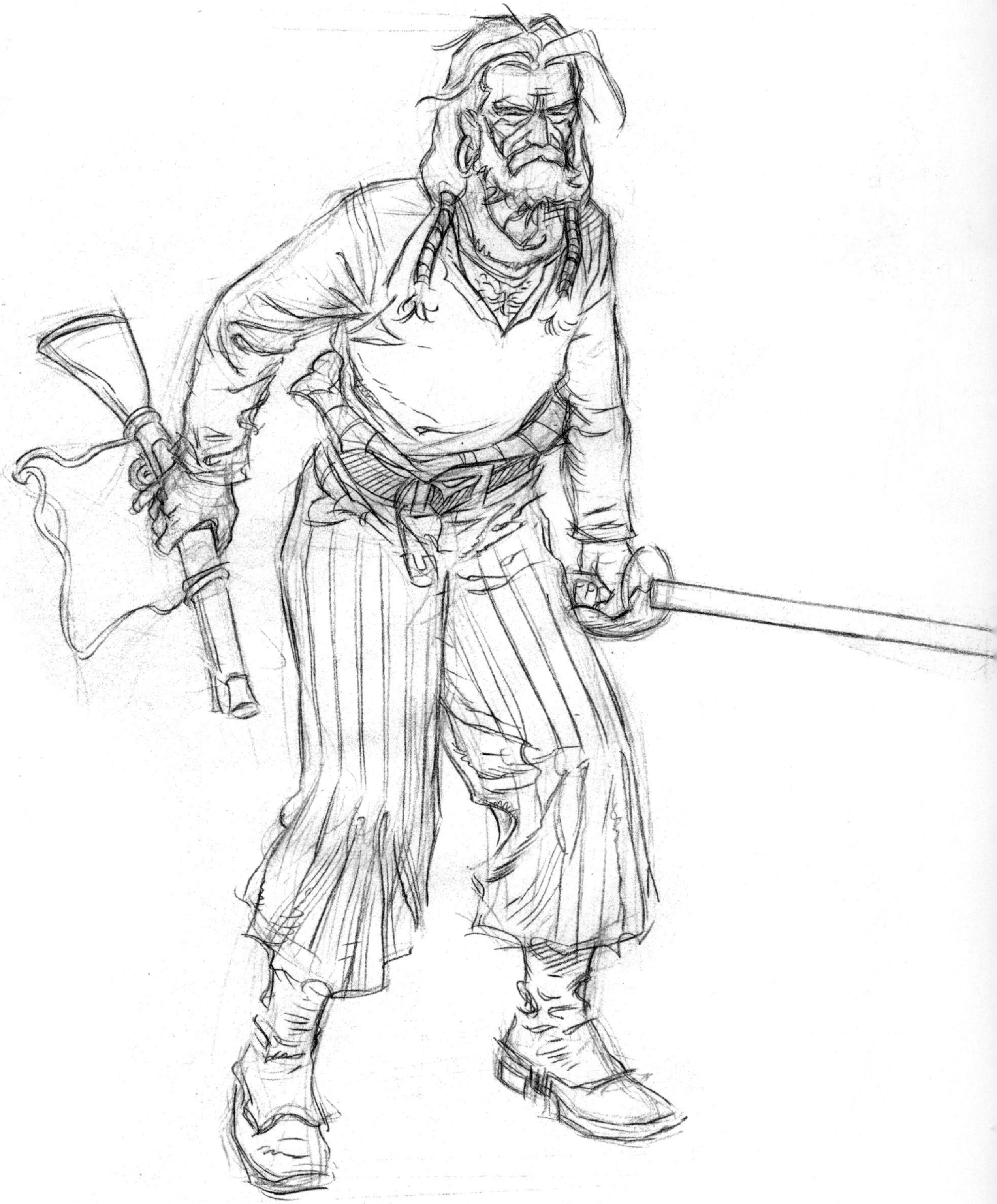

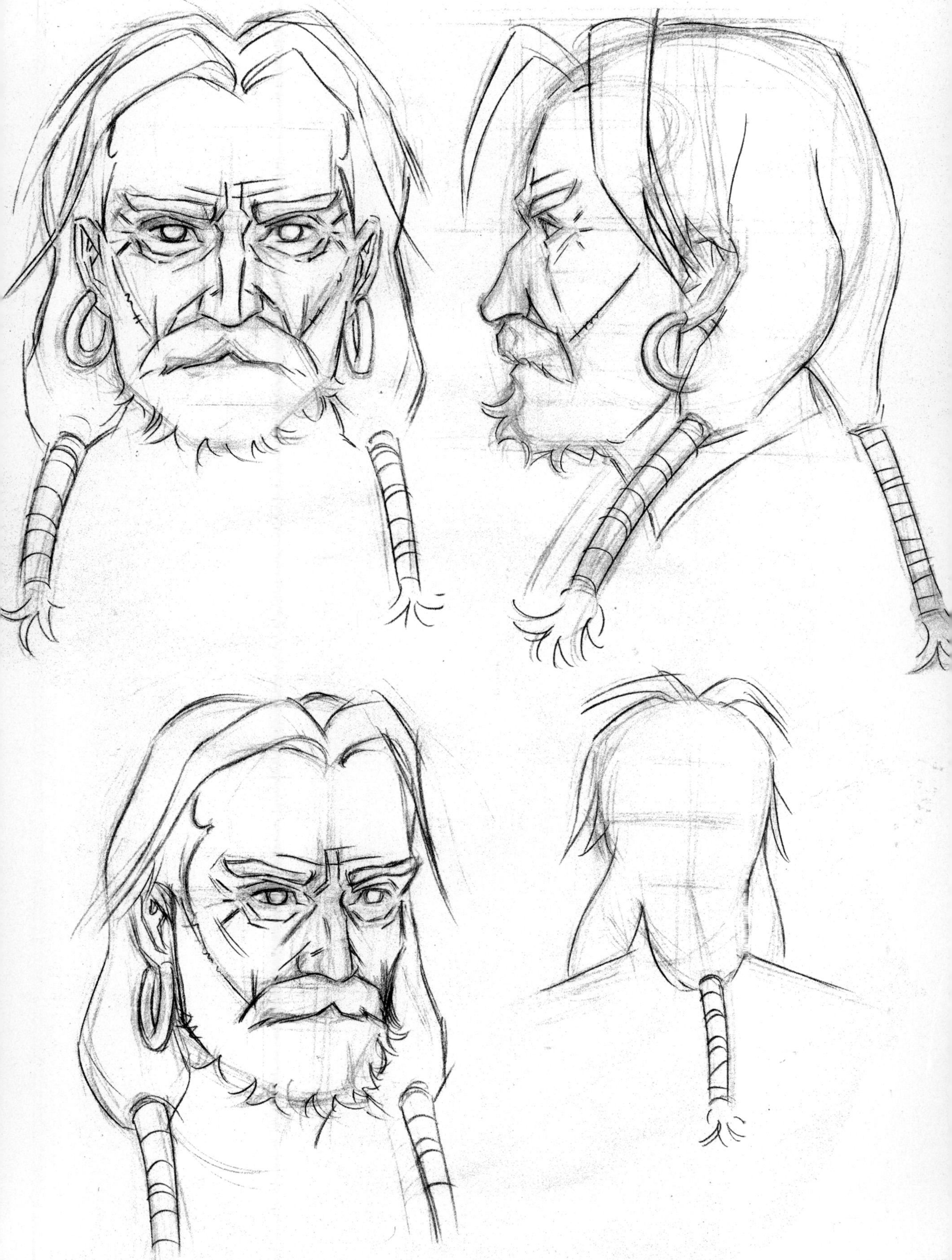

# IAN EDGINTON

Ian Edginton is a relatively recent name to appear in *2000 AD*, but like his *Leviathan* and *Scarlet Traces* co-creator D'Israeli, his impact has been immediate. Debuting with occult pirate series *The Red Seas*, Edginton has gone on to create the aforementioned series as well as *Interceptor*. He has also written *Judge Dredd*, a Kleggs one-off, and *Strange Cases*.

Edginton's work prior to coming to the Galaxy's Greatest Comic covers a wide range of genres — from Dark Horse's *Aliens* series to *The Authority, Blade, Deadline, The Establishment, Foxfire, Planet of the Apes, Ultraforce* and *Terminator*.

# STEVE YEOWELL

Steve Yeowell has been a massively popular *2000 AD* artist, since his debut as artist of the classic *Zenith*. He is also co-creator of *Maniac 5, Red Fang, Red Razors* and *The Red Seas*, and has pencilled *Armitage, Black Light, DeMarco, Devlin Waugh, Future Shocks, Judge Dredd, A Life Less Ordinary, Nikolai Dante, Pussyfoot 5, The Scarlet Apocrypha, Sinister Dexter, Tharg the Mighty* and *Vector 13*.

His work outside the Galaxy's Greatest Comic includes *Batman, Doom Patrol, The Invisibles, Sebastian O, Skrull Kill Krew, Starman* and *X-Men*.